Reed C. Richardson
University of Utah
Professor, Management and Economics
Former Director, Institute of Industrial Relations

COLLECTIVE BARGAINING BY OBJECTIVES
A Positive Approach

Second Edition

P9-DBY-764

Prentice-Hall, Inc., Englewood Cliffs, New Jersey 07632

Library of Congress Cataloging in Publication Data

RICHARDSON, REED C. (date)
   Collective bargaining by objectives.

   Bibliography: p.
   Includes index.
   1. Collective bargaining.   2. Collective
bargaining—United States.   I. Title.
HD6971.5.R53 1985   331.89'1'0973   84-15093
ISBN 0-13-140476-8

TO JUDITH

Editorial/production supervision
   and interior design: **Joan Foley**
Cover design: **Ben Santora**
Manufacturing buyer: **Ed O'Dougherty**

Printed in the United States of America

10 9 8 7 6 5 4 3 2 1

ISBN 0-13-140476-8   01

Prentice-Hall International, Inc., *London*
Prentice-Hall of Australia Pty. Limited, *Sydney*
Editora Prentice-Hall do Brasil, Ltda., *Rio de Janeiro*
Prentice-Hall Canada Inc., *Toronto*
Prentice-Hall of India Private Limited, *New Delhi*
Prentice-Hall of Japan, Inc., *Tokyo*
Prentice-Hall of Southeast Asia Pte., Ltd., *Singapore*
Whitehall Books Limited, *Wellington, New Zealand*

CONTENTS

iii

PART II

COLLECTIVE BARGAINING PROCESS: NEGOTIATION   69

PART III

COLLECTIVE BARGAINING PROCESS: CONTRACT ADMINISTRATION   177

PART IV

COLLECTIVE BARGAINING PROCESS: RESOLUTION OF CONFLICT 249

19

FOREWORD
to the Second Edition

When Reed Richardson wrote his first edition of *Collective Bargaining by Objectives*, he was breaking new ground. He picked up a tested principle of management—Managing by Objectives—and applied it with professional skill to the collective bargaining relationship. No experienced practitioner would ever concede that negotiation and labor relations are perfectly systematic, but Richardson makes it clear that they need not be performed entirely by intuition and visceral reactions to the other side.

This second edition picks up and improves on the first edition in several important ways. It does not, of course, drop any of the very intelligent and practical tools of defining objectives by both parties before the negotiations get under way. Rather, it hones those methods through attention to better preparation by the parties before negotiation begins, making it clear that contract-to-contract collection of facts and data is an important part of the entire bargaining process. The idea of the CBO log is an original and valuable contribution. It is not merely another chart, but has an underlying assumption of rationality and a system that can help turn confrontation into agreement, with both sides emerging as winners.

Collective bargaining in the future, Richardson proposes, will be more information-based and less founded on rhetoric and tricks in the actual bargaining process. The basic building block is, of course, the goals of the parties, and it is this theme which makes Richardson's work different—and in my opinion—well ahead of most books on bargaining.

George S. Odiorne
St. Petersburg, Florida

PREFACE

Collective bargaining, a term introduced by Beatrice Potter Webb in 1891, has traditionally been associated with the trade union movement. In terms of numbers of agreements negotiated and individuals directly concerned, the most common form of collective bargaining is still with trade unions. Dominated by private-sector unionism prior to the 1960s, collective bargaining has since undergone a dramatic change by its extension to federal, state, and municipal employees. Another product of the last decade has been the increasingly active role played by professional and state associations of employees in negotiating collective bargaining agreements. Although avoiding the name *union* or affiliating formally with the union movement, these associations have taken on many of the trappings of unions. What this means for collective bargaining is that the term is no longer synonymous with or limited to the trade union movement. What this also means is that the institution of collective bargaining has assumed a position of major importance among the institutions of our society. While limited in this book to that form of collective bargaining associated with employer-employee relations, it is important to note the spread to other areas: for example, community disputes outside the employer-employee field. In the employer-employee relations area alone, collective bargaining, through an estimated 150,000–160,000 negotiated agreements, directly affects some 22.5 million private and government wage and salary employees. When the multiplier and competitive effects of these collective bargaining settlements are also considered, the total impact of collective bargaining on the economy and other institutions is even more significant.

Only thirty years ago, the caption on a number of articles and research studies was "Is Collective Bargaining Obsolete?" Certainly, in the 1980s, despite the problems of recession and widespread unemployment, collective bargaining has proven that it is not an obsolete process but a viable and complementary process in reaching the goals and aspirations of a free society. Some of the more important reasons for this resiliency are: (1) the impact of broad attitudinal changes in our society during recent decades, (2) a growing acceptance of collective bargaining as a respectable and preferred vehicle for settling differences between employers and employees in all conceivable areas, (3) the lack of viable alternatives to collective bargaining in a free society, (4) the way the environment of a free society fosters and renders possible such collective action, and (5) the recent and important extension of collective bargaining rights to governmental employees.

Collective Bargaining by Objectives is about this vital institution of a democratic and free society. Rather than a theoretical examination of the collective bargaining process, the focus of the book is on the process itself: what is involved, how it works, how the parties can be effective within the framework of the process, and how productive efforts by many groups can render the process more efficient and useful as a key element in the workings of our society. The book is designed to be adaptive to a number of uses: (1) as a supplement to more broadly based books on labor relations; (2) as the central reading in courses specifically oriented to collective bargaining negotiations, grievance handling, or grievance arbitration; (3) as a guide to workshops and training programs in the areas of negotiation, grievance handling, and grievance arbitration; and (4) as a valuable source of information and guide for the practitioner faced with negotiating an agreement, processing a grievance, or representing one of the parties at an arbitration hearing.

More specifically as to content, the term _collective bargaining_ in employer-employee relations usually refers to two areas of activity: the negotiation of the terms of the agreement and the administration of these terms during the life of the agreement. A third area of activity is identified for the purposes of this book. This is the related activity of private and public means developed for the purpose of strengthening collective bargaining as a means of resolving conflict. Where not purposely considered an alternative to collective bargaining, these private and public aids to the resolution of labor-management conflict constitute a vital support to the collective bargaining process. Thus, in addition to Part I, which introduces the reader to labor-management relations and collective bargaining, there are three major divisions of the book proper: Part II, Negotiation; Part III, Contract Administration; Part IV, Resolution of Conflict.

But the book is intended to be more than just a source of information concerning the collective bargaining process. The highest priority is given in the subject matter and arrangement of material to the practical matter of bridging the gap for the reader between information on the one hand and the practice of collective bargaining on the other. A book providing merely information is like providing the tools for a building project without showing how to use them efficiently. This book presents a methodology for bargaining—a systematic and methodical step-by-step way of preparing for and carrying on bargaining to provide the link between information and use. The result is a more positive thrust to the entire procedure, increasing the effectiveness of the negotiator, experienced or inexperienced. The key to this methodology is that the common, ordinary tasks that have to be done to be effective in collective bargaining are placed within a systematic and easily followed framework. The methodology is called Collective Bargaining by Objectives (CBO) and is an adaptation of Management by Objectives (MBO) to the collective bargaining process. Key chapters in the development of this methodology are Chapters 7 through 14.

To facilitate the reader's understanding and to minimize the confusion that results from a lengthy and too-minute coverage, the main content of the book remains informative but as brief as possible. For a more intensive investigation into any area of the book, each subject includes a list of annotated reading materials.

The focus of the first edition of *Collective Bargaining by Objectives* has been retained. The purpose of the revision is to enhance and reinforce the existing format. Throughout this book, I have emphasized the continuing importance of the classical labor relations study, *Industrial Democracy* by Beatrice and Sydney Webb, © by The London School of Economics and Political Science. Part II has been reorganized to provide a clearer transition, in the CBO process of preparing for negotiations, from the first step of systematically assembling and organizing basic bargaining information to the final step, through the CBO methodology, of developing a blueprint for negotiations. The book has been carefully reviewed to update all relevant information and to provide the latest references to literature in the field through the annotated bibliography. Moreover, practical techniques and tools of value in collective bargaining are identified, when appropriate, with the particular collective bargaining function, such as techniques for maintaining proper grievance records, techniques for recording problems arising formally or informally in applying the contract, and a checklist for those who are preparing for negotiations to use in determining whether all essential areas have been covered in order to insure a proper performance.

For the person who wishes to use the book for a learning experience or training device in the practice of collective bargaining, the Appendix provides two negotiation games to be used in simulation training. Guidance for these games, based on the author's experience over a number of years, is included. The use of simulation is strongly recommended as a highly effective teaching or training device in applying the objectives (CBO) methodology.

Many people have been influential and helpful in this revision. Deserving special thanks are Teaching and Research Associate Ann Wendt and Professor Gary Hansen, who have worked closely with the author in determining the revisions needed and in providing essential research information to update the book. I am also grateful for the advice and reactions to the CBO approach from friends and colleagues Arben Clark, Sheel Pawar, Robert Henson, Gayland Moffat, George Odiorne, and Dale Yoder. To FMCS Commissioner of Mediation Tom Curdie, thanks for his close association and support. To cooperating groups such as the FMCS, AAA, Civil Service Commission, Federal Labor Relations Authority, Federal Impasses Panel, Prentice-Hall, and the Bureau of National Affairs, my deep appreciation. I should be ungrateful if I failed to mention the hundreds of graduate and undergraduate students and practitioner participants in seminars and workshops who have been exposed to the CBO method during the past twelve years and whose comments have been most useful and persuasive in determining some of the revisions. Also, thanks to the many representatives of management and labor organizations whose association, over three decades, has enriched my understanding of collective bargaining and arbitration in my role as an impartial arbitrator. Finally, to Linda Miles, Elizabeth Porter, Melissa Whitehead, James Peters, and Armin Watson, for their willingness to provide assistance whenever needed, a special thanks.

PART I

COLLECTIVE BARGAINING PROCESS: Background

Barter between individuals must be superseded by negotiations, through authorized representatives, between groups of workers and consumers. Individualist exchange must follow individualist productions, and give place to collective bargaining.

Beatrice Potter Webb   1891

But though Collective Bargaining prevails over a much larger area than Trade Unionism, it is the Trade Union alone which can provide the machinery for any but its most casual and limited application.

Sidney and Beatrice Webb, *Industrial Democracy*   1902

CHAPTER 1

EVOLUTION: 1790 to 1890

GENERAL INTRODUCTION

The objective in including a section on the evolution of collective bargaining in America is to provide a historical framework within which the remainder of the book may be more clearly understood.

Rather than an exhaustive account of collective bargaining, the emphasis is on an overview through the selective use of historical materials. The materials chosen are those that identify the significant changes in collective bargaining from one historical period to another, and the major environmental forces that have blended and molded collective bargaining into what it is today.

While the material is divided into two general periods of approximately a century each, there is a further identification of five subperiods for clarity. They are:

1. Foundation period: 1790 to 1890
2. Unilateralism to collective bargaining: 1890 to 1930
3. Collective bargaining and public policy: 1930 to 1945
4. Employer acceptance: 1945 to 1962
5. Collective bargaining, an institution: 1962 to the present

For purposes of clarification, the term *union* or *labor movement* is defined as the formal trade union movement. The term *employee organi-*

zation (especially pertinent to the contemporary period) is used in a broader sense to identify all forms of employee organizations, union or otherwise, engaged in collective bargaining or negotiation of labor-management agreements.

The term *collective bargaining* will be used throughout to identify developments in joint labor-management negotiation and/or administration of the labor agreement. It is recognized that the term did not originate until the end of the nineteenth century. It was coined by Beatrice Potter Webb to describe the bilateral negotiation process between labor and management.

FOUNDATION PERIOD: 1790 TO 1890

INTRODUCTION

It is customary to think of collective bargaining as coextensive with unionism; however, such was not the case in the first century of the American labor movement. More commonly, the relationship between employers and unions of the period was unilateral. The employees, through their union organization, normally looked upon their demands as being final demands, not subject to the give-and-take of negotiation or bargaining. As a result, employees approached employers with a "take it or we strike" attitude. The employer's approach was equally unilateral. If in a strong position, the employer simply ignored the union demands, or refused them and let the union action run its course. If in a weak position, the employer might accede to the union demands until a better day, when the tables could be turned on the union through a unilateral abolishment of the gains made.[1]

> The demands which the body drew up were demands which they expected to have met in full. They were not bargaining proposals, set two or three times higher than their settlement price, but an "actual bill of wages" sometimes printed and ready to be posted in the shops immediately upon acceptance. Compromise was therefore not intended. The union members had previously sworn among themselves not to work for less than the wages stated in their demands, and they were serious in that oath.
>
> This was not therefore a process of bargaining. It was a procedure for a trial of economic strength to determine whose wage decisions would prevail—the union's or the employer's.[2]

[1] In describing the historical development of collective bargaining in America, no serious labor historian can ignore the pioneering work of Neil W. Chamberlain, *Collective Bargaining* (New York: McGraw-Hill, 1951), and Vernon H. Jensen, "Notes on the Beginnings of Collective Bargaining," *Industrial and Labor Relations Review*, vol. 9, no. 2 (January 1956).

[2] Chamberlain, *Collective Bargaining*, pp. 6–7.

Collective Bargaining

By 1825, in a few trades and communities, the practice of unilateral imposition of terms had "given way to one of bilateral negotiation and the drafting of one-sided terms of surrender had in some instances been replaced by two-party agreements." However, "ultimatum rather than conferences was the prevailing practice of both unions and associated employers."[3]

Twenty-five years later, although instances of genuine negotiation between employers and unions were "only straws in the wind," more union officials and employers had gained experience in negotiation, and a few had even become advocates of collective bargaining as a policy of union-employer relations. The idea of collective bargaining was spreading. However, the panic of 1857 brought a temporary halt to both unionism and collective bargaining.

The end of the Civil War witnessed a renewal of union activity, this time at the national as well as the local level. As union activity intensified, interest in collective bargaining revived, although the development must be characterized as slight, and not the customary relationship between management and labor. But however slight it was in terms of overall union-management relations, there was a qualitative difference that had great portent for the future of collective bargaining. First, by 1890, three trades had been able to establish permanent systems of local trade agreements: the railway-operating brotherhoods, the Amalgamated Association of Iron and Steel Workers, and the bricklayers of Chicago. Second, the verbal agreements of earlier years were being replaced by written agreements. Jensen points to a third less obtrusive trend, but one of importance in the development of collective bargaining: the frequent espousal by unions and union leaders of arbitration or conciliation. Jensen indicates that more often than not, since the term *collective bargaining* had not yet come into use, what the parties meant was not arbitration or conciliation in the formal sense, but "a conciliatory rather than a belligerent approach to securing their demands," or a "joint meeting of workers and employers."[4] Jensen notes, "It is obvious that the term arbitration was used broadly enough, if not more or less synonymously, to include bargaining as well as intervention of third parties." He concludes, "Even so, the practice of this type of arbitration [third-party adjudication] was very limited."[5]

Thus by 1890 the idea and the practice of collective bargaining as evidenced by written agreements, even though not the customary relationship, were not only gaining ground in both thought and deed but were

[3]*Ibid.*, p. 14.
[4]Jensen, "Notes on the Beginnings of Collective Bargaining," p. 229.
[5]*Ibid.*, p. 231.

sufficiently well established to constitute a springboard for any future development.

A selective chronology of the recorded instances of collective bargaining negotiations is illustrative of the progress made.

1799	**The Journeymen Cordwainers of Philadelphia were locked out for refusing a decrease in wages. It was not long until the journeymen sued for peace. A compromise offer was submitted by the society and accepted by the employer. Negotiations ensued, and in the end the employers apparently agreed to the compromise.**[6]
1809	**An excerpt from a verbatim of negotiations between the journeymen and master printers of New York City reads:**

Minor changes were again made in the new bill of prices on October 7th, and finally . . . adopted as a whole and forwarded to the employers.

Upon receipt of the notification from the journeymen's society the master printers convened. . . . The meeting adopted a counter proposal . . . to submit to the union.

The Typographical Society met in general session on October 28th and received a report . . . "that the master printers . . . requested that a committee of the society might be appointed to confer with their committee in order, if possible, to effect an accommodation."

The committeemen . . . "reported that they had waited on committee of master printers . . . who met them with a frankness which was highly creditable to themselves and pleasing to the committee. They had made many concessions, and the committee, desirous of putting a speedy termination to our differences, has also consented to advocate some trifling concession on our part."[7]

The points at issue were then adjusted satisfactorily through further conferences with the employers.

1827	**In the conspiracy trial of the Philadelphia Journeymen Tailors, there is another, although less elaborate, account of a bargaining relationship:**

In September, 1825, a bill of prices was agreed upon by the journeymen tailors of this city. . . . It was submitted to several of the master tailors. . . . Such was this bill of prices, being really a compromise between

---

[6]John R. Commons et al., *History of Labour in the United States* (New York: Macmillan, 1918), I, p. 122.

[7]Adapted from Chamberlain, *Collective Bargaining*, p. 10. (Emphasis added.)

two conflicting interests, *by which* each party surren-
dered something and received a satisfactory equi-
valent.[8]

1847

Robert MacFarlane, editor for the *Mechanic's Mirror*,
declared: "It has always appeared to me . . . that a
plain, friendly relationship and statement of facts on
both sides would have reconciled both parties, *with a
little concession by each.*"[9]

1850s

Horace Greeley actively promoted collective bargaining.
Greeley's statement of "principles underlying the joint
union-management trade agreement system . . .
stands as a landmark in the history of the development
of Collective Bargaining in the United States."[10] A few
excerpts make this quite clear:

> 3. *We believe employers have rights as well as jour-
> neymen—that they too should hold meetings and form
> societies or appoint delegates to confer with like dele-
> gates on the part of the journeymen; and that by the
> joint action of these conferrers, fair rates of wages in
> each calling should be established and main-
> tained. . . .*
>
> 5. *We believe that strikes, or refusals of journeymen
> to work at such wages as they can command, are sel-
> dom necessary—that proper representations and con-
> ciliatory action on the part of journeymen would se-
> cure all requisite modifications. . . .*
>
> 6. *. . . . If journeymen alone regulate the prices of la-
> bor, they will be likely to fix them too high; if em-
> ployers alone fix them . . . they will as naturally fix
> them too low; but let the journeymen and employers in
> each table unite in framing, upholding and from time to
> time modifying their scale, and it will usually be just
> about right.*[11]

1869

The printers' union of New York attempted a unilateral
promulgation of a wage increase. The employers then
complained that they had had no chance to respond
before the printers struck. The strike continued for
eight weeks.

> Then informal and private conferences were called
> between leaders of both groups, and it was reported
> that "a spirit of mutual concession" prevailed. Finally,

---

[8]John R. Commons et al., eds., *A Documentary History of American Industrial Society*, (Cleveland, Ohio: Arthur H. Clark Co., 1910), IV, pp. 142–43. (Emphasis added.)

[9]*Ibid.*, VIII, p. 261. (Emphasis added.)

[10]Chamberlain, *Collective Bargaining*, p. 26.

[11]*Ibid.*, adapted from pp. 27–28. (Emphasis added.) From the *New York Daily Trib-
une*, April 13, 1853. This statement will be found in George A. Stevens, *New York Typographical Union* No. 6, New York State Department of Labor, Annual Report of the Bureau
of Labor Statistics (1911), part I, pp. 621–22.

after eleven weeks, a settlement was jointly reached and incorporated in a written agreement, *which among other provisions included the following:* "This scale shall not be altered except by a call for a mutual conference between a joint committee of employers and journeymen, *and no alterations shall take effect except upon one month's notice by either party to the other unless by* mutual consent."[12]

1866 & 1876   The Amalgamated Association of Iron and Steel Workers was a pioneer in the evolution of collective bargaining and the trade agreement. In the iron industry, an amalgamation took place in 1876 of three heretofore separate craft organizations—the United Sons of Vulcan (puddlers), the Associated Brotherhood of Iron and Steel Heaters (roughers, rollers, and catchers), and the Iron and Steel Hands—under the name of the Amalgamated Association of Iron and Steel Workers. *"The puddlers had had a trade agreement with the employers* upon the sliding scale principle since 1866—*the first national trade agreement in American labour history.* . . . So effective was this organization that *its pioneer trade agreement of 1866* was continued in most of the mills for a quarter of a century, and in a few of the remaining iron mills continues even down to the present time."[13]

1870–1871   In 1870, the Anthracite Board of Trade (representing coal operators) proposed a substantial cut in wages for the following year. The miners (anthracite), represented by the Workingmen's Benevolent Association, struck. Franklin B. Gowan, president of the Philadelphia and Reading Railroad, was asked to settle the differences. Through his services, *a compromise* (the "Gowan Compromise") *was reached between the parties.* The next year, further difficulties arose after a drop in coal prices. On July 29, 1870, the two groups *signed the first written agreement in the coal industry.*[14]

Later, negotiations took place over an agreement for the next year (1871) without success, and the miners resorted to arbitration. This settled all differences with the exception of wages. The wage issue was settled by further arbitration and agreements. Some changes were made without incident through 1874. Significantly for collective bargaining, the 1871 agreement included an arrangement for settlement of nonwage disputes without resort to a strike:

[12]*Ibid.,* pp. 32–33. (Emphasis added.) From Stevens, *New York Typographical Union,* p. 303.

[13]Commons et al., *History of Labour in the United States* (1918), II, p. 179. (Emphasis added.)

[14]Philip Taft, *Organized Labor in American History* (New York: Harper & Row, 1964), pp. 71–72.

> *All questions of disagreement in any district, ex-*
> *cepting wages, which cannot be settled by the parties*
> *directly interested shall be referred to a district board*
> *of arbitration, to consist of three members on each side,*
> *with power in case of disagreement to select an umpire*
> *whose decision shall be final. No colliery or district to*
> *stop work pending such arbitration.*[15]

1870   Jensen notes that an example of early joint relations in
                the shoe industry had been described as an early ex-
                ample of arbitration but, through the loose use of
                terms prevalent then, was really more akin to collec-
                tive bargaining. The arrangement

> *. . . at first, consisted of a committee of five from the*
> *union . . . and five from the employers, set up to*
> *meet . . . and talk over matters in an amicable manner;*
> *so that if possible, some agreement might be reached*
> *which would be mutually satisfactory. In 1870 the two*
> *committees worked out an agreement, and the men*
> *were jubilant, and considered they had gained a point*
> *in being recognized by employers as a body to be nego-*
> *tiated with on equal terms.*[16]

1875   Only two groups were able to develop a permanent sys-
                tem of trade agreements prior to 1887: the railway
                organizations, and the iron and steel workers.

                All too little attention has been given historically to
                the tremendous contribution of the railroad-operating
                brotherhoods to the development of collective bar-
                gaining and of protective labor legislation. In both
                areas, the railroad brotherhoods were pioneers and
                exercised an influence far beyond their numbers. In the
                1880s, they were the aristocracy of the trade union
                movement. Because of their strategic position in
                transportation, it is easy to understand why collective
                bargaining, written agreements, and favorable legisla-
                tion came earlier to the operating brotherhoods than
                to most of the labor movement.[17]

ENVIRONMENT

Environment is considered to be all those forces outside the collective
bargaining process that by their impact have influenced the character and
development of collective bargaining. Collective bargaining is an institu-

[15]Carroll D. Wright, *Industrial Conciliation and Arbitration* (Boston: Rand, Abery &
Co., 1881), pp. 138–40.

[16]Jensen, "Notes on the Beginnings of Collective Bargaining," p. 233. (Emphasis
added.) From *Eighth Annual Report of the Bureau of Labor Statistics*, Massachusetts, 1877,
pp. 27, 30.

[17]Reed C. Richardson, *The Locomotive Engineers, 1863–1963* (Ann Arbor: Bureau of
Industrial Relations, University of Michigan, 1963), pp. 196–97.

tional process given birth by the presence and interaction of two organized institutional groups: labor and management. Whatever tends to affect these two institutional groups in their relations with each other may also have an impact on their collective bargaining relationship. The status and character of collective bargaining as an institutional process at any given time is a function of the intermix of broad economic, social, and political forces as they affect society, and through society its institutions, and through these institutions processes such as collective bargaining. To attempt to picture the evolution of collective bargaining without considering the influence of environment would be to see the evolution only as a series of steps without understanding why the steps occurred.

Three points are clear in the description of collective bargaining in its first hundred years: (1) Collective bargaining was not the customary means by which labor and management reconciled their differences. (2) Its growth was not coextensive with the growth of the labor movement. (3) In spite of its minor role in labor-management relations from 1790 to 1890, the idea had taken hold, and the practice of collective bargaining had evolved sufficiently to provide a sound foundation for future expansion.

The fact that collective bargaining did develop in some instances is probably accounted for by the chance combination of circumstances, even though the overall environment was hostile. First, a basic step had been taken toward joint negotiations between labor and management simply by the emergence of labor organizations. This established a natural drive toward such negotiations, since the purpose of the labor organization was to represent its members with the employers. Second, given union organizations, wherever the labor organization and the employer found themselves evenly balanced in power, there was a natural impetus to consider breaking the stalemate through negotiation rather than force. Third, since collective bargaining is essentially a "moderate, businesslike process," whenever a particular labor organization and employer were inclined toward moderation and a businesslike approach to their problems, it was probable that a form of collective bargaining would emerge.

Most union-management situations in the nineteenth century were not characterized by collective bargaining relationships. It follows, therefore, that other environmental factors must have acted to retard the development of the process.

The nature of labor organizations, until the latter part of the nineteenth century, was often an obstacle in and of itself to the development of collective bargaining. The solid development of collective bargaining is in part a function of stable organization and continuity of relationships between employer and labor organization. It would be difficult to characterize the labor organizations of the nineteenth century as stable, since they seemed highly susceptible to destruction by depression and recession. Unions in this period have been described as experiencing "great difficulty . . . in staying organized for any purpose," and as being "highly unstable," and "mowed down and swept out of existence"[18] in every industrial crisis. Union membership in the period prior to the 1890s parallels the business cycle, periodically being weakened or destroyed by such recessions as those of 1817–20, 1837–52, 1857–62, 1873, and 1887. As long as unionism itself was highly unstable, there was not much of a chance, except in a few instances, that collective bargaining and negotiated contractual agreements could develop with any continuity.

Along with instability, a second characteristic of labor organizations delayed the development of collective bargaining. This was the lack of a unified approach to their common problems by labor organizations as a group. The type of unionism most conducive to the growth of collective bargaining is business unionism. Collective bargaining itself, as a moderate, businesslike process, thrives best in an atmosphere where the activities of both parties are based on a businesslike approach to problems. Although business unionism was evident in a few instances and seemed about to emerge on a broader scale at times, the full development and formalization of this concept did not emerge until the middle of the 1880s. The typical picture of organized labor's activities during the period was constant experimentation in search of workable goals and the best means to achieve those goals. This led workers into experimenting with economic action, political action, and social reform, the scene shifting from period to period as one particular type of action seemed more enticing than the others. At times, worker organizations appeared bent on turning into hybrid groups where they were at one and the same time espousing the concepts of Marxism, the goals and activities of uplift groups such as the Knights of Labor, and the "pure and simple trade unionism" of the craft trades. This mixed and changing bag of activities and objectives merely evinced the confusion and turmoil of a highly experimental period of labor. It is no small wonder that, as a result, the attention of workers' groups was more often than not turned in directions and to activities that were not favorable to the development of collective bargaining. Cooperation, political action, abolishment of the wage system, and achievement of the eight-hour day were often more high-sounding and alluring concepts than the slow, grinding process of economic pressure and collective negotiation typical of business unionism.

Attitudinal barriers to the emergence of collective bargaining were also significant during the trade union movement's first hundred years. America in this period was slowly emerging from the hold and influence of past customs and traditions in which the relationship between employer or master and employee was fixed; where the employer's role,

[18]Commons et al., *History of Labour in the United States* (1918), I, pp. 159–61.

fixed by the master-servant doctrines of past centuries, was an authoritarian role—a paternalistic relationship, in which the employee was not to know why nor to question, but to do. It underscored what was considered as not only a God-given right and obligation to rule, but the responsibility of the master to guide his employees in their conduct both on and off the job. It was a doctrine that was as demeaning to the position and rights of the employee as it was ennobling to the position and rights of the master or employer.

Therefore, as workers began to apply pressure for a voice in determining their employment relationship, it was a foregone conclusion that they would receive a negative response from their employers. Two aspects of the situation emphasize the importance of custom and tradition. First, the demands of the employees were initially couched in polite and respectful terms, conveying their hesitancy at breaking with old and customary relationships. The employer made it clear, by direct reference or inference, that he considered this pressure an effrontery to him and to all that the employees also should hold sacred. However, as workers' organizations became more active, and as the passage of time and changing events began to whittle away at the rigidity of old customs, the temerity over breaking with the past gradually began to disappear. Individual examples can always be cited of enlightened employers, even from the earliest days of union organization, but for a substantial group, custom and tradition continued to play an important part in these employers' opposition to unions. This employer hostility was somewhat different from that of later periods, when collective bargaining was making rapid progress. The hostility of the nineteenth-century employer to unionism was inextricably interwoven with the social fabric of a society based strongly on custom and tradition, instead of a simple economic conflict between two competitive groups.

SELECTED REFERENCES

The annotated references appended to each chapter are not meant to cover exhaustively all references to the subject matter of the chapter. Rather, I have selected basic readings that for most purposes will adequately cover the reader's quest for additional information. If the reader wishes to pursue any particular subject area in further depth, the readings chosen will provide references to additional reading materials.

Chamberlain, Neil W., *Collective Bargaining.* New York: McGraw-Hill, 1951. Professor Chamberlain's interpretation of the historical evolution of collective bargaining is basic reading for the interested student. No other writings before or since have analyzed the adaptation of collective bargaining to the changing social environment of which it is a part. Looking ahead from 1950, Chamberlain fully expected collective bargaining to continue to develop as a part of the process of social ferment.

Commons, John R., and associates, eds., *A Documentary History of American Industrial Society.* Cleveland, Ohio: Arthur H. Clark Co., 1910. For the serious student of labor history, this series of ten volumes reproduces many documents vital to an understanding of the evolution of industrial society. The series covers the period from the plantation system to 1880.

Commons, John R. et al., *History of Labour in the United States,* Vols. I and II. New York: Macmillan, 1918. Few labor historians would quarrel with the notion that the Commons series is the *sine qua non* source for any serious study of unionism and labor-management relations from colonial times to 1932. Volumes I and II provide a rich source of basic information on the development of labor relations to the end of the nineteenth century.

Dulles, Foster Rhea, *Labor in America,* 4th ed. Ill.: Harlan Davidson, 1984. For an easily read history of the American labor movement, this book is recommended to the reader. It serves as good background reading.

Jensen, Vernon H., "Notes on the Beginnings of Collective Bargaining," *Industrial and Labor Relations Review,* 9, no. 2 (January 1956), 225–34. Professor Jensen holds to the idea that, in contrast to the traditional view that the early years of unionism were characterized by intense conflict, the real picture was one of the development of collective bargaining as "a moderate, conservative process."

Millis, Harry A., and Royal E. Montgomery, *Organized Labor,* Vol. III. New York: McGraw-Hill, 1945. This book, in Chapters 2 to 4, still remains one of the best-structured accounts of the rise of unions from the 1790s to the 1930s.

Sloane, Arthur A., and Fred Witney, *Labor Relations,* 4th ed. Englewood Cliffs, N.J.: Prentice-Hall, 1981. This is an excellent source for additional background reading before turning to the simulation exercise using CBO.

Taft, Philip, *The Structure and Government of Labor Unions.* Cambridge, Mass.: Harvard University Press, 1954. Professor Taft deals with aspects of trade unions that he felt were sadly neglected. As a consequence, this book is concerned with a study of what goes on inside unions, how they conduct their affairs, to what extent there is competition for office, what they collect in dues, what they pay their officers.

Ulman, Lloyd, *American Trade Unionism—Past and Present: 1. The Development of Trades and Labor Unions,* Reprint no. 157, Institute of Industrial Relations, University of California, Berkeley, 1961. In this study, Lloyd Ulman discusses the development of some of the "major institutional forms that have characterized organized labor in the United States." In discussing these forms, the author relates them to "the objectives they were designed to further" and to some of the "environmental characteristics with which they were designed to cope.

————, *The Rise of the National Trade Union—The Development and Significance of Its Structure, Governing Institutions, and Economic Policies.* Cambridge, Mass.: Harvard University Press, 1955. Although some studies have been made of individual unions, it was left to Ulman to bring together into a comprehensive study the facts about the development of union government and policies and to show how the present national unions evolved into what they are.

CHAPTER 2

EVOLUTION: 1890
to the Present

FROM UNILATERALISM TO COLLECTIVE
BARGAINING: 1890 TO 1930

Labor-management relations moved into the dawn of a new era with the emergence of the twentieth century. Unilateral dealings on each side were replaced by collective bargaining, and the era of the trade agreement emerged. Collective bargaining became coextensive with the trade union movement wherever stable relationships were established between management and labor. The headway made and the acceptance achieved by collective bargaining signified that the "idea of joint partnership between organised labour and organised capital, which, even since the fifties, had been struggling for acceptance, finally came to fruition."[1] In like manner, the clarification of the concept of the trade agreement led "the way from an industrial system which was alternately either despotism or anarchy to a constitutional form of government in industry."[2] However, all was not quiet on the labor front. On the contrary, the successful establishment of collective bargaining and the trade agreement resulted from many hard-fought battles, some successful and some resulting in bitter defeat.

[1]John R. Commons et al., *History of Labour in the United States* (New York: Macmillan, 1918), II, p. 524.
[2]*Ibid.*, p. 520.

COLLECTIVE BARGAINING

The historical record shows that collective bargaining made headway beginning with the 1890s to the point where it was no longer a novel process. It was not long until it was instituted in "numerous individual establishments, in a number of industries on a local basis (such as the building trades and printing), and in ten or twelve industries on a national basis."[3] Although there were some major defeats for both union organization and collective bargaining in such industries as steel and meat packing, these were more than outweighed, in terms of the continuity of collective bargaining and the firm establishment of the trade agreement system, by the successes in such industries as mining, construction, transportation, printing, and clothing. Perhaps the most effective way to show the form and substance of collective bargaining and the trade agreements in this period is to look at some of the specific success stories.

The era of trade agreements, according to Commons, was launched by the epochal stove molders' agreement of 1891.[4] This agreement capped three turbulent, discontented decades replete with strikes and lockouts, in which the atmosphere was so highly charged that almost any issue might be a cause for war, and in which the two parties fought each other to a standstill! It is a small wonder that the agreement of 1891 was considered a landmark in the evolution of collective bargaining. The friction and unstable relations of the past were replaced by the principle of peaceful settlement of disputes. Under the agreement, when disputes arose, the parties were to attempt settlement directly. If this failed, then the dispute was to be submitted to a conference committee of six, three from each side. The decision of the conference committee was to be binding for one year. While the dispute was being processed, no change in the status quo was to be permitted. For the next eight years, the stove molders' agreement was a "lone road-post pointing the way and acting as an incentive for other industries to follow."[5]

Pointing in the same direction and also epochal in its impact was the so-called "interstate agreement" resulting from the bituminous coal strike of 1898 in the central competitive bituminous coal district.[6]

Statesmanlike conduct by union president John Mitchell during the anthracite coal strike in 1902 gave further support to the enthusiasm

---

[3]Neil W. Chamberlain, *Collective Bargaining* (New York: McGraw-Hill, 1951), p. 33.

[4]Commons et al., *History of Labour in the United States*, II, p. 480. Commons notes that the iron- and steelworkers had a trade agreement as early as 1866, but the trade was so strong "that its example had no power to make other trades aspire with confidence towards the same."

[5]*Ibid.*, p. 524.

[6]Selig Perlman and Philip Taft, *History of Labour in the United States, 1896–1932*, IV (New York: Macmillan, 1935), p. 25.

generated by the bituminous coal workers' success of 1898. Mitchell, despite the heaviest pressure, refused to sanction a sympathetic strike by bituminous coal miners in aid of the anthracite strikers. The ground for his refusal was that the bituminous miners were under an agreement, and to strike would be a breach of faith with the employer signatories to that agreement. His stand placed the onus for prolongation of the strike upon the anthracite operators and, most important, encouraged a much more sympathetic public attitude toward labor.

Building-trade unions in the meantime were experiencing significant advances. Comprising almost two dozen unions, the crafts expanded their holding in the building construction industry from an initial 68,000 members going into their second hundred years, to over 394,000 in 1904 and over 500,000 by World War I. Taft notes that the most stable unions in the United States were in the building construction industry.[7]

Just as epochal in their impact on the development of trade agreements were the agreements secured by the Ladies' Garment Workers Union and the Clothing Workers Union. An agreement resulting from the settlement of the Cloakmakers' strike of 1910 established, among a number of other important provisions, a board of arbitration: one representative from each side and attorneys from the two groups. The board was charged with considering and settling all grievances, and rulings of the board were to be final and binding. This brought to an industry "hitherto considered hopelessly anarchial" a form of industrial government.[8]

Not to be outdone, the railroad brotherhoods had also continued to build upon the sound foundation of collective bargaining and trade agreements established before the turn of the century. For example, the Locomotive Engineers had succeeded by 1920 in enlarging and extending written contracts to about 100 pages and to almost all the railroad systems of the country. By 1902, 118 carriers were covered by written contracts; by 1912, 243 carriers; and by 1916, 348 carriers.[9]

ENVIRONMENT

Even though collective bargaining was faced with the restraints of intense employer opposition and adverse court decisions, the environment within which it had to develop, beginning with the 1890s, was much more favorable and conducive to positive results than in earlier periods.

In the first place, unions had developed some permanence and continuity not known in earlier days. This was evinced in two ways. No

[7]Philip Taft, *Organized Labor in American History* (New York: Harper & Row, 1964), p. 203.

[8]Perlman and Taft, *History of Labour in the United States*, IV, p. 300.

[9]Reed C. Richardson, *The Locomotive Engineer, 1863–1963* (Ann Arbor: Bureau of Industrial Relations, University of Michigan, 1963), p. 363.

longer were unions characterized by spasms of union activity during prosperity phases of business cycles, followed by periods of disorganization
and decline during depression that in some instances completely destroyed union organizations. But the stability was more than the ability to
maintain organization and membership in the face of economic fluctua-
tions. It was also a stability of purpose and goals, born of the unity brought
on by the adoption of the new trade unionism philosophy. Now, in good
times and bad, instead of alternating between economic or trade union
action on the one hand and panaceas and politics on the other, the union
movement held steadily to its business unionism mode of operation. This
stability of both organization and mode of operation introduced a positive
factor in the drive for collective bargaining and trade agreements.

Second, business unionism by its very nature gave a positive thrust
to the drive for collective bargaining. It has been pointed out that collective bargaining is a conservative and businesslike process. It is easy, therefore, to conclude that with the adoption of the business unionism philosophy by the trade union movement, the "trade agreement" became the *sine
qua non* of American trade unionism and brought with it a natural and
positive emphasis on developing collective bargaining relationships.

Third, nothing succeeds like success. And success is more easily
achieved in an atmosphere where the developments taking place are understood, not novel. As a result of developments in iron, transportation,
and shoes in the 1870s and 1880s, and the rapid spread of the trade
agreement both geographically and by trade in the 1890s, neither the trade
agreement nor collective bargaining was foreign to the American mind.
Consequently, with the notable and successful formalization by the stove
molders, miners, railroad men, and garment workers of collective bargaining and the trade agreement in their industries, it raised the anticipation
and hopes of other workers that they too could accomplish the same
results. Both the penetration of these significant industries and the model
trade agreements that resulted were certainly an impetus and example for
others to follow.

Fourth, not only was the trade agreement no longer novel and therefore more easily accepted by the public, but the nature of developments in
the economy created a more favorable, if not at times sympathetic, public
attitude toward organized labor and its goals. A "clear gauge" of attitudinal change is shown by the McNamara dynamite case. Only an investigation was requested by the public, not revenge.[10] Other indications
of attitudinal changes are numerous. In the bituminous coal strike of
1897, "A great deal of public support had been won by the peaceful
attitude of the strikers," and in August of 1897, "the Governor of Indiana
publicly expressed his approval of the walkout and urged the citizens of

---

[10]Commons et al., *History of Labour in the United States*, II, p. 528.

his state to aid the strikers."[11] Moreover, Mitchell's statesmanship in the anthracite coal strike of 1902 not only came "as a pleasant surprise to a public which had little inkling that labor unions considered their contractual obligations as binding under all circumstances,"[12] but provoked discussion and publicity to the point where "the public at large became accustomed to view the labour question in a matter-of-course, non-hysterical light."[13] Taft observes:

> Prolonged unemployment, with its accompanying destitution and suffering, tarnished the reputation of business, and the public regarded, at least for a time, the workers' quest for greater security and higher pay as justifiable. Exposures of corporate derelictions made the demands of labor for some countervailing power appear reasonable. The friendlier public attitude toward labor was written into federal and state legislation.[14]

Finally, although the court system, imbued with the sacredness of private property rights, was restrictive in its decisions, the federal government itself assumed a more neutral stance. Laissez faire, the less government intervention the better, became the order of the day. Only one industry experienced government intervention—the railroads.

It should be remembered that the brotherhoods, because of their strategic position in the country's transportation system, were involved in frontier developments in labor-management legislation that, even though immediately confined to transportation, were to establish a pattern for much of the labor legislation dealing with collective bargaining enacted after 1932. The philosophy of government intervention in the affairs of the railroad industry, because of the high degree of public interest involved (illustrated by the Interstate Commerce Act of 1887), led directly to a parallel line of reasoning with respect to labor-management relations in the industry. If the railroad industry needed regulation in order to protect the public interest, then labor-management relations might likewise require government supervision in order to ensure uninterrupted service. Thus, the government set about establishing machinery to minimize labor disputes.

But the government did not inject itself into the field of railway labor relations as a regulatory force. Its approach was to provide machinery to facilitate, not force, a solution in disputes that the parties were unable to settle by private negotiation. Three acts were passed between 1888 and 1913, providing variously for the use of arbitration, mediation, and fact-

[11]Perlman and Taft, *History of Labour in the United States*, IV, p. 24.
[12]*Ibid.*, p. 48.
[13]Commons et al., *History of Labour in the United States*, II, p. 528.
[14]Taft, *Organized Labor in American History*, p. 162.

finding boards as instruments to solve disputes. The importance of these acts lay not in their practical accomplishment but in the precedent they set for government intervention in labor relations. Eventually, this led to the passage of the Railway Labor Act of 1926, which for many years was known as the "model act" because of its influence on the National Labor Relations Act and other legislation of the thirties. But beyond its serving as a model, it should be noted that the passage of the Railway Labor Act was a great landmark in the development of collective bargaining because, although confined to a single industry—transportation—the act enunciated for the first time public policy with respect to labor-management relations. Employers in an industry were for the first time guaranteed by legislation the right to organize and bargain collectively through representatives of their own choosing. Carriers and their employees were required to exert every reasonable effort to make and maintain agreements concerning rates of pay, rules, and working conditions, and to settle disputes, whether they arose from the application of the agreements or otherwise. Finally, clear recognition was given to the need for a difference in the methods of handling disputes arising over the terms of the agreement, and methods in disputes arising over interpretation of those terms. This marked the zenith of the contributions of both the railroad industry and the railroad brotherhoods to the development of collective bargaining. The brotherhoods, once known as the "aristocracy of the labor movement," and the senior brotherhood, the Locomotive Engineers—described by newspapers in the 1880s as the "most powerful labor organization in the country"—contributed much to the founding period of collective bargaining but now were soon to be eclipsed by the decline of their own industry and their overshadowing by unions in other industries.

COLLECTIVE BARGAINING AND PUBLIC POLICY: 1930 TO 1945

INTRODUCTION

No previous period in the history of American trade unionism, other than the Great Upheaval of 1886, matched the epochal importance of the 1930s in the development of collective bargaining and industrial self-government for the worker. With the passage of the National Industrial Recovery Act in 1933, followed in 1935 by the National Labor Relations Act, collective bargaining received a degree of public respectability that a century and a half of private efforts had been unable to achieve. The impact on the organizing and collective bargaining activities of the trade union movement was nothing short of phenomenal.

COLLECTIVE BARGAINING

The impact of the New Deal on labor's bargaining efforts was not only dramatic but, in many ways, the single most epochal development in the evolution of collective bargaining.

> *Within a brief span of six years, American workers in the basic industrial sector of the nation witnessed the transformation of their bargaining organizations from relatively impotent bodies into equal partners in the industrial system.*[15]

Not only had union organizing activities been raised by law to a respectability not known in the past, but collective bargaining and the trade agreement had now also achieved the same respectability.

It should be emphasized that by the enactment of the National Labor Relations Act, and through it, guarantee of the "full freedom of association, self-organization, and designation of representatives of their choosing," Congress was establishing the *means* to an *end*. The end or goal that Congress hoped to achieve through guarantee of the right of workers to organize was twofold: (1) an antidepression measure, and (2) the establishment of a system of industrial government through collective bargaining. The lack of the latter, said Congress, was to injure, impair, or interrupt commerce and to aggravate recurrent business depressions. Therefore, as a matter of public policy, Congress stated:

> *It is hereby declared to be the policy of the United States to eliminate the causes of certain substantial obstructions to the free flow of commerce and to mitigate and eliminate these obstructions when they have occurred by encouraging the practice and procedure of collective bargaining and by protecting the exercise by workers of full freedom of association . . . for the purpose of negotiating the terms and conditions of their employment or other mutual aid or protection.*[16]

The solid evidence of the spread of collective bargaining and trade agreements is found both in numbers and in the nature of the industries in which industrial government was established. The increase in membership of unions to almost 15 million by 1945 also meant that some 12 million more workers were covered and constituted an increase of 500 percent, not an insignificant change. Not available is the number of trade agreements in 1933, but in 1945 there were well over 100,000 different

[15]Walter Galenson, *The CIO Challenge to the AFL* (Cambridge, Mass.: Harvard University Press, 1960), p. xvii.

[16]National Labor Relations Act, Section 1. (Act of July 5, 1935, 49 Stat. 449)

trade agreements in operation at one time. The establishment of agreements in the steel and automobile industries reflects well the nature of change going on in individual industries:

> *If there is any single series of events in the labor history of this period which may be characterized as of momentous import, it is the organization of the steel industry . . . a crushing defeat by the United States Steel Corporation in 1901. . . . Yet by March, 1937, the United States Steel Corporation, long a symbol of anti-unionism, had signed a collective contract with an outside union, an action that had repercussions throughout American industry.*[17]

> *By entirely stopping production of all General Motors cars in January and February and obtaining recognition in the first written and signed agreement on a national scale which that great citadel of the open shop had ever granted to a labor union, the CIO . . . opened the way for the remarkable upsurge in sentiment for union organization which is now going on in many sections of the country.*[18]

ENVIRONMENT

Basically, the changes in the 1930s that were of such significance for trade unions and the spread of collective bargaining were not changes unrelated to the past. As with most significant historical changes, the process was one of slow evolution, a gathering of forces for change reaching back, in some instances, a considerable period of time. Eventually in the course of time, there is juxtaposition of these underlying forces for change and a catalyst of sufficient power to effect the desired changes. So it was with the tremendous ideological shifts of both the public and the government in the 1930s. Industrial unionism was not new. Labor legislation was not new. The need for social change that would recognize the rights of human beings relative to property was not new. Collective bargaining and the trade agreement were not new. But in the past, the full recognition of these needs was hindered by an environment that was generally hostile and obstructive. Now, in the 1930s, the juxtaposition of needs and historical events occurred. The catalyst was the crash of 1929 and the ensuing Great Depression. The impetus to change was a significant shift in public and governmental attitudes arising out of the economic and humanitarian needs of this unique, deep, and lengthy period of distress.

The Great Depression was not only the most severe depression in the history of the United States, but it caused a complete economic collapse, cutting across all economic classes and groups: "Great fortunes and the

---

[17]Galenson, *The CIO Challenge*, p. 75.

[18]*Ibid.*, p. 141. From Russel B. Porter in *The New York Times*, April 4, 1937, IV, p. 10.

widow's mite together disappeared."[19] It was more shocking in its effect than past depressions had been: "Leaders in all walks of life, including economists, were dumbfounded at the speed with which the glittering structure of prosperity had collapsed like a house of cards."[20] It raised real questions about the applicability of the shibboleths of the past to a modern industrial world:

> In 1928 they had been promised "a chicken in every pot and two cars in every garage," if they elected Hoover. In 1932, when the owner of a garage felt himself lucky to have a roof on it and a chicken to relieve its emptiness, he had ceased to reverence the old shibboleths of "rugged individualism" and the "immutable laws of economics."[21]

The individual stresses of the moment created a state of mind not only more oriented to human needs but susceptible to change. "No language is graphic enough to picture the want that stalked through the land as economic conditions became worse . . . no mind sufficiently keen to measure the human losses that resulted."[22]

It was thus in this atmosphere of doubt about the ideology of the past, and of intense pressures upon the government to find solutions to the economic stress and the primacy of human needs, that the great social legislation of the 1930s in the field of labor was made possible, although it must be admitted that the AFL was more the recipient than the initiator of change.

EMPLOYER ACCEPTANCE: 1945 TO 1962

One fact became clear in the postwar period: Collective bargaining had come of age. Initially, the move toward collective bargaining had been motivated by the need of workers, threatened by the increasing size and impersonal nature of the modern industrial organization, to make themselves heard through representation lest they be engulfed and lose their identity. The vehicle through which they gained representation and the hope for a collective bargaining relationship came with the formation of the labor organization. Over a century and a half, the growth of employee representation through collective bargaining was the chief beneficiary of

---

[19]James A. Barnes, *Wealth of the American People* (Englewood Cliffs, N.J.: Prentice-Hall, 1949), p. 68.

[20]Harold W. Faulkner, *American Economic History*, 8th ed. (New York: Harper & Row, 1954), p. 651.

[21]Fred O. Shannon, *America's Economic Growth* (New York: Macmillan, 1940), p. 744.

[22]Barnes, *Wealth of the American People*, p. 681.

the continuity and expansion of the trade union movement. Further progress was made when, in the 1930s, collective bargaining was given public respectability through a policy statement: "It is hereby declared to be the policy of the United States . . . [to encourage] the practice and procedure of collective bargaining . . ."[23] It remained for the postwar period to witness a final step—acceptance of collective bargaining as a permanent institutional process in American society. Finally, the entire evolution was nurtured to respectability through the instrumentality of an environment based on democracy.

No longer faced with the need to devote time and efforts to establishing the principle of collective bargaining, labor and management could turn their efforts toward improvement of it. The result was increasingly to professionalize the practice of collective bargaining. It was well established by this time that collective bargaining included two important elements: negotiation and contract administration. Moreover, the labor agreement became a more complex and technical document.

Finally, as forces of dramatic change began to affect the social and economic fabric of society, workers' lives and their needs were also affected and became more complex. As more complex matters became involved in labor-management relations, the viability and effectiveness of collective bargaining as a means of solving modern labor-management problems came increasingly under question and even attack.

COLLECTIVE BARGAINING

For collective bargaining, the events of 1945 to 1962 were somewhat disparate in impact. There were encouraging developments while, at the same time, there were some clouds on the horizon.

One encouraging result of the 1935 to 1945 expansion of both the trade union movement and collective bargaining was the broadening and deepening impact on the latter. Union organization not only extended collective bargaining to the major industrial employers of the country and through this brought larger numbers of workers under the trade agreement system, but also extended the role of collective bargaining geographically and occupationally. By the very nature of the widening and deepening process, collective bargaining became more and more firmly rooted in America's system.

The metamorphosis from unilateralism to acceptance of collective bargaining in principle was completed. The government had already accepted collective bargaining as necessary; the courts had made an abrupt turnabout from the obstructionist doctrine of individual freedom of contract to the primacy of the collective bargaining contract; the public no

---

[23]National Labor Relations Act, Findings and Policy, Sec. 1.

longer questioned collective bargaining or trade agreements; it remained only for the last bastion of resistance to the acceptance of collective bargaining to fall—that is, the employer. Within a few years after World War II, it became clear that employers had accepted collective bargaining and the trade agreement as more or less permanent fixtures of the American way of life.

This fact can be illustrated by two events between 1945 and 1950. One clear example of the change occurred in the bargaining relationships in the automobile industry. In 1937, members of the UAW had occupied the premises of the General Motors Corporation and were engaged in a sit-down strike. The reaction of GM was to request that Governor Murphy send in National Guard troops to expel the strikers and protect company property. In 1950, in contrast, the two former antagonists signed a now-famous agreement, the "Treaty of Detroit," in which they agreed to a labor contract of five years' duration with a no-reopening clause. The second event that illustrated employer acceptance of collective bargaining was the postwar labor-management conference called by President Truman, when compared to a similar conference called by Wilson after World War I. The World War I conference broke up over the unwillingness of the employers to accept unionism and, with it, collective bargaining as the sole vehicle for handling employee-employer problems. The employers felt that employees should be free to choose the nemesis of unions, the company representation plan, if they so desired. In contrast, the major issue in the second postwar conference was not over the right of unions to represent workers nor over their right to negotiate collective bargaining agreements. The issue debated most vigorously by the employers, and their major concern, was the scope and coverage of collective bargaining. The acceptability of the process of collective bargaining was not the issue, only how far it was to be allowed to encroach on what employers considered areas of management prerogatives.

A second development in collective bargaining occurred as a result of wartime wage controls. The War Labor Board, which was given the responsibility for controlling wage increases, had allowed unions to negotiate certain noncash benefits. The reasoning was that these benefits, since they were "at the fringe" of wages, would not have a direct and immediate impact on employee spending and therefore were not inflationary in character. The unions, finding an opening through which they could assuage their members' complaints, took vigorous action to keep this door open and to widen it. This then became the platform from which the so-called fringe-benefit movement was launched, destined to play such an important part, in time and in substance, during the negotiations of ensuing years. The impact of fringe items on collective bargaining varied, but there is no doubt that, overall, this movement introduced a rapidly expanding list of bargaining items to the negotiating table, greatly enlarged the length and complexity of labor agreements, and required a greater need for professional expertise on the part of negotiators. Most of the mandatory bargaining items added to negotiations over the years were a result of National Labor Relations Board (NLRB) or court decisions on disputed fringe items. Illustrative of the extent to which fringe items increased in numbers is the list of 101 of them compiled by Dale Yoder, admittedly only a partial list, under four general categories: (1) For Employment Security, (2) For Health Protection, (3) For Old Age and Retirement, and (4) For Personal Identification, Participation, and On-the-Job Motivation.[24]

The one dark cloud on the horizon in the late fifties concerned the viability of the collective bargaining process faced by increasingly complex employee benefit needs and the more complex technological and social problems of the period. There were those who felt that collective bargaining simply could not effectively deal with the broad national and international economic and social problems emerging at the end of the 1950s. Willard Wirtz, the secretary of labor, raised the challenge in a speech at the International Trade Fair in Chicago in 1961:

> In a world that has shrunk overnight and a national economy in which each part now depends on every other part and on the health of the whole, the continuation of private collective bargaining as the important force in the future it has been in the past, depends on the decision of the bargainers to exercise, or not to exercise, responsibility for the concerns that affect the whole economy. . . . The future of collective bargaining depends on whether its motive power and its procedures can be adjusted and revised to permit a large recognition and reflection of the common national interests.[25]

An independent study group of the Committee for Economic Development (CED), appointed to look into the matter of the effectiveness of collective bargaining in resolving the matters of the day, reported:

> In the quarter century that has elapsed since the mid-thirties, this form of industrial relations has been widely accepted in principle, but is now being criticized more and more in practice. In recent years particularly, collective bargaining has been a target in a cross-fire of mounting complaints about its past and present consequences and of increasing reservation about its future serviceability. Indeed, the fashion today in many quarters is to point to a crisis in Collective Bargaining and to dispense policy prescriptions for drastic change.[26]

[24]Dale Yoder, *Personnel Management and Industrial Relations*, 7th ed. (Englewood Cliffs, N.J.: Prentice-Hall, 1982), pp. 656–57.

[25]W. Willard Wirtz, "The Future of Collective Bargaining," address delivered at the International Trade Fair, Chicago, August 3, 1961, *Monthly Labor Review*, 84, no. 11, 1206.

[26]An Independent Study Group, *The Public Interest in National Labor Policy* (New York: Committee for Economic Development, 1961), p. 7.

ENVIRONMENT

The environment of the late forties and the fifties was mixed. On the one side was a nation adjusting from war to peace—a catch-up period for consumer groups deprived of many items during the wartime period, for workers seeking to catch up on wages and other benefits, for industry changing over to peacetime production but also considerably affected by advances in technology resulting from wartime technical and scientific progress. It was a period of contrasts in public attitudes, reflecting the pain of adjustment to all groups resulting from the inevitable crosscurrents and conflicts generated by interest groups, each seeking to maximize its own position. Also, there were the beginnings of a closer examination of values—by individuals and groups, ranging from economic values to human worth—that were to have such portent for the upheaval in values and relationships of the 1960s. Perhaps the most continuous and basic underlying influence, with widespread repercussions on economic, social, cultural, and human values, was the significant and rapidly changing technology of the nation. True, the basis for the technological changes was laid in the past. However, the rate of change in application of new technology—the technology of the computer and the space age—was what separates this period from others. The rapid rate of change brought to all of American society widespread repercussions, many of which were not to be really felt until later. In a way, the impact on the modern world of the 1950s was much like the impact of the Industrial Revolution in the late nineteenth century, except that society was a little, but not much, better prepared to adapt to the change in the 1950s. Even so, those living in any such period are too close to the scene to be aware of the full implication of such major changes in technology and their disruption of economic and social relationships and patterns. While the adaptation may not be as dramatic as in the past, it is still painful in many ways. It is in this kind of a changing atmosphere—(1) rapid technological change, (2) a questioning attitude about unions and collective bargaining, and (3) a society in the throes of major change in attitudes and in institutional and personal relationships—that trade unionism and collective bargaining moved from the 1950s into the changing and new world of the 1960s and 1970s.

COLLECTIVE BARGAINING, AN INSTITUTION: 1962 TO THE PRESENT

With greater historical perspective, it may well be that the period since 1962 will be viewed as one of the three most important periods, rivaling the periods of the 1880s and the 1930s in its impact on the fundamental character of the labor movement and collective bargaining. In common to all three periods was the imbalance caused by rapidly changing technology: large-scale production in the 1880s, mass production starting in the 1920s, and the technology of the computer and space age in the 1950s and 1960s.

Partly a manifestation of these imbalances, but also a result of long-standing, deeply rooted social problems was the embarrassing anomoly, as the nation moved into the 1960s, of a substantial part of the population—20 to 30 million—who, because of discrimination, lack of education, or lack of skills, either could not find employment, or if employed, could not earn enough to rise above poverty levels. Structural employment, a result of technological change, was the increasing problem of matching people to jobs. The juxtaposition of these serious economic and social problems with the increasing assertiveness on the part of many groups who considered themselves victims gave rise to aggression. The civil rights movement undoubtedly sparked this greater assertiveness. This was followed in the 1960s by various student movements, the young peoples' questioning the values of their elders, the increased vocalness and activity of the feminist movement and of groups caught up in the issue over representation, such as teachers, policemen, firemen, and other public employees. Moreover, structural changes in employment were eroding the central industrial base of trade unionism. This, combined with rising educational levels among workers and a younger working population, meant significant changes in the membership composition of unions, increasing the inflow of younger and better educated members and of professional, technical, and clerical white-collar workers. And with the extension of collective bargaining rights in 1962 to federal workers, the influx of public-sector employees brought about further change in union membership. Finally, added to the changing environment for collective bargaining was the Pandora's box of problems of the 1970s and 1980s—inflation, unemployment, energy shortages, pollution of the environment, foreign competition, and international tensions, plus a splurge of social legislation in reaction to many of the group movements that brought the government much more intimately into the substance of collective bargaining in areas such as civil rights, pay, safety, and health and welfare, to name a few.

It is small wonder there were those in the 1950s and 1960s who doubted the ability of the institution of collective bargaining to survive in this complex and changing environment. A cursory review of collective bargaining since the 1960s reveals that, not only has collective bargaining as a vital functioning institution of American society survived, it has achieved a status of respectability. So-called concessionary bargaining, the object of much attention during the recession of the early 1980s, attests to the viability and adaptability of collective bargaining to meet changing situations. It should be pointed out that concessionary bargaining functioned within the traditional system of free collective bargaining, not outside it. The question today is not whether collective bargaining can survive as an institution, but what can be done to insure that it will be an even more productive functioning unit of American life. While not diminishing its viability in the face of emerging complexities, the following developments of the 1960s to the 1980s affirm the growing acceptability of collective bargaining in its own right:

1. While faced with many internal problems and major adjustments to a changing clientele and a myriad of *new* problems, the traditional private sector unionism still holds to collective bargaining and the labor agreement as the *sine qua non* of the trade union movement.

2. The relative decline of traditional private-sector unionism was offset, in part, by the extension of collective bargaining rights to federal, state, and municipal workers through legislative enactments in a majority of states and by presidential order at the federal level. These official moves by federal and state governments brought whole new areas of employers and employees under the umbrella of collective bargaining contracts, and in so doing widened the coverage and acceptability of collective bargaining. Of equal import, the government extended organizing and bargaining rights to its own employees for the first time. This it had failed or refused to do when extending the same rights to employees in the private sector more than twenty-five years earlier. Both federal and state governments now placed themselves squarely behind the process of collective bargaining. Such a commitment to public employees could not help but raise the practice to a more prestigious level. Indeed, in quick order, the federal and state governments effected more change in public employer-employee relations than in any comparable period in the past. For example, it is estimated that over 80 percent of federal employees have elected to be brought under collective bargaining contracts, something not achieved in private sector unionism in some two hundred years of endeavor.

3. A new dimension has also been added since the 1960s to the expanding acceptance of collective bargaining. This is the advent of the professional or state association as negotiator of collective bargaining agreements for its members. District, state, and federal associations of teachers are examples. While avoiding the name *union* or formal affiliation with the union movement, these associations have taken on many of the trappings of unions, not the least of which is their function of negotiating the terms and conditions of employment for their members. Community groups have also availed themselves of further collective bargaining in solving joint problems through negotiation, thus expanding collective bargaining's scope and usage.

4. Finally, as a result of the willingness of many groups to experiment with new methods, collective bargaining remains vital and operative. Some issues and situations are not amenable to crisis bargaining or

frequent strikes. Such issues are finding solutions more and more through innovative changes in bargaining procedures (see Part IV, Management of Conflict). Less attention is being paid today to alternatives and substitutes for collective bargaining and more to innovative methods of improving the effectiveness of collective bargaining. Pessimism and negativeness toward the institution of collective bargaining is being replaced more and more with a positive attitude wherein collective bargaining is viewed as the only constructive vehicle in a free society to resolve employer-employee problems.

SELECTED REFERENCES

Barkin, Solomon, *The Decline of the Labor Movement.* Santa Barbara, Calif.: Center for the Study of Democratic Institutions, 1961. Written as a contemporary account by a knowledgeable witness of the labor movement's travail at the end of the 1950s.

Beirne, Joseph A., *Challenge to Labor.* Englewood Cliffs, N.J.: Prentice-Hall, 1969. A labor leader articulates the responsibility of the labor movement to serve as an effective spokesman not only for union members but for all workers in the pluralistic balances of forces in American society. He sees the labor movement's role in preserving and fortifying American "pluralism" as vital to our democratic processes.

Bowen, William C., and Orley Ashenfelter, eds., *Labor and the National Economy,* rev. ed. New York: Norton, 1975. The editors note that there has been more and more of a recognition by all groups over the last two decades of the extent to which the success of our economic system depends on the workings of labor markets. The essays included in this pamphlet address themselves to the labor markets and such issues as efficiency, labor problems of minorities and women, and inflation and unemployment.

Brody, David, ed., *The American Labor Movement.* New York: Harper & Row, 1971. A series of essays on the American labor movement, with an integrative theme. The editor was charged with the responsibility of selecting some of what he considered the best, most persuasive writings bearing on the American labor movement. For a penetrating look at some of the significant aspects of American labor in the late nineteenth century and early twentieth century, this book earns high marks.

Brooks, Thomas R., *Walls Come Tumbling Down—A History of the Civil Rights Movement, 1940–1970.* Englewood Cliffs, N.J.: Prentice-Hall, 1974. While no single development accounts for major changes in the social framework and attitudes of society, certainly there is justification in pointing to the civil rights movement as one of the catalysts that induced the changes, in the 1960s, in people's attitudes and relationships.

Chamberlain, Neil W., *Collective Bargaining.* New York: McGraw-Hill, 1951. Chapter 20 examines the role of collective bargaining in American society. Chamberlain raises the question of the need for synthesis between the group activity or cooperative approach of collective bargaining and the old systematic reliance on individual competition.

Derber, Milton, and Edwin Young, eds., *Labor and the New Deal.* Madison: University of Wisconsin Press, 1957. A definitive work on the rise of organized labor under the New Deal.

Fleming, Robin W., "Collective Bargaining Revisited," in *Frontiers of Collective Bargaining,* eds. John T. Dunlop and Neil W. Chamberlain. New York: Harper & Row, 1967. A thoughtful and careful coverage of the evolution of collective bargaining from the thirties to the mid-sixties. Discussed are such subjects as structural problems, bargaining in the public sector, the new context for bargaining in the private sector, and interest-dispute handling.

Galenson, Walter, *The CIO Challenge to the AFL.* Cambridge, Mass.: Harvard University Press, 1960. An excellent and highly recommended study of the emergence and rise to power of the CIO.

Gross, James A., *The Makings of the National Labor Relations Board,* Vol. I. Albany: State University of New York Press, 1974. The author notes the ever-increasing importance of administrative agencies as vital and pervasive forces in our society and the need for a major study of such groups. This study looks into the events of 1933 to 1937, leading to and following the establishment of the NLRB.

Perlman, Selig, and Philip Taft, *History of Labour in the United States, 1896–1932,* Vol. IV. New York: Macmillan, 1935. Continuing in the mold of the other three volumes of the Commons series on labor history, the Perlman and Taft volume provides a wealth of detailed and well-documented materials on the development of labor relations from the depression of the 1890s to the early 1930s. An outstanding feature of the book is the first chapter's "Conclusions from Past Experimentation."

Taft, Philip, *The A. F. of L. in the Time of Gompers.* New York: Harper & Row, 1957. The first to receive full access to AFL files and records, Professor Taft makes a notable contribution to the information about the rise of the AFL and its activities up to the death of Gompers in 1924.

———, *The A. F. of L. From the Death of Gomper to the Merger.* New York: Harper & Row, 1959. This constitutes the second phase of Professor Taft's study of the AFL. While not addressed directly to collective bargaining during the period, it does provide a useful framework through which a better understanding of the union movement and, with it, collective bargaining can be obtained.

———, *Organized Labor in American History.* New York: Harper & Row, 1964. A good general history of organized labor, with considerable information about the growth of collective bargaining and the trade agreement.

Taylor, Benjamin J., and Fred Witney, *Labor Relations Law,* 4th ed., chapters 1–11. Englewood Cliffs, N.J.: Prentice-Hall, 1983. Excellent coverage of the evolution of the law of collective bargaining from the early stages when, more often than not, the law was a hindrance to the growth of collective bargaining, up to the emergence of public policy intended to encourage collective bargaining.

Ulman, Lloyd, *American Trade Unionism—Past and Present: 1. The Development of Trades and Labor Unions; 2. Unionism and Collective Bargaining in the Modern Period,* Reprint no. 157, Institute of Industrial Relations, University of California, Berkeley, 1961. Professor Ulman brings to the reader a penetrating and informative look at the union movement and collective bargaining in the decade and a half following World War II.

CHAPTER 3

LEGAL FRAMEWORK:
An Overview

The purpose of this chapter is to outline the general framework of law that sets the legal boundaries and rules of the game for collective bargaining negotiations at the federal, state, and local levels and in the private and public sectors.

The legal framework of collective bargaining negotiations may be found in the Railway Labor Act (RLA), for railroad workers and airline employees; the National Labor Relations Act as amended by the Labor Management Relations Act of 1947 (LMRA 1947), covering all other areas of the private economy subject to federal law;[1] the Civil Service Reform

---

[1]The Railway Labor Act covers railroad and airline workers and was initially passed in 1926. It has been amended several times since.

The National Labor Relations Act (Wagner Act) was enacted in 1935 at the demise of the National Industrial Recovery Act of 1933 (NIRA). The NLRA has been amended and supplemented by additional legislation—the Labor Management Relations Act of 1947 (Taft-Hartley), the Labor Management Reporting and Disclosure Act of 1959 (Landrum-Griffin), and, more recently, Public Law 93-360 (Health Care Industry) in 1974.

Excluded prior to 1974, all private health-care institutions, whether or not operated for a profit, have been brought under the NLRA. Government-operated health facilities such as federal, state, county, and city hospitals are still excluded. Under this new legislation, private health-care institutions are covered in the same manner as other private concerns, except for special provisions to minimize work stoppages because of the critical nature of the services rendered by these institutions. Special procedures established by the amendment are covered in Part IV of this book, "Resolution of Conflict." Private health-care institutions include hospitals, convalescent hospitals, health-maintenance organizations, health clinics,

Act of 1978, Title VII (hereinafter CSRA 1978, Title VII), covering federal employees;[2] and various state laws covering employer-employee activities in both private and public employment not subject to federal law.[3] These statutes are the product of a long period of evolution reaching back almost two hundred years. The most recent antecedents, and those having the most direct bearing on the statutes of the present day, are found in the legislation of the late nineteenth and early twentieth century in the railway labor field. These legislative acts served as a basis of experience and a language model for the labor legislation of the last four decades.

Beginning with the Arbitration Act of 1888, the use of arbitration and investigative boards in work stoppages was introduced. Mediation and conciliation were added by the Erdman Act of 1898. The Newlands Act followed in 1913, continuing both arbitration and mediation, and then was succeeded by the Transportation Act of 1920, which established a Railway Labor Board empowered to investigate and report the facts of disputes. Railway labor legislation reached heights it has never capped in the Railway Labor Act of 1926. This act, still operative, was for many years considered the model for emerging legislation on employer-employee matters. The most notable feature of the act was the legal right it gave to railway workers to organize, choose representatives, and engage in collective bargaining without "interference, influence or coercion." This was to serve as the cornerstone philosophy of the National Labor Relations Act of 1935 and subsequent legislation in both private and public areas.

LEGAL FRAMEWORK: NATIONAL LEVEL

Although a more detailed examination of the law in both private and public sectors will be made at appropriate points in later chapters, it may be useful here to mention some of the major areas covered by statutes, orders, or regulations that establish the overall legal framework for collective bargaining. Attention is confined initially to those employees covered

---

nursing homes, extended-care facilities, or other institutions devoted to the care of sick, infirm, or aged persons.

Hereinafter, the term *NLRA* will be used to identify the National Labor Relations Act as amended in 1947, 1959, and 1974. Where *Taft-Hartley* is used, it will be to identify portions of the 1947 law adding new titles to the labor relations statutes.

[2]Collective bargaining rights were first extended to federal employees by Executive Order 10988 in 1962. Other EOs in 1969, 1971, and 1975 augmented the original EO. These EOs were replaced in 1978 by CSRA, Title VII.

[3]There are twelve states with labor relations laws patterned after the NLRA and the LMRA 1947. In the public sector, forty states and the District of Columbia have extended collective bargaining coverage to state and/or municipal employees.

by the NLRA and CSRA 1978, Title VII. It is well to emphasize that this legal framework reflects essentially the same philosophy as that covering railway and airline workers under the Railway Labor Act. Ten areas are chosen to illustrate the coverage of the NLRA compared with the coverage of CSRA 1978, Title VII. State statutes covering public and private employees, while similar to the respective national laws, will be treated separately because of the difficulty of treating forty separate states having legislation. The areas to be compared under the NLRA and CSRA 1978, Title VII, are:

1. Purpose and policy
2. Parties to collective bargaining
3. Rights of parties to collective bargaining
4. Administration of statute
5. Collective bargaining representative
6. Appropriate bargaining unit
7. Duty to bargain
8. Enforcement—unfair labor practices
9. Contract administration—grievances and arbitration
10. Management of conflict

1. Purpose and Policy   Collective bargaining in both the private and public sectors is unequivocally encouraged by public policy.

NLRA	CSRA 1978, Title VII
Section 1 declares that, in order to mitigate and eliminate obstructions to the free flow of commerce, it is the policy of the U.S. to protect "the practice and procedure of collective bargaining."	Section 7101(a) declares that "labor organizations and collective bargaining in the civil service are in the public interest."

2. Parties to Collective Bargaining   Defining who is an employer, an employee, or a labor organization for collective bargaining purposes is vital under the statutes. It is absolutely necessary to know to what the statute applies in order to understand the rights, obligations, and procedures enunciated in the statutes.

NLRA	CSRA 1978, Title VII
Section 2(3) defines *employee* as any employee of an employer subject to federal law, including those out of work because of a legal strike, but excludes agricultural laborers, workers in do-	Section 7103 (a) defines *employee* as an individual employed in an agency, or out of work because of an unfair labor practice. Not included are supervisors, members of the armed forces, aliens

mestic service at home, independent contractors, supervisors, and those subject to the Railway Labor Act.

Section 2(2) defines *employers* as any employer subject to federal law, including their agents, but excludes federal and state governments or subdivisions, the Federal Reserve, wholly owned government corporations, nonprofit hospitals, persons under the Railway Labor Act, and labor organizations unless acting as an employer.

Section 2(5) refers to *labor organization* as any employee organization "which exists for the purpose, in whole or in part, of dealing with employees concerning grievances, labor disputes, wages, rates of pay, hours of employment, or conditions of work."

and noncitizens occupying a position outside the U.S., Foreign Service employees, and employees on strike in violation of Section 7311.

Section 7103(a)(3) defines *employer* as an executive agency, including the Library of Congress and GPO, but excluding the GAO, FBI, CIA, NSA, TVA, FLRA, Impasses Panel, Foreign Service, and certain intelligence and security operations.

Section 7103(a)(4) defines *labor organization* as an "organization composed in whole or in part of employees, in which employees . . . pay dues, and which has as a purpose the dealing with an agency concerning grievances and conditions of employment." It excludes organizations sponsored by an agency, or organizations that assist or participate in a strike against the government or advocate the overthrow of the government, or organizations that discriminate with regard to membership because of "race, creed, national origin, sex, age, preferential or nonpreferential Civil Service status, political affiliation, marital status, or handicapping condition."

3. Rights of Parties to Collective Bargaining The central focus of statutes prior to CSRA 1978, Title VII, was directed to rights of employees. Title VII of CSRA 1978 introduces the rights of management by statute.

NLRA

Section 7 enunciates the rights of employees as the "right to self-organization, to form, join or assist labor organizations, to bargain collectively through representatives of their own choosing, or to engage in other concerted activities for the purpose of collective bargaining or other mu-

CSRA 1978, Title VII

Section 7102 states that "Each employee shall have the right to form, join, assist any labor organization, or to refrain from any such activity, freely and without fear of penalty or reprisal. . . ." This also includes the right to act as a representative of an organization and to "engage in collec-

tual aid or protection, and shall also have the right to refrain. . . .

The NLRA does not cover management rights. Management rights become a part of the labor agreements only by negotiation.

tive bargaining with respect to conditions of employment through representatives chosen by the employees."

Section 7106 specifically addresses the rights of management or the agency to determine such matters as mission, budget, organization, number of employees, and internal security practices. Also, in accordance with applicable laws, much the same as management rights clauses in private-sector contracts, this section grants management the right to hire, assign, direct, lay off, discipline, contract out, and promote, to name a few.

Labor organization rights are covered under 5. *Collective Bargaining Representative.*

4. Administration of Statute   Each statute is administered by an agency of the executive branch of the government.

NLRA

Section 3(a) provides for the administration of the NLRA by an executive agency, the National Labor Relations Board, consisting of five members appointed by the president with approval of the Senate. This section also provides for the appointment of a general counsel, who is the prosecuting arm of the administering authority. The board is responsible for adjudicating appeals of unfair labor practices and administers the representation procedures of the statute.

CSRA 1978, Title VII

Section 7104 provides for the Federal Labor Relations Authority. A general counsel is also provided for. Appointment and functions are mostly similar to the NLRB and its general counsel, except in one area: The FLRA, under certain circumstances, hears appeals from arbitration decisions—Sec. 7105(a)(2)(H).

5. Collective Bargaining Representative   Through provision of an election process for certifying the bargaining representative of the employees, the statute also provides a vehicle for the labor organization to gain protection of certain rights under the law.

NLRA

Section 9 provides a means of certifying the collective bargaining representative for employees in an appropriate unit by evidence that at least 30 percent of the employees in the unit wish to be represented by the labor organization. Such evidence must be followed by a secret ballot resulting in a majority of the unit employees' favoring the labor organization.

Section 9 also provides that the labor organization may be designated as representative of employees in the unit by consensus of the parties.

Section 9 provides that the labor organization designated becomes the *exclusive* collective bargaining representative of all the employees of the unit, without regard to membership in the organization.

Section 9 provides a bar against an election during any twelve-month period wherein a valid election has already occurred. The contract bar doctrine also may bar an election for up to three years during a valid contract.

CSRA 1978, Title VII

Section 7111 contains similar provisions.

Section 7111(g) contains similar provisions.

Section 7114(a)(1) provides for exclusive representation of "the interests of all employees in the unit it represents without discrimination and without regard to their organization membership."

Section 7111(f) identifies three bars to election: when a valid election has been held during the preceding twelve months, when exclusive rights have been granted an organization within the preceding twelve months, and when a contract has been in effect for less than three years.

6. Appropriate Bargaining Unit   The designation of the appropriate bargaining unit is directly linked to collective bargaining and the representation process. Before the election of a bargaining representative (just discussed), the employees to be represented must be the ones who may vote, and the ones to be covered by the agreement must be designated.

NLRA

Section 9(b) provides the fullest freedom to employees in the exercise of their rights, and grants to the NLRB the authority to determine whether the bargaining unit "shall be the employer, craft

CSRA 1978, Title VII

Section 7112(a) extends similar authority to the FLRA to determine if the appropriate unit should be on "an agency, plant, installation, functional or other basis." A community of interests

unit, plant, unit, or subdivision thereof."

Section 9(b) provides for exclusion of certain employees in certain circumstances; for example, professional employees, craft employees, guards.

among the unit employees is the objective.

Section 7111(b) excludes certain employees from the appropriate unit, such as, supervisors, confidential employees, personnel employees other than purely clerical, professional, intelligence and security, and audit employees.

7. Duty to Bargain   The duty to bargain is inextricably woven into the ultimate objective of collective bargaining: the consummation of a collective bargaining agreement.

NLRA

Sections 8(a)(5) and 8(b)(3) require that the employer and employee bargaining representatives bargain with each other. Section 8(d) includes in the above a mutual obligation to meet at reasonable times, to confer in good faith with respect to "wages, hours, and other terms and conditions of employment, or the negotiation of an agreement, or any question arising thereunder and the execution of written contracts incorporating any agreement reached." This does not compel consensus to a proposal or require a concession.

NLRB and court decisions have resulted in three bargaining items: mandatory, permissive, and prohibited. These will be explained in Chapter 10, "Bargaining Items."

No comparable provision may be found in the NLRA.

CSRA 1978, Title VII

Sections 7103(a)(12), 7114(a)(4), and 7114(b)(2) establish similar requirements for bargaining in good faith, with one exception. The exception is the subject matter for bargaining. This refers to what may be bargained, if presented by either party, as "conditions of employment affecting such employees." "Conditions of employment" under Section 7103(a)(14) means "personnel policies, practices, and matters, whether established by rule, regulation, or otherwise, affecting working conditions."

Bargaining items that are prohibited are prohibited political activities, position classifications, and any other matters specifically provided for by statute, such as wages. Although time has not allowed the formulation of a list comparable to the private sector, such a list is beginning to emerge through decisions of the FLRA. These will be explained in Chapter 10, "Bargaining Items." Section 7117(a) provides that the parties may bargain on matters subject to a government regulation if it can be shown that "no compelling need exists for the rule or regulation."

8. Enforcement—Unfair Labor Practices   Citing a party for an unfair labor practice is the means the authorities use to enforce the statutes governing collective bargaining in the private and federal government sectors.

NLRA	CSRA 1978, Title VII
Section 8(a)(1–5) generally restrains employers from interfering, restraining, or coercing employees in the exercise of their collective bargaining rights under the statute. It also restrains the employer from interfering with the employees' organization or employee membership therein, and from refusing to bargain with the certified representative of its employees.	Section 7116 provides for similar restraints against any attempts by employer or labor organization to interfere, restrain, or coerce employees in the exercise of their rights. In addition, it is an unfair labor practice for either the employer or the labor organization to refuse to cooperate during impasse procedures, or for the labor organization to discriminate in terms or conditions of membership on the basis of race, color, creed, national origin, sex, age, preferential or non-preferential civil service status, political affiliation, marital status, or handicap. The labor organization is also prohibited from participating in a work stoppage that interferes with an agency's operations.
Section 8(b) through (e) requires that labor organizations or their representatives bargain in good faith with the employer, uphold their contractual commitments, and desist from any attempts to influence the employer's choice of a bargaining representative or to cause the employer to discriminate against an employee for any reason other than not paying his dues and fees. Section 8 also declares it an unfair labor practice for the labor organization to engage in illegal strikes, boycotts, or picketing, or to force the employer to recognize any but the duly authorized representative of the employees.	

9. Contract Administration—Grievances and Arbitration   Contract administration refers to the mechanism for joint and peaceful resolution of questions or problems arising in the day-to-day application of the labor agreement. The vehicle for contract administration is the jointly negotiated grievance procedure. Statutory recognition of the right of an employee to grieve is explicit.

NLRA	CSRA 1978, Title VII
Section 9(a) acknowledges the right of an employee to present a	Section 7121 explicitly provides that agreements covering feder-

grievance to the employer without the intervention of the bargaining representative. However, any adjustment must comply with the contract, and the bargaining representative must be allowed to be present. Section 201 alludes to a grievance procedure, but the main emphasis is upon a terminal procedure for grievances.

al employees must contain a grievance procedure. This procedure is to include a terminal step, that is, binding arbitration. Provided also is the right of individual employees to process their own grievances, although the bargaining representative must be assured the right to be present. Section 7521(c) identifies some matters not subject to the grievance procedure. Section 7521(d), (e), and (f) covers alternative choices of the grievance procedure or statutory procedures on some matters.

Section 7105(a) allows the parties to appeal some arbitration decisions to the LMRA for review.

10. Management of Conflict   Impasse and other types of conflict resulting from negotiations have also received the attention of the lawmakers in both private-sector legislation and federal-employee legislation.

NLRA

Section 201 establishes an independent agency, the Federal Mediation and Conciliation Service, to provide assistance to the parties in their negotiations. Section 206 provides aid to the parties whenever a strike or lockout assumes the proportions of a national emergency. Aid is in the form of a board of inquiry, eighty-day injunction, and secret ballot on last offer.

CSRA 1978, Title VII

Since federal employees may not strike (Sec. 305, LMRA), it is natural that a high priority should be allotted to alternate procedures to resolve negotiation impasses. Section 7119 provides for a Federal Service Impasses Panel charged with providing "services and assistance to agencies . . . in the resolution of negotiation impasses." The panel is empowered to recommend procedures to the parties to resolve the impasse, assist the parties by whatever procedures it may deem appropriate, and, if all else fails, it may "take whatever action is necessary" not inconsistent with the statute. It reminds the author of what used to be called the "bag-of-tools" approach.

LEGAL FRAMEWORK: STATE AND LOCAL

Although twelve states have labor relations laws comparable to either the Wagner Act or Taft-Hartley, or both, the real focus of action is with the state statutes, orders, and regulations extending bargaining rights to public employees. Forty states and the District of Columbia have extended bargaining rights to public employees, although some states provide that the public employer need only "meet and confer" with the union. But the practical result is often similar to that under the duty to bargain. Only ten states have no bargaining rights by law, regulation, or order for public employees, although in most of these same states bargaining does occur, for example, with teachers.

The legal framework for private and public employee bargaining at the state level is generally comparable to the NLRA and to CSRA 1978, Title VII, at the federal level. Rather than attempt to compare the approach to collective bargaining matters of all forty states and the District of Columbia, the statutes of four states widely separated geographically (Hawaii, Minnesota, New York, and Iowa) will be used to illustrate the general features of their comprehensive public-employee bargaining laws.

Public Policy The Taylor Act, Ch. 392, Civil Service Law, 1967, is illustrative of a public-policy approach at the state level:

> Section 200, Statement of policy. *The legislature of the state of New York declares that it is the public policy of the state and the purpose of this act to promote harmonious and cooperative relationships between the government and its employees and to protect the public by assuring, at all times, the orderly and uninterrupted operations and functions of government. These policies are best effectuated by (a) granting to public employees the right of organization and representation, (b) requiring the state, local governments and other political subdivisions, to negotiate with, and enter into written agreements with employee organizations representing public employees which have been certified or recognized, (c) encouraging such public employers and such employee organizations to agree upon procedures for resolving disputes, (d) creating a public employment relations board to assist in resolving disputes between public employees and public employers, and (e) continuing the prohibition against strikes by public employees and providing remedies for violations of such prohibition.*

The Hawaiian public-employee statute, Act 171.L.1970, reads similarly:

> Section 89-1 *The legislature declares that it is the public policy of the State to promote harmonious and cooperative rela-*

tions between government and its employees and to protect the public by assuring effective and orderly operations of government. These policies are best effectuated by (1) recognizing the right of public employees to organize for the purpose of collective bargaining, (2) requiring the public employers to negotiate with and enter into written agreements with exclusive representatives on matters of wages, hours, and other terms and conditions of employment, while, at the same time, (3) maintaining merit principles and the principle of equal pay for equal work among state and county employees . . . and (4) creating a public employment relations board to administer the provisions of this chapter.

Parties to Collective Bargaining Definition of the parties (employers and employees) is tailored in two ways: (1) the types of employers and employees found in state and local government units, and (2) the employer units covered by state law or order. Illustrative of state coverage are these excerpts from the Taylor Act:

Section 201(b)(a) The term "government" or "public employer" means (i) the state of New York, (ii) a county, city, town, village or any other political subdivision or civil division of the state, (iii) a school district or any governmental entity operating a public school, college or university, (iv) a public improvement or special district, (v) a public authority, commission, or public benefit corporation, or (vi) any other public corporation, agency or instrumentality or unit of government which exercises governmental powers under the laws of the state.

Section 201(5) The term "employee organization" means an organization of any kind having as its primary purpose the improvement of terms and conditions of employment of public employees [can include associations].

Section 201(7) The term "public employee" means any person holding a position by appointment or employment in the service of a public employer, excluding . . . persons holding positions by appointment or employment in the organized militia of the state and persons who may reasonably be designated from time to time as managerial or confidential.

Employee Rights Employee rights of self-organization, or of forming, joining, or assisting any organization and of bargaining collectively are the same as those at the federal level. However, in contrast to the private sector, the legal framework of most of the states prohibits public employees the right to strike and in the remainder of states allows the strike only under special rules. The Minnesota Employment Relations Act, 1971, illustrates a prohibition against work stoppages:

> Sec. 179.64. Strikes: (1) No person holding a position by ap-
> pointment or employment in the government of the state of Min-
> nesota, or in the government of any one or more of the political
> subdivisions thereof, or in the service of the public schools, or of
> the state university, or in the service of any authority, commis-
> sion or board or any other branch of the public service . . . may
> engage in a strike.

The Hawaiian statute provides the right to strike under certain
conditions:

> Sec. 89-12(a) Participation in a strike shall be unlawful for
> any employee who (1) is not included in an appropriate bargain-
> ing unit for which an exclusive representative has been cer-
> tified . . . , or (2) is included in an appropriate bargaining unit
> for which process for resolution of a dispute is by referral to
> final and binding arbitration.
>
> (b) It shall be lawful for an employee, who is not prohibited
> from striking under paragraph (a) and who is in the appropriate
> bargaining unit involved in an impasse, to participate in a strike
> after (1) requirements . . . relating to the resolution of disputes
> have been complied with in good faith, (2) the proceedings for
> the prevention of any prohibited practice have been exhausted,
> (3) sixty days have elapsed since the fact-finding board has
> made public its findings and any recommendations, (4) the ex-
> clusive representative has given a ten-day notice of intent to
> strike to the board and to the employer.
>
> (c) Where the strike occurring, or about to occur, endangers
> the public health or safety, the public employer concerned may
> petition the board to make an investigation. If the board finds
> that there is imminent or present danger to the health and safety
> of the public, the board shall set requirements that must be
> complied with to avoid or remove any such imminent or present
> danger.

Unfair Labor Practice   In addition to those included in federal law,
the Iowa statute lists other unfair labor practices: denying the rights accompanying certification or exclusive recognition; refusing to participate
in good faith in any agreed-upon impasse procedures; engaging in a lockout; and picketing in a manner which interferes with ingress and egress to
the facilities of the public employer.

Collective Bargaining Representative   State laws delegate the same
authority to the duly constituted representative of employees in an appropriate bargaining unit but, in addition, recognize public-employee associations as legitimate representatives along with unions.

Appropriate Bargaining Unit   As in federal laws, the procedures
for establishing the appropriate bargaining unit as well as the bargaining

representative are spelled out. The Hawaiian statute is interesting because it designates the appropriate bargaining units in some detail:

> *Sec. 89-6(a). All employees throughout the State within any of the following categories shall constitute an appropriate bargaining unit:*
>
> (1) Nonsupervisory employees in blue collar positions;
> (2) Supervisory employees in blue collar positions;
> (3) Nonsupervisory employees in white collar positions;
> (4) Supervisory employees in white collar positions;
> (5) Teachers and other personnel of the department of education under the same salary schedule;
> (6) Educational officers and other personnel of the department of education under the same salary schedule;
> (7) Faculty of the University of Hawaii and the Community College system;
> (8) Personnel of the University of Hawaii and the Community College system, other than faculty;
> (9) Registered professional nurses;
> (10) Nonprofessional hospital and institutional workers;
> (11) Firemen;
> (12) Policemen; and
> (13) Professional and scientific employees, other than registered professional nurses.

Coverage The type of coverage of public-employees' statute or order varies among the states. Ten states provide no coverage for public employees; twenty-one extend bargaining rights to state and municipal employees, firemen, policemen, and teachers; four extend bargaining rights to four of the preceding categories; six, including the District of Columbia, to three of the groups of employees; three to two groups; and seven states extend bargaining rights to only one group of employees. Looked at in another way, twenty-eight states extend bargaining rights to state employees; thirty-five, including the District of Columbia, to municipal employees; thirty-nine, including the District of Columbia, to firemen; thirty-one, including the District of Columbia, to policemen; and thirty to teachers.

Impasse-Settlement Procedures The states, in their statutes and orders, have been much more active and detailed in their approaches to impasse-settlement procedures. They include traditional techniques and also various combinations in the use of mediation, fact finding, and arbitration.

The Iowa Public Employment Relations Act provides a good example of a state's comprehensive dispute-resolution procedure:

Section 19. Impasse Procedures—Agreement of Parties. As the first step in the performance of their duty to bargain, the public employer and the employee organization shall endeavor to agree upon impasse procedures no later than one hundred twenty days prior to the certified budget submission date of the public employer. If the parties fail to agree upon impasse procedures under the provisions of this section, the impasse procedures provided in sections 20, 21 and 22 of this Act shall apply.

Section 20. Mediation. In the absence of an impasse agreement between the parties or the failure of either party to utilize its procedures, one hundred twenty days prior to the certified budget submission date, the board shall, upon the request of either party, appoint an impartial and disinterested person to act as mediator. It shall be the function of the mediator to bring the parties together to effectuate a settlement of the dispute, but the mediator may not compel the parties to agree.

Section 21. Fact-Finding. If the impasse persists ten days after the mediator has been appointed, the board shall appoint a fact-finder representative of the public, from a list of qualified persons maintained by the board. The fact-finder shall conduct a hearing, may administer oaths, and may request the board to issue subpoenas. The fact-finder shall make written findings of facts and recommendations for resolution of the dispute and, not later than fifteen days from the day of appointment, shall serve such findings on the public employer and the certified employee organization.

The public employer and the certified employee organization shall immediately accept the fact-finder's recommendation or shall within five days submit the fact-finder's recommendations to the governing body and members of the certified employee organization for acceptance or rejection. If the dispute continues ten days after the report is submitted, the report shall be made public by the board.

Section 22. Binding Arbitration. 1. If an impasse persists after the findings of fact and recommendations are made public by the fact-finder, the parties may continue to negotiate or, the board shall have the power, upon request of either party, to arrange for arbitration, which shall be binding. . . . The submission of the impasse items to the arbitrators shall be limited to those issues that had been considered by the fact-finder and upon which the parties have not reached agreement. With respect to each such item, the arbitration board award shall be restricted to the final offers on each impasse item submitted by the parties to the arbitration board or to the recommendation of the fact-finder on each impasse item. . . . A majority of the panel of arbitrators shall select within fifteen days after its first meeting the most reasonable offer, in its judgment, of the final offers on each impasse item submitted by the parties, or the recommendations of the fact-finder on each impasse item. The selections by the panel of arbitrators and items agreed upon by the public employer and the employee organization, shall be deemed to be the collective bargaining agreement between the parties.

WHAT DETERMINES THE SECTOR EACH STATUTE COVERS?

Whether the employer is a private- or public-sector employer, whether the employees in either case are covered by a labor law, and if so, by which law or laws—these are questions that can be answered only by checking each employer's status against several criteria:

1. Is the employer engaged in interstate or intrastate commerce? If the former, the employer is covered by federal law; if the latter, by state law. One exception should be noted, since it vitally affects an employee's labor-relations rights and protection. If the employee is in a right-to-work state, the right-to-work law of the state is universally applied whether or not, for other purposes, the employee comes under federal or under state law exclusively.

2. Is the employer in private industry, in transportation (railroads and airlines), or in the public sector? If the employer is in interstate commerce and outside the railroad and airline industries, the NLRA applies; if in railroads or airlines, the RLA applies. If the employer is a public employer at the federal level other than the U.S. Postal Service, Title VII of CSRA 1978 applies; if at the state or municipal level, state public-employee laws apply. If the employer is in intrastate commerce and a private employer, appropriate state labor-relations laws apply. Again, state right-to-work laws apply to all employers regardless of the previous distinctions.

3. Other criteria determining an employer's status under the law would be the distinction between industrial employers and agricultural (extractive) employers, the latter not covered by labor laws; and the distinction between union and association representation of employees, the latter recognized by some state laws but not by federal law, and the former recognized by both state and federal laws.

SUBSTANTIVE FEATURES OF THE AGREEMENT AND OTHER STATUTES

By mandate, restriction, and exclusion, the statutes discussed up to this point have established a legal framework within which the process of negotiating an agreement must function. Other statutes, many of them products of the social and human-rights movements of the 1960s, add another dimension to the negotiation of the agreement. Rather than influencing the process itself, these statutes have influenced the substantive features—the subject matter—of the agreement.

Representative of these statutes and the negotiation matters they affect are (1) the Fair Labor Standards Act of 1938, as amended, covering wage and hour limitations; (2) the Civil Rights Act of 1969, concerning discrimination in employment because of race, color, religion, or national origin; (3) the Equal Opportunity Act of 1972, applying to all personnel actions affecting employees or applicants for employment and their right to be free from any discrimination based on race, color, religion, sex, or national origin; (4) the Equal Pay Act of 1963, prohibiting discrimination in the payment of wages on the basis of sex for equal work on jobs whose performance requires equal skill, effort, and responsibility and that are performed under similar working conditions; (5) the Occupational Safety and Health Act (OSHA), 1970, requiring that the employment and place of employment be free from recognized hazards that are likely to cause death or serious physical harm to employees; (6) the Employee Retirement Income Security Act of 1974, which establishes regulations covering retirement plans and minimum vesting and funding standards; and (7) the Vietnam Era Veterans Reemployment Act of 1974, which requires reemployment of veterans meeting certain requirements of their former positions and, if they are qualified, either restoration of seniority or employment in a position of like seniority, status, and pay.

SELECTED REFERENCES

Employment Practices. New York: Commerce Clearing House, Inc. An excellent source of information on federal and state laws banning discrimination in employment on account of race, color, religion, sex, national origin, and age. Equal-pay rules are covered in detail. This is a continuing and up-to-date service.

Fair Employment Practices. Washington, D.C.: Bureau of National Affairs, Inc. This continuing series provides comprehensive coverage of federal and state laws that prohibit discrimination in employment based on race, color, religion, national origin, sex, and age.

Federal Wages–Hours. New York: Commerce Clearing House, Inc. An up-to-date and continuing service concerning rules, statutes, regulations, and forms; government-contract wage-hour rules; administrative and court decisions; and current comment on wage-hour developments.

Getman, Julius G., and John D. Blackburn, *Labor Relations—Law, Practice and Policy,* 2nd ed. Mineola, N.Y.: The Foundation Press, Inc., 1983.

Industrial Relations Guide. Englewood Cliffs, N.J.: Prentice-Hall, Inc. Biweekly reports in this continuing series explain the impact of new developments and new trends in collective bargaining and arbitration. The basic text of the loose-leaf volume, updated periodically, includes a complete explanation of the nature of labor arbitration, plus descriptions of past awards and thousands of sample contract clauses. "New Ideas" articles are written by outside experts in the field on subjects of interest to management and labor alike.

Labor Law Course, 25th ed. Chicago, Ill.: Commerce Clearing House, Inc., 1983.

Labor Cases. New York: Commerce Clearing House, Inc. A continuing service that includes full-text federal and state court decisions on labor law.

Labor Relations. Washington, D.C.: Bureau of National Affairs, Inc. This is a continuing series covering the problems arising under federal and state labor laws. Here, the numerous rulings of the National Labor Relations Board, state boards, and the courts have been combed, sorted, and put into nonlegal language. Provisions and procedures of the Occupational Safety and Health Act are also included.

Labor Relations Guide. Englewood Cliffs, N.J.: Prentice-Hall, Inc. This service, updated weekly, is particularly useful for business executives, lawyers, personnel managers, and consultants who want information that quickly and easily answers day-to-day labor relations questions. Important decisions of the National Labor Relations Board, the Equal Employment Opportunity Commission, the Occupational Safety and Health Administration, and the courts are reported promptly in easy-to-understand language. The service includes an explanation of labor laws—wage hour, the NLRA, the Civil Rights Act, age discrimination, Vietnam Era Veterans Reemployment Act, OSHA, garnishment, state labor laws, and others—and provides the full texts of federal laws and executive orders.

Law of Labor Relations. Washington, D.C.: Bureau of National Affairs, Inc. A comprehensive series that provides a current account of court opinions and decisions of the National Labor Relations Board.

Levine, Marvin J., *Comparative Labor Relations Law.* Morristown, N.J.: General Learning Press, 1975. Most readers would relate the title of this book to an intercountry comparison. Instead, and in a timely way, the author's concern is between the two major sectors of labor relations activity in America—the private and public sectors. This unique text "examines the extent to which private industry labor law standards and precedents are applied to federal, state, and local governmental level."

Morris, Charles J., ed., *The Developing Labor Law,* 2nd ed. Washington, D.C.: Bureau of National Affairs, Inc., 1983. This book, a product of a diverse group composing the section of labor relations law of the American Bar Association, is outstanding as a chronicle of the developments of the law under the National Labor Relations Act. It is the product of some sixty prominent specialists in labor relations law and will be kept current by annual supplements.

NLRB Decisions. New York: Commerce Clearing House, Inc. A continuing service that includes comprehensive digests of new NLRB decisions.

Public Personnel Administration: Labor-Management Relations. Englewood Cliffs, N.J.: Prentice-Hall, Inc. Focusing on public-sector collective bargaining, this service explains laws, methods, rulings, clauses, and established precedents (including summaries of arbitration awards). Biweekly reports provide news of developments in this complex area. Sections of the basic text include "New Ideas," "Collective Bargaining Problems and Answers," "Annotated Public Employment Relations Laws and Regulations," "Union Contract Clauses," and Arbitration Awards Analyzed."

Rothschild, Donald P., Leroy S. Merrifield, and Harry T. Edwards, *Collective Bargaining and Labor Arbitration,* 2nd ed. New York: Bobbs-Merrill, 1979.

Smith, Arthur B., Jr., "The Impact on Collective Bargaining of Equal Employment Opportunity Remedies," *Industrial and Labor Relations Review,* 28, no. 3 (April 1975), 376–94. The author discusses the seniority-system cases under Title VII and the impact this has on the substantive features of collective bargaining.

State Labor Laws. Washington, D.C.: Bureau of National Affairs, Inc. A comprehensive and up-to-date compilation of state laws dealing with the fields of labor relations, employment regulations, and wages, hours, and child labor. In addition, there is included a directory of the agencies that administer and enforce the laws.

Sullivan, Charles A., Michael J. Zimmer, and Richard F. Richards, *Federal Statutory Law of Employment Discrimination,* Charlottesville, Va.: Bobbs-Merrill, 1980. A comprehensive presentation of federal employment discrimination laws and their court interpretation.

Taylor, Benjamin J., and Fred Witney, *Labor Relations Law,* 4th ed. Englewood Cliffs, N.J.: Prentice-Hall, 1983. A most readable coverage of the legal framework within which collective bargaining operates. A significant contribution of the book is that it assumes that the law of labor relations will have little meaning to the reader if he cannot see it against the dynamics of labor unions and collective bargaining—i.e., the labor relations environment within which the legal structure operates. Hence, the book strikes a balance between the law of collective bargaining and current problems of labor relations. Both the private and public sectors of collective bargaining are covered.

Wages and Hours. Washington, D.C.: Bureau of National Affairs, Inc. A continuing series that deals with the application of the federal and state wage-hour laws to business enterprise.

Wage-Hour Guide. Englewood Cliffs, N.J.: Prentice-Hall, Inc. This volume includes the texts of both the Equal Pay Law and the Wage-Hour Law. Information is provided on who is covered, who is exempt, wages and overtime, child labor restrictions, records-investigations, enforcement methods, government contracts, and related topics. A regular report explains current developments. A "Current Matter" section contains administrative opinions and digests of court decisions.

CHAPTER 4

PLAYERS
IN COLLECTIVE
BARGAINING

The term *players* in collective bargaining negotiations refers to those individuals, groups, agencies, or boards that may play a role at one point or another in the negotiation process. This includes the main players—employers and employee representatives—plus others such as the national and state labor relations boards, mediators, arbitrators, fact-finders, and, in the public sector, the Federal Labor Relations Authority and the Federal Service Impasses Panel. There are still others, such as the courts, the legislatures, and various agencies dealing with employment or human rights. But these groups are usually less directly related to the negotiation process as such, although they may have an important influence on the legal environment and particular substantive features of the negotiated labor agreement.

EMPLOYER

With respect to collective bargaining negotiations, the term *employer* may refer to an employer bargaining on a single-firm basis, a single employer bargaining on a multiple-plant basis, a single employer negotiating on a companywide basis, or a group of employers bargaining on an association basis. The employer may likewise be negotiating on an areawide, regional, industrywide or nationwide basis. Public-sector employers may organize for negotiations on a plant or installation, craft, function, or other basis at the federal level. At the state level, *public employer* may mean a state or political subdivision, including a town, city, borough, district, board of regents, school board, public or quasipublic corporation, housing authority, or other authority established by law.

EMPLOYEE REPRESENTATIVE

The union or *employee representative* organized for negotiations might mean a local union, an international union, or joint or multiunion bargaining by local or international unions negotiating at the local, regional, or national level. Employee associations also perform these functions in many states, some protected and some not protected by labor laws. However, the bargaining process and objectives are essentially the same in both associations and unions.

From the foregoing it can be seen that the way labor and management combine for collective bargaining varies considerably over a wide variety of arrangements, such as negotiations between (1) a local, one-plant company and a local union; (2) a division of a company and a local union; (3) a single plant of a company and a local union; (4) an employers' council or association of employers and a local union; (5) a single company and/or joint council or coalition of local unions; (6) an association of employers and a joint council or coalition of local unions; (7) employers in a region (such as trucking) and all local unions of an international union within the region (Teamsters' Master Agreement); (8) a company representing a number of plants and an international union; (9) a single company and a coalition of international unions; (10) a single employer, separately with each of a number of local unions; (11) a coalition of companies on an industrywide basis and a single international union; (12) a government installation and a union or unions; (13) a state government and a state employees' association or union; (14) a municipal government and one or more associations or unions of its employees, such as policemen, firemen, sanitation workers, or office employees; or (15) a school board and a teachers' association.[1]

This does not exhaust all the combinations, but it does illustrate the variety of collective bargaining combinations. The form used by labor or management in any particular situation reflects in part historical circum-

---

[1]In 1967, it was estimated that 1.2 percent of collective bargaining agreements covered units of 1,000 or more employees but 50 percent of all covered workers; 98.8 percent of contracts were for units of less than 1,000 workers; 36 percent of contracts were on a multiplant–single-employer basis; 28 percent on a single-employer–single-plant basis; and 36 percent on a multiemployer basis. Lloyd Ulman, ed., *Challenges to Collective Bargaining* (Englewood Cliffs, N.J.: Prentice-Hall, 1967), p. 25.

stances but most certainly is a product of the needs of the parties to fit their bargaining and their contract to the nature of their own industry, firm, agency, and employee-representative situation.

THIRD PARTIES

NATIONAL LABOR RELATIONS BOARD

To protect the rights prescribed by the NLRA and to remedy unfair labor practices, Congress established the National Labor Relations Board (NLRB). The NLRB is organized into two major divisions, the five-member board itself and the office of the general counsel. The five members of the board, appointed by the president with the approval of Congress, hear and decide unfair labor practice cases prosecuted by the general counsel that have not been settled at earlier steps of the complaint procedure. In addition, the board determines questions concerning representation elections that are referred to it from the regional offices. The board function is primarily a judicial function. The office of general counsel was established in 1947 to separate the prosecuting function (earlier under the board) from the judicial function. The general counsel and his staff, who investigate, have the sole discretion to prosecute, and do prosecute all unfair labor practice cases. The general counsel's staff also conducts representation elections to determine whether a union is to be certified as the bargaining agent for a unit of employees. The regional offices of the NLRB are under the general supervision of the general counsel. It is with him and his staff, especially in the regional offices, that most public contacts with the NLRB are made.

Most of the day-to-day work of investigating and processing unfair labor practice charges and conducting representation elections devolve upon the regional offices located in twenty-eight major cities throughout the country under authority granted them by the NLRB and the general counsel.

If, during the collective bargaining negotiations, any individual or organization feels that the law has been violated, an unfair labor practice charge may be filed against the offending party, alleging a violation of the NLRA.[2] This complaint is filed with the regional office of the NLRB. The charge is then investigated by an agent from the regional office, and upon completion of this investigation, the regional director decides whether a formal complaint is warranted. If there is substance to the charge, an

---

[2]Kenneth C. McGuiness, *Silverberg's How to Take a Case before the National Labor Relations Board*, 3rd ed. (Washington, D.C.: Bureau of National Affairs, 1967). See also the annual reports of the NLRB.

informal settlement may be reached. Failing this, the regional director issues a formal complaint. A formal hearing is then held before a board trial examiner, who issues a decision and a recommended order based on his findings of fact in the case. Appeals from this decision may be made to the NLRB, and from there, matters of enforcement or appeal go to the circuit court of appeals. It must be emphasized that the interpretative function of the board, even though the board has no direct enforcement powers itself, plays an extremely important role in what the parties may or may not do during the bargaining process and on the scope of their bargaining activities. In some areas, such as the meaning of the phrases "other concerted activities for the purpose of collective bargaining or other mutual aid or protection," or "confer in good faith with respect to wage, hours, and other terms and conditions of employment," the board, through its interpretations, has expanded significantly the role of collective bargaining.

CIVIL SERVICE REFORM ACT OF 1978, TITLE VII *Law governing federal collective bargaining.*

In the federal sector, the counterpart of the NLRB is a function of the Federal Labor Relations Authority. The authority is composed of three members, appointed by the president, with the advice and consent of the Senate. The authority is charged with the responsibility of establishing policy, providing guidance, and carrying out the purposes of Title VII. More specific functions include determining appropriate bargaining units, conducting representation elections, adjudicating unfair labor practices, resolving exceptions to arbitrators' awards, and whatever else is necessary to effectively administer Title VII. Parallel to the private sector (NLRA), Title VII of CSRA also provides for a general counsel, whose main responsibilities are to investigate and, where needed, to prosecute unfair labor practice complaints, or to perform other duties the authority may prescribe. Unlike the NLRA, Title VII provides for a Federal Services Impasses Council to assist in the resolution of negotiation impasses. This is to provide an alternative course of action to the strike, which is forbidden to federal employees.

STATE LABOR RELATIONS BOARDS

Most states also have agencies established to administer state labor laws.[3] These agencies come under a number of titles, but essentially they are to the state what the National Labor Relations Board is to the federal sector.

[3]See sections in the Prentice-Hall, Commerce Clearing House, and Bureau of National Affairs services covering state labor relations laws or the states directly. The University of Hawaii, Industrial Relations Center, has published some excellent material on public-sector bargaining at the state and local levels.

For example, in Colorado, the Industrial Commission administers state labor laws; in Connecticut, it is the State Board of Labor Relations (which administers laws covering both public and private sectors); Hawaii has an Employment Board; and New York operates through a Labor Relations Board. For the public sector, the responsibility for administration varies. There is no state board in California, but there are Employee Relations Boards to administer local labor relations in the city of Los Angeles and Los Angeles County. In Kansas, a new Public Employee Relations Board administers public-sector labor relations.

FEDERAL MEDIATION AND CONCILIATION SERVICE

The FMCS is an administrative arm of the executive branch of the federal government.[4] Through it, the parties may obtain the services of a federal mediator (located in regions throughout the country) to assist them in resolving differences and breaking impasses.

A longstanding concept, but one that has taken on added meaning in recent years, is "preventive mediation." Under this concept, the mediator maintains a continuing dialogue with the parties in order to smooth relations and put out fires before, rather than after, the fact.

It should be noted that the mediator does not serve a judicial function; he cannot adjudicate or decide or impose a decision on the parties. His sole function is to use his good offices as a representative of the government, acting in a neutral capacity, and his expertise in labor relations to aid the parties in reconciling their differences and arriving at an amicable settlement of their contract. As William E. Simkin, former director of the FMCS, notes, the mediator "may cajole, he may recommend, but the parties always have the right to say 'no,' even on most procedural matters."[5] Simkin describes the mediator as one who performs "a continuum of possible functions of an impartial person in the collective bargaining relationship beginning with the common notions about conciliation and going across the scale to, but not including, arbitration."[6] Mediators come from a variety of backgrounds in labor relations—union, management, and education—but have one thing in common: They enter the service from a broad base of practical experience.

The Federal Mediation and Conciliation Service is also available in the resolution of negotiation disputes in the public sector, since no comparable body was established under Executive Order 11491 or Title VII. However, when voluntary efforts such as mediation fail to resolve a nego-

---

[4]William E. Simkin, *Mediation and the Dynamics of Collective Bargaining* (Washington, D.C.: Bureau of National Affairs, 1971). See also annual reports of FMCS.

[5]*Ibid.*, p. 28.

[6]*Ibid.*, p. 27.

tiation impasse, either party may request that the matter be considered by the Federal Service Impasses Panel, a new body established under the executive order. The panel, at its discretion, may consider the matter and recommend a way of resolving it or may settle the impasse by appropriate action. Arbitration or fact finding by a third party may be turned to by the parties if such action is authorized or directed by the panel.

ARBITRATION

The nation's arbitrators are private individuals whose main function is to arbitrate appealed grievances (rights disputes) rather than disputes arising from collective bargaining negotiations (interest disputes). Occasionally, an arbitrator will be brought in on a contract-negotiation problem, but for the most part both parties shy clear of using an arbitrator on such problems, because it means a third party imposing on them the terms that will be incorporated in their contracts. Arbitration is a judicial process and, as such, is more appropriate to situations where an interpretation of existing language is needed that could not be decided by the parties through their normal grievance procedures. The arbitrator—after being selected from names secured from the Federal Mediation and Conciliation Service, the American Arbitration Association, various state agencies, or direct contact with private individuals—holds hearings, takes testimony, hears arguments of both parties over a specified issue, and then after study renders a decision, interpreting the clause or clauses in question or the action of the party under a particular clause of the contract. The decision of the arbitrator is final and binding on the parties, may be enforced through appeal to the courts, and may be overturned by court action only if it involves a misuse of authority. The courts do not inquire into the reasoning of the arbitrator on the facts presented, nor into the decision based on that reasoning, except where there is evidence that the arbitrator has exceeded his authority or has been guilty of procedural error. The Supreme Court reasons:

> The refusal of courts to review the merits of an arbitration award is the proper approach to arbitration under collective bargaining agreements. . . . an arbitrator is confined to interpretation and application of the collective bargaining agreement: . . . when the arbitrator's words manifest an infidelity to this obligation, courts have no choice but to refuse enforcement of the award.[7]

In addition to providing for arbitration in negotiation disputes with the approval of the Federal Service Impasses Panel, Title VII also allows a

[7]*U.S. Steel Workers of America v. Enterprise Wheel and Car Company*, 363 U.S. 593 (1960).

negotiated procedure in the labor agreement for the arbitration of grievances over the interpretation or application of the agreement if invoked by either party to the agreement. Departing from private-sector practice in the use of arbitration, the order allows either party to file exceptions to an arbitrator's award with the Federal Labor Relations Authority for final determination.

Fact Finding

Fact finding involves the introduction of a third party of neutrals or disinterested parties to a dispute situation. Their responsibility under rules established either by the parties or by statute is to investigate, ascertain the facts, determine positions of the parties, and report their findings with or without a recommended settlement. The rationale in the use of the fact-finders is that it somehow introduces the public interest, brings the facts to light, establishes a basis either for the parties to continue negotiations or for the marshalling of public pressures on the parties to settle, or serves as a basis for a public body to order a settlement on the basis of facts gathered by disinterested parties. The use of the fact-finding technique is fully covered in Part IV.

Joint Study Committees

Admittedly, the main parties involved in joint study committees are labor and management themselves. But it should be recognized that in the use of such committees, either on a one-time problem-solving assignment or as a continuously functioning committee, the use of neutrals as members has proved a very effective device in a number of instances. Full coverage of this committee approach with the involvement of neutrals will be found in Part IV.

SELECTED REFERENCES

Baer, Walter E., *Labor Arbitration Guide.* Homewood, Ill.: Dow Jones-Irwin, 1974. The author brings to the reader a comprehensive account of the basic features of the arbitration process.

Barbash, Jack, *American Unions, Structure, Government and Politics.* New York: Random House, 1967. An informative and easily read account of unions as a government system. Professor Barbash brings the reader a combined union-government-academic experience in his interpretation of unionism.

Bloom, Gordon F., and Herbert R. Northrup, *Economics of Labor Relations,* 9th ed. Homewood, Ill.: Richard D. Irwin, 1981. A readable account of the structure and function of unions in Chapter 3. Chapter 4 contains two sections well worth reading for information concerning the setting of union and management policy for collective bargaining.

Current References and Information Services for Policy Decision-Making in State and Local Government Labor Relations—A Selected Bibliography. U.S. Department of Labor, November 1971. With the rapidly changing picture in state government collective bargaining activities, publications pointing to sources of information, such as this one, are of vital importance.

A Directory of Public Employee Organizations—A Guide to the Major Organization Representing State and Local Public Employees. U.S. Department of Labor, 1974. Information is provided on each organization listed as to its headquarters, jurisdiction, type and purpose of organization, organizational structure, membership, supporting groups, work-stoppage policy, publications, conventions, and year of origin.

A Directory of Public Management Organizations. U.S. Department of Labor, November 1971. This DOL publication includes a guide to national organizations of state and local governments and associations of public officials with an interest in public-employee–management relations.

Gifford, Courtney D., ed., *Directory of U.S. Labor Organizations, 1982–83 Edition.* Washington, D.C.: Bureau of National Affairs, Inc. This publication is updated periodically and includes a listing of national unions, employees' associations, the AFL-CIO, other federations, and state labor organizations. In addition, a summary of developments since the last directory and statistics on the labor movement are included.

Hardman, J. B. S., and Maurice F. Neufeld, eds., *The House of Labor— Internal Operations of American Unions.* Englewood Cliffs, N.J.: Prentice-Hall, 1951. Two objectives guided the organization of this book's material: "(1) to acquaint persons outside of organized labor with the 'inside' of the American Labor movement, its performance, and motivation; and (2) to present to the participants in union activity an over-all view of their group activities in the promotion of union objectives."

Maggiolo, Walter A., *Techniques of Mediation in Labor Disputes.* Dobbs Ferry, N.Y.: Oceana Publications, 1971. A complete picture of the mediator and what he does.

McGuiness, Kenneth C., *Silverberg's How to Take a Case before the National Labor Relations Board,* 4th ed. Washington, D.C.: Bureau of National Affairs, Inc., 1976. For those engaged in collective bargaining in the private sector, this book constitutes a definitive source on the NLRB and how the parties may use its services.

Morris, Charles J., ed., *The Developing Labor Law,* 2nd ed. Washington, D.C.: Bureau of National Affairs, Inc., 1983. The chapters included in Part VII give a comprehensive view of the administration of the NLRA by the NLRB and the role of the courts in such administration.

Simkin, William E., *Mediation and the Dynamics of Collective Bargaining.* Washington, D.C.: Bureau of National Affairs, Inc., 1971. Few people have the credentials to talk about mediation that this author, a former director of the FMCS, has. This is not just a description of the mediation function but a book aimed at understanding and analyzing the mediation process.

State Labor Laws. Washington, D.C.: Bureau of National Affairs, Inc. A series that is kept up to date on the agencies that administer and enforce the laws, and the laws that establish and define the powers and duties of these agencies.

Yoder, Dale, and Paul D. Staudohar, *Personnel Management and Industrial Relations,* 7th ed., chapter 13. Englewood Cliffs, N.J.: Prentice-Hall, 1982. A readable account of union theory, policy, and practice. Understanding the union—how it is organized and functions, and its relationship to management—is vital to an understanding of the collective bargaining relationships of the parties.

CHAPTER 5

THE COLLECTIVE BARGAINING AGREEMENT

The collective bargaining agreement is included at this point to aid the reader in developing a better understanding and perspective of the chapters that follow concerning the negotiation process. The agreement is the objective and result of the negotiation process. With a fuller understanding of the end product, the agreement, each step in the negotiation process as it unfolds takes on new meaning because it is judged against the foreknowledge of the final product.

The collective bargaining agreement may be described in a number of ways. It is a compromise between the self-interests of the two parties that they have agreed upon as a guide to their relationships on certain matters for a specified period of time. In this sense, it is a form of constitutional government introduced into the work relationship. Justice Douglas, in delivering the majority opinion in the *Steelworkers v. Warrior Navigation Co.* segment of the "Trilogy,"[1] addressed himself to the significance of the collective agreement:

> It is a more than a contract; it is a generalized code to govern a myriad of cases which the draftsmen cannot wholly anticipate.

[1] On June 20, 1960, the U.S. Supreme Court handed down three decisions of great import to the arbitration process. The three cases, each involving the United Steelworkers of America, have come to be known as the "Trilogy" cases. They include: Warrior & Gulf Navigation, American Manufacturing, and Enterprise Wheel & Car Corporation cases.

> *[It] is an effort to erect a system of industrial self-government.*
>
> *[It is a choice] between having that relationship governed by an agreed-upon rule or law or leaving each and every matter subject to a temporary resolution dependent solely upon the relative strength of any given movement, of the contending forces.*
>
> *It calls into being a new common law—the common law of a particular industry of a particular plant. [363 U.S. 574 (1960)]*

The Webbs would call it the introduction of industrial democracy to the workplace, since it represents the joint voice of labor and management as to how their relationship should be governed. More specifically, its substantive terms not only define such basic matters as wages and hours, but include a whole myriad of complex rules regulating almost every aspect of the employment relationship—even to maternity leave, garnishment of wages, location of plant, patent rights, and political activity. When signed, the collective agreement constitutes a contract between the parties—the employer, the union, and the employees within the bargaining unit.

A LEGAL CONTRACT

That Congress viewed the collective agreement as a legally enforceable contract is attested to by Section 301(a) of the Labor Management Relations Act of 1947:

> *Suits for violation of contracts between an employer and a labor organization representing employees in an industry affecting commerce as defined in this Act, or between any such labor organizations, may be brought in any district court of the United States having jurisdiction of the parties, without respect to the amount in controversy or without regard to the citizenship of the parties. [Emphasis added.]*

Regardless of the nitpicking that some writers engage in when trying to distinguish between the nature of a collective agreement and that of commercial agreements, the fact remains that Congress makes it clear that the collective agreement is a contract and is between two parties—"an employer and a labor organization representing employees." The agreement signed by the parties remains legally binding upon all three—the employer, the union, and the employees—unless they legally remove themselves or are removed from its coverage. In the case of the union, this would mean, for example, that the union was decertified and was no longer the bargaining agent for the employees of a designated appropriate bargaining unit, or that upon renegotiation of the agreement, the parties failed to reach a settlement. In the latter instance, the contract, and with it, legal responsibility, would then cease to exist. In the case of employees who belong to the designated appropriate bargaining unit, whether they belong to the union or not, there is a legal responsibility to comply with the provisions of the collective agreement as long as they continue as employees. They may, of course, remove themselves from legal responsibility by quitting or severing their employment relationship.

Congress intended that there also be a clear relationship between the union and the employees in a bargaining unit relative to the collective agreement, by stating in Section 9(a):

> Representatives designated or selected for the purpose of collective bargaining by the majority of the employees in a unit appropriate for such purposes, shall be the exclusive representatives of all the employees in such a unit for the purpose of collective bargaining in respect to rates of pay, wages, hours of employment, or other conditions of employment.

As long as the union has met the requirements of the law as to certification as bargaining representative and, upon the completion of the negotiations, has met its own requirements of ratification by its membership, the collective agreement so signed is a binding contract on both the union and the employees in the bargaining unit. The inviolate nature of this representation is further emphasized by the later language of Section 9(a), in which employees within the bargaining unit are granted the right to individually process their own grievances if they so desire, without the participation of the union, as long as any settlement does not violate the terms of the collective agreement of which the union as their signator is a party.

ENFORCEMENT OF THE COLLECTIVE AGREEMENT

It is clear by both practice and legal decisions that the collective agreement is a legal contract enforceable by law. Several avenues of recourse are provided, either by the parties or by legislation. The most frequent method of enforcement of provisions of the agreement is through grievance arbitration. This is a method that usually uses an outside third party as the sole judge, or a combination of an arbitration board made up of representatives of the two parties plus an outside neutral. In most instances, this amounts to little difference from the single-arbitrator approach, since the outside neutral arbitrator in effect hears the case, writes it up, and makes a decision. However, the point is that this method of enforcement of the contract is a legal recourse established under the contract or agreement itself. About 94 percent of collective agreements provide for arbitration of grievances not settled by the parties themselves. Ninety-nine percent of these provide that arbitration shall follow automatically if the grievance process has been exhausted, and/or that it may be invoked by either party. Sample arbitration clauses may illustrate the process:

> . . . *if the above [grievance] procedure in its entirety does not result in a satisfactory adjustment of any grievance arising under this Agreement, the grievance may be submitted to arbitration at the instance of either party.*

The binding nature of the arbitrator's decision is also usually stated in the agreement:

> *The decision of the arbitrator shall be final and conclusive and binding upon employees, the Company and the Union: subject to the right of the Company or the Union to judicial review, any lawful decision of the arbitrator shall forthwith place into effect.*

Although it has been stated earlier, it is important to emphasize that the arbitrator's decision is final and binding upon the parties, may be enforced through appeal to the courts, and may be overturned by court action only if it involves a misuse of authority. The courts do not inquire into the reasoning of the arbitrator as he reviews the facts presented, nor into the decision based on that reasoning, except where there is evidence that the arbitrator has misused or exceeded his authority substantively or procedurally.

The courts have also held that under certain circumstances, the National Labor Relations Board may, ancillary to its main function of enforcing the law against unfair labor practices, rule on matters related to a violation of the collective agreement that would normally be subject to the arbitration procedure. For example, the board was involved in a case where the charge was refusal to sign a contract (an unfair labor practice). In making a decision on this charge, the board also ruled on an ancillary payment of certain benefits that if not made would have constituted a breach of contract by the employer (the defendant). Other than these special instances, primacy is given to the arbitration procedure to enforce the agreement.[2]

Finally, Section 301 makes it clear that final recourse may be had to the courts to enforce the collective agreement. Either party may resort directly to the courts when violation of the agreement does not involve

---

[2]See Benjamin J. Taylor and Fred Witney, *Labor Relations Law*, 2nd ed. (Englewood Cliffs, N.J.: Prentice-Hall, 1975), p. 659.

arbitration of, for example, when a party refuses to go to arbitration under an arbitration clause of the contract. Damages caused by an unlawful strike (no-strike clause in contract) may be resolved in the court also. Finally, appeal to the courts may be resorted to in order to enforce arbitration awards.

Under Section 301, collective agreements are enforceable in both federal and state courts, although primacy in enforcement and the issuance of injunctions is given under the law to the federal district courts.

CONTENTS OF THE COLLECTIVE AGREEMENT

Some agreements run only twenty or thirty pages; others are well over a hundred pages. To describe the agreement in detail is an impossible task within the confines of a chapter. However, a good idea of the agreement can be gained by looking at the main items and types of provisions. This approach will serve to acquaint the reader with the general content. More details will follow in the chapters on negotiation and contract administration, but an in-depth understanding can come only through becoming involved in negotiations and contract administration. Aside from examining collective agreements individually, comprehension of the various items of bargaining may be gained through the excellent, detailed, and up-to-date services published by the Bureau of National Affairs, Commerce Clearing House, and Prentice-Hall. These are most objective and exhaustive in their coverage.

Beal and Wickersham assert that the agreement serves four primary functions, and "no matter what the number of pages or clauses, or the order of presentation, every complete union agreement shows this pattern."[3] It is the fundamental pattern of collective bargaining in the United States. The four areas are union security and management rights, the wage and effect bargain, individual security, and administration.

Dale Yoder gives the major areas of a collective agreement as:[4]

Preamble and purpose	Union label or shop card
Term, life, duration	Holidays
Bargaining unit	Vacations
Recognition (form, type)	Leaves
Union security (form)	Reporting, call-in, etc.
Management rights	Shift differentials
Wages	Discharge

[3]Edwin F. Beal and Edward D. Wickersham, *The Practice of Collective Bargaining*, rev. ed. (Homewood, Ill.: Richard D. Irwin, 1963), p. 320.

[4]Dale Yoder, *Personnel Management and Industrial Relations*, 6th ed. (Englewood Cliffs, N.J.: Prentice-Hall, 1970), p. 440.

Reopening	Benefits
Hours	Safety
Grievances	Apprenticeship
Strikes, lockouts	Amendment

An even more detailed picture of the myriad of subjects and their variations found in agreements can be obtained by scanning the main topical division of the "Contract Clause Finder" that accompanies the Bureau of National Affairs (BNA) service, *Collective Bargaining Negotiations and Contracts:*[5]   ↑*private*

Absence from work	Negotiations
Accidents and illness	New employees
Accidents within plant	Night work
Admission of members to union	Non-union goods
Admission of union reps.	Notice of amendment and termination
Age limitations	
Agency shop	Occupational sickness and accident
Amendment and duration	
Annual wage	"Open shop"
Apprenticeship	Overtime
Arbitration	Parties to contract
Assignability of contract	Patent rights
Automatic increases	Pay guarantees
Automatic renewal of contract	Payroll data
Back pay	Pensions
Bargaining agent	Physical examination
Bargaining unit	Picketing
Bonuses	Piece work
Boycotts	Plant removal
Bulletin boards	Plant rules
Bumping	Political activity
Call-in pay	Posting information
Change in hours	Preferential hiring
Check-off	Premium pay
Classification of employees	Probationary employees
Clean-up time	Production standards
Closed shop	Profit-sharing plans
Coercion	Promotion, demotion, transfer
Company rules	Recall from layoff
Contracting work out	Recognition
Cooperation between union & mgt.	Regular rate of pay

---

[5]*Collective Bargaining Negotiations and Contracts* (Washington, D.C.: Bureau of National Affairs, Inc., Service Current), pp. 32:11–32:16.

Coverage of contract
Damaged goods
Damages—breach of contract
Dangerous work
Death in family leave
Deductions from wages
Demotion
Differentials in wages
Disabled employees
Discharge, discipline
Disciplinary action
Discounts to employees
Discrimination
Dismissal compensation
Disputes
Dues to collect
Duration of contract
Early retirement
Employer associations
Encouragement of union member-
    membership
Enforcement of contract
Expenses incidental to work
Firing
Foremen
Funeral leave
Garnishment of wages
Get-ready time
Government regulations
Grievances and arbitration
Handicapped workers
Hazardous work
Health and sanitation
Health & welfare plans
Hiring halls
Hiring—new employees
Holiday
Hours and overtime
Hours guarantees
Illness
Incentive systems
Income maintenance
Injury on job
Insurance

Rehiring
Reinstatement
Relief periods
Relocation of business
Renewal of agreement
Reopenings
Resignation of employees
Rest periods
Retirement plans
Retroactive pay
Retroactivity
Return to work
Rules
Runaway shop
Safety
Sale of business
Saving provisions
Scheduling hours or production
Security for performance of agree-
    ment
Security risks
Seniority
Severance pay
Sharing of work
Shifts of work
Shop stewards & committeemen
Sick leave
Spoiled work
Standby time
Strikes and lockouts
Subcontracting
Superseniority
Supplement unemployment pay
Supervisory employees
Technological displacement
Temporary employees
Termination
Time studies
Tools
Training and apprenticeship
Travel time
Transfers
Trial periods
Unemployment benefits

Job evaluation
Jury duty
Layoff, rehiring, work sharing
Leave of absence
Legal services
Limitations on production
Living quarters
Loans to employees
Location of plant
Lockouts
Lunch periods
Maintenance of membership
Make-up time
Management & union rights
Maternity leave
Meal allowance
Mediation
Medical service
Membership in union
Military service
Minimum wage guarantees
Modification of agreement
Modified union shop
"Most favored employer" clauses
Restrictions on conduct of business

Uniforms and tools
Union activity on company time and property
Union label
Union-management cooperation
Union representatives
Union rights and responsibilities
Union security
Union shop
Unit for bargaining
Vacations
Vesting
Veterans
Violation of contract
Visits by union representatives
Voting time
Wages
Waiting time
Waivers of bargaining rights
Warnings to employees
Welfare plans
Work by employer
Work permits
Working conditions
Work sharing
Workweek

It is also important to recall from the discussion in Chapter 3, "Legal Framework," that the contents of the collective bargaining agreement vary between the private sector and the public sector (federal, state, and local) because of the more restrictive approach of statutes governing collective bargaining in the public sector as to what is a bargainable subject. Notable differences between provisions of federal sector contracts and provisions of private sector contracts are the subjects of wages, union security, right to strike, and what may be reserved to the unilateral decisions of management. Differences between the contents of state and local or public-sector agreements and private-sector agreements vary according to state laws. Most state statutes prohibit the right to strike. However, in contrast with the federal sector wherein all employees are prohibited from striking, there are nine state statutes that permit a limited right to strike. The degree to which state statutes allow the negotiation of cost items, including wages, varies. However, there is more flexibility at the state and local level to negotiate wage settlements. Union security, forbidden under federal statutes for federal government employees, may be negotiated into agreements between state and local employees and their employers. Four state statutes specifically permit the union shop. Nine states permit the agency shop, and one state specifically permits maintenance of membership clauses. Even more important to union security arrangements under state and local agreements is the decision by the U.S. Supreme Court—*Abood* v. *Detroit Board of Education,* Case No. 7501153 (1977)—authorizing agency-shop clauses in public-employee contracts as long as the fee paid to a labor organization is not used for political purposes. State statutes, the same as the federal statute, also restrict bargainable subjects by granting broader areas of unilateral control to management under management reserved-rights clauses. To provide specific contrast between subjects of public-sector contracts and subjects of private-sector contracts, the following list of topics typical of federal-sector agreements and of state- or local-sector agreements is offered:

Federal-Sector Agreements	State- and/or Local-Sector Agreements
Annual leave	Affirmative action
Appropriate matters	Agency shop
Arbitration	Assignment of work
Assignment of temporarily disabled employees	Authorized agents
Cafeteria committees	Bilingual bonus
Changes in agreement	Bulletin boards
Committees	Call-back pay
Communications	Cancelled work
Compensation (promotions)	Caseloads
Controller performance	Change-off of equipment
Court leave	Clean-up period
Definitions	Consultation and training
Details and assignments	Cost of living
Disciplinary/adverse actions	Court claims and accident reports
Disposition of unit work	Disability compensation
Distribution and publicity	Disciplinary action
Dress code	Dues check-off
Dues withholding	Duration of contract
Duration and changes	Employee benefits
Eating facilities	Employee lists
Effect of the agreement	Employee paycheck errors
Employee assistance program	Employee representation
Employee disability program	Extra work
Employee performance evaluation	Full understanding modifications—waiver
Employee publications	Grievance procedures
Employee representation	Grievances—general in character

Employee rights
Equal employment opportunity
Excused absences
Familiarization flying
Federal personnel manuals
FLSA amendments
Grievance procedure
Hazards and environmental pay
Health and safety
Hiring criteria
Holiday closure
Holiday work
Holidays
Hours of work and basic work week
Incentive awards program
Informal review of job description
Jury duty and court leave
Labor-management cooperation
Leave for special circumstances
Leave of absence
Leave without pay—union officials
Loans
Local supplements to master agreement
Management rights
Maternity leave
Medical examinations
Merit promotion
Moving expenses
Names of employees and communications
Negotiation during agreement
Noncompetitive temporary promotion
Nondiscrimination
Official personnel folder
Official time—union representatives
On-the-job training
Overtime
Parking
Participation in wage surveys
Parties to the agreement
Payroll withholding of dues

Holiday pay limitation
Holiday work
Holidays
Hospitalization, medical insurance and optical care
Hours of work
Implementation
Instruction rate
Insurance
Job bids
Jury duty and witness leave
Labor management and safety committees
Late time
Layoff benefits
Layoff or reduction procedure
Leaves of absence
Longevity pay
Management rights
Meal periods
Military-leave vacation
Miscellaneous benefits
Missing assignments
Nondiscrimination
Nonplatform assignments
Obligation to support
Out-of-class assignments
Overtime compensation
Parking
Part-time and seasonal employees
Payroll deductions and dues
Pension plan contribution
Personal leave without pay
Personnel files
Personnel policies and procedures
Position classification study
Posting notices
Productivity
Provisions of FLSA
Provisions of law
Purpose
Recognition
Relief time
Renegotiation

Performance evaluation
Position classification
Position descriptions
Printing of the agreement
Productivity
Promotions and transfers
Provisions of law and regulation
Purpose of the agreement
Realignment of the work force
Recognition and coverage
Recruiting members
Reduction of force
Reopeners
Repromotion
Retirement and death benefits
Return rights from overseas location
Rights of the parties
Rosters
Sick leave
Special tools, clothing, services
Studies and testing of employees
Temporary assignments and associated per diem
Training—TDY
Travel and per diem
Union benefits
Union conventions, board of directors, and regional meetings
Use of employer facilities
Wages—premium
Washington field relations
Watch schedules
Working hours

Report and turn-in
Rest periods
Retirement benefits
Runs—definition
Safety and health
Salaries
School schedule
Selection of work
Seniority
Shift differential
Sick leave, funeral leave, and hospital benefits
Special pay practices
Spread premium
Strike and work stoppages
Successor interest
Technological change
Term
Tool, uniform, and automobile allowance
Transfer
Transfer vacation
Uniform
Union representation
Union rights
Vacation
Wage differential
Wages—wage schedule
Work schedules
Workweek—off days

SELECTED REFERENCES

Feller, David E., *A General Theory of the Collective Bargaining Agreement.* Reprint No. 372, Institute of Industrial Relations, University of California, Los Angeles, 1973. Professor Feller notes that a definitive theory of the rights created by the collective bargaining agreement has never developed in American law. There have been analogies drawn from time to time, and particular answers have been provided in suits between unions, employers, and employees, but nowhere has a unified theory been developed that attempts to relate these particular answers to each other in a coherent manner. In this article, the author sets himself to the task of developing just such a theory.

Livernash, E. Robert, "Special and Local Negotiations," in *Frontiers of Collective Bargaining,* eds. John T. Dunlop and Neil W. Chamberlain. New York: Harper & Row, 1967. Professor Livernash deals with negotiation situations involving more than a single agreement between the parties: special supplemental agreements (pensions, benefit plans) and local agreements under a master agreement.

Morris, Charles J., Ed., *The Developing Labor Law,* 2nd ed. chapter 17. Washington, D.C.: Bureau of National Affairs, Inc., 1983. The legal enforceability of the collective bargaining agreement and the relationship of the NLRB to the court system are dealt with here.

Taylor, Benjamin J., and Fred Witney, *Labor Relations Law,* 4th ed., chapter 15. Englewood Cliffs, N.J.: Prentice-Hall, 1983. This is good coverage of the legal status of the labor agreement and the internal enforcement procedures that are usually included in labor agreements.

PART II

COLLECTIVE BARGAINING PROCESS:
Negotiation

When we come to the settlement of the terms upon which a new general agreement should be entered into, an entirely different set of considerations is involved. Whether the general level of wages in the trade should be raised or lowered by 10 per cent; whether the number of boys to be engaged by any one employer should be restricted, and if so, by what scale; whether the hours of labor should be reduced, and overtime regulated or prohibited—are not problems which could be solved by the most perfect calculating-machine. Here nothing has been decided, or accepted in advance by both parties, and the fullest possible play is left for the arts of diplomacy. In so far as the issue is left to Collective Bargaining there is not even any question of principle involved. The workmen are frankly striving to get for themselves the best terms that can permanently be extracted from the employers. The employers, on the other hand, are endeavoring, in accordance with business principles, to buy their labor in the cheapest market.

Sidney and Beatrice Webb, *Industrial Democracy* 1902

CHAPTER 6

INTRODUCTION
TO PART TWO

MEANING OF COLLECTIVE BARGAINING

Parts II, III, and IV deal with topics that, while treated separately, are essentially elements of one process: collective bargaining. Beatrice Potter Webb introduced this term in 1891.[1] When the Webbs later popularized the term *collective bargaining* in the great classic, *Industrial Democracy*,[2] it had a more restricted meaning than it has today. Primarily, the Webbs and the American writers of the day were applying the term *collective bargaining* to the negotiation process. The Webbs, in discussing "the method of collective bargaining," noted first the meaning of the term *individual bargain*[3] as applying strictly to a situation between an employer and workingmen individually under which the terms of employment were determined. They then proceeded to describe, in contrast, what they meant by "the method of collective bargaining":

> But if a group of workmen concert together, and send representatives to conduct the bargaining on behalf of the whole

[1]Beatrice Potter, *The Co-operative Movement in Great Britain* (New York: Scribner's, 1891), pp. 216–17.

[2]Sidney and Beatrice Webb, *Industrial Democracy* (London: Longmans, Green, 1902), p. 173.

[3]*Ibid.*

> body, the position at once changes. Instead of the employer
> making a series of separate contracts with isolated individuals,
> he meets with a collective will, and settles, in a single agree-
> ment, the principles upon which, for the time being, all work-
> men of a particular group, or class, or grade, will be engaged.[4]

Even though collective bargaining was used initially to describe negotiations, another collective bargaining function that was later to be of
equal importance was beginning to emerge. This was the incorporation in
the trade agreement of machinery to resolve disputes that might arise
during the contract period over the meaning and application of the agreement—the process now known as contract administration. It should be
recognized that yet a third collective bargaining function has also been
developing. This third element involves the use of techniques and devices
outside the regular negotiation and contract-administration procedures
aimed at strengthening both processes—techniques such as mediation,
arbitration, fact finding, and continuous bargaining. Insofar as these supplementary aids are aimed at facilitating and strengthening collective bargaining and are not considered as substitutes, they should be recognized
as formal elements of what we call collective bargaining. This is the reasoning behind the three-way division of materials that follows: Part II,
"Negotiation"; Part III, "Contract Administration"; Part IV, "Resolution
of Conflict."

NEGOTIATION AND THE COLLECTIVE
BARGAINING AGREEMENT

Of immediate concern is the negotiation stage of collective bargaining. As
background, it is understood that collective bargaining negotiation is a
multifaceted process that takes on somewhat the coloration of the time,
place, and participants involved. This is why there are many variations in
the contract results from one bargaining situation to another, even where
the same union is involved but with different firms, or where the locals of
the same international are dealing with essentially similar firms but in
different geographic areas. Other differences are related to community,
economic, political, and social influence; in the way the employer is
organized; in production methods and technology; in the nature of the
product; in the industry environment (manufacturing, transportation, service, construction, and government, and their subcategories); in historical
circumstances; in the legal atmosphere (legislation, court decisions, arbitration decisions, grievance settlements); and not least, in the personalities and predilections of negotiators from one bargaining situation to

[4]*Ibid.*

another. All these are a part of the forces influencing the specific nature of the trade agreement and language that results from any particular collective bargaining negotiation. In sum, collective bargaining negotiation is not an easily described process nor does it lend itself to being reduced to what one might describe as a typical situation. It is the product of many environmental forces that shape its nature, some general and some unique to the particular negotiation.

COLLECTIVE BARGAINING BY OBJECTIVES

In the arrangement of material for this book, the practical matter of bridging the gap between information and its use is the first consideration. Two major conditions are required to effect successful collective bargaining negotiations. The first is preparatory, establishing the groundwork for effective negotiations. The second brings to bear the intrinsic bargaining skills of the negotiator. However, effectiveness at the bargaining table is more than the intrinsic bargaining skills of the negotiator—personality and experience. It is more succinctly described as a compound of the prior preparation for negotiations and the intrinsic bargaining skill of the negotiator. Consequently, proper preparation cannot be overemphasized. Preparation, in turn, is enhanced greatly by the method of preparation.

Part II is devoted to a step-by-step procedure starting with gathering and organizing bargaining information, then developing this information into a plan of action or blueprint for negotiations (CBO), and finally, to applying this blueprint to the actual negotiations.

Chapter 7 introduces the reader to the important task of developing bargaining information. Of particular concern are such questions as: When should such information be assembled? Where may such information be found? What kinds of information should be assembled? How this information can be organized and assembled so as to insure easy accessability in developing the blueprint for negotiations and for reference during the actual negotiating is the subject of Chapter 8, "A CBO Log."

Chapter 9 through Chapter 13 provide the reader with a methodology for formulating a plan of action or blueprint for negotiations from the assembled bargaining information described in Chapters 7 and 8. This methodology is termed *collective bargaining by objectives* (CBO). It is an adaptation of *management by objectives* (MBO) to the negotiation process. It is the bridge between information gathered and its use at the negotiation table. The key to this methodology (CBO) is that the ordinary tasks that must be completed preparatory to negotiations are placed within an easily perceived framework. Moreover, by the discipline this methodology generates, it assures that the negotiators, in advance of negotiations, will familiarize themselves with all aspects of the subject matter to be bargained. It is not a seat-of-the-pants approach to negotiations, but one based upon preparation and knowledge. Additionally, it results in a plan of action or blueprint *in advance* of negotiations. Because CBO is a goals-oriented methodology, the negotiator knows not only where he is headed and why, but, with as reasonable certainty as good preparation can provide, knows the possible range of actual results. This is not a defensive bargaining methodology, but a positive bargaining methodology for the negotiator based on sound preparation, providing known goals within a predetermined possible settlement range. Finally, it should be noted that CBO is a bargaining methodology. Experience and feedback over the last twelve years of its use indicates it is adaptable to any negotiating situation.

Chapter 14 is directed to the final preparation prior to the parties sitting down at the bargaining table. A new aid, a checklist for the negotiator, is included in this chapter. This is to help the negotiator determine whether all preparations for an effective negotiation session have been completed. Chapter 14 also discusses the use of a bargaining book.

Chapter 15 is addressed to the actual negotiation. The legal framework of the negotiation, bargaining format and procedures, negotiations stages, and conduct of negotiations are described. Bargaining homilies, rather than specific formulas or bargaining techniques, are enunciated. The use of CBO as a means of evaluating results of the negotiation is described last in Chapter 15.

SELECTED REFERENCES

Allen, Robert E., and Timothy J. Keaveny, *Contemporary Labor Relations,* Reading, Mass.: Addison-Wesley, 1983. Parts one and three provide general coverage of the evolution of public policy and the collective bargaining process.

Anderson, Arvid, "Labor Relations in the Public Service," in *Employee and Labor Relations, ASPA Handbook of Personnel and Industrial Relations,* eds. Dale Yoder and H. G. Heneman, Jr. Washington, D.C.: Bureau of National Affairs, Inc., 1979. Chairman of the New York City Office of Collective Bargaining since 1968, Arvid Anderson speaks with the voice of experience and authority on public-sector labor relations.

Beal, Edwin F., and James P. Begin, *The Practice of Collective Bargaining,* 6th ed. Homewood, Ill.: Richard D. Irwin, 1982. As noted by the authors, this latest edition preserves the integrity of treatment of theory and principles underlying practice that has been the hallmark of past editions. It also contains an excellent section on cases.

Bent, Alan Edward, and T. Zane Reeves, *Collective Bargaining in the Public Sector.* Menlo Park, Calif.: The Benjamin/Cummings Publishing Co., 1978. The authors examine the phenomenon of public-sector unionism and its relationship to public personnel administration and civil service. The role of public-employee unionism in the political process is not confined in this study to the institutional or legal framework but is broadened to include an analysis of the "profound ways by which public employee unions are reshaping contemporary political power relationship at all levels of government."

Bloom, Gordon F., and Herbert R. Northrup, *Economics of Labor Relations,* 6th ed. Homewood, Ill.: Richard D. Irwin, 1969. Chapter 4 contains excellent sections on the economic and social settings of collective bargaining.

Davey, Harold W., Mario F. Bognanno, and David L. Estenson, *Contemporary Collective Bargaining,* 4th ed. Englewood Cliffs, N.J.: Prentice-Hall, 1982. Professors Davey, Bognanno, and Estenson provide the reader with a remarkable blending of the academician and the practitioner. The reader will find the material not only understandable but down to earth.

Dilts, David A., and Clarence R. Deitsch, *Labor Relations.* New York: Macmillan, 1983. The authors emphasize that the "commonality of interests, cooperation, and trust" are the "key to the solution of many of the problems currently facing labor and management." Basic economic tools are used in a straightforward and simplified fashion as an aid to the understanding of pressing labor relations issues and problems.

Fossum, John, *Labor Relations—Development, Structure, Process,* rev. ed. Dallas, Tex.: Business Publications, Inc., 1982. This book is directed to the synthesis of some of the research efforts of both institutionalists and behaviorists. It constitutes a careful, well balanced account of the general field of labor relations suited to the needs of readers of all persuasions.

Gibbons, Muriel K., et al, eds., *Portrait of a Process—Collective Negotiations in Public Employment.* Fort Washington, Pa.: Labor Relations Press, 1979. A collection of essays by different authors, constituting what the editors describe as "An unretouched portrait of public employment labor relations as it exists in the United States."

Herman, E. Edward, and Alfred Kuhn, *Collective Bargaining and Labor Relations.* Englewood Cliffs, N.J.: Prentice-Hall, 1981. This book "provides an in-depth coverage of a number of areas that are either omitted or underemphasized" in other texts, such as the bargaining unit, preparing for bargaining, costing, and power.

Hildebrand, George H., "The Public Sector," in *Frontiers of Collective Bargaining,* eds. John T. Dunlop and Neil W. Chamberlain. New York: Harper & Row, 1967. The author raises and discusses many of the issues relative to bargaining in the public sector, such as special features of public-sector bargaining, what to do about impasses, and the question of relative bargaining power.

Kassalow, Everett M., *Trade Unions and Industrial Relations: An International Comparison.* New York: Random House, 1969. The author is convinced that the comparative method provides new insights for social scientists examining American industrial relations. This is an excellent examination of industrial relations—trade unions and collective bargaining—on a comparative basis between Europe and America. He addresses such collective bargaining topics as the agreement, scope of bargaining, legislation, bargaining methods, and union security.

Ryder, Meyer, S., Charles M. Rehmus, and Sanford Cohen, *Management Preparation for Collective Bargaining.* Homewood, Ill.: Dow Jones-Irwin,

1966. This study was motivated by the apparent lack of writings on management preparation for collective bargaining. It is based on an extensive survey of practices of firms and is most detailed about the preparation process.

Shafritz, Jay M., *Dictionary of Personnel Management and Labor Relations*. Oak Park, Ill.: Moore Publishing Company, 1980. A much-needed addition to labor relations literature. The author approaches his subject generically, neither favoring nor discriminating in his treatment of the public sector or private sector.

Slichter, Sumner H., James J. Healy, and E. Robert Livernash, *The Impact of Collective Bargaining on Management*. Washington, D.C.: The Brookings Institution, 1960. Even after so many years, this study still stands out as one of the penetrating looks at the impact of collective bargaining on management policy and practice represented by a cross section of 150 companies, 25 industry associations, and 40 unions. The book is divided according to substantive areas of management policy and practice, such as hiring, training and apprenticeship, seniority, work sharing and layoff, and promotion, to name a few.

Somers, Gerald G., ed., *Collective Bargaining: Contemporary American Experience*, Madison, Wis.: Industrial Relations Research Association, 1980. A detailed description and analysis of contemporary collective bargaining in ten major industries, authored by ten distinguished individuals in the collective bargaining field, with a commentary by Jack Barbash. The study is considered in a sense to be an update of *How Collective Bargaining Works*, a classic edited by Harry A. Millis and published in 1940.

Stieber, Jack, *Public Employee Unionism: Structure, Growth, Policy*. Washington, D.C.: The Brookings Institution, 1973. Professor Stieber examines the various types of unions and associations representing employees in state and local sectors of government, exclusive of schoolteachers and transit employees. The study is concerned with the impact of the structure, growth patterns and policies upon collective bargaining. Included are topics such as the organization of employees in public service, conflict and cooperation, collective bargaining, the strike issue, and emerging patterns.

Weber, Arnold R., ed., *The Structure of Collective Bargaining*. New York: Free Press, 1961. An excellent look at the role of collective bargaining in the decision-making process of our economic system. The focus of the book is on trends and problems in the structure of collective bargaining, covering such topics as the size and scope of bargaining units and the power function between managements and unions in the making of decisions. Industries covered are steel, chemical, airline, construction, and farm equipment.

Wolfbein, Seymour L., ed., *Emerging Sectors of Collective Bargaining*. Braintree, Mass: D. H. Mark, 1970. The 1950s and 1960s were among the most momentous periods in the evolution of collective bargaining. This book, which includes names such as Dunlop, Taylor, Ross, and Moskow, looks at the emerging sectors of collective bargaining and the new internal structures and responses resulting.

Worman, Max S., Jr., *Critical Issues in Labor*. New York: Macmillan, 1969. A useful source of background information concerning the changing character and challenges of the labor-management developing issues, experimental techniques, behavioral approaches, and changing attitudes related to collective bargaining, and what all this means for labor in a free society.

Zagoria, Sam, ed., *Public Workers and Public Unions.* Englewood Cliffs, N.J.: Prentice-Hall, 1972. From a broader approach to the role, development, and structure of public-sector bargaining, this study then turns more specific with articles on the municipal employer, the school board, the union leader, and the budget director. The book concludes with the problem areas of impasses, strikes, politics at the bargaining table, and race relations.

CHAPTER 7

GATHERING AND ASSEMBLING BARGAINING INFORMATION

This chapter, gathering and assembling the raw data or basic bargaining information, begins the preparatory process. The final step in the preparatory process, the development of a blueprint or plan of action through CBO, depends on the quality of the initial gathering-and-assembling process for its success as a tool for successful bargaining.

Essential to effective gathering and assembling of bargaining information is knowing *when* to begin gathering information, *how* to gather and assemble the information for effective use, and *what* information is most essential to the successful development of a plan of action for negotiations. *When* one should begin gathering bargaining information may be answered simplistically: At the time the current contract is ratified, start to assemble information for the next negotiations, whether they will occur in one year, two years, three years, or even further down the line. To put off is to forget. To fail to gather and record important information daily, or at least as often as possible, for the next negotiations is to lessen the quality or usefulness of the information as a bargaining tool. This usefulness is increased by recording the information, with appropriate observations, at the time it is available—not a week, a month, or a year or so later. Time dims the memory and questions the accuracy of what did occur and how it should be recorded.

How one should gather and assemble the bargaining information may also be answered simply: Develop a system, whether it be a set of large loose-leaf pages appropriately identified by subject areas or a file classified by subject areas. The essential goal should be *retrievability*. *How* also refers to the sources of the bargaining data. A list of sources is essential. Both the location of sources for material and hints on successful techniques for assembling bargaining information are treated more fully with the discussion of what types of bargaining information to assemble. In addition, the Selected References to this chapter identify major sources of bargaining data. What kinds of bargaining data to assemble depends on the compiler's capabilities for gathering such information, the type of bargaining situation (size of the bargaining unit, work performed by those served by the bargaining unit, availability of information at the national, regional, or local level), the economic situation, and the general bargaining climate.

The first task is to determine the kind of bargaining information necessary to the development of an effective plan of action for negotiations. Since the need for information will vary from one bargaining situation to another, the types of data discussed in the following section are not intended to be exhaustive. Rather, they provide a broad spectrum of types of bargaining data useful in most negotiations. Techniques for recording and assembling data are provided to stimulate the thinking of readers regarding the proper sources for their own situation and how best to assemble the data. This chapter deals with the broad task of gathering and assembling data and emphasizes securing the right kinds of information and rendering it accessible through a system. Chapter 8 reveals a technique for synthesizing and extracting information vital to the coming negotiations on a continuous basis and in a form that renders it immediately accessible for the final preparatory step to negotiations—the development of a blueprint or plan of action through CBO.

TYPES OF BARGAINING INFORMATION

1. INFORMATION FROM THE LAST NEGOTIATION

Much help in preparing for the next negotiation may be derived from an immediate assessment of the negotiations leading to the ratification of the current contract. It is vital that the bargaining team and other concerned personnel make a written critique of the negotiations leading to the current contract as soon as this contract is ratified. The critique will provide a record of first-hand observations of those aspects of the just-completed negotiations affecting the welfare of the employer or labor organization so that this information may be incorporated into the planning for the next negotiations, however far into the future they may be. What should be recorded? A far-from-exhaustive list, but one suggestive of the direction the critique should take would include such matters as:

1. Strategy that paid off or did not pay off
2. Preparation that paid off or did not pay off

3. Information that should have been part of the preparation but was neglected
4. Bargaining items dropped from negotiations but bound to be of concern at the next negotiations
5. Bargaining items conceded in the course of trade-offs or in the course of consummating the contract but not viewed as being in the best interests of the party concerned
6. Observations anent personalities of those at the bargaining table
7. Items negotiated that, viewed by the labor organization upon retrospect, appear unduly restrictive of employee benefits or rights
8. Items negotiated that are viewed by the employer as unduly costly or limiting of managerial authority
9. Contract language that appears conflicting upon reading or rereading the entire contract

The time that the direct participants are available is the time to critique the contract language, item by item, for intent and meaning. This should reveal printing errors or language faults the parties did not perceive in the thick of negotiations. Typing the contract with a large-enough left margin for notes and numbering each line of the contract consecutively on each page is illustrated in Form 7-1. The critique group

FORM 7-1

1	the matter to the final step of the grievance procedure.
2	ARTICLE 14: ARBITRATION PROCEDURES
3	
4	Only grievances which have been timely processed by the
5	Union through the grievance steps in Article 12 or 13 and
6	which allege a violation of this agreement (including a
7	claim alleging unjust suspension or termination) may be
8	carried to arbitration.
9	All reasonable efforts should be made to avoid the
10	expense and trouble of arbitration. Within thirty-five (35)
11	calendar days of request for arbitration, the parties shall
12	either agree upon an arbitrator or shall request a panel of
13	names from the Federal Mediation Service, and within seven
14	(7) calendar days after receipt of such panel shall select
15	the arbitrator by alternately striking names from the panel
16	with the first strike determined by lot. Extensions of up
17	to seven (7) calendar days may be granted for either party
18	if written or verbal request is made within forty-eight (48)
19	hours of the original deadline. If the Union fails timely
20	to select an arbitrator, the grievance shall be deemed
21	withdrawn.
22	Parties shall reduce to writing their agreed positions
23	with respect to facts and issues, and any disputed facts or
24	issues.
25	The arbitrator shall have no power to change this
26	Agreement nor to impose any terms or conditions the arbitra-
27	tor might think the parties should have agreed upon.
28	
29	
30	

should examine each line carefully, inserting appropriate notes into the open part of the page to indicate the meaning and intent of the language from each point of view. If more space is needed, a blank facing page may be added. This is especially important with respect to new language or to language already in the contract but the subject of discussion among the parties at the last negotiations. Such a critique *by those actually involved in negotiations* is invaluable in the ongoing process of applying the contract and preparing for the next negotiations. Moreover, it assures that a record will be available to those who may have to conduct future negotiations without the benefit of first-hand knowledge of the manner the contract's language came into being and how it was interpreted by those who fashioned it. Otherwise, any advantage in preparing for the next negotiations is vitiated through loss of memory, or too often, simply because the people directly involved are no longer around.

2. COMPARISON WITH OTHER CONTRACT SETTLEMENTS

Another vital information source in preparing for negotiations is other contract settlements. In obtaining this kind of information, two cautions should be observed. First, data on other contract settlements should be current. It does no good to argue one's position on the basis of out-of-date settlements. Second, one must be selective in gathering data concerning other contract settlements for purposes of comparison. With more than 150,000 contracts being negotiated every two to three years, the person who is not selective courts the danger of quickly entering into an unmanageable situation. Even more acute is the problem that the less selective one is in obtaining data from other settlements, the more irrelevant such data becomes. Selectivity means starting with those outside contract settlements that have the sharpest impact and relevance to the outcome of one's own negotiations. These would be the contract settlements involving firms or agencies having similar products or services. In terms of the market, these are the groups in most direct competition with one's own product or service. There should also be a sensitivity to contract settlements by employers who hire from the same labor market as one's own, even though the product or service may differ. Moving beyond the settlements with immediate relevance requires greater and greater selectivity and attention to what is manageable. But it is possible to glean useful information for one's own negotiations from a broader selective input of settlements when the objective is to discern pattern settlements on a regional or national basis or to identify new bargaining subject areas wherein contract settlements are being extended.

Granted, there are difficulties in acquiring other contracts, but this may often be overcome through the assistance of national labor organizations, trade or employer organizations, or government or research groups with access to information on contract settlements, either regional or national. If other contracts are available, one successful technique in rendering the material easy to use is through a comparative contract clause book, illustrated in Form 7-2. The party using this visual means of comparing different contracts, provision by provision, can extend the number of contracts being compared by a horizontal accordian extension of each sheet of comparisons. This provides easy access to comparisons by bargaining items or subjects through a quick scan. Other forms of comparative information anent contract settlements are issued in publications or distributed studies of trade associations, national labor organizations, general employer groups, and research and governmental groups. These provide comparisons of contract settlements on regional or national levels in more limited areas. For example, one such study included for transit systems on a regional basis a comparison of settlements directed at the number of employees under the agreement, expiration date of the agreement, wages by classification, days of vacation, sick-leave benefits, paid holidays, uniform allowance, and contribution per employee into health and pension funds. Another contract, between the Paper and Allied Products Industry and its employees, identified the employer, the union, and the number of employees covered; the current general wage increase and date; and related information on wage and benefit changes. Illustrative of union sources is one national union's publication that revealed, on an industrywide basis for 137 cities, a comparison of the basic hourly rate plus vacation, health and welfare contributions, pension fund contributions, apprenticeship funds, other contractual benefits, the total package, the increment termination, and the agreement termination.

FORM 7–2
Clause Book Contract Comparisons

SMITH-FIELD, INC. *Article XI—Holidays*	*BREWERY COOPERATIVE* *Article XX—Holidays &* *Overtime*	*NECTAR BREWING* *COMPANY* *Part V—Fringe Benefits*
Section 1. The following shall be considered as holidays: New Year's Day, Washington's Birthday, Good Friday, Memorial Day, Fourth of July, Labor Day, Veteran's Day, Thanksgiving	1. (a) The day before New Year's day, Presidents' Day (3rd Monday in February), Good Friday, Decoration Day, Fourth of July, Labor Day, Veterans' Day, (Fourth Monday in October), Thanksgiving	Section 1. Paid Holidays The following days shall be considered holidays: New Year's Day (January 1st), Washington's Birthday (the third Monday in February), Memorial Day (the last Monday in May), Independence Day

3. EVOLUTION OF THE COLLECTIVE BARGAINING
   AGREEMENT

In addition to the comparison of one's collective bargaining agreement
with other settlements, a vital source of information for bargaining purposes is how one's own agreement has evolved over the various time
periods it has been in effect. This is important not only in ascertaining
when and how particular provisions of the contract have changed over the
various contract periods, but also is a means of catching errors or conflicts
in language that might not otherwise be noticed until an incident brings
them to the attention of the parties. Intent may also be adduced from
knowing the direction of changes in language. Moreover, if information is
available as to changes in contract language and provisions over time and
it is combined with the critiques of the bargaining teams who negotiated
each past contract, a picture may emerge as to the meaning and intent of
the various provisions of the agreement as they have evolved. As an arbitrator with several decades' experience, the writer remembers many
incidents in which knowing how a provision entered the contract and
what was intended at the time was a crucial factor in determing its proper
application. More often than not, there was no readily available information nor individuals with first-hand knowledge of the negotiations effecting a particular contract.

A useful technique in portraying the contract evolution, provision
by provision, is illustrated in Form 7-3. This format, through the use of a

FORM 7–3
Clause Book Contract Evolution

1978 *ARTICLE XII—* *SENIORITY*	1981 *ARTICLE XVII—* *SENIORITY*	1984 *ARTICLE XVII—* *SENIORITY*
Section (a) Definition	Section (a) Definition of Seniority	Section (a) Definition of Seniority
Seniority at the mine shall be recognized in the industry on the fol- lowing basis: Length of service and qualification to perform the work.	Seniority at the mine shall be recognized in the industry on the fol- lowing basis: length of service and the ability to step into and perform the work of the job at the time the job is awarded.	Seniority at the mine shall be recognized in the industry on the fol- lowing basis: length of service and the ability to step into and perform the work of the job at the time the job is awarded.
	In awarding bids on job postings, the parties agree that management will not show favoritism or discrimination. To help senior Employees	In awarding bids on job postings, the parties agree that management will not show favoritism or discrimination. To help senior Employees

FORM 7–3 (*Continued*)

1978 ARTICLE XII— SENIORITY	1981 ARTICLE XVII— SENIORITY	1984 ARTICLE XVII— SENIORITY
	achieve promotion, they shall be given preference to the extent practicable in the filling of temporary vacancies as set out in section (c) of Article XIX (Classification).	achieve promotion, they shall be given preference to the extent practicable in the filling of temporary vacancies as set out in section (c) of Article XIX (Classification).
Section (b) Reduction in Work Force In all cases where the working force is to be reduced, employees with the greatest seniority shall be retained providing they are qualified to perform the work.	Section (b) Reduction in Work Force In all cases where the working force is to be reduced, Employees with the greatest seniority at the mine shall be retained provided that they have the ability to perform available work.	Section (b) Reduction in Work Force In all cases where the working force is to be reduced, Employees with the greatest seniority at the mine shall be retained provided that they have the ability to perform available work.
	Section (c) Layoff Procedure In all cases where the working force is to be reduced or realigned, management shall meet with the mine committee at least 24 hours in advance and review the available jobs and the individuals to be laid off, retained or realigned. Within five (5) days after an Employee is notified that he is to be laid off, he must fill out a standardized form and submit it to mine management. On this form, the laid-off Employee shall list: (1) his years of service at the mine;	Section (c) Layoff Procedure In all cases where the working force is to be reduced or realigned, management shall meet with the mine committee at least 24 hours in advance and review the available jobs and the individuals to be laid off, retained or realigned. Within five (5) days after an Employee is notified that he is to be laid off, he must fill out a standardized form and submit it to mine management. On this form, the laid-off Employee shall list: (1) his years of service at the mine;

contract evolution clause book, is similar to that already discussed for comparing contracts of different employers. It provides horizontal comparison, article by article, for the various periods the contract has been in force for this particular bargaining unit. For example, changes in the definition of *seniority* can be readily detected in Form 7-3 for the contracts of 1978, 1981, and 1984. When no changes occur from one contract to another, it is sufficient to indicate no change.

4. Costing the Contract

A cost breakdown of the contract is undeniably one of the most important types of information to assemble in preparing for negotiations. Contract costing can be assembled in a number of forms, depending on the specific use for each cost. Costing of the contract can be historical, showing costs totally and functionally, and variations from contract to contract. It is important in the give-and-take of bargaining to depict not only total changes in contract costs over time but how various components of the total cost may be changing from contract to contract. It is not only necessary to accurately cost out the current contract in a form revealing a complete picture of all costs included, but also to monitor the current contract regularly to determine whether the anticipated costs of the various components are within the cost projections calculated at the time of ratification. This leads to the costing of the proposed contract changes at the next negotiations, serving as the bellwether for the negotiating party, compared with past costs and present capabilities or needs, in determining strategy and ranges of acceptability for each bargaining item. There are many forms that the parties may use to construct a cost picture, depending on each one's particular inclinations and resources. Costing is sometimes used to differentiate between wage costs and benefit costs; some costing includes a breakdown of costs to differentiate between contractual costs and legislated costs. Another not unusual breakdown of benefit costs shows those with no direct payment to the employee (insurance, pension), those for which no time is worked (vacation, holidays, funeral leave, jury duty, sickness and accident insurance, paid lunch, and excused paid time), and premium pay (overtime, shift differential). There is also a rather interesting breakdown of costs by article of the contract. Under this last, each article is identified numerically (1 through 37); the subject of each article is stated (Article 1, Duration, to Article 37, Pension); and the cost, if any, assigned to the specific article.

A most important consideration in costing out the contract or contract proposals, one that determines the usefulness of contract cost information, is the *method* used. This method can range from the relatively simple to the complex, depending on the nature of the information desired. The following method of costing illustrates a more simplified approach to securing certain significant cost figures. Several types of cost factors are recognized in this costing-out process: (1) direct payroll costs (cost of work and nonwork paid time), (2) changes in costs that are a direct function of changes in the direct wage rate, (3) nonpayroll costs, and (4) nonwork paid time. Nonwork paid time is included in (1) but separated out in (4) because of the importance of knowing the difference between increases in cost attributable to productive effort and increases resulting from nonwork paid time.

Changes in Costs

I. Direct Payroll—Annual

   Straight-time earnings—36¢ per hour general increase   *2,080 = 40hrs×52wk*
     100 employees
     100 × 2,080 hrs. × 36¢ =
   Premium earnings, second-shift established differential—10¢ per
       hour   *(eg. graveyard shift)*
     30 employees involved
     30 × 2,080 hrs. × 10¢ =
   Overtime: Overtime costs increased by increased straight-time rate,
       average straight-time rate increase 36¢
     36¢ × 12,000 overtime hrs. × .5 overtime rate =   *estimate*
   Bonus—none
   Other direct payroll cost increases
       Total Increase in Direct Payroll Costs =

Tax

II. Added Costs Directly Resulting from Higher Payroll Costs—Annual

   FICA—9.35% times increase in average straight-time earnings below
     $35,700 annually, 100 employees
     100 × 36¢ × 5.85% × 2,080 =
   Federal and state unemployment insurance tax
     Number of employees × 4,200 × tax rate (2.5 to 4.5%) =
   Workmen's compensation
     (Total cost or estimate)
   Other
       Total Additional Direct Payroll Costs =

Fringe Benefits

III. Nonpayroll Costs—Annual

   Insurance—company portion
     Health insurance, no change
     Dental insurance, none
     Eye care, none
     Life insurance—added employer contribution
       $100 per year
       $100 × 100 employees =
   Pension Costs
     Fully vested pension reduced from 25 years and age 65 to 20 years
       and age 62
     Estimated additional cost per year =
   Miscellaneous
     Tuition reimbursements
     Service rewards
     Suggestion awards
     Loss on employee cafeteria
     Overtime meals
     Cost of parking lots
     Company parties
     Personal tools
     Personal safety equipment
     Personal wearing apparel
   Profit sharing
   Other
       Total Additional Nonpayroll Costs, Annual =

COST ITEMS -

non-cost items: seniority discipline

public -ers have better benefits than private -ers. ∴ public used to get lower wages

IV. Changes in Nonwork Paid Time
  Holidays—2 new holidays added to 6 already in contract
       100 employees × 8 hrs. × 2 holidays × Average new wage
          ($6.14) =Vacation, new category added—4 weeks (160 hours
  annual vacation)
             with 20 or more years service; former top was 3 weeks after 15;
             average number of employees affected annually, 15
       15 × 40 × Average new wage ($6.14) =
   Paid lunchtime—paid ½ lunchtime added to contract
       100 employees × ½ hr. × days worked yearly (236) × Average
          new wage ($6.14) =
   Paid wash-up time, none
   Coffee breaks, no change
  Paid time off for union activity—new, one hour per week per shop
          steward
       10 shop stewards × Average new wage shop stewards ($7.29) ×
          1 hr. × 52 weeks =
   Paid sick leave
   Paid time off over and above workmen's compensation paid time,
          none
   Jury-service time off, no change
   Funeral-leave time off, no change
   Paid time off for safety or training, no change
   Other
             Total change in hours paid for but not worked, annual =

V. Financial Data Derived from Costing Out
   Total increase in contract costs
       I + II + III
   Average total increase in contract costs per employee payroll hour
       I + II + III ÷ 2,080 hours
   Average total increase in direct payroll costs per man-hour
       I + II ÷ 2,080 hours ÷ 100 employees
   Average total increase in nonpayroll costs per payroll-hour, per
          employee
       III ÷ 2,080 hours ÷ 100 employees
   Average total increase in nonwork paid time per payroll-hour per
          employee
       IV ÷ 2,080 hours ÷ 100 employees
   Average total increase in direct payroll costs per prod. (worked) hour
          (per employee)
       I + II ÷ 1,888 hours ÷ 100 employees
   Average total increase in nonpayroll costs per prod. (worked) hour
          (per employee)
       III ÷ 1,888 hours ÷ 100 employees
   Average total increase in nonwork paid time per prod. (worked) hour
          (per employee)
       IV ÷ 1,888 hours ÷ 100 employees

   The use of computers has greatly enhanced the process of costing a
contract, the variations in the data's presentation, and certainly the timeliness and availability of the data.

For those seeking more detailed information and advice on costs, there are such excellent sources as Granof's *How to Cost Your Labor Contract,* and Morse's *How to Negotiate the Labor Agreement.* See Chapter 12's Selected References for full details.

5. INFORMATION ON BARGAINING-UNIT EMPLOYEES

It is obvious that substantial portions of the collective bargaining agreement cannot be negotiated without data regarding the numbers and characteristics of employees who constitute the bargaining unit. Of course, the employer will not want to limit employee information to the bargaining unit since its range of concern with employee costs extends to total costs of the entire work force. However, for purposes of isolating the costs of past, present, and proposed collective bargaining contracts, the immediate focus for both parties is on the employees covered by the contract.

In determining what bargaining-unit employee information to assemble, those portions of the contract that can only be costed out if certain types of information are available must be identified. For example, direct wage costs require data on employees belonging to the bargaining unit as to number, classification, wage rate, and hours of work. Hospital and medical benefits for employees would depend not only on numbers, but on age and family composition. The following list indicates the use of employee information in various types of contract provisions or bargaining items.

Bargaining Item	Employee Information
HEALTH AND WELFARE	
Life insurance	Age and sex
Medical insurance	Age, dependents, marital status and spouses' employment
Pension/retirement plans	Age, sex, seniority date
Safety	Accident information by employee, department, job
PAY FOR TIME NOT WORKED	
Holidays	Employee absences, the day before and/or after a holiday
Leaves of absence (short term and long term)	Utilization information and types of leave for each employee and department
UNPAID LEAVE	
All types	Utilization by employee and department
WAGES	Job classification, seniority
WORK ASSIGNMENT	
Promotion and transfer	Employee skills and job growth goals

Shift changes	Child care responsibilities
Work site transfers	Mobility problems, i.e., home owner, dual-career family
VACATIONS	Seniority
CHECK-OFF	Union members in bargaining unit
PAID TIME FOR COLLECTIVE BARGAINING ACTIVITIES	Union officers and shop stewards
ALL BENEFITS OF CONTRACT	Employees in the bargaining unit

6. GENERAL ECONOMIC DATA

As with employee information, determining what types of economic information to assemble and in what form depends upon its use. This requires that one first look to the various contract provisions and from these provisions arrive at a determination as to what types of economic information will be necessary in preparing for negotiations. Selectivity is important. Otherwise, gathering economic information would not only be unmanageable in terms of the time involved but also in the ability to use the information. For example, economic information concerning the consumer price index would be most appropriate in negotiating a cost-of-living clause in the contract or in negotiating wages. Data on wages by occupation and industry would be useful information in negotiating the wage package. Information from the Bureau of Labor Statistics (BLS) on current changes in wages and supplementary benefits agreed to in collective bargaining is vital information in supporting positions on these items during negotiations. Other useful types of information published by the government reflect studies of benefit plans, both frequency of use and provisions of individual plans; productivity measures by major sectors; occupational health and safety; labor turnover; occupational outlook and labor force projections; to mention a few.

7. THE LEGAL FRAMEWORK OF COLLECTIVE BARGAINING

Chapter 3 covers the legal framework of collective bargaining. As said, this is a multifaceted framework of several statutes covering different groups of employers and employees. The statutes and groups include, for purposes of review:

> *The National Labor Relations Act of 1935,* amended by the *Labor Management Relations Act of 1947* and the *Labor Management Reporting and Disclosure Act of 1959,* covering employers and their employees in interstate commerce
>
> *Civil Service Reform Act of 1978, Title VII,* covering federal agencies and their employees

Railway Labor Act of 1926, covering express companies, sleeping-car companies, carriers by railroad, or companies directly or indirectly controlled by railroads and engaged in transport (other than trucking) and every common carrier by air subject to the *Interstate Commerce Act*

State Collective Bargaining Statutes, covering one or more state employees, municipal employees, firefighters, policemen, and teachers (forty states)

State Labor Laws similar to the *LMRA of 1947* at the federal level, covering employer-employee relations in intrastate commerce

Federal Statutes such as the *FLSA of 1938, Civil Rights Act of 1969, Equal Opportunity Act of 1972, Equal Pay Act of 1963, Occupational Safety and Health Act of 1970, Employee Retirement Security Act of 1974,* and the *Veterans' Re-Employment Rights Act of 1975*—all having an impact upon the substance of labor agreements

State Right-to-Work Statutes restricting the inclusion of union security clauses in labor agreements in certain states

Inasmuch as both the process of collective bargaining (determining the bargaining unit, representation, negotiating and administering the agreement) and the substance of what may be negotiated are influenced by these statutes, it is vital in preparing for negotiations and during the actual negotiations to be aware of the framework of law.

There is, however, a special problem in keeping abreast of developments in law affecting collective bargaining. It is difficult enough for the layman to keep up with the meaning of these statutes as they are affected by court and administration decisions alone, let alone understand the "legalese." For larger employers and national labor organizations with in-house counsels or counsels under contract, the matter can be handled. For smaller employers and labor organizations, the cost of in-house or outside counsel may well be prohibitive. It is important, therefore, for those who do not have the expert advice, to be aware of sources wherein, at nominal cost, they may obtain information concerning amendments in legislation or interpretations of legislation that could affect their particular bargaining situations. Smaller national unions can turn to the parent federation, such as the AFL-CIO; local unions can turn to their national affiliates; small employers can look to their trade or employer associations operating in some instances as local employer councils or regional or national organizations. Other excellent and current sources of information are the many publications of private (some nonprofit) and governmental groups. Since it is impossible to list all of these sources, a few, solely for illustrative purposes, are included:

Regular services covering legislative and legal changes affecting collective bargaining published by Prentice-Hall, Commerce Clearing House, Bureau of National Affairs, Bureau of Labor Statistics, the Federal Labor Relations Authority; Cor-

*nell's Industrial and Labor Relations publications, as well as
publications of many other universities; publications of the
American Society of Personnel Administration and other similar groups; the labor law journals of a variety of universities;
and the regular publications of the American Arbitration Association. A good book such as Prentice-Hall's* Labor Relations
Law *by Taylor and Witney can do much to allay confusion.*

8. CONTRACT EXPERIENCE

Because of the direct daily connection between the application of the
contract and its ongoing interpretation, the application becomes one of
the most vital, if not the most vital, source of information in preparing for
negotiations. It is this daily testing and implementing of the contract that
elicits better than anything else what each provision of the contract means
to each party and the interests each represents. Does a particular provision mean what party members thought it meant at the time they signed
the final agreement? Does the agreement protect both parties' vital interests—the union and employee rights on the one hand, and the right to
manage on the other? What has been omitted from the contract that experience now dictates should be included? What contract provisions does
experience now reveal should be deleted? All of these messages to the
employer and to the employees and their representatives emerging from
application of the contract become a most important part of preparing for
negotiations.

Two important sources related to contract administration, one formal and the other informal, provide the major sources of information
about how the contract is working out as it comes up against the day-to-
day employer-employee problems.

The more formal source of information feedback comes from the
results of grievance processing. Grievance processing includes two levels
of feedback. The first level includes the grievances that are settled by the
parties prior to the terminal step of arbitration. The second level includes
the grievances settled by arbitration. The result of grievance processing is
either a joint decision or a neutral's decision. In either case, the decision
applies and interprets some aspect of the contract as it relates to a problem
arising under the employer-employee relation. Each settlement, each decision, is a record, therefore, of a settlement of a difference of opinion
between the parties as to how a particular provision of the contract should
apply. The decision becomes, in effect, a precedent and a part of the
contract by interpretation, as though it had been written into the contract.
If the effect of the decision is adverse to the interests of one of the parties,
it signals to that party that that particular provision should be changed at
the next negotiations in order to neutralize the adverse effect or to swing
the balance in favor of their own particular interests. As a source of data

critical to needed amendments in the contract at the next negotiations, the grievance settlements should not be minimized. It follows that the degree to which this source will be useful for the next negotiations is directly commensurate to the care the party takes to record and file such settlements, the care the party takes to examine the implications of the settlement with regard to impact upon its own interests, and the care the party takes to establish a retrieval system for such bargaining information.

The second source of information deriving from the administration of the contract is informal and more difficult to get at unless the party takes the time to establish an operative communication and retrieval system. This source involves the actions before the formal grievance stage of contract administration. Many questions about the meaning of the contract language are answered before they ever become a formally filed written grievance. More often than not, there is no record of such occurrences, generally between an employee and his foreman or among the employee, steward, and foreman. Or, if a notation is recorded on the foreman's log, often such information is not fed back to those who must develop the plan for the next negotiations. The same is true, perhaps even more so, when union steward or employee feedback to the union negotiators is concerned. Viewed alone, these on-the-floor settlements of contract problems may appear too insignificant to bother with. However, repeated incidents of questions of contract language often signal defects in language or structure that deserve as much attention as the more obvious incidents being processed through the grievance procedure. Repeated discussions of a particular contract provision, such as work assignment, safety, or absences, should lead to questions about the language of the appropriate provision and whether such situations might be avoided by modifying the language. If this on-the-spot procedure is to be valuable in discovering potential problems in contract language, a workable retrieval system between first-level participants and those who are charged with preparing for negotiations at higher levels demands priority. For the union, this retrieval system requires cooperation of all employees, particularly shop stewards. For management, the foremen and supervisors who deal directly with the employees must shoulder much responsibility.

One retrieval system with considerable merit is the use of a "living contract." This kind of retrieval system is in the form of a contract under constant scrutiny as it is applied. It is also linked to a feedback system. Usually the feedback is to a key functionary in the personnel office or in the union. Here the information is consolidated so that a complete picture is produced as to how each provision of the contract is working out. Notations are entered on an actual contract adjacent to the provision or provisions in question, resulting in an immediate identification of those parts of the contract requiring attention.

The current contract is typed as illustrated in Form 7-4, double-

FORM 7–4
Living Contract

```
 1      Any regular operator requesting to work overtime must
 2    sign the overtime list which shall be posted in each division.
 3    Overtime will be rotated among the signers.
 4      Any operator failing to be relieved shall not be re-
 5    quired, without the operator's consent to work more than one
 6    and one-half (1-1/2) hours before being relieved. If the opera-
 7    tor agrees to more than one and one-half (1-1/2) hours of extra
 8    work a minimum of two (2) hours work or pay for two (2)
 9    hours shall be provided.
10          ARTICLE 37 MINIMUM PAY FOR EXTRA WORK
11      Any regular operator having worked a regular run and
12    performing extra work before or after a regular run or being
13    called for extra work during the interim of two periods of
14    a regular run shall be paid one and one-half (1-1/2) times
15    their regular straight-time rate for such extra work with
16    a minimum of two (2) hours time.
17      Any regular operator called for extra work not other-
18    wise herein outlined, shall be paid time and one-half, with
19    a minimum of two (2) work hours.
20      Operators, after having worked a regular run and being
21    called for special work, will be allowed thirty (30) minutes
22    for meals before such work, if possible; if not, they will
23    be allowed thirty (30) minutes time after four (4) hours of
24    such work. Special work is defined as any work not a regular
25    run or regular tripper.
26      Any regular operator who is temporarily displaced from an
27    assigned run because of no fault of the operator, shall
28    be paid eight (8) hours or the amount of that regular run.
```

---

spaced on numbered lines and with wide margins. In fact, if more space is needed for notations, a complete blank page facing the living contract provisions can be inserted into a loose-leaf notebook.

In the case of the employer's use of this method, the labor relations director would distribute copies of the living contract to all managers and supervisors (line supervisors) of bargaining unit employees at the postnegotiation contract training session. Each of the managers or supervisors is asked to record briefly all informal contract experiences pertaining to specific provisions of the contract, in the space opposite the particular provision or particular language in the living contract. Line supervisors keeping the records are then asked to meet regularly with representatives of the labor relations department during the contract term to review the informal experiences they have noted in their own copies of the living contract regarding day-by-day application of the contract. The notes kept by line personnel in their own copies of the living contract are then periodically transferred to a master living contract in the director's office. This method of collecting informal information assures early notification of contract interpretation problems before they result in a griev-

FORM 7–5
Living Contract

I.2-insert "posted on the bulletin
board in each division."

I.5-add comma after consent.

check II. 11-16, Art. 37 for
conflict with II. 12-17, Art. 36.
Suggest deletion of 12-17.

Take out second para of 37.

II.26-28 Booth-"displacement
can occur anytime somebody
fills a regular operators run."

I.27 should read "their assigned
run."

1 Any regular operator requesting to work overtime must
2 sign the overtime list which shall be posted in each division.
3 Overtime will be rotated among the signers.
4 Any operator failing to be relieved shall not be re-
5 quired, without the operator's consent to work more than one
6 and one-half (1-1/2) hours before being relieved. If the opera-
7 tor agrees to more than one and one-half (1-1/2) hours of extra
8 work a minimum of two (2) hours work or pay for two (2)
9 hours shall be provided.
10   ARTICLE 37 MINIMUM PAY FOR EXTRA WORK
11 Any regular operator having worked a regular run and
12 performing extra work before or after a regular run or being
13 called for extra work during the interim of two periods of
14 a regular run shall be paid one and one-half (1-1/2) times
15 their regular straight-time rate for such extra work with
16 a minimum of two (2) hours time.
17 Any regular operator called for extra work not other-
18 wise herein outlined, shall be paid time and one-half, with
19 a minimum of two (2) work hours.
20 Operators, after having worked a regular run and being
21 called for special work, will be allowed thirty (30) minutes
22 for meals before such work, if possible; if not, they will
23 be allowed thirty (30) minutes time after four (4) hours of
24 such work. Special work is defined as any work not a regular
25 run or regular tripper.
26 Any regular operator who is temporarily displaced from an
27 assigned run because of no fault of the operator, shall
28 be paid eight (8) hours or the amount of that regular run.

ance. More important for the process of preparing for negotiations, the living contract provides critical data for formulating contract proposals at the next negotiations. To illustrate, one page of the master living contract might appear as in Form 7-5.

9. Miscellaneous Bargaining Information

Perhaps, with the writer's emphasis on gathering *facts*, any suggestion of gathering data through the grapevine or from scuttlebut and other conversations might seem out of place. However, with judicious use this information may be important not only in obtaining a general "feel" for the climate of the next negotiations, but in deciding what bargaining items the other party is most likely to introduce and some notion of the priorities of the other party. A more specific use can be made of verbal conversation if it is properly recorded and documented. For example, one manager of human resources, also the chief negotiator, has developed the habit of noting each conversation with union officials in a calendar book. These conversations, as they relate to specific bargaining items and sections of the contract, are recorded. Relevant information from the calendar book is combined with other bargaining information, article by article, in a bargaining book, to be discussed in Chapter 14. Thus, when discussions concerning a particular contract provision occur again, the manager does not need to depend on memory alone, but can respond, "I note in a conversation on July 7, 1983, at approximately 11 A.M. you said '_____.' "

CONCLUSION   *Nothing like a good, brief summary*

The way that this vital bargaining information may be rendered more readily accessible is covered in Chapter 8.

SELECTED REFERENCES

Allen, Robert E., and Timothy J. Keaveny, *Contemporary Labor Relations,* Menlo Park, Calif.: Addison-Wesley, 1983. Chapter 9, Collective Bargaining: From Preparation to Agreement, emphasizes the importance of preparation.

Annual reports—Highly recommended as sources of information for negotiations are the annual reports of such groups as the FLRA, the FMCS, and the National Labor Relations Board.

Beal, Edwin F., and James P. Begin, *The Practice of Collective Bargaining,* 6th ed. Homewood, Ill.: Richard D. Irwin, 1982. Beal and Begin emphasize the importance of proper preparation, pp. 217–21.

Campo, Arnold F., "Entering into Negotiations," in LeRoy Marceau, *Dealing with a Union,* pp. 86–99. New York: American Management Association, Inc., 1969. Contains information sources and advice on preparing for negotiations for both labor and management.

Collective Bargaining Negotiations & Contracts. Washington, D.C.: Bureau of National Affairs, Inc. A current and continuing service that provides information on bargaining trends and techniques, current settlements, basic patterns in union contracts, and facts for bargaining. An invaluable source for the negotiator who needs information on trends in contract settlements or the language of specific provisions of union contracts. Along with this major service, the BNA also issues a condensed account of *Basic Patterns in Union Contracts* in pamphlet form (8th ed., 1975).

Contract Clause Manual. St. Louis Region, U.S. Civil Service Commission, February 1975. Useful information concerning various types of contract clauses that have been incorporated into federal-sector collective bargaining contracts.

Davey, Harold W., Mario F. Bognanno, and David L. Estenson, *Contemporary Collective Bargaining,* 4th ed. Englewood Cliffs, N.J.: Prentice-Hall, 1982. Excellent coverage of the preparation for negotiations in Chapter 5. The authors give special treatment in the Appendix to Chapter 5 to calculating settlement costs, pp. 135–48. This is highly recommended.

Fossum, John A., *Labor Relations—Development, Structure, Process,* Dallas, Tex.: Business Publications, Inc., 1982. Chapter 10 is devoted for the most part to preparation for negotiations.

Gifford, Courtney, ed., *Directory of U.S. Labor Organizations, 1982–83 Edition.* Washington, D.C.: Bureau of National Affairs, Inc., 1982. Excellent information concerning labor organizations, their membership, collective bargaining activities, and other data. The BNA has taken over the responsibility for this publication from the DOL.

Government Employee Relations Report. Washington, D.C.: Bureau of National Affairs, Inc. The BNA provides in this service a weekly reporting for subscribers on federal, state, and local developments, including union demands for recognition; bargaining-unit determination; contract negotiations; new clauses in public-sector contracts; grievance settlements; arbitration awards; statistical data on earnings, hours of work, cost of living, and employment in the public sector; and federal and state legislation affecting public employees.

Government Union Review, A Quarterly Journal on Public Sector Labor Relations. Vienna, Va: Public Service Research Foundation. For up-to-date information on public-sector collective bargaining.

Handbook of Labor Statistics. Washington, D.C.: U.S. Department of Labor, Bureau of Labor Statistics. A wealth of information on employment, unemployment, hours, productivity, compensation, earnings by industry, social insurance, consumer price index, union membership, work stoppages, labor relations, occupational injuries and illnesses, gross national product, and national income. Of special value is the listing in the Appendix of Sources of Additional Data. This is a yearly publication.

Herman, E. Edward, and Alfred Kuhn, *Collective Bargaining and Labor Relations,* Englewood Cliffs, N.J.: Prentice-Hall, 1981. The authors devote Part IV to preparation for bargaining (Chapter 9) and costing of labor contracts (Chapter 10). This is an excellent treatment of these topics and is highly recommended reading.

Journal of Collective Negotiations in the Public Sector, Farmingdale, N.Y.: Baywood Publishing Company. For up-to-date information on public-sector collective bargaining.

Journals, professional. Highly recommended as sources of information are the *Industrial and Labor Relations Review* (Cornell), *Industrial Relations* (Berkeley), the *Arbitration Journal* (American Arbitration Association), and the various labor law journals.

Labor-Management Relations in the Federal Service. Washington, D.C.: U.S. Federal Labor Relations Council, 1975. Among those involved in federal-sector labor relations, this is a useful and informative publication. Included are the EOs applying to federal-sector labor relations, and reports and recommendations that have led to changes in these laws. Thoroughly informative.

LAIRS, Labor Agreement Information Retrieval System. Office of Labor–Management Relations of the U.S. Civil Service Commission. The file is composed of data, in various forms, extracted from federal labor agreements, third-party determinations, and statistical reports submitted regularly by federal agencies.

Marting, Elizabeth, ed., "A Step-by-Step Guide to the Preparatory Process," in *Understanding Collective Bargaining,* pp. 96–109. New York: American Management Association, Inc., 1958. A basic discussion of what must be done to prepare for negotiations, covering advance preparations, facts required for bargaining, contract termination notice, reviewing the union's proposals, company proposals and final preparation.

————, **ed.,** "Getting Ready to Talk Contract," in *Ibid.,* Part II. An older but excellent discussion of the negotiation process. Part II is a combination of articles by both practitioners and academicians. Selwyn H. Torff, Clive B. McKee, Fred D. Hunter, Hjalmar Rosen, R. A. H. Rosen, and Monroe Berkowitz blend their efforts in bringing to the reader a down-to-earth approach to adequate preparation, a key to effective bargaining, the negotiating teams, and a step-by-step guide to preparatory process.

Monthly Labor Review. Washington, D.C.: U.S. Department of Labor, Bureau of Labor Statistics. One of the best government sources of bargaining information.

Peters, Edward, *Strategy and Tactics in Labor Negotiations,* 3rd ed., pp. 90–98, 108–14. Swarthmore, Pa.: Personnel Journal, 1966. For years a mediator, Mr. Peters brings his practical experience and ability to articulate the nuances of collective bargaining to bear on negotiable issues and fringe issues.

Proceedings. Highly recommended as sources of information are the proceedings of the National Academy of Arbitrators, the Industrial Relations Research Association, the Society of Professionals in Dispute Resolution.

Public Personal Administration: Labor-Management Relations. Englewood Cliffs, N.J.: Prentice-Hall, Inc. Focusing on public-sector collective bargaining, this service explains laws, methods, rulings, clauses, and established precedents (including summaries of arbitration awards). Biweekly reports provide news of developments in this complex area. Sections of the basic text include "New Ideas," "Collective Bargaining Problems and Answers," "Annotated Public Employment Relations Laws and Regulations," "Union Contract Clauses," and "Arbitration Awards Analyzed."

Ryder, Meyer S., Charles M. Rehmus, and Sanford Cohen, *Management Preparation for Collective Bargaining.* Homewood, Ill.: Dow Jones-Irwin, 1966. Excellent coverage of practices of firms surveyed, covering such subjects as final preparation, subjects, strategic aspects of preparation, intercompany cooperation, and joint union-management preparation.

Siegel, Abraham J., ed., *The Impact of Computers on Collective Bargaining.* Cambridge, Mass.: M.I.T. Press, 1970. A collection of articles, critical in some aspects of the role computers may play in collective bargaining but generally supportive of the positive role to be played by computers in the preparatory process for negotiations.

Taylor, Benjamin, J., and Fred Witney, *Labor Relations Law,* 4th ed., chapter 14. Englewood Cliffs, N.J.: Prentice-Hall, 1983. Excellent coverage of the subject of bargaining as controlled by law and agency decisions.

Union Contracts, Arbitration. New York: Commerce Clearing House, Inc. A continuing service that includes specimen contracts, arbitration procedures, and current information on contract terms being negotiated.

U.S. Department of Labor publications. The publications of DOL are a gold mine of information for the negotiator in both the public and private sectors. Included are such publications as *Characteristics of Construction Agreements, 1972–73* (BLS Bulletin 1819), 1974; *Collective Bargaining Agreements in the Federal Service, Late 1971* (BLS Bulletin 1789), 1973; *Municipal Collective Bargaining Agreements in Large Cities* (BLS Bulletin 1759), 1972; *Negotiation Impasse, Grievance, and Arbitration in Federal Agreements* (BLS Bulletin 1661), 1970; *Grievance Procedures* (BLS Bulletin 1425-1), 1964; *Calendar of*

Major Contract Expirations and Reopenings (December or January issues of the MLR); *Wages Calendars* (a yearly bulletin); *Work Stoppages* (a yearly bulletin); *Collective Bargaining Summary* (industry summaries); *A Directory of Public Employment Relations Boards and Agencies* (November 1971); *Scope of Bargaining in the Public Sector* (1972); *Arbitration Procedures* (Bulletin No. 1425–6), 1966; *Grievance and Arbitration Procedures in State and Local Agreements,* 1975; *Characteristics of Major Collective Bargaining Agreements,* July 1, 1974; and *Understanding Grievance Arbitration in the Public Sector,* 1974.

CHAPTER 8

A CBO LOG:
Provides
Accessibility
of Bargaining
Information

Chapter 7 addressed the extremely critical need to develop a broad base of bargaining information when formulating a plan or blueprint for action before the actual negotiations. Chapter 7 emphasized when to collect bargaining information—continuously—what information to gather, the sources, and how to assemble the information in order to use it most effectively. A proper filing or notebook system, divided by subject and with master controls for each type of information to insure its availability, was advocated. After the information has been gathered, two additional considerations are paramount to rendering it usable in formulating the plan or blueprint for action. Much time would be lost if the information was just filed, even with a good filing system, and if there was no ongoing system for extracting from the raw data those particular bits that could become a vital part of the final planning for the next negotiations. This second phase of preparing for negotiations emphasizes a technique for recording and extracting vital bargaining information in summary form, so as to render it more quickly accessible to those responsible for preparing for negotiations. The technique discussed here dovetails with the methodology used when preparing the plan or blueprint for action discussed in Chapters 9 to 13.

This technique is in the form of what the author chooses to identify as a Collective Bargaining by Objectives Log, CBO Log for short. Form 8-1 shows the CBO Log, which is best handled through a loose-leaf notebook,

FORM 8–1
Collective Bargaining by Objectives Log
A Guide for Systematically Extracting and Providing Accessibility of Bargaining Information

IDENTIFICATION NUMBER AND DATE	SUBJECT MATTER	CONTRACT CLAUSE IDENTIFICATION*	SOURCE OF INFORMATION**	GENERAL BARGAINING OBJECTIVE FOR NEXT NEGOTIATIONS	REMARKS AND CROSS-REFERENCING

*If no clause in present contract insert word none.
**Examples: grievance settlement, arbitration award, supervisor or shop steward input, other contract settlements, etc.

using as many pages as needed and filing chronologically and numerically.

As information flows in, whether from the critique of the last negotiation, from information concerning outside contract settlements, or from a grievance concerning a particular section of the contract, if the recorders or the planners anticipate that any part of that information could be important to the next negotiations, they should extract and record that information in sequence in the CBO Log. Types of information considered pertinent to the next negotiation might be a contract problem revealed by the critique of the last negotiation, the nature of other contract settlements, changes in economic conditions, new local laws, an application of the contract resulting in a grievance, changes in technology, or work-force adjustments, to name a few. Anything that can be identified as an item of probable import to the next negotiations and planning for such negotiations, should be recorded. One of the most important values of the CBO Log is its emphasis on the continual logging of facts vital to the next negotiations while the information is fresh. Having an understanding of what is involved and what needs to be done at the next negotiation is at a maximum. The second value of the CBO Log is that it records facts necessary for planning negotiations, and that it forces the planner or recorder to project a general objective to be achieved relative to each item recorded. This general objective can then be easily translated to the range of objectives or acceptable range of settlements used in the CBO plan or blueprint for action. While providing information in a form that can mesh with the process of formulating the CBO blueprint for negotiations, the CBO Log also provides ready access to the source of the information for backchecking and identifying the particular sections of the contract concerned. The CBO Log also provides a means of quickly bringing together through cross-referencing all of the logged information on a single subject, say holidays, from the confirmation of the last contract to the beginning of renegotiations for a new contract. This gives those planners responsible for developing the final blueprint prior to negotiations a condensed but specific view of each bargaining subject that will be involved in the negotiations based on the total information collected between contracts and assembled as outlined in Chapter 7.

The clearest way to illustrate the use of the CBO Log is through the following example, with only the names changed.

ILLUSTRATION: RECALL TO WORK AFTER
REDUCTION IN FORCE AND LAYOFFS

In the face of a general slump in sales because of a decline in the market, the XYZ Corporation reduced some of its operations, with a resultant reduction in the number of employees. The labor agreement, Section

14.10, *Lay Offs Other Than Temporary*, establishes the method and order of reduction of force from the departments involved in the cutback operations:

(a) Reduction, other than on a temporary basis, in the number of employees in a job classification . . . shall first be accomplished on the basis of Departmental seniority, with those employees having the least Departmental seniority on the job involved in the reduction the first to be laid off therefrom.

(b) An employee removed from his job in accordance with paragraph (a) above shall be reassigned (in the reverse order of his line of promotion) to his most recently held permanent job within said Department to which he is entitled on the basis of Departmental seniority. In the event no such job is available, he shall be assigned to replace any employee within said department having less Departmental seniority, provided he has the skill and ability necessary to do the required work efficiently.

(c) In the event of a reduction in the total number of employees within a Department, other than on a temporary basis as provided for in Section 14.9, employees oldest in terms of Departmental seniority will be retained as needed in such Department provided they have the required skill and ability to efficiently perform the work required.

(d) An employee on layoff from a Department lasting ten (10) work days or more may exercise his plant seniority across department lines on common labor or base rate jobs.

When the reduction in force was concluded, 130 employees had been laid off from Department A. Of the 130 employees, 20 had been able to avail themselves of Section 14.10(d) above and had bumped into common-labor or base-rate jobs in another department.

One month after the reduction in force and resulting layoffs, business began to pick up again and the employer was faced with the problem of recall. Section 14.11 of the agreement, *Rehire After Lay Off*, covers the recall procedure:

(a) When employees in Departments other than in the . . . Department . . . are recalled to work therein following lay off they shall be called back to work in the reverse order to that in which they were laid off giving due consideration to their skill and ability to satisfactorily perform the required work and efficiency of operation. Such re-employment privilege, however, shall not exceed twenty-four (24) months following their date of layoff. The refusal or failure to respond within five (5) calendar days to such offer of re-employment shall terminate any obligation of the Employer hereunder.

It was readily apparent that the provision above adequately covered all employees who were laid off not only from the department but also from the company because they did not have enough seniority to exercise the bumping right of Section 14.10(d). There was, however, a real question as to what sections of the agreement covered recall of the twenty employees who had bumped into jobs in another department and were still working. The question was whether Section 14.11(a) applied to the recall of these employees or whether they were to be considered as transfers subject to Section 14.8, *Inter-Departmental Transfers*, which states:

> (a) *Departmental Transfers at Employee Request.* Employees transferred from one department to another at their own request shall be considered new employees with regard to Department seniority standing in the Department to which transferred. Employees transferred back to their former Department at their own request will begin to accrue Department seniority in the Department to which transferred as of the date of such transfer.

When the matter could not be resolved concerning which section, 14.11(a) or 14.8(a), applied to the recall of the twenty employees still working but in another department, the parties answered the question of the immediate situation by means of a "Memorandum of Understanding," which established a recall method satisfactory to both parties. This memorandum was to apply to the specific recall of the twenty employees and had no future implications with respect to establishing precedence. When the district organization of the union later filed an exception to the use of the memorandum, the problem went to arbitration. The arbitrator ruled that the memorandum was legally established and proper within the agreement as it applied to the one-time situation.

The danger to the union in the current construction of the contract is that employees who exercised their bumping rights to move into other departments during a reduction in force might well be construed to be transfers—14.8(a)—rather than layoffs—14.11(a). If this were to happen, the union members who chose the route of bumping into other departments would at that point lose seniority accumulated in their original department instead of retaining seniority for twenty-four months as provided in Section 14.11(a). When a recall to their original departments was announced, the workers who bumped into other departments would have to bid in as new employees without seniority. In effect, they would have been reduced from the head to the bottom of the seniority list among those who had been laid off from the department.

If the union were using the CBO Log, it would enter the information as shown in Form 8-2. This completed page of the CBO Log illustrates the recording of this layoff and recall contract problem and includes, for illustration, other entries that might be typical for a union. It will be noted from a perusal of the recorded information that, not only does the CBO Log enhance the efficiency of the system of preparing for negotiations, it insures from the beginning that the recorder will begin to think in terms of objectives or bargaining goals relative to each bargainable item entered, while that item is still fresh and the original parties are present.

The first four columns of the CBO Log are self-explanatory; however, comments need to be added concerning the last two columns. It should be emphasized that setting an objective or goal for the next negotiations relative to each item listed in the CBO Log is practical. First, the goal is in writing. A record is preserved no matter who might need to use the information to prepare for the next negotiations. Second, because this information will be valuable at contract time, the recorder is more keenly aware of the implications of the entry and the reason why it should be recorded immediately rather than at a later time, when the memory may have dimmed or the parties concerned are no longer available. It also should be observed that at this point only the general objective is recorded. There is no attempt to establish a range of optimistic (O), realistic (R), and pessimistic (P) goals at this time. This will be done when the negotiation time arrives, with the development of the final blueprint or plan of action using the CBO method. At that time, based on the bargaining climate and the strategy agreed upon, each of the objectives recorded in the CBO Log are identified within the familiar O, R, and P framework.

The last column in the CBO Log is *Remarks and Cross-Referencing*. Additional comments relative to the entry may be added here. However, the main value of the column is its function as a cross-reference for entries dealing with like subjects. In this way, the user can expeditiously bring together all of the entries regarding Recall from Layoff, for instance, because they will all be cross-referenced to number 1 on the CBO Log. Again, as emphasized earlier, one of the principle purposes in developing the CBO Log is to increase the accessibility to important bargaining information. If preparation is a key to successful negotiations, developing a system for gathering and organizing information in easily accessible form is a key to successful preparation.

Form 8-3 provides a second illustration of the CBO Log, this time as it might appear if an employer were filling it out.

It is not enough merely to develop an efficient system for gathering and organizing bargaining information. Using this data to develop a blueprint or plan of action for negotiation is also essential. This is the purpose of the Collective Bargaining by Objectives methodology proper, developed in Chapters 9 to 13.

FORM 8-2
Collective Bargaining by Objectives Log
A Guide for Systematically Extracting and Providing Accessibility of Bargaining Information

IDENTIFICATION NUMBER AND DATE	SUBJECT MATTER	CONTRACT CLAUSE IDENTIFICATION*	SOURCE OF INFORMATION**	GENERAL BARGAINING OBJECTIVE FOR NEXT NEGOTIATIONS	REMARKS AND CROSS-REFERENCING
1 5/8/83	Recall from Layoff	Art 14.11 (a) Art 14.8 (a)	Arbitration RE FMCS 75K/7915	Modify 14.11 (a): Layoff for purposes of recall is to be construed as layoff from a department and is to include those employees who, during a reduction of force, have exercised their plant seniority to bump into base-rate and common-labor positions in other departments. Remove any conflict between <u>transfer</u> and recall articles.	
2 8/6/83	Seniority Date and Probationary Period	Article 2.2 Article 3.1	Grievance R-176	Modify language of Probationary Clause so that, instead of "seniority beginning retroactive 8	

104

3 8/25/83	Steward Job Protection	Article 2.9	Arbitration RE AAA 256731	months from completion of probationary period," it reads: "Seniority is retroactive to date of hire." Modify language to read "the" steward instead of "a" steward.	See Ident. No. 1 5/8/81
4 9/4/83	Sick Leave—Pregnancy	Article 18.5	Statutes	Modify language on pregnancy leave to comply with statutes, e.g., must be consistent with other sick-leave provisions.	
5 2/8/84	Job Sharing	Article 23.7	Impact of Reduction of Force, Membership Feedback	Modify language governing reduction of force to include an initial sharing of work to a minimum of 35 hours a week before reducing work force.	
6 3/17/84	Portal-to-Portal Pay	New Provision	Employee Feedback	Bargaining unit members object to unpaid time necessary to travel from gate to jobs—in some cases as much as 20 minutes.	

*If no clause in present contract insert word none.

**Examples: grievance settlement, arbitration award, supervisor or shop steward input, other contract settlements, etc.

FORM 8–3
Collective Bargaining by Objectives Log
A Guide for Systematically Extracting and Providing Accessability of Bargaining Information

IDENTIFICATION NUMBER AND DATE	SUBJECT MATTER	CONTRACT CLAUSE IDENTIFICATION*	SOURCE OF INFORMATION**	GENERAL BARGAINING OBJECTIVE FOR NEXT NEGOTIATIONS	REMARKS AND CROSS-REFERENCING
1 6/10/83	Stewards' Time	None	Shop Foremen	Stewards using excessive time for union business (beyond grievance handling). Add provision to limit amount of time stewards may use and restrict time paid by the Company for stewards to handle grievances.	
2 8/10/83	Pension	None	Last Negotiation	Develop pension plan Peck's can afford that will be acceptable to the Union.	
3 8/20/83	Hours of Labor	Article 9(a)	Cost-effectiveness—Accounting Dept.	Extend workweek to 6 or 7 days or add additional shifts to reduce overtime expenses and to produce more effective equipment utilization.	
4	Hiring of New	Article 2(a)	Employment	Modify language to allow fill-	

10/1/83	Employees to fill vacancies			ing of vacancies by merit rather than present language that allows less-qualified Company employees priority over new hires in filling vacancies.
5 6/10/84	Safety	Article 8	Last Negotiation	Management control over safety has been compromised by safety provision requiring bilateral decisions on safety problems. Renegotiate language to give Management unilateral control over safety with the Union having consultation rights only.
6 7/7/84	Guaranteed Employment	None	Comparison of contract settlements	Security is high priority for employees what with the high levels of unemployment. Prepare a position for the next negotiations in which any employment guarantees are linked to efficiency and productivity commitments by the employees.

*If no clause in present contract insert word none.
**Examples: grievance settlement, arbitration award, supervisor or shop steward input, other contract settlements, etc.

CHAPTER 9

INTRODUCTION TO COLLECTIVE BARGAINING BY OBJECTIVES

Developing a blueprint or plan of action is the final step in the process of preparing for negotiations. The methodology used is Collective Bargaining by Objectives (CBO), a modification of Management by Objectives (MBO). Central to CBO is its planned approach to negotiations and the compiling of all relevant materials and information concerning the items to be bargained. Essential elements of the CBO methodology are identified in Form 9-1. It will be noted that all of these elements—identification of items to be negotiated, individual item priorities, a range for each item of predetermined bargaining goals from optimistic to pessimistic, and the initial bargaining position to be assumed for each item by the party using the methodology—are common-sense elements of bargaining. The way the objectives approach influences negotiating effectiveness is not in the identification of the common-sense elements. These are known. *The difference is placing what is common sense within a methodology that provides a systematic framework for approaching collective bargaining negotiations.* The formalizing or structuring outlined here is not at the expense of flexibility in strategy and tactics so vital to negotiation. This approach continues to allow flexibility, albeit within a more tangible framework and set of goals. What it does is introduce discipline and system to the negotiator's actions and preparation.

The positive results are contingent upon the willingness of the negotiator *to adhere completely to the methodology outlined.* The lazy nego-

FORM 9–1
Collective Bargaining by Objectives
A Guide for Systematic Data Preparation and Planning Negotiations

Bargaining Items*	Priorities**	RANGE OF BARGAINING OBJECTIVES			Initial Bargaining Position	EVALUATION RESULTS		
		Pessimistic	Realistic	Optimistic		P	R	O

*Classify items in two groups: financial and nonfinancial
**Relative priority of each bargaining item to all other bargaining items

tiator, the seat-of-the pants negotiator, or the negotiator who leaves results to chance or assumes that formulae as to what to say and how to act and react will serve him in such a variable climate as collective bargaining negotiations will find little comfort in the discipline and orderliness this methodology demands.

A brief explanation of Form 9-1 is presented here to provide the reader with a complete picture of the CBO process; the various components are discussed in more detail in subsequent chapters.

OVERVIEW

Column 1, *Bargaining Items,* is for the listing of all those items or contractual subjects, whether introduced by the employee or the employer representative, that the parties will consider during the course of the collective bargaining negotiations—wages, vacations, holiday, promotions, seniority, insurance, and so on. These bargaining items should be separated into two listings—one for all cost or financial items, the other for noncost or nonfinancial items. As many CBO sheets should be used as are necessary for a complete listing of the bargaining items.

Priorities, column 2, refers to the relative importance of each bargaining item in the system of priorities of the party concerned. For every item, a priority rating is determined based on its value or importance relative to all other items on the bargaining agenda.

Columns 3, 4, and 5, *Range of Bargaining Objectives,* are for the purpose of establishing a range of actual objectives for each bargaining item listed in column 1. The range includes columns for realistic (column 4), optimistic (column 5), and pessimistic (column 3) objectives. This range should constitute, in the best judgment of the party, an actual, not hypothetical or theoretical, *settlement range.* For example, objectives entered in column 4 for each item are those that the party believes realistically can be achieved. This is the negotiator's *realistic* goal—not what he hopes or guesses will be achieved, but what he fully expects will be the most probable final settlement on that particular bargaining item.

The *optimistic* goal for the particular item would be what the negotiator thinks can be achieved, as a real and preferred possibility, but whose odds are not as favorable as those for the realistic objective. The *pessimistic* goal would be a possible outcome if everything did not go as well as expected—not as favorable as either the realistic or optimistic, but definitely within the acceptance range of the party. It is important to emphasize that the range represented by the pessimistic, realistic, and optimistic positions is a preconceived and acceptable bargaining settlement range, not an impasse range or a strike or lockout range, although, as a result of the give-and-take of bargaining, any of these may occur. Above all, these objectives are a strictly confidential part of the negotiator's blueprint of goals and objectives and should be treated as such and never revealed to the opposing bargaining representative.

Initial Bargaining Position, column 6, is the visible stance (the initial proposal or counterproposal) that the negotiator presents to the other party at the outset of negotiations on each item, whether it is an item the negotiator introduced or one the other party introduced. This must not be confused with the range of objectives just mentioned (columns 3, 4, and 5), which must be confidential to the party concerned if its strategy is to be successful.

Columns 7, 8, and 9, *Evaluation Results,* are a checklist to be used after negotiations have been concluded to compare results achieved (pessimistic, realistic, or optimistic) with original objectives set for each bargaining item. This may be used for other useful purposes also, such as assessment of effectiveness of strategy and tactics relative to each item during the negotiations just concluded. This will be explained later.

POSITIVE COLLECTIVE BARGAINING

The following positive advantages to collective bargaining negotiations result from the use of the CBO methodology:

1. While structuring the approach to collective bargaining negotiations, the objectives approach is not at the expense of the flexibility so necessary to the give-and-take of negotiations.
2. It gives the negotiating team a real sense of direction and tangible goals (objectives) by which team members may measure their progress during negotiations.
3. It provides a more meaningful basis for data preparation, because positions and goals are specifically identified.
4. The range of bargaining objectives is in reality a settlement area toward which the negotiating team works, rather than the range, so often described by writers of the field, whose minimum and maximum represent conflict or breakdown. The latter introduces negativism into the approach of the bargaining team, whereas the objectives approach effects a positive tone and thrust.
5. The team has a ready-reference, easy-to-scan blueprint that provides a confidential guide to strategy and tactics for all cost and noncost bargaining items, individually and/or collectively.
6. The identification of not just one goal but a range of possible settlement goals on each bargaining item requires by its very nature a more detailed and careful analysis.
7. Limiting the objectives approach to methodology makes it equally applicable and useful to private-sector bargaining, public-sector bargaining, or, for that matter, any type of bargaining situation.

8. Nothing is introduced into the methodology that is foreign to the normal bargaining situation.

9. It provides a better means of evaluating past negotiations as a useful experience base from which to launch a more effective plan for the next round of negotiations.

10. It may be used equally well as an effective tool for actual negotiations or as a simulation device to train negotiators.

11. It provides (a) the individual parties with a safe and effective mechanism (agreed-upon settlement range) for delegating authority to their bargaining teams, and (b) a built-in means of establishing a rewards system for successful negotiators.

SELECTED REFERENCES

Odiorne, George S., *Management by Objectives.* New York: Pitman, 1969. George S. Odiorne is well known as a leading advocate of the system known as Management by Objectives. Not only has he been an effective proponent of MBO on the lecture circuit, in the classroom, and as a leading consultant to business corporations, but he has actively involved himself in the installation of MBO systems. It was through a close association with Dean Odiorne that I saw the potential of adapting the system of MBO to the process of collective bargaining (CBO).

CHAPTER 10

BARGAINING ITEMS

Column 1 of the bargaining-by-objectives form requires a listing of all items that have been introduced by either the employer or the union for negotiation: wages, overtime, sick leave, vacations, promotion, discipline, insurance, management rights, and so on.

For its maximum usefulness as a confidential guide to negotiation, all economic or financial items should be listed in one major grouping. This would include all those items for which a recurring money outlay can be identified, such as wages, vacations, and holidays. All noncost items should be listed in a separate but contiguous grouping. These would include such items as seniority, grievance procedure, and management rights.

Differences and similarities between private-sector and public-sector bargaining items will be identified where appropriate in the material that follows.

PRELIMINARY AND FINAL IDENTIFICATION OF BARGAINING ITEMS

Usually, the union takes the initiative in introducing items for negotiations, although there is nothing in the law that requires this procedure. The union introduction of the items is most often in the form of an initial request for contract modification sixty days or more prior to the termination of the existing agreement. The bargaining items could also be introduced as part of a first-time contract demand if there had been no prior collective bargaining agreement between the parties. Demands of the union might be in the form of additions, deletions, clarifications, or other changes in the expiring agreement.

When the company responds to these initial demands of the union, the full agenda of items to be considered at the bargaining table is established. The company response may be merely a counterproposal or response to the specific items introduced by the union, or it may include this response plus additional items the company feels should be considered. There is nothing in collective bargaining law or practice that prevents the company from introducing items of its own that it wants considered at the bargaining table, or even taking the initiative by giving the initial sixty-day notice to the union.

It can readily be seen that there are two preliminary steps before the listing of bargaining items becomes final for either of the parties. Step 1 for the union is accomplished when it presents its initial demands to the company. Step 2, completing the union's list of any additional items to be considered at the bargaining table, is accomplished when the union receives management's response. Similarly, step 1 for management is taken when the union position is formalized and all the items the union wishes to consider have been introduced. Step 2, completing the company's list of items to be considered, is taken after the company has made its formal response to the union.[1] At this point, the listing of items for bargaining, but *only* that listing, will be identical for both parties. The rest of the information on the bargaining form will differ for the two parties in line with their separate and confidential priorities and objectives. It is essential that every item or subitem that is to be a subject for bargaining be listed on the bargaining form within one of the two general categories, financial or nonfinancial. By way of illustration, Form 10-1 shows a few items of what the first column of the bargaining form might include.

APPLICATION OF LAW TO BARGAINING ITEMS

PRIVATE SECTOR

The law has a direct bearing on the negotiation items that the parties put on the bargaining table. Three categories relative to subjects or items for bargaining are recognized:

---

[1]There may be more than one exchange before the list of items to be negotiated is finalized.

FORM 10-1
Collective Bargaining by Objectives
A Guide for Systematic Data Preparation and Planning Negotiations

---

*BARGAINING ITEMS**

(Financial Items)
Holidays

Wages

Insurance

—
—
—

—

(Nonfinancial Items)
Union Security

Probationary
  Period
Arbitrator Cost

---

*Classify items in two groups: financial and nonfinancial

1. Mandatory bargaining items
2. Voluntary or permissive bargaining items
3. Illegal or prohibited bargaining items

The last two may be disposed of with less discussion than the first. Voluntary or permissive bargaining items refer to those middle-range items that are neither mandatory nor illegal. Crucial to an understanding of voluntary items and collective bargaining is the fact that these become a part of negotiations only through the joint agreement of both parties. Neither party can be compelled against its wishes to negotiate over voluntary items, nor can the signing of a contract be held up as a result of one party's refusal to bargain on a voluntary item. Moreover, adamant refusal to bargain about a voluntary subject or to include it in the final agreement is not illegal. Finally, either party may propose a voluntary item for bargaining, the parties may bargain in good faith on the item, and if both parties agree, they may include the item in the final contract.

Illegal bargaining items are those that are forbidden by law. A closed shop, a hot-cargo clause, a hiring hall giving preference to union members, or a union security clause in a right-to-work state are examples of illegal subjects for bargaining.

Mandatory bargaining items are those over which the parties must bargain if they are introduced to the bargaining table by either party through the demand and/or counteroffer process. The number of mandatory bargaining items has been constantly expanding over the past fifty years as more and more subjects have been declared by the NLRB and the courts to come within the meaning of the National Labor Relations Act's definitions of wages, hours, and other conditions of employment.

Court and NLRB decisions have declared some seventy basic items as mandatory for bargaining purposes. It is obvious that the list would be many times as long if all the subcategories of these items were listed. Included are nineteen classified under "wages," three under "hours," and the remainder under "other terms and conditions of employment." The items are as follows:

Wages

Hours

Discharge

Arbitration

Holidays—paid

Vacations—paid

Duration of agreement

Grievance procedure

Layoff plan

Reinstatement of economic strikers

Change of payment from hourly base to salary base

Union security and check-off

Work rules

Merit wage increase

Work schedule

Lunch periods

Rest periods

Pension plan

Retirement age

Bonus payments

Price of meals provided by company

Group insurance—health, accident, life

Promotions

Work assignments and transfers

No-strike clause

Piece rates

Stock-purchase plan

Work loads

Change of employee status to independent contractors

Management-rights clause

Cancellation of seniority upon relocation of plant

Discounts on company products

Shift differentials

Contract clause providing for supervisors' keeping seniority in unit

Procedures for income tax withholding

Severance pay

Nondiscriminatory hiring hall

Plant rules

Safety

Prohibition against supervisor's doing unit work

Superseniority for union stewards

Check-off

Partial plant closing

Hunting on employer forest reserve where previously granted

Seniority

Layoffs

Transfers

Change in operations resulting in reclassifying workers from incentive to straight time, or cut work force, or installation of cost-saving machine

Plant closing

Job-posting procedures

Plant reopening

Employee physical examination

Union security

Bargaining over "Bar List"

Truck rentals—minimum rental to be paid by carriers to employee-owned vehicles

Musician price list

Arrangement for negotiation

Change in insurance carrier and benefits

Plant closedown and relocation

Profit-sharing plan

Motor-carrier—union agreement providing that carriers use own equipment before leasing outside equipment

Overtime pay

Agency shop

Sick leave

Employer's insistence on clause giving arbitrator right to enforce award

Company houses

Subcontracting

Discriminatory racial policies

Production ceiling imposed by union

Most-favored-nation clause

PUBLIC SECTOR: FEDERAL

Title I of the NLRA as amended sets forth general policy concerning employee rights: "Employees shall have the right to self-organization, to form, join, or assist labor organizations." Similar rights are also extended to federal employees through the Civil Service Reform Act (CSRA 1978, Title VII): "Each employee shall have the right to form, join, or assist any labor organization . . . freely and without fear of penalty or reprisal." Both directives also protect the right to refrain from such activity. Both directives also protect the right to bargain collectively through representatives of the employees' own choosing. The NLRA as amended says: "Employees shall have the right to bargain collectively through representatives of their own choosing. . . ." In the words of CSRA 1978, Title VII, the right to self-organization includes engaging "in collective bargaining with respect to conditions of employment through representatives chosen by the employees."

Up to this point, the treatment of employee rights and bargaining was somewhat the same for private and federal sectors. It is in the implementation of these rights that differences of treatment under the regulations begin to appear. Attention here is confined to differences that affect the collective bargaining process between the federal and private areas, with particular focus on the way the NLRA as amended and CSRA 1978,

Title VII, have different effects on the subject matter of collective bargaining negotiations in their particular areas.

The preceding section examined in some detail the items for bargaining in the private sector—mandatory, permissive, and prohibited—which evolved through interpretation of Section 8(c) of the NLRA as amended: "to bargain collectively is the performance of the mutual obligation of the employer and the representatives of the employees to meet at reasonable times and confer in good faith with respect to *wages, hours and conditions of employment.*" (Emphasis added.) It is the interpretation of the NLRB and the courts of the phrase "wages, hours and conditions of employment" that has resulted in the present listing of mandatory, permissive, and prohibited items for negotiation in the private sector.

Mandatory items for bargaining in the private sector have expanded by interpretation, as noted earlier, from a relatively short list of subjects in the late 1930s and early 1940s into a list of subjects of considerable length today. Although there has been some easing of restrictions on bargainable subjects in the federal sector between the enactment of Executive Order 11491 (1969) and its successor, CSRA 1978, Title VII, the expansion of the scope of bargainable subjects during the last twenty years has not proceeded as quickly as occurred in the private sector during its initial expansion period from the middle 1940s to the middle 1960s. This can be explained by the differences conceived by the legislators between the private sector and the federal sector in the field of labor relations. Part of this results from a desire to prevent conflict within a dual system; that is, conflict between collective-bargaining related subjects and already established laws and regulations affecting employer-employee relations. Another part of it results from the question of sovereignty and the functioning of government bodies under the law; and part of it results from the less flexible nature or ability of government compared to the private sector in responding to the demands of employee groups. At any rate and for whatever reason, the scope of bargainable subjects in the federal government remains more restricted than in the private area. Private-sector legislation merely enunciates a broad guideline—wages, hours, and conditions of employment—whereas the legislation governing federal government employer-employee collective bargaining has restricted quite specifically the scope of bargainable subjects in a number of ways, ranging from mandatory to *optionally bargainable*[2] (at the option of the employer), permissive, prohibited, and illegal. Thus, a freer hand has been given the NLRB and the courts to develop the specifics of the meaning of *bargainable* and *nonbargainable* subjects, whereas the authority and the courts under CSRA 1978, Title VII, are left with the greater problem of somehow, through interpretation on a case-by-case basis, developing a specific list of man-

---

[2]Taylor and Witney coined this term.

datory, permissive, and prohibited (and shades in between) bargaining subjects much more proscribed by statutory language than is true of private-sector legislation. What the scope of bargaining is conceived as for the federal sector in the current period will be dealt with in two ways. Presented first is the same type of three-way breakdown—mandatory, permissive, and prohibited—used to identify the scope of bargaining in the private sector. This takes the form of a summary review of the scope of bargaining in the federal sector as delineated in CSRA 1978, Title VII. This includes the guidelines established by statute in determining what subjects are bargainable, what are not bargainable, and what may be bargainable under certain conditions. Second, a list based on a case-by-case sampling of decisions of the FLR Authority concerning bargainability of certain matters is appended to indicate the manner of developing the scope of bargaining through interpretation of the statutory language.

Title VII and the Scope of Bargaining

Category	CSRA 1978, Title VII
Mandatory bargaining subjects	Mandatory bargaining subjects are those subjects the parties have a mutual obligation to bargain for in good faith if presented by either party at the bargaining table. Note that this does not "compel either party to agree to a proposal or to make a concession." Section 7103(a)(12) addresses mandatory bargaining subjects as "conditions of employment affecting" employees in an appropriate unit of an agency. Section 7103(a)(14) defines *conditions of employment* affecting such employees as "*personnel policies, practices and matters,* whether established by rule, regulation, or otherwise, *affecting working conditions.*" (Emphasis added.) Section 7117(a) and (b) qualifies the words *rule* and *regulation* by allowing only those rules and regulations that are (a) not "inconsistent with any Federal law or any Government-wide rule or regulation" and (b) only when "no compelling need . . . exists for the rule or regulation." The agency may inform the FLR Authority that no compelling need exists, or the FLR Authority may so determine on its own volition.
Permissive bargaining subjects	Permissive bargaining subjects are usually defined as those not required by law to be negotiated if introduced, but, because they are neither mandatory nor prohibited, may be negotiated by consensus of the parties. In the private sector, this would be described as the grey area between mandatory and prohibited bargaining subjects. This is also true in the main for the federal sector, except that Title VII specifies some subjects that may be bargained but only at the election of one of the parties, *management.* Section 7106 is a statutory statement of management rights reserved to governmental agencies.

This is in contrast to the private sector, where such rights appear only if negotiated into the contract. Section 7106(a) details the rights reserved to management. These will be discussed under *Prohibited or Illegal Bargaining Subjects*. Section 7106(b), however, extends to management the right, at its own election, to negotiate such matters as "the numbers, types, and grades of employees or positions assigned to any organizational subdivision, work project, or tour of duty"; the "technology, methods, as means of performing work"; the "procedures which management observe in exercising any authority under this section"; and "appropriate arrangements for employees adversely affected by the exercise of any authority under this section by such management officials."

Prohibited or illegal bargaining subjects

The commonality of "prohibited" and "illegal" bargaining subjects is that under Title VII neither may be included in the subjects to be negotiated at the bargaining table. An item is "prohibited" because the statute prohibits the negotiation of the item either directly or by relegating to management exclusive unilateral control over certain areas of employer-employee relations. An item is "illegal" when the statute prohibits the negotiation of the item because it would be a violation of law to do so. The specificity of the statute as to what subject areas may not be introduced at the bargaining table aids in determining what bargaining subjects are mandatorily negotiable. Section 7103(a)(14) of the CSRA mandates that the conditions of employment do not include policies, practices, and matters relating to "political activities prohibited under subchapter III of chapter 73" of Title VII; or relating to "the classification of any position"; or relating to "the extent such matters are specifically provided for by Federal statute." Section 7121(c) adds retirement, life insurance, health insurance; a suspension or removal under Section 7532; or any examination, certification, or appointment. These are not only prohibited bargaining subjects, but their introduction at the negotiation table would be illegal. Section 7106(a) states that, subject to the qualification of 7106(b) regarding optionally negotiable subjects (explained under *Permissive Bargaining*), the employer has the exclusive management right to "determine the mission, budget, organization, number of employees, and internal practices of the agency." Also, subject to the qualification of Section 7106(b) and in accordance with applicable laws governing the following functions, the employer has the exclusive management right to "hire, assign, direct, layoff, and retain employees in the agency"; to "suspend, remove, reduce in grade or pay, or take other disciplinary action against such employees"; to "assign work"; to "make determinations with respect to contracting out"; to "determine the personnel by which agency operations shall be conducted"; to fill positions and to select for appointments from "among properly ranked and certified candidates for promotion" or "any other appropriate source"; and to "take whatever actions may be necessary to carry out the agency mission during emergencies." Other prohibited areas for bargaining, identified in Section 7117, would be those rules or regulations that are "Government-wide" or when a "compelling need (as determined under regulations prescribed by the Authority) exists" for certain agency rules or regulations. Also excluded are conditions of employment "to the extent such matters are specifically provided for by Federal statute"— Section 7103(a)(14)(C). Wages and benefits are important matters covered by law and not subject to negotiation according to the above language. It should be noted that, with respect to wages, there is one exception. Public Law 92–392, Section 9(b), August 19, 1972, provides an exception for certain employees and their agencies from the prevailing rate system used for other government employees. These groups, principally in the Department of Interior and the Department of Energy, are granted special authority by statute to continue the negotiation of "wages and related matters" inasmuch as these groups have "traditionally negotiated such matters" and are "covered by savings clauses of subsection 9(b)." This exemption was continued for these groups in the CSRA, Ocotber 13, 1978, PL 95–454, Title VII, Section 704, 92 Stat. 1218.

Determining the negotiability of bargaining proposals under CSRA 1978, Title VII, is still in the developmental stage. A list as decisive as the one included earlier for the private sector is not possible. This is because, in the development of the negotiability of items proposed for bargaining in the private sector since the Wagner Act, the National Labor Relations Board has had to deal only with the interpretation of a single phrase, "wages, hours, and other terms and conditions of employment." In contrast, under the CSRA, the interpretation by the authority as to what must, may, or may not be negotiated concerns the phrase "conditions of employment," defined as "personnel policies, practices and matters, whether established by rule, regulation, or otherwise, affecting working conditions." This, in turn, is limited or restricted further by other provisions of the statute that directly exclude some bargaining items from conditions of employment; that allot priority to law and certain rules and regulations over the negotiability of other bargaining items; that exclude from negotiability some topics held to be exclusively within the control of management; that leave negotiation of other items to the exclusive election of management; and that allow still other bargaining items to be negotiated only if they concern procedure or application, rather than substantive matters. The result is that determining whether a particular proposal is or is not subject to negotiation is often much more complex to interpret under CSRA 1978, Title VII, than under the NLRA.

Yet, knowledge of what must, may, and may not be negotiated under the provisions of CSRA is vital to those who must negotiate contracts in the federal sector. No definitive list is available as a guide. Where can such information be obtained? Certainly, for those who have the time and resources, a subscription to the *Decisions of the Federal Labor Relations Authority* is one solution. Another source for this information can be found by checking the subject matter of existing contracts in the federal sector. A typical list of what may be found in federal agreements is included in Chapter 5. This offers a good idea of those items which have passed muster under the law and have been held negotiable as "conditions of employment" under CSRA. To further aid the reader in determining the direction the authority appears to be following in its identification of mandatory, permissive, and prohibited bargaining items under CSRA, provided next is a sampling of decisions since the authority took over the responsibility of administering federal-employee collective bargaining with the passage of CSRA in 1978. The examples are categorized so as to highlight decisions of the authority, especially with respect to the CSRA provisions that limit or condition the meaning of "conditions of employment."

Mandatory Bargaining Items

When the bargaining proposal concerns a *condition of employment*, Section 7103(a)(12) and (14):

- A bargaining proposal concerning registration of privately owned, duty-free vehicles
- A bargaining proposal for ration control involving subsistence, commissary exchange, and other essential facilities and services that must be furnished to employees
- A bargaining proposal that the agency may terminate a program implementing the Federal Employees Flexible Work Schedules Act of 1978 only under certain circumstances
- A bargaining proposal to situate employees in order to minimize distractions and to effect changes, to the extent the agency has discretion to recommend such changes to an architect in order for a building to conform to fire and safety requirements
- A bargaining proposal that bargaining-unit employees not be required to register their privately owned vehicles pursuant to agency regulations
- A bargaining proposal for an agency to implement an open-space office design
- A bargaining proposal with respect to office size, design, book shelves, file cabinets—all not shown to have been provided for any technical purpose

- A bargaining proposal concerning individual office doors, floor-to-ceiling partitions for two-person offices, shower and locker facilities only incidental to the performance of an agency's work
- A bargaining proposal with regard to the initial date or starting and ending times of a first-aid facility already planned in a new building
- A bargaining proposal to require an agency to take whatever action it can to insure that employee cafeteria prices do not rise faster than employees' income and to post comparisons

When the bargaining proposal is addressed to the *procedures* management will observe in exercising its authority, Section 7106(b)(2):

- A bargaining proposal, otherwise consistent with law and regulations, relating only to particular aspects of performance appraisal systems, such as procedures and appropriate arrangements, but not to identification of critical elements or establishment of performance standards
- A bargaining proposal of a plan to prescribe procedures that management is to follow to produce a final ranking of eligible candidates and prescribe the number of eligibles who will be referred for consideration
- A bargaining proposal that, prior to management's instituting disciplinary action against a union representative or officer for engaging in union activity or inappropriate behavior, discussions will be held with the union representative and, if not settled then, with the area director and the local president or metro representative
- A bargaining proposal concerning merit promotion procedures for positions within the bargaining unit
- A bargaining proposal as to the manner of notifying employees by inspectors of certain procedures, privileges, and obligations in relation to an investigation that could lead to discipline
- A bargaining proposal to establish a procedural time limit for completion of a promotion roster
- A bargaining proposal that employees below the journeyman level in a career ladder will be promoted to the next higher level upon meeting the qualification requirements and demonstrating the ability to perform at a higher grade after the agency has already issued the decision to select and place the employee in a career ladder position
- A bargaining proposal requiring an agency, when filling a vacant position from the certificates of eligible candidates, to make a selection within two weeks or cancel the vacancy
- A bargaining proposal to grant employees the opportunity to volunteer for work normally performed by other employees prior to requiring any of them to do the work

When the bargaining proposal provides for *appropriate arrangements* for employees adversely affected by the exercise of management's authority, Section 7106(b)(3):

- A bargaining proposal for maximum utilization of existing vacancies in the event of a reduction in force

- A bargaining proposal to require strict compliance with applicable laws and regulations
- A bargaining proposal to the effect that standards of performance will make allowances for factors beyond the control of the employee
- A bargaining proposal to require that part-time employees be utilized only when it is not practical nor prudent to use full-time employees
- A bargaining proposal to minimize the effects on bargaining-unit employees of contracting-out decisions that are to be applied in accordance with the laws
- A bargaining proposal concerned with the application of critical elements and performance standards established by management when the proposal is not excluded by law or contrary to any governmentwide regulation
- A bargaining proposal that hours of work will not be reduced without just cause
- A bargaining proposal that the agency agrees to develop reasonable performance standards for unit employees
- A bargaining proposal that all performance standards will be fair and equitable and consistent with classification standards for any certain job

When bargaining proposals are ministerial or do not interfere with management's authority as enunciated in Section 7106 or with applicable laws, Section 7106(a) and (b)(1):

- A bargaining proposal for a "crediting plan" to evaluate educational qualifications of candidates eligible for further consideration; to establish a system for ranking candidates based on educational qualifications, performance appraisals, awards received; and to apply computer codes to educational records of eligibles for ranking purposes
- A bargaining proposal requiring that performance appraisal be based solely on those duties enumerated in the employees' job descriptions
- A bargaining proposal to require that performance standards and critical elements be consistent with the duties and responsibilities contained in a properly classified position
- A bargaining proposal that temporary duty assignments be based upon seniority
- A bargaining proposal for a procedure to define the initial area of consideration and expansion of that area for filling positions
- A bargaining proposal that employees may obtain outside employment if it does not conflict with duties and does not result in discredit, criticism, or conflict of interests
- A bargaining proposal to require that an employee detailed to a higher grade position for more than sixty days be temporarily promoted on his or her sixty-first day
- A bargaining proposal to incorporate the statement of the mission under a different section
- A bargaining proposal to use interchangeable terms, Duty Officer or GCO
- A bargaining proposal that requires the agency to grant full considera-

tion for vacancies to employees within the bargaining unit but does not preclude the agency from expanding the area of consideration for selection from any other appropriate source

- A bargaining proposal to establish the work hours in a day, core time days and hours, and maximum hours per day that may be worked under a flexible work scheduling arrangement, but not the number, types, and grades of employees
- A bargaining proposal to require the agency to pay travel expenses for employees who travel on official time
- A bargaining proposal of a crediting plan to effectuate more precise evaluation criteria for qualifications for promotion
- A bargaining proposal concerning the starting time and ending time of work shifts

When bargaining proposals are consistent with federal law, governmentwide rule or regulation, and rules or regulations for which a compelling need exists, Section 7117(a)(1) and (2):

- A bargaining proposal of criteria the agency will use when reassigning employees who have been adversely affected by a reduction in force and the agency does not show a compelling need exists for a regulation covering the matter
- A bargaining proposal that the agency grant to the union a block of eighty hours' official time each year for union representatives to attend union-sponsored training programs of mutual benefit
- A bargaining proposal for overtime that did not concern a matter specifically provided for by federal law and did not violate Section 7106(a)(1) of the statute
- A bargaining proposal to provide an employee with the opportunity to improve performance so that a contemplated adverse action based on previous unsatisfactory performance would not be effected
- A bargaining proposal that management should not, in assigning work, act contrary to law or regulation
- A bargaining proposal to require employee appraisals on an annual basis when 5 USC 4302(a)(1) mandates performance appraisal systems for periodic appraisal
- A bargaining proposal for flexitime if this would not interfere with management rights
- A bargaining proposal defining a performance standard and a critical element
- A bargaining proposal that, for purposes of applying Section 7(k) of the Fair Labor Standards Act, 1938 (FLSA), a work period should consist of seven days

When bargaining proposals concern the scope of the grievance procedure, Section 7103(a)(9); Section 7121(a), (b) to (f):

- A bargaining proposal for a grievance procedure including matters relating to appeals of adverse actions of National Guard technicians
- A bargaining proposal to include within the scope and coverage of the

negotiated grievance procedure matters relating to appeals of adverse actions as well as provide choice of appeal through the grievance procedure or the statutory procedure
- A bargaining proposal to render adverse actions appealable to the VA or under the negotiated grievance procedure

When bargaining proposals relate to representation rights and duties, Section 7114 and Section 7131:

- A bargaining proposal to negotiate grievance procedure when grievance procedure fails to expressly exclude appeals of adverse actions involving National Guard technicians or separation of employees during probation periods from the grievance procedure
- A bargaining proposal to include under the negotiated grievance procedure those promotions and placement actions taken according to Army Civilian Personnel Regulations
- A bargaining proposal to include under the negotiated grievance procedure reduction in force, reductions in grade or pay based on acceptable performance, or any other adverse action involving National Guard technicians
- A bargaining proposal for grievance procedure that did not expressly exclude matters concerning the separation of employees during probation periods from coverage by the grievance procedure
- A bargaining proposal to incorporate "prohibited personnel practices" and "merit system principle" provisions of the CSRA into the agreement
- A bargaining proposal that union membership solicitation may occur during period of time that management has determined performance of job functions is not required
- A bargaining proposal for the use of official time by a union representative to prepare for collective bargaining and impasse resolution

Permissive and "At the election of the agency" Bargaining Items

When the bargaining proposal is not related to a condition of employment of employees in the bargaining unit, Section 7103(a)(2)(B)(iii):

- A bargaining proposal that management take into consideration the union's recommended punitive or remedial actions against management officials and supervisors who violate rights of employees
- A bargaining proposal that each employee be permitted to rate his or her supervisor twice each year
- A bargaining proposal to apply merit promotion procedures to the filling of positions outside the bargaining unit
- A bargaining proposal for promotion procedures for nonbargaining unit supervisory positions

When the bargaining proposal refers to the numbers, types, and grades of employees, Section 7106(b)(1):

- A bargaining proposal to bar employees from working alone in certain health and safety situations
- A bargaining proposal to freeze hiring until all Reduction in Force (RIF) actions have been completed
- A bargaining proposal to impose a freeze on filling vacancies until bargaining-unit employees involved in a transfer of functions have had an opportunity to request reassignment, received a response, and have had time to indicate their willingness
- A bargaining proposal to impose a freeze on outside hiring in the event of a realignment of the work force

When the bargaining proposal refers to the positions assigned to any organizational subdivision, work project, or tour of duty, Section 7106(b)(1):

- A bargaining proposal to require an agency to maintain two-person crews for safety reasons while employees are in a travel duty status

When the bargaining proposal refers to the technology of performing work, Section 7106(b)(1):

- A bargaining proposal to require management to provide certain employees with a telephone
- A bargaining proposal concerning the equipment or facilities planned for a new building
- A bargaining proposal to provide a secure storage area for the official weapons unit employees are authorized to wear during the performance of their duties

When the bargaining proposal refers to the methods or means of performing work, Section 7106(b)(1):

- A bargaining proposal that employees maintain completed logs in accordance with the Veterans Administration maintenance of records
- A bargaining proposal that employees refrain from inserting unofficial personal comments in logs

Prohibited or Illegal Bargaining Items

When the bargaining proposal conflicts with management's authority to determine the mission, budget, organization, number of employees and internal security practices, Section 7106(a)(1):

- A bargaining proposal to require the agency to establish its organizational structure in a manner to assure promotional opportunities for its civilian technician employees
- A bargaining proposal to limit the number of civilian positions in the

agency capable of being converted into positions occupied by military personnel

- A bargaining proposal that would require the agency to structure its organization in a manner to assure promotional opportunities for certain employees
- A bargaining proposal to modify organizational structure in order to afford promotional opportunities for certain employees without regard to classification
- A bargaining proposal to reorganize a division to create four work sections instead of two and require that each work section be assigned a section coordinator

When the bargaining proposal conflicts with management's authority to hire, assign, direct, layoff, and retain employees, Section 7106(a)(2)(A):

- A bargaining proposal to specify the number and types of vacancies to be reserved for filling through the upper mobility program
- A bargaining proposal to prohibit assignment of duties performed by employees in one classification to employees in another classification
- A bargaining proposal requiring negotiations to determine the substance of performance standards for any position
- A bargaining proposal requiring that particular performance standards and critical elements be established through negotiation
- A bargaining proposal to bar the agency from including certain enumerated subjects in performance standards for bargaining-unit employees
- A bargaining proposal to establish mandatory conditions for an agency to meet before reducing specified categories below specified hours of work per week

When the bargaining proposal conflicts with management's authority to suspend, remove, reduce in pay, or take other disciplinary action, Section 7106 (a)(2)(A):

- A bargaining proposal that, if contemplated disciplinary actions against a union representative or official cannot be worked out at the area-direct level, management's recourse shall be to the authority

When the bargaining proposal conflicts with management's authority to assign work, Section 7102(a)(2)(B):

- A bargaining proposal to change the mandatory nature of agency operating instructions and change to guidelines
- A bargaining proposal to eliminate performance of various duties by GCOs such as insuring adequate tools and logs are maintained, modifying assignment of work, keeping physical locations neat and clean, and allowing absence from the work area
- A bargaining proposal to change mandatory work requirements to permissive work requirements
- A bargaining proposal to change the time duties are to be performed from specific times to other times

- A bargaining proposal to eliminate specific duties
- A bargaining proposal to assign work to a particular employee or preclude assignment of work to any other employee
- A bargaining proposal to prevent management from assigning certain types of training on weekends and holidays
- A bargaining proposal to limit management's ability to assign nurses to certain duties unless "urgent or needful situations" arise
- A bargaining proposal requiring that work assignments of firefighters be consistent with their primary function
- A bargaining proposal to prescribe duties employees can be assigned to on certain days
- A bargaining proposal that the agency assign the responsibility to resolve conflicts in assignments of researchers to the division chief

When the bargaining proposal conflicts with management's authority to contract out, Section 7106(a)(2)(B):

- A general proposal concerning contracting out

When the bargaining proposal conflicts with management's authority to determine the personnel needed to conduct agency operations, Section 7106(a)(2)(B):

- A bargaining proposal to designate the particular management officials who would represent an agency on rating and ranking panels

When the bargaining proposal conflicts with management's authority to select from among properly ranked and certified candidates or any other appropriate source, Section 7106(a)(2)(C):

- A bargaining proposal requiring union participation in determining the knowledge, skills, and abilities for successful performance of the work of a position
- A bargaining proposal to require management to repromote employees who have been demoted as a result of a reduction in force
- A bargaining proposal to place a union representative on the agency's Position Management Committee
- A bargaining proposal for recruitment that would prevent the agency from expanding the area of consideration or selecting from any other appropriate source if three highly qualified candidates were identified
- A bargaining proposal to require the agency to select an applicant from among technicians and train him for the position when a technician from the full-time force does not meet mandatory qualifications for the announced position
- A bargaining proposal to prevent the agency from selecting employees from OPM (Office of Personnel Management) certificates unless they are also on the agency's merit promotion certificate

- A bargaining proposal that management cannot accept any applications outside the agency with respect to vacancies
- A bargaining proposal to compel the agency during a reduction in force to select "qualifiable bargaining-unit candidates when filling an existing vacancy"
- A bargaining proposal to require that management, in filling a vacant bargaining position, select a participant from, or laterally transfer only from, the agency's "Classification and Placement Plan"

When the bargaining proposal is outside the duty to bargain because it is not a condition of employment, Section 7103(a)(12), (14); Section 7114(b)(2); Section 7121(c)(5):

- A bargaining proposal concerning employee use of the agency recreational facilities and picnic area
- A bargaining proposal to prevent management's disclosure of confidential medical information to certain officials
- A bargaining proposal to require supervisors to maintain certain records to be shown to and initialed by affected employees
- A bargaining proposal to designate certain positions as "special" for pay purposes
- A bargaining proposal to extend coverage of the negotiated grievance procedure to include direct challenges to the agency's identification of the critical elements and establishment of performance standards
- A bargaining proposal that would authorize hazard pay differentials to certain categories of General Schedule employees
- A bargaining proposal that work in excess of forty hours per week performed on Sunday be paid at twice the basic rate
- A bargaining proposal that concerns the obligation to bargain (Unfair Labor Practice)

When a bargaining proposal concerns nonbargaining-unit groups or is limited to certain individuals within the bargaining unit, Section 7114(a)(1):

- A bargaining proposal to negotiate procedures for filling supervisory vacancies
- A bargaining proposal to allow members of the bargaining unit who are released from competitive levels to bump other employees during a RIF who are within the same subgroup in other competitive levels but are not all part of the bargaining unit
- A bargaining proposal that each employee be permitted to rate his or her supervisor twice a year when management does not elect to negotiate on the subject
- A bargaining proposal that duty time be allowed for union-sponsored training
- A bargaining proposal to require the agency to use competitive procedures of its Merit Promotion Plan in filling supervisory or management positions with bargaining-unit employees

When the bargaining proposal is inconsistent with any federal law or any governmentwide rule or regulation, Section 7117(a)(1):

- A bargaining proposal to preclude the agency from revising unit position descriptions regardless of the duties actually assigned to the positions or employees, unless the revised duties are consistent with current professional levels of the positions
- A bargaining proposal to negate OPM time-in-trade proposals, to the effect that, in order to advance from a competitive or excepted position to a competitive position, the employee must serve one year in a position in the next lower grade for the line of work
- A bargaining proposal to require the agency to allocate reserved parking spaces to employees who meet certain conditions, notwithstanding mandatory priorities already established by governmentwide regulations to dictate allocation
- A bargaining proposal to list holidays, including holidays not recognized under federal law
- A bargaining proposal for an agency shop

When a bargaining proposal is inconsistent with a rule or regulation for which a compelling need exists, Section 7117(a)(2):

- A bargaining proposal to require an agency to use seniority, as listed on tenure lists of competitive areas, as the sole determinant of employees who would be affected by a RIF when such a proposal is inconsistent with agency regulations for which there is a compelling need
- A bargaining proposal that a technician's retention standing in a RIF be based solely on the technician's civilian performance appraisal

When the bargaining proposal provides for two appeal procedures, Section 7121(d):

- A bargaining proposal to permit the filing of a discrimination complaint under both the statutory appeal procedure and the negotiated grievance procedure

When the bargaining proposal provides for statutory or negotiated grievance appeals on all subjects covered by the grievance procedure, Section 7121(d)(3):

- A bargaining proposal to grant to bargaining-unit employees the option to choose either the negotiated grievance procedure or the statutory procedure with respect to any matter covered by the grievance procedure

When the bargaining proposal interferes with the employee's right to appeal on his own, Section 7121(b)(3)(B):

- A bargaining proposal to require concurrence of the union before a grievance is filed

PUBLIC SECTOR: STATE AND LOCAL

The limitations on the scope of bargaining continue to be carried over from the federal to the state and local sectors. It should be observed, however, that between the two sectors of public-employee bargaining, the federal is the more restricted in its scope. For the most part, at either federal or state and local levels of public-employee bargaining, sufficient time has not elapsed to allow as definitive a list of mandatory and prohibited bargaining items to develop as have done so in the fifty years of private-sector bargaining under the NLRA. Nevertheless, one state, Nevada, has chosen not to wait for interpretive decisions on bargaining scope; it has specifically spelled out the scope of mandatory bargaining and those subject matters that are not within the scope of mandatory bargaining but are reserved to the local-government employer. Nevada's Local Government Employee-Management Relations Act, Section 288.150(2), "The Scope of Mandatory Bargaining," is limited to:

(a) Salary or wage rates or other forms of direct monetary compensation,

(b) Sick leave,

(c) Vacation leave,

(d) Holidays,

(e) Other paid or nonpaid leaves of absence,

(f) Insurance benefits,

(g) Total hours of work required of an employee on each workday or workweek,

(h) Total number of days' work required of an employee in a workyear,

(i) Discharge and disciplinary procedures,

(j) Recognition clause,

(k) The method used to classify employees in the negotiating unit,

(l) Deduction of dues for the recognized employee organization,

(m) Protection of employees in the negotiating unit from discrimination because of participation in recognized employee organizations consistent with the provisions of this chapter,

(n) No-strike provisions consistent with the provisions of this chapter,

(o) Grievance and arbitration procedures for resolution of disputes relating to interpretation or application of collective agreements,

(p) General savings clauses,

(q) Duration of collective bargaining agreements,

(r) Safety,

(s)   Teacher preparation time,
(t)   Procedures for reduction in work force.

Section 288.150(3) lists those matters that are not a subject of mandatory bargaining as:

(a)   The right to hire, direct, assign or transfer an employee, but excluding the right to assign or transfer an employee as a form of discipline,

(b)   The right to reduce in force or lay off any employee because of lack of work or lack of funds, subject to paragraph (t) of subsection 2,

(c)   The right to determine:
(1)   Appropriate staffing levels and work performance standards except for safety considerations;
(2)   The content of the workday including without limitation workload factors, except for safety considerations;
(3)   The quality and quantity of services to be offered to the public; and
(4)   The means and methods of offering those services.

BARGAINING ITEMS: THE SUBSTANCE OF THE AGREEMENT AND SOCIAL LEGISLATION

Federal, state, and local legislative bodies have enacted numerous laws and regulations which affect the substantive elements of the collective bargaining contract. These laws and regulations establish minimums the employer must provide, in accordance with specific conditions. Therefore, the well-prepared negotiator must have a comprehensive understanding of the laws and regulations and their impact upon the organization's collective bargaining contract.

The following list provides basic contract provisions and relevant federal laws. This is not intended to be exhaustive. The reader is also reminded that for every federal law regulating contract substance, there may be one or more state or local laws and regulations.

Contract Provision	Federal Statute
Disability insurance	Pregnancy Discrimination Act
	Workers' Compensation
Equal employment opportunity	Age Discrimination Act
	Executive Order 11246
	1964 Civil Rights Act
	Vocational Rehabilitation Act
Hours	Davis-Bacon Act

	Fair Labor Standards Act
	Service Contract Act
	Walsh-Healey Act
Layoff	Unemployment Insurance
Leave of absence	Pregnancy Discrimination Act
Medical insurance	Health Maintenance Act
	Pregnancy Discrimination Act
Military leave of absence	Selective Service Act
	Vietnam Era Veterans Reemployment Act
Overtime	Davis-Bacon Act
	Fair Labor Standards Act
	Service Contract Act
	Walsh-Healey Act
Pensions/retirement	Employee Retirement Income Security Act
	Social Security Act
Safety	Mine Safety Act
	Occupational Safety and Health Act
Seniority	1964 Civil Rights Act
	Pregnancy Discrimination Act
	Selective Service Act
	Vietnam Era Veterans Reemployment Act
Wages	Davis-Bacon Act
	Equal Pay Act
	Fair Labor Standards Act
	Service Contract Act
	Walsh-Healey Act
	Age Discrimination Act
Work assignments	1964 Civil Rights Act
	Vocational Rehabilitation Act

SOURCES FOR DEVELOPING BARGAINING ITEMS

The items or subjects of negotiation are formally introduced to the bargaining table through the initial demand and counterproposal process of the two parties as described at the beginning of this chapter. Inasmuch as the collective bargaining contract can be changed only periodically, usually when the agreement terminates (every two or three years) or is reopened for negotiation, it is extremely important to both parties that all subjects in the contract needing revision be introduced. If an item is overlooked, there might be a wait of one, two, or three years, or longer before another opportunity to negotiate changes or effect new terms in the agreement appears. Failure to negotiate timely modifications to the agreement can prove costly to one or both parties in the form of poor management-employee relations, serious impairment of the rights of either or both parties, or excessive costs. Reasons for introducing certain bargaining items vary considerably. Some language changes are effected to facilitate smooth administration of the contract; some bargaining subjects are added to rectify mistakes in language, not noticed at the time of the last negotiations, that have proven costly either in money terms or in loss of rights; some bargaining items of lesser significance are offered as trade-offs; some bargaining items serve as a matter of pure strategy, perhaps to test the wind for future negotiations on items that will not float at the present time; some bargaining items are necessary to update the contract to competitive conditions, economic conditions, social conditions, or legal changes; some subjects are required to correct ambiguities, some to create ambiguities or to leave the meaning flexible to adapt to changing times. There are many reasons. All should be considered before either party closes the door on the introduction of bargaining items for the current negotiation.

A full review of all bargaining matters to be introduced at negotiations brings out the importance of adopting and following an efficient system for gathering and organizing bargaining information. This is covered in Chapters 7 and 8. It is the primary source of bargaining items for the next negotiations and includes, as covered in Chapter 7: the results of a review of the last negotiations; what is happening in other contract negotiations; economic, social, and legislative conditions; changes in both the labor and product markets; and experience in administering the agreement during its period, to name a few. The exchange of the parties prior to actual negotiations formalizes the list of bargaining subjects and caps the lengthy period of preparation that began at the end of the preceding negotiations. Proper attention to the preparatory process covered in Chapters 7 and 8 can do much to develop a systematic approach to identifying and covering completely all items to be introduced.

Identifying the bargaining subjects is but the first step in developing the CBO blueprint or plan for the negotiations. The next step in the CBO methodology is assigning priorities to each of the bargaining items. This is essential in preparing for negotiations and developing strategy, regardless of which party will introduce each bargaining subject.

CHAPTER 11

PRIORITIES

Column 2 of Form 9-1, "Collective Bargaining by Objectives," requires the negotiating party to think out carefully and identify by number or some other form of ranking the importance to that party of each bargaining item in relation to all others on the agenda. Priority does not necessarily relate directly to whether the item is introduced by the company or the union, or whether it is a cost or noncost item. It may be of higher priority to the company in terms of its objectives, financial and otherwise, to resist a particular demand introduced by the union, or to achieve a settlement on the item below the union position, than to achieve settlement on another item that the company itself introduced but that has less impact on the company operation. The priority given to the bargaining items need not be a consecutive listing. Some items might have about the same relative priority as others. Ranking the items by relative priority or importance to the bargaining party, therefore, might be done consecutively, with no two items the same, or by groups of items. The key is to establish an identification method that is easily followed, but most of all *to establish the priorities*, whatever the method used. Both the identification of priorities that is so extremely important for strategy considerations and the thinking process necessary to establish a relative priority system are positive steps for successful negotiations.

The *how* of setting priorities must be related to the individual party's value system. Criteria that might be considered are the importance of the bargaining goals established for each individual bargaining item as they relate to such measures as cost or income, continuing relations of the union and the company, continuing employer-employee relations, ease of implementation and administration, precedent established for future negotiation, and personal prestige of the parties. Establishing relative priorities on all items on the bargaining agenda is an individual matter and, therefore, requires that each party (1) know its own goals and/or value structure, and (2) be able to relate each item on the bargaining agenda specifically to such goals and value structure.

When one considers that initial demands and counteroffers, setting of bargaining goals, strategy and tactics, trade and compromise—in fact, the entire give-and-take of the collective bargaining negotiation process—are all inextricably connected with a priority system, it is hard to avoid the conclusion that establishing priorities is of vital importance to negotiation success. The key element in the objectives approach is that these priority values are pinned down and *known prior to negotiations*; otherwise, there can be only one result for the bargaining party: confusion and fumbling, during both the preparatory process and the actual negotiations.

Attempting to ascertain the priority system of the other party before and during negotiations is equally important and a part of the goal of any successful negotiator, but this is more logically discussed later, in the section on the formal negotiation process. It should not be necessary to point out that each party's priority system should be kept highly confidential to that party, since it is so closely related to bargaining strategy.

Determining the relative priority of each bargaining item completes the second stage of the objectives approach. To illustrate, priorities might appear as in Form 11-1 for an employer, whereas the union, in contrast, might consider union security its number-one priority, and holidays a number three or four. For manageability and ease in the give-and-take of negotiations, it is suggested that the range of priorities be confined to ten or fewer categories. Otherwise, as the range of priorities is increased, the value of the priority system as a strategical device may break down under the weight of inconsequential differences in the comparative worth of the various bargaining items. For example, trying to consider differences between an item with a numerical priority of thirty-seven compared with one with priority of thirty-five during the often fast-moving flow of bargaining would be onerous. It is much easier to handle differences among item priorities within a range of ten. The more the representatives of each party have to think through the relative importance of each bargaining item under consideration, the better their understanding of the particular bargaining item will be and the more positive their approach to negotiating on that item will become.

FORM 11–1
Collective Bargaining by Objectives
A Guide for Systematic Data Preparation and Planning Negotiations

PRIORITIES**	
BARGAINING ITEMS*	PRIORITIES**
(Financial Items) Holidays	5
Wages	1
Insurance	2
—	
—	
—	
—	
(Nonfinancial Items) Union Security	2
Probationary Period	8
Arbitrator Cost	6

*Classify items in two groups: financial and nonfinancial
**Relative priority of each bargaining item to all other bargaining items

CHAPTER 12

RANGE OF BARGAINING OBJECTIVES

It must be reemphasized that the range of objectives (columns 3, 4, and 5 in Form 12-1) is (1) a potentially acceptable settlement range; (2) a range starting from the most desirable (optimistic) to the least desirable (pessimistic) type of settlement, which constitutes an actual set of goals toward which the company or the union negotiates positively; and (3) an unchanging set of goals, once negotiations begin, unless there is a change in the basic assumptions on which the goals were first established. The positiveness with which the party negotiates is as closely linked to unwavering goals as to any other factor influencing bargaining success.

REALISTIC BARGAINING OBJECTIVE

It is easiest and most efficient for the party to start out by first establishing the realistic objective or bargaining goal (expected final settlement) for each bargaining item listed in column 1. This realistic objective is established by assessing all the factors and forces that are anticipated to enter into a final settlement on that particular item, including patterns and trends in pertinent local, regional, and national settlements and the extent to which the party feels it can defend its position. Another force is the bargaining climate—that is, relations between the parties. These relations result from the position of the union relative to its membership, the guidelines being set by the local union or its parent international, the personalities involved at the bargaining table, economic and political conditions within the union and the company and in the community and the nation, the relative bargaining strength of the two parties, employee attitudes, community attitudes, how it fits into the overall strategy in the negotiation of other items, and any other factor the party perceives might affect the bargaining outcome on any particular item. For example, suppose the present contract allows for six holidays. In assessing the situation, the company makes an estimate, looking at the matter practically and basing its estimate on research and analysis, that the final settlement anent holidays will *most likely* be one additional holiday, or seven in all. The key to the CBO approach is that the realistic objective, the most likely outcome in management's opinion, is founded on its own independent research and analysis and not on its reaction to what the union demand is or might be. Each objective established is formulated after careful research and analysis of the bargaining information accumulated through the process described in Chapters 7 and 8. The ability to achieve the objective or goal (realistic in this instance) is not then dependent upon chance or luck but is backed by solid facts and reasoning. The negotiator knows that each objective so set has been carefully considered in light of all relevant information that might affect the bargaining outcome of that particular item. Knowing this, the negotiator can pursue the objective with the confidence that it is an obtainable goal. Confidence is an important part of the CBO approach. Knowing rather than guessing what objectives are obtainable engenders a positiveness in the negotiator. It enables the negotiator, regardless of whether the item is introduced by his party or by the other party, to put aside tentative thoughts about the negotiations and to proceed positively and vigorously toward the goals set, rather than reacting to the other party's game plan.

Form 12-1 illustrates how the company records its realistic objective of "seven days" in column 4. The same procedure would be followed by the union in setting its realistic bargaining objective for holidays. The union, based on its independent research and analysis, might arrive at "eight days" as its realistic bargaining objective. This figure, like the company's, has been arrived at after proper research and analysis and would be what the union expects the settlement outcome to be, not what the union asks or reveals, or what the company makes visible to begin with. It is and must be an objective the union can pursue as a realistic objective. As with the priorities recorded in column 2 of the CBO form, the realistic bargaining objective, as well as the optimistic and pessimistic objectives to be considered later, must be kept confidential. By setting the realistic objective at the level considered most probable as the final outcome, the first step in establishing a range of bargaining objectives is completed.

FORM 12–1
Collective Bargaining by Objectives
A Guide for Systematic Data Preparation and Planning Negotiations

BARGAINING ITEMS*	PRIORITIES**	RANGE OF BARGAINING OBJECTIVES		
		Pessimistic	Realistic	Optimistic
(Financial Items)				
Holidays	5	1 Floating 1 Birthday	1 Floating	No Change
Wages	1	Cost: $.10/hour 8%	Cost: $.05/hour 6.5%	Cost: 0 5%
		Cost: $.84/hour	Cost: $.67/hour	Cost: $.51/hour
Insurance	2	100% paid by company $100 deductable	Employee Pay: Single $5.45 Single + 1 $6.93 Family $8.76	Employee Pay: Single $5.76 Single + 1 $7.32 Family $9.73
		Cost: $.125/hour	Cost: $.11/hour	Cost: $.105/hour
——— ——— ——— ——				
(Nonfinancial Items)				
Union Security	2	Union Shop	Modified Union Shop	Agency Shop
Probationary Period	8	30 days	60 days	90 days
Arbitrator Cost	6	Employer Pay 60/40	Split Costs 50/50	Loser Pay 60/40

*Classify items in two groups: financial and nonfinancial
**Relative priority of each bargaining item to all other bargaining items

141

OPTIMISTIC BARGAINING OBJECTIVE

The establishment of an optimistic bargaining objective essentially derives from the study and setting of the realistic objective. The optimistic bargaining objective is merely looking on the brighter side of settlement possibilities relative to each bargaining item—the "frosting-on-the-cake" concept. The chance of achieving the optimistic objective is not as great as that of achieving the realistic objective but is still a distinct and attainable possibility. It is crucial to the establishment of the bargaining-objective approach that the party clearly understand that the optimistic goal must be a distinct possibility—within the range of possible bargaining settlements, according to the best judgment of the party. For example, as shown in Form 12-1, column 5, using the previous example concerning holidays, the company might establish its optimistic settlement goal as "no change" from the old contract on holidays—that is, holidays remain at six a year, a distinct possibility according to company analysis. The union, on the other hand, in setting *its* optimistic goal, might consider nine holidays, an addition of three, a distinctly obtainable objective if everything goes better than expected at the bargaining table.

PESSIMISTIC BARGAINING OBJECTIVE

The pessimistic bargaining objective for any bargaining item must also be an objective that is a distinct possibility, even though less probable than the realistic objective. It, too, is most easily derived from the considerations that gave rise to the establishment of the realistic goal for a particular item. It is simply a lesser settlement that the party may have to accept, if reluctantly, if all does not go quite as planned in the negotiations. Using the previous example of holidays, the pessimistic objective for the company might be a settlement at eight holidays, or an increase of two over the old contract, as in Form 12-1, column 3. The union might consider seven holidays as its pessimistic objective, one that is less desirable but nevertheless within the range of possibilities for which it might settle.

There are two primary reasons for using a range of objectives rather than a single objective approach for each bargaining item. The first reason recognizes the practical side of bargaining—the need for flexibility to accommodate the give-and-take of negotiations if one goal is not achieved. The optimistic becomes a preferred goal, which the party has already determined is obtainable if negotiations go just right. It does not, however, constitute the most probable settlement, only the most preferable. If the optimistic goal is not achieved, the party is not at a stone wall but has yet another objective—already acknowledged in the preparation for negotiations as the most likely settlement level—to pursue. Should this realistic goal not be achieved, the party has anticipated that it may need to fall back on another goal, less desirable but determined in advance as acceptable so long as a majority of the settlements do not fall into this part of the range. The key to the range is that each objective constitutes a positive goal, thus bolstering the positive quality of the bargaining but still allowing the flexibility of movement so important to successful negotiations.

The second feature of the range-of-objectives concept is that the negotiating party with its chief nonnegotiating principals, whether the company or the union, will have arrived prior to negotiations at a consensus on the range of settlement for the entire contract, as long as there is a reasonable balance among the three levels of objectives, preferably with the balance leaning toward the realistic-optimistic objectives. With this concensus, authority may be delegated to the negotiating committee to negotiate a settlement on each bargaining item and for the contract as a whole as long as the negotiators work within the range agreed upon. Through this method, higher authority has delegated authority without losing control over the final settlement.

COSTING THE CONTRACT CHANGES

Determining the cost of changes in the contract is an absolutely essential ingredient in determining bargaining objectives. For the company, it is added costs; for the employees, it is added income. Eventually both parties in a contract renegotiation come to the point where the cost of the package becomes the crucial factor in reaching an agreement. The mechanics of costing the contract are discussed in Chapter 7. It is suggested that, as an adjunct to the setting of objectives for each item, each objective for each item should be costed out and either a total cost figure or per-hour figure entered immediately below the objective on Form 12-1. This renders the form even more useful as a blueprint for negotiations since the negotiating party can determine at a glance not only what each position will add to costs or benefits and what the range of costs or benefits will be for each item, but also the total cost of the package of financial items. This will not substitute for the final precise costing-out process, but it does give perspective to the financial implications of certain moves at the bargaining table.

SUMMARY OBSERVATIONS

Inasmuch as the range of bargaining objectives is the main difference between the use of the CBO methodology and other approaches to negotiations, it is considered important to note and to reemphasize some of the main features of this methodology.

1. Of vital importance in using the objectives approach is the confidentiality of the information concerning priorities and especially objectives. This becomes the focal point from which all the actions of the parties in the negotiations emanate, and the bargaining-by-objectives form becomes a ready reference from which to determine position, tactics, and progress being made. Grouping all financial items, as explained earlier, on either an hourly or a total-cost basis provides a ready source for the company or the union to determine the money impact of trades and compromises on money items and the effect on the total money package. By tying this initially to its own range of bargaining objectives, each party will have done some preparatory work and thinking prior to negotiation.

2. The identification of objectives becomes the basis for a more organized and careful approach to gathering and assembling data to support the party's bargaining position. It should really enhance the usefulness of data, whether organized in bargaining books or some other way. Because the party must consider a range of bargaining objectives (possible settlements), the objectives approach enhances and broadens the whole process of preparation for bargaining. The party is forced to do more positive thinking and is, therefore, better prepared and has more clearly in mind where it expects and wants to go than by any other approach to bargaining.

3. The establishment of objectives as definitive, as required under the objectives approach, offers a safe and effective way for management or the union to delegate authority to its bargaining team. Of great importance is that the authority is a flexible authority—the bargaining range of objectives—which is so necessary to effective strategy and negotiating. All the party must do is take the time to sit down with its bargaining team, agree on the range of objectives for each individual bargaining item, and then delegate authority to its team to settle within the range, except where too many of the settlements are falling in the pessimistic range. In this case, there should be further assessment by the party in authority and the bargaining team, because the assumptions on which the original goals were established may have changed, or perhaps there is a decided weakness in the bargaining team itself. Nothing is more frustrating to the negotiating process than for a party to have to sit across the bargaining table and attempt to bargain with a party that lacks bargaining authority. It is an exercise in futility.

4. It is recognized that, by nature, not all items lend themselves to a three-way range of objectives. This is particularly true with some of the noncost bargaining items. Where this is the case, the party should at least establish two positions for the bargaining item, either a realistic-pessimistic range or an optimistic-realistic range. This is crucial both in terms of having positive objectives in mind while negotiating, and in terms of the way in which such prior consideration and thought of the particular bargaining item enhances preparation prior to negotiations.

5. Objectives should not be altered unless assumptions change—firmness and clarity are a strength.

6. Concerning the meaning of the bargaining-objectives range, it is well to point out that this range has no particular meaning with respect to strike or lockout points. Introducing strike or lockout considerations into the methodology would introduce a negativism that would undermine the overall usefulness of the objectives approach. The emphasis and focus of bargaining by objectives is to approach negotiations with positive and attainable goals and to relegate decisions on strikes, lockouts, and such considerations to strategy and tactics that might result from the actual negotiation process rather than being a major factor in the establishing of objectives. The objectives approach, while not ignoring pressure tactics, is based primarily on the achievement of goals through sound preparation and a careful, systematic approach to negotiation.

7. The very process required by the objectives approach—identifying the bargaining items, establishing priorities, and deciding on a range of achievable objectives—introduces positiveness because it not only systematizes what must be done but also *requires* a high degree of thought, analysis, and preparation before negotiations. There is nothing theoretical about the methodology. It is a practical and workable concept based on what must be done. The negotiator, through this methodology, enters negotiations knowing what he is doing, where he is going, and how strong his position is—not just generally, but relative to each item on the agenda. He is not "flying by the seat of his pants."

8. Finally, it must be emphasized that the objectives approach introduces a methodology or systematic way of negotiating that is useful in any negotiation. It may be and has been used for such bargaining activities as negotiating government contracts, budgets, insurance claims, and purchase of real estate, to name a few.

SELECTED REFERENCES

Burtt, Everett Johnson, Jr., *Labor Markets, Unions, and Government Policies.* New York: St. Martin's Press, 1963. Good background reading for the objectives of unions in collective bargaining (Chapters 11–12).

Granof, Michael H., *How to Cost Your Labor Contract.* Washington, D.C.: Bureau of National Affairs, Inc., 1973. Professor Granof, an accountant, fills a long-delayed need by addressing himself to the cost implications of the labor contract. He feels that the cost implications are too important to be left to the labor relations specialist. Yet the book is not a "how-to-do-it" manual. Instead, it approaches contract evaluation from the premise that there must be an explicit integration of plans relative to collective bargaining with those pertaining to other functions of the company.

McKee, Clive B., "Climate-Key to Effective Bargaining," in Elizabeth Marting, ed., *Understanding Collective Bargaining,* pp. 73–74. New York: American Management Association, Inc., 1958. Emphasizes the importance of management's bargaining objectives being carefully discussed and definite targets set before negotiation begins.

Morse, Bruce, *How to Negotiate the Labor Agreement,* 9th ed. Detroit: Trends Publishing Co., 1981. The author discusses the development of an employer's objectives and relates these to the final proposals.

Peters, Edward, *Strategy and Tactics in Labor Negotiations,* 3rd ed., pp. 31–54. Swarthmore, Pa.: Personnel Journal, 1966. Here the author is concerned with two topics: setting a realistic goal and criteria for a realistic goal. From his years of experience in negotiations as a leading mediator on the West Coast, the author ties goal setting to his experience on the firing line.

CHAPTER 13

INITIAL BARGAINING POSITIONS

As stated earlier, the initial bargaining positions of the parties are the visible position each takes at the outset of negotiations that is reflected in the initial demands of the union and the response or counteroffer of the employer. These are not the same as the range of bargaining objectives recorded in columns 3, 4, and 5 of the objectives form. The range of objectives, to reiterate, constitutes the confidential goals that the party actually expects to achieve in the final settlement. Under no circumstances should these be made visible to the other party, since this knowledge would destroy the bargaining leverage and the strategy based on these final goals.

A number of approaches are evident from observation of negotiations throughout the country. In some situations, the initial bargaining position (demand and response) may be close to what the parties have set as their objectives and expect to settle for finally. This approach creates the distinct possibility of a narrower negotiating range between the parties, although this may not be true without exception. This is more akin to the Boulware approach. In other instances, the parties' initial positions are based on the philosophy that the more the union asks for, the more there is to be gained, and the less offered by the company, the less will have to be given. This may result in a wide negotiating gap between what have been set as objectives and what the union and the employer demand and offer respectively. Other situations are characterized by combinations of these two approaches, sometimes differing according to the particular bargaining item.

The only general kind of guide for the negotiator is to very carefully examine each item for which objectives have been established, and from this examination determine where the first visible position on each item must be in order for the party to have a good chance to achieve the optimistic objective, a strong possibility of settling at the realistic-objective level, and a reasonable possibility that the settlement will not be at the pessimistic-objective level. Establishing the initial bargaining position is such an individual matter that more specific advice than this is not very useful. I do contend, however, that having gone to the trouble of accomplishing the spadework necessary to establish bargaining objectives, and having gone through the careful thought process required to establish such objectives, a party is in the best position possible to establish a logical and meaningful initial or visible position on each item to present to the other party at the start of negotiations. The objectives process minimizes the uncertainty in determining the initial bargaining position, and at the same time relates this initial posture more meaningfully to final attainable goals.

The initial bargaining position may be illustrated as in column 6 of Form 13-1 (the company, in this instance). The union's initial demand on holidays might be for nine, as indicated earlier; or if the union representatives expect a hard time in securing their objectives relative to holidays, they might very well set their initial position at ten or eleven. The visible position that either party takes relative to any particular item then depends on how difficult the parties estimate the negotiation will be in reaching, most preferably, their optimistic goal, and more probably, their realistic goal. It is this estimate of the amount of "haggling" or "horse trading" they must go through to achieve their objectives that determines whether their initial position (demand or counterproposal) is a position close to or wide of the optimistic. Of course, neither party should assume a position that is ridiculous on its face because the other party will treat it for what it is worth, and serious negotiation will not proceed until the position is brought somewhere within the realm of reality.

CONCLUSION

Determining the initial position on all bargaining items also completes the CBO methodology. With the completion of the bargaining items, priorities, range of bargaining objectives, and initial bargaining position, the negotiator has established a blueprint or plan of action for the negotiations. Developing strategy to achieve the goals established through the CBO method is a natural consequence of the preparation that began with

FORM 13–1
Collective Bargaining by Objectives
A Guide for Systematic Data Preparation and Planning Negotiations

BARGAINING ITEMS*	PRIORITIES**	RANGE OF BARGAINING OBJECTIVES				Initial Bargaining Position
		Pessimistic	Realistic	Optimistic		
(Financial Items)						
Holidays	5	1 Floating 1 Birthday Cost: $.10/hour	1 Floating Cost: $.05/hour	No Change Cost: 0		No Change
Wages	1	8%	6.5%	5%		3%
		Cost: $.84/hour	Cost: $.67/hour	Cost: $.51/hour		Cost: $.30/hour
Insurance	2	100% paid by company $100 deductible Cost: $.125/hour	Employee Pay: Single $5.45 Single + 1 $6.93 Family $8.76 Cost: $.11/hour	Employee Pay: Single $5.76 Single + 1 $7.32 Family $9.73 Cost: $.105/hour		Employee Pay: Single $6.06 Single + 1 $7.70 Family $10.24 Cost: $.10/hour
— — — —						
(Nonfinancial Items)						
Union Security	2	Union Shop	Modified Union Shop	Agency Shop		Agency Shop
Probationary Period	8	30 days	60 days	90 days		120 days
Arbitrator Cost	6	Employer Pay 60/40	Split Costs 50/50	Loser Pay 60/40		Loser Pay

*Classify items in two groups: financial and nonfinancial
**Relative priority of each bargaining item to all other bargaining items

the gathering of information and was consummated with the completion of the CBO methodology. The foundation is laid for approaching negotiations on a positive note, knowing that the blueprint or plan of action is based upon sound preparation and factual data.

There are, however, some preparations that need to be attended to before actually engaging in negotiations. These concern procedural matters anent the negotiations, a bargaining book to compile the supporting data for the goals established through CBO, and a checklist to determine whether all preparations have been completed. This is the task addressed in Chapter 14.

SELECTED REFERENCES

Bloom, Gordon F., and Herbert R. Northrup, *Economics of Labor Relations,* 9th ed. Homewood, Ill.: Richard D. Irwin, 1981. This includes a short but useful section on the union's formulation of demands.

Dunlop, John T., and James J. Healy, *Collective Bargaining—Principles and Cases,* pp. 54–57. Homewood, Ill.: Richard D. Irwin, 1955. A short but informative discussion of the relationship of the initial positions of the parties to each other.

Marting, Elizabeth, ed., "A Step-by-Step Guide to the Preparatory Process," in *Understanding Collective Bargaining,* pp. 106–8. New York: American Management Association, Inc., 1958. Brief but important material on union and management proposals.

CHAPTER 14

FINAL PREPARATIONS:
A Checklist
and Bargaining Book

Chapters 7 through 13 demonstrated a system for preparing for collective bargaining negotiations. This discourse carried the reader from gathering and assembling data through extracting from that data bargaining information vital to the next negotiations, to developing the final plan of action. The plan of action or blueprint for negotiations is based on a methodology the author has called Collective Bargaining by Objectives or CBO. This system of preparing for negotiations has resulted, to this point, in identifying bargaining items, in setting priorities on each bargaining item, in establishing a range of bargaining objectives for each bargaining item (an acceptable settlement range for the negotiating party concerned), and in determining what will be revealed to the party as the initial position of each bargaining item. All of this sequence—from the initial gathering of bargaining data to creating a plan of action through CBO—is predicated on the value of factual support for positions and goals. The emphasis is on using, instead of a "heck and by guess" approach to goals, an approach brought about by realistic goals. In doing so, guesswork as to results is replaced by facts and by knowledge and confidence that the goals are rational, reasonable, supportable, and attainable. A negative, defensive, rear-guard action typical of some negotiations, and resulting from insufficient preparation and a lack of known supportable goals, is thus precluded. In using the CBO method, it is vital that no position on a bargaining item should be revealed to the other party nor formal bargaining on any item commence until the spadework has been completed: the identifying of and agreeing to bargaining items, the establishing of priorities for each bargaining item, the delineating of a range of bargaining objectives for each item, and the pricing out of each objective so established. Finally, after these steps of deriving an initial position on each bargaining item, these positions may be revealed to the other side.

Completing the CBO blueprint prior to formal negotiation is a must. This provides not only a positive thrust to negotiations but is the basis for the overall planning and strategy. However, before formal substantive negotiations begin, there are yet other tasks to attend to. Procedures and the conduct of negotiations must mutually be agreed upon. What the size and composition of the bargaining team should be in order to accomplish the task most efficiently must be determined. Facilities for the negotiations are important. The chief negotiator needs to use the most effective device to assemble the bargaining information to be used during the negotiations to support and explain the position taken on each bargaining item and to assure that the objectives established for each bargaining item will be achieved.

CHECKLIST

To assure that all preparatory steps have been completed before formal negotiations anent substantive matters commence—CBO blueprint, composition of bargaining team, facilities, procedures—it is recommended that each party develop a checklist, such as shown in Form 14-1.

THE BARGAINING BOOK

The device most commonly used to assemble materials to be used during negotiations is what is known as a bargaining book. There are many versions, but all have certain common features. Usually they are in the form of a large loose-leaf notebook, or notebooks. Keeping the data contained in the bargaining book to manageable size is emphasized. Relevancy of the information to the objectives set for each bargaining item is a key determinant of what to include. Accessibility of information places a premium not only on keeping the amount of information to manageable proportions but also on organizing the materials so they are consonant with the bargaining format to be followed.

Although each bargaining book will be organized to fit the needs and preferences of the individual charged with the task of negotiating a new contract, it is usual to include two types of bargaining data: general information, with forms to facilitate the recording of the proceedings; and

FORM 14–1
Checklist for Final Preparations *(Check as Completed)*

CBO

_____ CBO Form completed for each bargaining item

_____ CBO Form completed in <u>sequence</u>, e.g., Item, Priority, Range of Objectives, Initial Position

_____ No less than two of the three objectives (P, R, and O) identified for each item; all three objectives identified for financial items

_____ Each objective priced out for each item, plus totals of columns

_____ Factual data supporting the choice of the bargaining objectives readily available

_____ Approval of range of objectives by organizational leadership

_____ Bargaining team has authority to negotiate and agree within range of objectives

BARGAINING TEAM

_____ Information on those who will be representing other party

_____ Size and composition of one's team consonant with effective negotiation*

_____ Team fully informed of bargaining information, goals, format, plan, roles

FACILITIES

_____ Adequacy of facilities for negotiations, caucuses, staff, equipment, small group discussions

NEGOTIATION SESSIONS

_____ Time, frequency, length of negotiation

_____ Chairman, cochairman, roles

_____ Provision for exchange of bargaining items if not completed earlier

_____ Limitation of size and composition of negotiating teams

_____ Limitation of nonparticipants

PROCEDURES

_____ Bargaining agenda, order of introducing bargaining items

_____ Cutoff date for introducing new bargaining items

_____ Caucuses: initiation, frequency, time limits

_____ Tabling and recalling bargaining items

_____ Signing off bargaining items parties have agreed upon

_____ Reintroducing bargaining items signed off

_____ Continuous update of contract as negotiations proceed—techniques: scribes, word processor**

_____ Transcribing negotiations

_____ Press and other media coverage

_____ Communications with employees

---

*The objective is to provide necessary expertise without cluttering the bargaining scene by the unwieldy size of the bargaining team.

**The author knows of a negotiation where one party installed a word processor in a room near where negotiations were taking place. By this means, an entirely new updated contract was provided for the negotiators each day as the negotiations proceeded.

more detailed, article-by-article information related to specific bargaining items.

The following is illustrative of what might be entered in the general bargaining information section of the bargaining book.

General Bargaining Information

1. Assuming the use of the CBO methodology, the completed CBO forms should appear first in the bargaining book to provide at a glance the bargaining items arrived at by the parties, the bargaining priority assigned each item to be negotiated by each party using the form, the range of objectives serving as the bargaining goals established for each item by the particular party, the cost of each goal in the settlement range or range of objectives, and finally, derived from these steps, the initial bargaining position established for each item to be negotiated. This is the master plan. All other bargaining information in the bargaining book is support for reaching the goals established in the CBO blueprint for negotiations.

2. This section should also include a detailed and complete cost breakdown of the current contract. The form of this breakdown may vary according to the particular needs of the negotiating party. It may be a cost breakdown, article by article, of the contract. It may be a breakdown by functional areas such as direct payroll costs (straight-time earnings, premium earnings, overtime); added costs resulting from payroll costs (FICA, unemployment insurance, worker's compensation); nonpayroll costs (insurance, pension, miscellaneous costs such as tuition reimbursements, overtime meals, personal tools), and nonwork paid time (holidays, vacations, paid lunch, paid washup, coffee breaks, paid sick leave, jury service, paid time off for safety or training). It might be a cost breakdown by gross pay and fringe benefits. Or it might be a breakdown of benefit costs by contractual benefit costs and legislated benefits. Many negotiators are taking advantage of computer facilities to develop a fairly sophisticated program that provides cost breakdowns for almost every purpose of the negotiator. Computer programming of contract costs also provides a means of updating costs of a contract on a daily basis as negotiations proceed. For management, it is also important to include cost and revenue information concerning the operations of the firm or, if in government, the agency.

3. Also included in the general section of the bargaining book should be a consolidated listing in two columns of the bargaining items introduced by the union and those introduced by the employer. Each bargaining item listed is identified as to page and section of the contract where it is found or, if new, where it is to be inserted. The listing of bargaining items in this way also serves as a basis for the parties to negotiate the order of taking up each bargaining item during sessions.

4. Work sheets to record progress should be prepared and included

in the general materials. These are used as the negotiations proceed. Although the work sheets vary as to content, they should provide, at the least: columns for articles and sections consecutively as they are being negotiated; the present language of articles or sections identified; the union's proposal for each of the bargaining items identified by article and section; and management's proposal for these same bargaining items. Also, there should be a column for notes as to the progress of negotiations; vital information such as the tabling of a bargaining item and the date it was tabled; any item referred to a committee for further work, the date it was referred, and any special instructions to the committee; the date consensus on a bargaining item is reached and acknowledged by the initials of each negotiator; trade-offs; bargaining items dropped or combined with other bargaining items; and any other notes that should be made a matter of record as the negotiations proceed. Wisdom supports the keeping of such bargaining notes. Otherwise, differences inevitably surface later during negotiations as to actions or decisions occurring earlier that were only verbal. A final column of value, especially for the employer, is one identifying the final cost (benefit to the employee) of each bargaining item signed off by the parties. As the language of each bargaining item signed off by the parties is agreed upon, this should be recorded in final form, dated, and acknowledged by the initials of the chief negotiator for each party. While the sign-off of each bargaining item does not signify final approval of the entire contract, it is a way of putting that bargaining item aside as completed, unless both parties agree later that there is a reason to reopen negotiations regarding any completed bargaining item. This signing-off process furnishes a written record that the negotiation on that particular item is completed. This record is indisputable, unlike what might possibly be the case if the completion of the bargaining on the item is only acknowledged verbally. Final approval of the contract, as previously noted, is only accomplished by the ratification procedures each party must follow within its own framework or rules of administration. Whether separate pages in a loose-leaf book are used to record the completed language of each bargaining item, or a copy of the living contract is used and modified in the agreed-upon language, it is advisable to keep all the signed-off provisions of the contract together so that, at the end of the negotiations, they constitute the new contract, with appropriate signatures ready for final ratifying.

5. The general section of the bargaining book should also contain the agreed-upon procedures for negotiation. These should be in writing and initialed by the parties in order to dispel any procedural questions that might arise in the midst of negotiations.

6. Finally, the general section should contain any general economic information or results of other bargaining settlements deemed supportive of the overall contract negotiations. Economic information and other bar-

gaining settlements supportive of specific bargaining items should be included in the second part of the bargaining book with other data relating to the specific bargaining items.

The second and larger part of the bargaining book is divided into segments, tabbed individually by articles of the contract. Within each article, consecutively identified, is inserted all bargaining information appropriate to the successful negotiation of that particular article. This is where the careful prenegotiation preparations described in Chapters 7 through 13 are justified in both time and effort for the negotiator. The emphasis throughout the entire preparations was on gathering the right sorts of information, synthesizing that data to provide immediate accessibility, and formulating a plan for negotiations, the CBO blueprint. From this preparation, it should not be difficult to identify those types of supportive data relating to each article to be negotiated, and to transfer that supportive information into the segment devoted to that particular article in the bargaining book. To illustrate the types of information, depending on the nature of the article to be negotiated, that could be included under one article or another in the section tabbed according to the article in the bargaining book, the following list of data, by no means exhaustive, is presented.

Article-by-Article Bargaining Information

1. Any information from the critique of the last negotiations that would be supportive of the party's position anent a particular article
2. A summary of grievance or arbitration settlements relating directly to the article
3. A summary of the feedback from supervisors (if management) or stewards (if a labor organization) of incidents or problems arising in the application of a particular article that did not reach the formal grievance system and were reported through the living contract feedback system
4. Notations of verbal conversations with the other party relating to the application of an article, these would include notes of conversations, entered daily, from phone calls, meetings, etc.
5. All correspondence between the parties relative to an article
6. Economic and other general data supporting a party's position regarding an article, such as cost-of-living data, wage and salary data, technological change, structural changes in employment, product market information, labor market information, productivity, turnover, absenteeism, to name a few
7. News clippings relevant to an article
8. A record of working time activities of officers and stewards of the labor organization, time spent by management representatives on contractual subjects

9. Company rules or policies, such as rules on absenteeism, discipline, safety

10. Records on absenteeism for various reasons—sick leave, excused and unexcused, personal leave, disability

11. Vacation data by job classification and for all employees

12. Wage and employee compensation data—current wage rates, new wage rates, contractual benefits, no direct payment to employees, pay for time not worked, premium payment for hours worked, and legislated benefits

13. Insurance and pension plan costs by individuals covered, monthly costs, annual costs, cost breakdown by plan number, department and employee and employer contributions; should include a list of bargaining-unit employees by name, social security number, length of service, age, marital status, size and ages of family

14. Committee reports related to particular articles such as the Accident Review Committee

15. Information from court decisions, administrative decisions, or statutes bearing on the language or negotiability of particular articles; especially the social legislation and its interpretation as it relates to what might and might not be included in labor contracts

16. Any changes in management policy or procedure having direct bearing upon the implementation of articles of the contract

17. A list of union officers and stewards usually found in an article, such as Union Recognition

18. The evolution of contractual language; can either be inserted into each segment by article or incorporated within a supplementary loose-leaf book

19. Letters of understanding relating to particular articles

20. Other settlements of competitors, or patterns in the settlement of particular contract provisions that could support either party's position on an article or provision

With the completion of these final preparations, the party is now ready to pursue negotiations on substantive issues. It is paramount here that the entire bargaining team, not just the chief negotiator, be completely familiar with the bargaining information accumulated within the bargaining book. Meetings for this purpose are essential. Further, it is essential that strategy and tactics founded on the data and objectives established through CBO be firmed up as much as possible, given the necessity for flexibility as negotiations proceed. Attention is next paid to the formal negotiations.

SELECTED REFERENCES

Each of the writers identified here discusses the use of a bargaining book on the pages noted.

Davey, Harold W., Mario F. Bognanno, and David L. Estenson, *Contemporary Collective Bargaining,* 4th ed., pp. 113, 133. Englewood Cliffs, N.J.: Prentice-Hall, 1982.

Fossum, John, *Labor Relations,* pp. 252–53. Dallas, Tex.: Business Publications, Inc., 1982.

Herman, E. Edward, and Alfred Kuhn, *Collective Bargaining and Labor Relations,* pp. 220–23. Englewood Cliffs, N.J.: Prentice-Hall, 1981.

Morse, Bruce, *How to Negotiate the Labor Agreement,* p. 5. 9th ed. Detroit, Mich.: Trends Publishing Co., 1981.

CHAPTER 15

COLLECTIVE BARGAINING PROCESS: Negotiation

All the foregoing discussions have focused on obtaining background knowledge, preparing basic data, developing expertise, and using a sound methodology as a foundation for the actual negotiations at the bargaining table.

With this as background, attention is now focused on the actual negotiation process, using the tools already developed. Three aspects of the process are delineated: (1) the legal framework for negotiation; (2) bargaining format and procedures; and (3) the negotiation process.

LEGAL FRAMEWORK: PRIVATE SECTOR

Central to the legal framework governing the negotiation process is the injunction that the parties must bargain in good faith, as per Sections 8(a)(5), 8(b)(3), and 8(d) of the National Labor Relations Act as amended.

As defined by Section 8(d), this requirement means:

> (d) For the purposes of this section, to bargain collectively is the performance of the mutual obligation of the employer and the representative of the employees to meet at reasonable times and confer in good faith with respect to wages, hours, and other terms and conditions of employment, or the negotiation of an agreement, or any question arising thereunder, and the execu-

tion of a written contract incorporating any agreement reached if requested by either party, but such obligation does not compel either party to agree to a proposal or require the making of a concession: Provided, That where there is in effect a collective-bargaining contract covering employees in an industry affecting commerce, the duty to bargain collectively shall also mean that no party to such contract shall terminate or modify such contract, unless the party desiring such termination or modification—

(1) serves a written notice upon the other party to the contract of the proposed termination or modification sixty days prior to the expiration date thereof, or in the event such contract contains no expiration date, sixty days prior to the time it is proposed to make such termination or modification;

(2) offers to meet and confer with the other party for the purpose of negotiating a new contract or a contract containing the proposed modifications;

(3) notifies the Federal Mediation and Conciliation Service within thirty days after such notice of the existence of a dispute, and simultaneously therewith notifies any State or Territorial agency established to mediate and conciliate disputes within the State or Territory where the dispute occurred, provided no agreement has been reached by that time; and

(4) continues in full force and effect, without resorting to strike or lockout, all the terms and conditions of the existing contract for a period of sixty days after such notice is given or until the expiration date of such contract, whichever occurs later.

Since the passage of the Taft-Hartley Act in 1947, there has been no major federal legislation that affects bargaining in good faith; rather, it has been up to the National Labor Relations Board and the courts to interpret the meaning of the law and decide when an employer or employees' representative has acted in good or bad faith. However, neither the board nor the courts have spelled out in precise language the criteria they use for this determination. Instead, there is a large body of decisions rendered over the years that collectively identify some informal guidelines. It must quickly be added, however, that a very large grey area has cropped up as the result of court and board interpretations.

Generally, the courts and the board have established that the totality of bargaining is taken into consideration when determining good faith. In other words, one violation or one charge of an unfair labor practice will not necessarily constitute a refusal to bargain, but a series of charges or violations might. Based on decisions to date, it is usually the employer upon whom rests the burden of proof. He is the one who most frequently has to justify good-faith intentions.

As interpreted by the NLRB and the courts, determining a violation of Section 8(d), good-faith bargaining, includes consideration of the following types of bargaining behavior:

1. *Surface Bargaining.* This involves merely going through the motions of bargaining, without any real intent of completing a formal agreement.
2. *Concessions.* Even though Section 8(d) does not require the making of a concession, the court and board definitions of good faith suggest that willingness to compromise is an essential ingredient.
3. *Proposals and Demands.* The board will consider the advancement of proposals as a factor in determining overall good faith.
4. *Dilatory Tactics.* The law requires that the parties meet and "confer at reasonable times and intervals." Obviously, refusal to meet at all with the union does not satisfy the positive duty imposed on the employer.
5. *Imposing Conditions.* Attempts to impose conditions that are so onerous or unreasonable as to indicate bad faith will be scrutinized by the board.
6. *Unilateral Changes in Conditions.* This is viewed as a strong indication that the employer is not bargaining with the required intent of reaching an agreement.
7. *Bypassing the Representative.* An employer violates his duty to bargain when he refuses to negotiate with the union representative. The duty of management to bargain in good faith involves, at a minimum, recognition that the statutory representative is the one with whom the employer must deal in conducting bargaining negotiations.
8. *Commission of Unfair Labor Practices during Negotiations.* Such action may reflect upon the good faith of the guilty party.
9. *Providing Information.* Information must be supplied to the union, upon request, to enable it to understand and intelligently discuss the issues raised in bargaining.
10. *Bargaining Items.* Refusal to bargain on a mandatory item or insistence on a permissive item to an impasse is usually viewed as bad-faith bargaining.[1]

LEGAL FRAMEWORK: FEDERAL SECTOR

Under Section 7101, Findings and Purpose, CSRA 1978, Title VII, Congress finds that "labor organizations and collective bargaining in the civil service are in the public interest." Collective bargaining is viewed in Section 7103(a)(12) as:

> . . . *performance of the mutual obligation of the representative of an agency and the exclusive representative of em-*

[1]Adapted from Charles J. Morris, ed., *The Developing Labor Law* (Washington, D.C.: Bureau of National Affairs, Inc., 1971), pp. 271–310.

*ployees in an appropriate unit in the agency to meet at reason-
able times and to consult and bargain in a good-faith effort to
reach agreement with respect to the conditions of employment
affecting such employees and to execute, if requested by either
party, a written document incorporating any collective bargaining agreement reached, but the obligation referred to in this
paragraph does not compel either party to agree to a proposal or
to make a concession.*

Section 7103(a)(14) defines "conditions of employment" as "personnel policies, practices, and matters, whether established by rule, regulation, or otherwise."

Section 7114(b) (1) to (5) spells out congressional intent as to the
meaning of the phrase "to negotiate in good faith":

*The duty of an agency and an exclusive representative to
negotiate in good faith under subsection (A) of this section shall
include the obligation—*

(1) to approach the negotiations with a sincere resolve to reach
a collective bargaining agreement;

(2) to be represented at the negotiations by duly authorized
representatives prepared to discuss and negotiate on any
condition of employment;

(3) to meet at reasonable times and convenient places as frequently as may be necessary, and to avoid unnecessary
delays;

(4) in the case of an agency, to furnish to the exclusive representative involved, or its authorized representative, upon
request and, to the extent not prohibited by law, data—

(A) which is normally maintained by the agency in the
regular course of business;

(B) which is reasonably available and necessary for full
and proper discussion, understanding, and negotiation of subjects within the scope of collective bargaining; and

(C) which does not constitute guidance, advice, counsel,
or training provided for management officials or supervisors, relating to collective bargaining; and

(5) if agreement is reached, to execute on the request of any
party to the negotiation a written document embodying the
agreed terms, and to take such steps as are necessary to
implement such agreement.

Section 7116(a)(5) and (b)(5) declare that it is an unfair labor practice
for an agency or a labor organization to refuse to negotiate in good faith
with the other party. This means that it is an unfair labor practice for
either party to refuse to bargain over conditions of employment as defined
by the statute. The scope of the phrase "conditions of employment" is
narrowed by some statutory exceptions. Excepted by Section 7103(a)(14)

from the obligation to bargain are subjects such as political activity, classification of any position, and matters specifically provided for by federal statute. Section 7106(a) also proscribes certain subject areas from mandatory negotiation, placing them under the unilateral control of management but leaving it to the unilateral election of the employer, under Section 7106(b), to negotiate on certain of these proscribed areas if the employer so desires. As noted in Chapter 3, reserving certain subject areas by statute as management rights or under the exclusive control of the employer differs sharply from the private sector, where management rights appear in the contract only if management is able to insert such rights through negotiation. Section 7106(a) and (b) read:

(a) Subject to subsection (b) of this section, nothing in this chapter shall affect the authority of any management official of any agency—

    (1) to determine the mission, budget, organization, number of employees, and internal security practices of the agency; and

    (2) in accordance with applicable laws—

        (A) to hire, assign, direct, layoff, and retain employees in the agency, or to suspend, remove, reduce in grade or pay, or take other disciplinary action against such employees;

        (B) to assign work, to make determinations with respect to contracting out, and to determine the personnel by which agency operations shall be conducted;

        (C) with respect to filling positions, to make selections for appointments from—

            (i) among properly ranked and certified candidates for promotion; or

            (ii) any other appropriate source; and

        (D) to take whatever actions may be necessary to carry out the agency mission during emergencies.

(b) Nothing in this section shall preclude any agency and any labor organization from negotiating—

    (1) at the election of the agency, on the numbers, types, and grades of employees or positions assigned to any organizational subdivision, work project, or tour of duty, or on the technology, methods, and means of performing work;

    (2) procedures which management officials of the agency will observe in exercising any authority under this section; or

    (3) appropriate arrangements for employees adversely affected by the exercise of any authority under this section by such management officials.

Finally, in determining what agency rules and regulations are to fall under the phrase "bargaining in good faith over conditions of employment," Section 7117 of CSRA 1978, Title VII, applies the criterion of "compelling need." Governmentwide rules or regulations are automatically ruled out as bargainable subjects. However, rules or regulations at the agency level or at the primary national subdivision level of an agency, to the extent they are not inconsistent with federal law or any governmentwide rule or regulation, shall be subject to the bargaining-in-good-faith requirement of the statute if the Federal Labor Relations Authority rules "that no compelling need (as determined under regulations prescribed by the Authority) exists for the rule or regulation." The purpose behind the amendment was to remove unnecessary constriction of "meaningful negotiations at the local level on personnel policies and practices and matters affecting working conditions," to "permit a wider scope of negotiations," and to avoid the issuance of "overprescriptive" higher-level agency regulations that are "not critical to effective agency management or the public interest."[2]

BARGAINING FORMAT AND PROCEDURES

There is no foolproof prescription for the procedure a party should follow in negotiations. The choice of procedure needs to be flexible to fit the bargaining situation. Moreover, it should be recognized that procedure is a negotiable item. Each party in successive negotiations tends to develop its own particular approach and pattern of bargaining. Some guidelines might be suggested from bargaining experience, but only in a very general sense if flexibility is to be maintained.

The first step beyond the preparatory work of establishing bargaining items, priorities, and objectives (columns 1 through 5 of the objectives approach) is the presentation of the initial bargaining positions of the parties. This is a visible step, as stated before (column 6). The step may be accomplished at a prenegotiation session or as a part of the first stage of the negotiation process. The parties' presentation or exchange of positions through demand and counteroffer or response brings into focus, pinpoints, and completes the list of bargaining items to be negotiated (column 1). It has been customary for the union to take the initiative by presenting to the company its proposal for changes in the contract. It must be emphasized that this is not a legal requirement. There is nothing to prevent the employer from taking the initiative and making the first move. Whether an employer should or should not do this depends upon the

---

[2]*Labor-Management Relations in the Federal Service* (Washington, D.C.: U.S. Federal Labor Relations Council, 1975), p. 38.

particular strategy the employer chooses to follow. The union presentation may be formal or informal, in detailed language, or by bargaining items only. This is followed by a company response or counteroffer in which the company, at its option, may make a formal counteroffer, respond in general to the union, and demand and/or make proposals of its own in addition to the bargaining items raised by the union.

At this point, the parties *must* be sure that the bargaining priorities and objectives on each negotiation item are fully firmed up in their own minds *before* actual negotiations begin.

Also, as noted in Chapter 14, prenegotiation meetings should establish rules and procedures for the negotiations, time and place of meetings, length of meetings, rules concerning conduct of meetings, and, last but certainly not least, the order of presentation of the bargaining items, procedures in dealing with each item, method of approval of items, and other matters of purely procedural nature. These are negotiable matters. At this stage in the bargaining it is also important that the parties reach an understanding as to whether additional bargaining items may be introduced during the negotiations, except by joint agreement. As a matter of practical necessity, not of law, the parties have usually followed the practice of not allowing new items to be introduced during the negotiations unless both parties agree. This is to avoid the chaos and disruption to negotiations that such a practice might create.

NEGOTIATING

Once the bargaining items to be considered have been established and procedural guidelines have been agreed upon, the parties are ready for the actual negotiations. As long as the negotiations fall within the sixty-day notice period, the parties in the private sector must "continue in full force and effect, without resorting to strike and lock-out, all the terms and conditions of the existing contract. . . ."[3] In the public sector, the same status quo is effected by CSRA 1978, Title VII, Section 6116(b), enjoining the labor organization from calling or engaging in a strike, work stoppage, slowdown, or picketing of an agency in a labor-management dispute. Although state public-employee statutes are not so explicit about notice periods, they do, in effect, accomplish the same result. Most of the states with such statutes prohibit strikes, and those with a limited right to strike have alternative impasse procedures that delay strike action while efforts are made to settle the dispute.

The actual process during the weeks or months from start of negotiations to ultimate resolution, signified by a signed agreement, varies con-

[3]NLRA, Sec. 8(d)(4).

siderably in detail and in the emotional level at which it is conducted. The differences in the negotiation process are products of the personalities of those involved, the labor-management situation at the outset of negotiations, outside events, bargaining techniques and strategy followed, and the relative power positions of the parties. However, most negotiations have the following common elements: (1) a settling-in stage, (2) a consolidation stage, (3) a finalization stage, and (4) a mopping-up stage.

Settling-in Stage   During the initial phases of the negotiations, the parties do a great deal of jockeying for position, acquainting themselves with the issues, and testing out the bargaining climate. All this is done without either party's committing itself too far until it fixes on the other party's position. Quite often, this involves discussing the items, with only minor commitments forthcoming, frequent caucusing to assess and analyze moves being contemplated, and a general tightening up on support for positions.

Consolidation Stage   From the first stage, the parties then move to more detailed discussion of items, some agreements and trade-offs on items of lesser priority to both parties (mainly noneconomic items), and the beginning moves toward packaging economic or financial items. Again, one witnesses joint discussions at the bargaining table, parties caucusing on items under discussion, meeting together again to further move toward agreement, further caucusing, and finally agreement and sign-off of items or setting items aside for later consideration.

Finalization Stage   In this stage, the range of negotiation items has been significantly reduced, fewer but higher-priority items are being dealt with, the parties settle in to harder bargaining, the feeling of impending impasse or final settlement is much more pervasive, and packaging the remaining items becomes more and more dominant. It is also at this point that the parties begin to opt for other types of pressure or intervention in order to effect a final settlement and avoid an impasse. It is in this stage that a union may (although there is an increasing tendency not to do so) threaten a strike deadline. It is also at this stage that a federal mediator or other outside intervention may be called in or, if the situation is governed by statutes, be called upon to head off any sort of work stoppage (by mediation, fact-finding, arbitration).

Although strikes do take place during negotiations, and even though crisis bargaining is still in evidence in many situations, the whole climate of collective bargaining seems to be changing with regard to these types of bargaining and bargaining pressures. More and more, the parties are seeing the futility of the strike except in very special circumstances and are moving to alternative approaches such as early bargaining, joint study committees, mediation-arbitration, and voluntary arbitration of unresolved issues (see Part IV). More and more, the statutory procedures are looking to alternative ways of resolving conflict without resort to the strike. Although there is an element of compulsion in the statutory procedures, the intent seems to be not compulsion, but a real desire to find viable alternatives to work stoppages. Except in instances of danger to health, safety, or national welfare, all these alternatives are aimed not at denying the *right* to strike, but at reducing or eliminating the *need* to strike.

Mopping-up Stage The agreement has been reached. The parties heave a big sigh of relief. The frustrations and the tedious time-consuming work of negotiation are over. Yet, the work is not completely over if the parties want to be spared grief in the coming months during which they will be living under the agreement. The final stage is to be sure that what they have agreed upon is put in language that conveys the intent of their agreement on each bargaining item and will not elicit grievances because of its sloppy construction.[4]

CONDUCT OF NEGOTIATIONS

The conduct of the actual negotiations by either party is certainly enhanced and firmed up by the objectives approach described earlier. The negotiator, through this methodology, is provided with a positive and known framework within which to develop strategy and techniques. However, there is no single formula or guide from which the negotiator may draw, other than experience and observation, that tells him what to do in each specific situation. The negotiator is required to be at one and the same time a poker player; a master at timing; an expert at divining the other party's intent and visualizing his own moves far ahead; a master at persuading and, where needed, applying pressure; and finally, a professional in labor relations who sees the consequences of what happens at the bargaining table in both the legal sense and the labor relations sense. In short, collective bargaining has evolved from the older, table-pounding trial of economic strength into both an art and a profession. The effective negotiator is indeed a professional in his field.

Even experience cannot guarantee that a basically inept person will do a good job. But for the individual who has the potential of developing the personal qualities of a good negotiator, experience can mean the difference between success and lack of success. In the meantime, the negotiator should be wary of neatly capsulized packages or formulas on strategy and tactics supposedly guaranteeing success at the bargaining table. The human factor in negotiating, complicated by all other factors affecting the situation, is too variable to lend itself to such neat packaging.

---

[4]LeRoy Marceau, *Drafting a Union Contract* (Boston: Little, Brown, 1965). Drafting the language of the contract is one of the most crucial parts of negotiation and should never be relegated to a secondary position out of relief that an agreement has been reached.

This is the reason for the emphasis in this book on proper preparation as the foundation for developing strategies. This is a stable factor, having the value to successful negotiation and strategy development of remaining constant from one bargaining situation to another. The use of specific strategies, the subject of many publications on the art of bargaining and bargaining tactics, must be approached with caution and good judgment during actual bargaining. Acknowledging the value of high-quality books such as Walton and McKersie's *A Behavioral Theory of Labor Negotiations*, Yoder and Staudohar say:

> This text is highly recommended for its many worthwhile illustrations of how to use strategy and tactics effectively in a variety of circumstances. There is no such thing as a "cook-book" approach or "magic formula" to being an effective negotiator, but this text is one of the best available guides.[5]

The best advice to negotiators must be cautionary in nature. Such advice, when bolstered by experience and guided or strengthened by the systematic and logical approach to bargaining suggested herein, is the best assurance that the negotiator, inexperienced or experienced, will be doing the best job for his party that he can, under the conditions within which he must operate. Perhaps the best way to describe these cautionary bits of advice is to call them "bargaining homilies."

BARGAINING HOMILIES

- Be sure that you have set *clear objectives* on every bargaining item and that you understand on what ground the objectives were established.
- *Do not hurry.*
- When in doubt, *caucus.*
- Be *well prepared* with firm data support for clearly identified objectives.
- Always strive to keep some flexibility in your position—don't get yourself out on a limb.
- Do not concern yourself with only what the other party says and does— *find out why.* Remember that economic motivation is not the only explanation for the other party's conduct and actions.
- Respect the importance of *face saving* for the other party.
- Constantly be alert to the *real intents* of the other party—with respect not only to goals, but also to priorities.
- Be a good *listener.*
- Build a reputation for being *fair* but *firm.*

---

[5]Dale Yoder and Paul D. Staudohar, *Personnel Management and Industrial Relations,* 7th ed. (Englewood Cliffs, N.J.: Prentice-Hall, 1982), p. 479. (Emphasis added.)

- Learn to control your *emotions*—don't panic. Use emotions as a tool, not an obstacle.
- Be sure as you make each bargaining move that you know its *relationship* to all other moves.
- *Measure each move* against your *objectives.*
- Pay close attention to the *wording* of every clause negotiated; words and phrases are often the source of grievances.
- Remember that collective bargaining negotiations are by their very nature part of a *compromise* process. There is no such thing as having all the pie.
- Learn to *understand* people and their personalities—it may mean a payoff during negotiations.
- Consider the *impact of present negotiations* on negotiations in *future* years.

EVALUATION OF BARGAINING RESULTS

The last columns (7, 8, and 9) of the bargaining by objectives form provide a systematic way of evaluating bargaining experience.

For each bargaining item indicated in the appropriate column—P (pessimistic), R (realistic), or O (optimistic)—the final settlement is compared to the original bargaining objective established for that item. If the settlement achieved was the realistic one, then check column 8; if optimistic, check column 9; if pessimistic, check column 7. Form 15-1 is an example of an employer's objectives and results. Based on its own objectives, the union would probably come up with a different picture of results when checking columns 7, 8, and 9. It should be noted that on some items settled at the realistic level, the results might be the same for both parties if they had established identical realistic objectives originally.

Next, for each item determine why the end result was P, R, or O. If on a particular item the optimistic objective was achieved, what happened during negotiations to bring about such a result? Analysis of bargaining results at the R and P levels for any particular item should also be carried through the same procedure. From this exercise, the party should be able to determine the kinds of strategies and tactics that proved successful in negotiations and those that did not. Notes should be taken to serve as a basis for doing a better job at the next negotiations. Furthermore, if the analysis is accomplished immediately after the negotiations have concluded and while recall is still at a maximum, the benefits to be derived by the party will be much greater and more useful when negotiation ensues.

As a spinoff from using the objectives approach, this final comparison of bargaining results to bargaining objectives can, if used with care, serve as a basis for a rewards system for successful negotiators.

FORM 15-1
Collective Bargaining by Objectives
A Guide for Systematic Data Preparation and Planning Negotiations

BARGAINING ITEMS*	PRIORITIES**	RANGE OF BARGAINING OBJECTIVES			Initial Bargaining Position	EVALUATION RESULTS		
		Pessimistic	Realistic	Optimistic		P	R	O
(Financial Items)								
Holidays	5	1 Floating 1 Birthday Cost: $.10/hour	1 Floating Cost: $.05/hour	No Change	No Change		X	
Wages	1	8% Cost: $.84/hour	6.5% Cost: $.67/hour	Cost: 0 5%	3% Cost: $.30/hour		X	X
Insurance	2	100% paid by company $100 deductible Cost: $.125/hour	Employee Pay: Single $5.45 Single + 1 $6.93 Family $8.76 Cost: $.11/hour	Employee Pay: Single $5.76 Single + 1 $7.32 Family $9.73 Cost: $.105/hour	Employee Pay: Single $6.06 Single + 1 $7.70 Family $10.24 Cost: $.10/hour			X
(Nonfinancial Items)								
Union Security	2	Union Shop	Modified Union Shop	Agency Shop	Agency Shop	X		
Probationary Period	8	30 days	60 days	90 days	120 days		X	
Arbitrator Cost	6	Employer Pay 60/40	Split Costs 50/50	Loser Pay 60/40	Loser Pay			X

*Classify items in two groups: financial and nonfinancial
**Relative priority of each bargaining item to all other bargaining items

THE CBO SYSTEM: PREPARING FOR NEGOTIATIONS

The negotiations are completed. A new agreement is signed. The period of application or contract administration is initiated. At the same time, the period of preparing for the next negotiations begins. The record of the negotiations just completed is one of the sources for bargaining information. Chapter 7, "Gathering and Assembling Bargaining Information," describes the process of preparing for negotiations that goes on from contract to contract. It *is* an ongoing process—preparing for negotiations, negotiating an agreement, and then returning to the preparations for the next negotiations.

SELECTED REFERENCES

Atherton, Wallace N., *Theory of Union Bargaining Goals.* Princeton, N.J.: Princeton University Press, 1973. As the author indicates, this book is not about bargaining theory. It is concerned with the union's application of theory to the formulation of goals, which it will then try to achieve "by bargaining with and putting economic pressure on the employer." The author treats the contributions of such writers as Reder, Berkowitz, Dunlop, Fellner, Carter, Ross, Mason, and Higgins and then proceeds to treat two elements: (1) the role of expected strike lengths as determinants of a union's goals, and (2) the task a union faces in trying to find a compromise sufficiently satisfactory to all or most of its members to keep the union together.

Bacharach, Samuel B., and Edward J. Lawler, *Bargaining—Power, Tactics, and Outcomes.* San Francisco, Calif.: Jossey-Bass Publishers, 1981. The authors assert that "For too long bargaining theory has neglected or assumed away the calculative thought pattern of actors in bargaining." The authors in this volume treat bargaining actors as conscious decision makers who think, and act accordingly, about what they are doing.

Bartos, Otomar J., *Process and Outcome of Negotiations.* New York: Columbia University Press, 1974. The author states that the purpose of the book is to describe, justify, and test various theories of negotiation. Although labor-management relations are included, the negotiation process is viewed in a broader setting. The author first looks at some theories and hypotheses of negotiation and then experiments in negotiation. He then proceeds to the process of negotiation (models and tests of models) and the strategic aspects of negotiation (models of outcome, tests of the models, and toughness and outcome). Finally, he moves to a comprehensive view of negotiation and notes that any such model should be future-oriented as well as past-oriented—i.e., the model should not only provide a base from which to predict what negotiators will do but also advise them what they ought to do. He concludes that because it is impossible to build a symmetric model of negotiation, it is also impossible to build a faultless normative model.

Bent, Alan Edward, and T. Zane Reeves, *Collective Bargaining in the Public Sector.* Menlo Park, Calif.: The Benjamin/Cummings Publishing Company,

1978. Considerable emphasis is given by the authors to the unique features of public-sector collective bargaining.

Burtt, Everett Johnson, Jr., *Labor Markets, Unions, and Government Policies.* New York: St. Martin's Press, 1963. Brief but good coverage of the traditional views of economists over the years with respect to wage determination. These views include the subsistence theory, wage-fund theory, marginal-productivity theory, Marshall's emphasis upon the general interdependence of supply and demand forces, bargaining theories, and modern theories of wage determination that approach influencing factors such as macro and micro, long and short run, and market structures in a much more sophisticated manner.

Chamberlain, Neil W., *Collective Bargaining,* 2nd ed., New York: McGraw-Hill, 1965. In Chapter 6, Chamberlain reduces the nature of the bargaining process to three basic theoretical types: (1) the marketing theory, (2) the government theory, and (3) the managerial theory. Chapter 10 contains an excellent examination of the meaning and the role of bargaining power in determining negotiation results. Chamberlain discusses bargaining power from the standpoint of both the union's ability to cause disagreement to be costly to the employer and the employer's ability to cause disagreement to be costly to the union. In the process, he examines the contributions of such stalwarts as Pigou, Commons, Simons, Slichter, Dunlop, Lindblom, and Hicks, but the main contribution of Chapter 10 is Chamberlain's own penetrating analysis of the facts and fallacies of bargaining power. Indeed, he points out that bargaining power is not always measured in terms of the cost it imposes on the other party; it may also be viewed in terms of reducing the cost to the other party of agreeing with the first party.

Cross, John G., *The Economics of Bargaining.* New York: Basic Books, 1969. Believing that intensive work must be done in many allied disciplines individually before the "theory of bargaining" emerges, Cross makes it clear in his title that he is concerned only with the economic aspects of bargaining. The basic premise of the author is that it is possible to treat the bargaining process in terms of economic variables and to come out with a determinate and useful theory.

Davey, Harold W., Mario F. Bognanno, and David L. Estenson, *Contemporary Collective Bargaining,* 4th ed., Englewood Cliffs, N.J.: Prentice-Hall, 1982. There is an excellent treatment of contract negotiation in Chapter 5, "Contract Negotiation: Principles, Problems, and Procedures."

de Menil, George, *Bargaining: Monopoly Power versus Union Power.* Cambridge, Mass.: M.I.T. Press, 1971. The author points out that markets that do not fit the standard economic models are difficult subjects for economic analysis. The labor market is a case in point. The purpose of the book is to develop a bargaining theory of wage determination. The author discusses other bargaining theories and chooses the Nash model for development of his own theory.

Dunlop, John T., *Industrial Relations Systems.* New York: Holt, Rinehart & Winston, 1958. A must for any reader interested in delving more deeply into industrial relations theory. Dunlop is concerned with a theoretical construct for industrial relations systems. All industrial relations systems have certain common properties and structures and respond to specified influences.

Fischer, Harry C., *The Uses of Accounting in Collective Bargaining.* Institute of Industrial Relations, University of California, Los Angeles, 1969. Rightfully, the author points out the importance of accounting to negotiations, where so much of the subject matter is concerned with cost items. The author notes that language in which the employer's ability to pay is expressed is in accounting terms. This pamphlet is intended as an introduction to that language.

Fossum, John A., *Labor Relations.* Dallas, Tex.: Business Publications, Inc., 1982. Chapter 9 discusses bargaining theory. Chapter 10 addresses bargaining tactics and bargaining on specific issues.

Gilroy, Thomas P., et al., *Educator's Guide to Collective Negotiations.* Columbus, Ohio: Charles E. Merrill, 1969. The authors have directed this book to the needs of the local school district and the parties involved in negotiation sessions. It provides a good background and some down-to-earth information about the process of negotiation in education.

Heneman, H. G., Jr., and Dale Yoder, *Labor Economics.* Cincinnati, Ohio: South-Western Publishing, 1965), pp. 628–34. Yoder and Heneman summarize current collective bargaining theory: identification of ranges or bands of possible compromise, union and employer preference functions, and schedules that reflect the comparative costs of agreement and disagreement.

Herman, E. Edward, and Alfred Kuhn, *Collective Bargaining and Labor Relations.* Englewood Cliffs, N.J.: Prentice-Hall, 1981. As they note in the Preface, the authors are concerned with the lack of emphasis, in other texts, on power, bargaining power, negotiating, and the strike. These areas are given in-depth coverage in this book. Part V is concerned with bargaining power, negotiations, and impasses.

Hilgert, Raymond L., and Sterling H. Schoen, *Labor Agreement Negotiations.* Cincinnati, Ohio: South-Western Publishing, 1982. The authors, through the use of simulation, put students behind the bargaining table and enable them to experience the negotiation process firsthand. Participants set objectives and then try to attain the objectives at the bargaining table. Because it is self-contained, the simulation adds another negotiation game that can be used with Collective Bargaining by Objectives.

Karrass, Chester L., *Give and Take: The Complete Guide to Negotiating Strategies and Tactics.* New York: Thomas Y. Crowell, 1974. The author includes 200 strategies and tactics as a guide to negotiation. He notes that this is the first complete guide to practical negotiating strategies, tactics, and countermeasures. As director of the Center for Effective Negotiating, the author responds to what he considers is the most frequently asked question: "What works at the table?"

Knee, Robert C., and Robert C. Knee, Jr., *Collective Bargaining Clauses.* Cincinnati, Ohio: W. H. Anderson, 1975. The authors provide a practical guide to the negotiator by their selection of clauses that they feel are either standard or realistic approaches to the area of negotiations.

Kochan, Thomas A., and Hoyt N. Wheeler, "Municipal Collective Bargaining: A Model and Analysis of Bargaining Outcomes," *Industrial and Labor Relations Review,* 29, no. 1 (October 1975), 46–66. Kochan and Wheeler report on the result of an attempt to formulate and operate a model of collective bargaining outcomes.

Levin, Noel Arnold, *Successful Labor Relations—An Employer's Guide.* New York: Fairchild Publications, 1967. David Cole's comment in the introduction epitomizes the reason for including this book. Cole states, "Arnold Levin is realistic and rational, and his book reflects this. While he has good practical advice for management representatives, he does not neglect the philosophical

and long-range implications and objectives." Written as advice for management, the author's excellent coverage of the negotiation process and his practical suggestions can also be used by unions.

Mabry, Bevars D., *Labor Relations and Collective Bargaining.* New York: Ronald
Press, 1966. Professor Mabry includes an information treatment of the theory
of collective bargaining in Part II. He touches not only on the nature of collective bargaining but also on the pure theory of bargaining, bargaining models,
and the economics of bargaining at both the micro and macro levels.

McClean, Alan A., "Personnel Policy Formulation and Psychiatry," *Reprint Series*
No. 129, Ithaca, N.Y.: New York State School of Industrial and Labor Relations, 1962. Collective bargaining, according to the psychiatrists, involves
demands that may symbolize needs quite different from their apparent mean-
ings or dobjectives.

McGregor, Douglas, *The Professional Manager,* pp. 186–87. New York: McGraw-
Hill, 1967. McGregor advances a synthesized behavioral-science approach to
collective bargaining theory. He outlines three possible strategies for dealing
with conflict: "divide and rule," "the suppression of differences," and "the
working through of differences."

McMahon, Edward J., "The Negotiation Process," in *Dealing with a Union,*
LeRoy Marceau. New York: American Management Association, Inc., 1969.
An informative discussion of the steps and strategies of the negotiation
process.

Marceau, LeRoy, *Drafting a Union Contract.* Boston: Little, Brown, 1965. The
author properly notes that there are many books written about ways to facilitate agreements but a real dearth of information on how to draft a union
contract properly. Marceau notes that the function of the draftsman is to
"prevent rather than to resolve labor disputes." This book offers an excellent
step-by-step approach to drafting the contract.

Marshall, Howard D., and Natalie J. Marshall, *Collective Bargaining.* New
York: Random House, 1971. A thorough study in Chapter 5 of the strategies of
collective bargaining.

Marting, Elizabeth, ed., "At the Bargaining Table," in *Understanding Collective
Bargaining,* Part III. New York: American Management Association, Inc.,
1958. Excellent down-to-earth discussion of the techniques of bargaining, pit-
falls for the unwary, blueprint for the bargaining sessions, and how to handle
crisis bargaining.

Morely, Ian, and Geoggrey Stephenson, *The Social Psychology of Bargaining,*
London, England: George Allen & Unwin, 1977. This book deals with some of
the social and psychological factors influencing negotiation for agreement.
The authors are concerned with structure in the process of bargaining.

Morris, Charles J., ed., *The Developing Labor Law,* 2nd ed., Washington, D.C.:
Bureau of National Affairs, Inc., 1983. Chapter 11 provides a complete examination of the injunction of the NLRA that the parties have a duty to bargain in
good faith. The explanation is in terms of both the evolution of the good-faith
bargaining concept and the current state of the law with respect to indicia of
good- and bad-faith bargaining.

Morse, Bruce, *How to Negotiate the Labor Agreement,* 9th ed., Detroit: Trends
Publishing Co., 1981. Morse provides brief (83 pages) and practical advice on
preparing for bargaining, organizing negotiations, and conducting
negotiations.

Neal, Richard G., *Negotiations Strategies, A Reference Manual for Public Sector Negotiations.* Perrysburg, Ohio: Richard Neal Associates, 1981.

———, *Bargaining Tactis,* Vols. 1 and 2, 1983. Carefully constructed and organized. The author takes a realistic approach to the use of tactics and strategies, noting that the tactics and strategies discussed in the three manuals have to be used with good judgment and in the proper setting. A wealth of advice in the use of strategy and tactics in the applied sense may be found within the covers of these manuals.

Peters, Edward, *Strategy and Tactics in Labor Negotiations,* 3rd ed. Swarthmore, Pa.: Personnel Journal, 1966. One would be hard put not to recommend the entire book, it is so full of on-the-firing-line types of information from an experienced practitioner. For the actual negotiations, the reader is referred to the chapters on "Collective Bargaining: A Science or an Art?"; "The Essential Nature and Purpose of Negotiations"; "From Bargaining Position to Final Offer"; "Prestige, Power, and Paternalism"; "Sign Language"; "Settlement"; "Bargaining in Good Faith"; and "Strike Negotiations."

Prentice-Hall Industrial Relations Guide. Englewood Cliffs, N.J.: Prentice-Hall, Inc. This service of Prentice-Hall offers a complete guide that is updated continually and provides vital information to the negotiator or IR representative on arbitration awards, union contract clauses, useful information concerning negotiating a contract, and new developments in the field.

Prentice-Hall Editorial Staff, *Manual for Drafting Union Contracts.* Englewood Cliffs, N.J.: Prentice-Hall, 1968. Prentice-Hall fulfills a vital need with this handy guide to drafting a union contract. Not only is the importance of a carefully written contract emphasized, but Prentice-Hall takes the reader step by step through the areas of the contract, such as union recognition and parties, union security and representation, grievance, arbitration and strikes, wages and working time, seniority, and working conditions and benefits.

Raiffa, Howard, *The Art and Science of Negotiation.* Cambridge, Mass.: The Belknap Press of Harvard University Press, 1982. With his disciplinary roots in mathematical analysis and game theory, and his extensive teaching experience in the Harvard Graduate School of Business Administration in competitive decision making, the author was in a natural position to apply his analytical skills to the process of negotiation and to translate this in-depth understanding of the negotiation process into "practical guidelines for negotiators and 'intervenors'." Raiffa avers that there is an art and a science of negotiation and that blending the practical side of negotiating with simple mathematical analysis can be to the advantage of disputants and intervenors alike. Raiffa addresses negotiating in all contexts through an extensive use of specific cases.

Repas, Bob F., *Collective Bargaining in Federal Employment,* 2nd ed. Industrial Relations Center, University of Hawaii, Honolulu, August 1973. The publication was especially crafted for the use of the union that seeks recognition and subsequent negotiation of an agreement with an agency of the federal government. Repas includes a wealth of information plus practical advice to the prospective negotiator.

Rothenberg, Herbert, and Steven B. Silverman, *Labor Unions—How To: Avert Them, Beat Them, Out-Negotiate Them, Live with Them, Unload Them.* Elkins Park, Pa.: Management Relations, Inc., 1973. The authors, whose days are fully occupied representing the interests of management in their labor relations problems, make no apology for the title of their book. It is frankly written out of an impatience of the authors, both attorneys, with the attitude of many firms of "not rocking the boat" and of "quiet surrender and acceptance" in their dealings with labor organizations. In their own words, the scope and the purpose of the book "is to demonstrate not only that it is possible to successfully stand up against a labor union, but how to avoid those mistakes and miscalculations which frequently result in the employer's loss of a dispute which could otherwise have been won."

Somers, Gerald G., ed., *Essays in Industrial Relations Theory.* Ames: Iowa State University Press, 1969. Professor Somers sums up the approach of the book by noting that each chapter is directed to a significant theoretical aspect of the industrial relations field, and the combination of all the chapters contributes to the development of the conceptual framework envisaged by the industrial relations theoreticians.

Stevens, Carl M., *Strategy and Collective Bargaining Negotiation.* New York: McGraw-Hill, 1963. A volume that significantly contributes to collective bargaining literature by applying theoretical tools to the negotiation process. Provides a way to interpret the strategy of the parties and their tactics at all stages of the contract negotiation process.

Summers, Clyde W., "Ratification of Agreements," in *Frontiers of Collective Bargaining,* eds. John T. Dunlop and Neil W. Chamberlain. New York: Harper & Row, 1967. A thorough discussion of the function and problems of ratification of the agreement.

Thompson, Arthur A., and Irwin Weinstock, "Facing the Crisis in Collective Bargaining," *MSU Business Topics,* 16, no. 3 (Summer 1968), 37–43. Thompson and Weinstock have developed a model of employer and union strategies in which employers follow the McGregor Theory Y and union representatives are Theory-X-oriented.

Walton, Richard E., and Robert B. McKersie, *A Behavioral Theory of Labor Negotiations.* New York: McGraw-Hill, 1967. The authors are concerned in this book about labor negotiations in particular and social negotiations in general. Four sets of activities are identified that the authors believe account for almost all the behavior in negotiations and constitute the framework for their theory of labor negotiations. The activities identified are called "distributive bargaining," "integrative bargaining," "attitudinal structuring," and "intraorganizational bargaining."

Weisberger, June, *Examples of Language and Interpretation in Public Sector Collective Bargaining Agreements: A Guide for Public Officials and Other Interested Parties.* IPE Monograph no. 3. Institute of Public Employment, Ithaca, N.Y.: New York State School of Industrial and Labor Relations, February 1975. The author has brought together some useful information. The title is self-explanatory.

PART III

COLLECTIVE BARGAINING PROCESS: Contract Administration

Finally, we see the whole machinery for collective bargaining seriously hampered, except in two or three trades, by the failure to make the vital distinction between interpreting an existing wage contract, and negotiating the terms upon which a new general agreement should be entered into.

Sidney and Beatrice Webb, *Industrial Democracy* 1902

CHAPTER 16

THE GRIEVANCE

The introduction of industrial democracy to the workplace, so highly heralded by the Webbs, was the primary result of the rise of unionism and the subsequent development of collective bargaining relationships. Collective bargaining introduced a process of *joint determination of the rules* under which the employer-employee relationship would be governed. But determination of the rules alone, would have resulted in the establishment of the structure of industrial government without the viability that such government requires to be fully effective on a day-by-day basis. Consequently, to the negotiated terms under which the parties would be governed was added a second process, more interpretive in nature: the *right to grieve* through machinery established in the collective bargaining agreement. The right to grieve created the means by which the terms negotiated could prove viable under the stresses and strains of everyday application. The point to be made, then, is that an operative type of industrial democracy between employers and employees depends not only upon jointly determined rules governing the relationship, but equally so upon *a process by which differences over the interpretations of the terms may be verbalized and jointly settled*. Without the right to grieve, the concept of industrial democracy would have been only partially realized. Supreme Court Justice Douglas stated that the grievance machinery under a collective bargaining agreement "is at the heart of the system of industrial self-government."[1]

A grievance may be broadly defined as a real or imagined wrong or cause for complaint. As used within the framework of collective bargaining contract administration, the cause for complaint requiring an adjustment between the parties is a real or imagined violation of the rights of a party—employer, employee, or union—as stipulated by the terms of the collective agreement or by past practice. The *primary focus* of the grievance process is upon the protection of the rights of the employee. However, it also provides an avenue through which either the union may grieve on its own behalf or for the bargaining-unit employees, or the employer may grieve if he feels that his rights under the agreement are being violated.

In order to give maximum exposure to the legal nature of the grievance, the sources from which grievances arise, and some types of grievances, this chapter confines itself to the grievance and nothing more. Ensuing chapters will deal with the machinery established to expedite the resolution of grievance questions.

THE GRIEVANCE: LAW AND POLICY

The right of an employee or group of employees to grieve matters related to their employment is strongly supported by both the NLRA and CSRA 1978, Title VII for private- and public-sector employees respectively. Protecting the right to grieve as a basic right, grievance procedure or no grievance procedure, is clearly enunciated.

The right of "any individual employee or a group of employees . . . to present grievances to their employers" was established first by the National Labor Relations Act of 1935.[2] While this established a legal pattern for recognition of the right to grieve, it was rather too general. It did not give enough recognition to (1) the status of the majority union as the sole representative of workers in the bargaining unit, and (2) the binding nature of the labor agreement on the employees in the bargaining unit, on the union, and on the employer. By interpretation, the National Labor Relations Board was trying to enforce both principles, but this was a poor substitute for a clear statement through the law. Congress, in the

---

[1]*Labor Arbitration Reports* (Washington, D.C.: Bureau of National Affairs, Inc., 1961), Vol. 34 LA 563.

[2]Benjamin Taylor and Fred Witney, *Labor Relations*, 4th ed., (Englewood Cliffs, N.J.: Prentice-Hall, 1983), p. 431.

Taft-Hartley amendments of 1947, attempted to make both the language and the intent of the law clear. The amendments nullified the old NLRB doctrine dealing with the presentation and adjustment of grievances and in its place established two standards for all grievance-procedure structures: (1) The individual worker must still be allowed to present his grievance on an individual basis if he so chooses. (2) The employer must be allowed to make an adjustment of a grievance so presented, provided the adjustment is not inconsistent with the terms of the collective bargaining agreement covering the bargaining unit. The second point constitutes the major shift in the old NLRB doctrine. Originally, the employer had to invite the representative of the employee to be present for both the presentation and the adjustment of the grievance. Under the Taft-Hartley amendments, the bargaining-unit representative does not have to be present during the adjustment but must be given the opportunity to be present during the proceedings. But, to reiterate, the individual employee and the employer may not agree to an adjustment of the grievance *that is not consistent with the labor agreement.*

Public-sector policy for federal employees leaves no question as to congressional intent with respect to the right of an employee to grieve when there is a collective bargaining agreement. CSRA 1978, Title VII, mandates that there shall be a procedure for the settlement of grievances with arbitration as a terminal settlement point. Section 7121(a)(1) states: "Any collective bargaining agreement shall provide procedures for the settlement of grievances, including questions of arbitrability." Moreover, with only two exceptions for alternative procedures at the option of the employee, this section also provides that "the procedures shall be the exclusive procedures for resolving grievances which fall within its coverage."

The same sort of reasoning found in the NLRA and CSRA 1978, Title VII, is carried over in the state laws with respect to the right of an employee to grieve. Most of the state laws grant the right to grieve to an employee within a bargaining unit with or without the presence of the bargaining representative. As with the NLRA and CSRA 1978, Title VII, if the employee chooses to grieve directly without using his bargaining representative, he cannot make any settlement that contravenes the labor agreement then in effect.

For example, Minnesota's Employment Relations Act provides in Section 179.65:

> Nothing . . . shall be construed to limit, impair or affect the right of any public employee or his representative to the expression or communication of a view, grievance, complaint or opinion on any matter related to the conditions or compensation of public employment.

Connecticut's Municipal Employee Relations Act, in Section 7.468(d), also provides:

> *An individual employee at any time may present a grievance to his employer and have the grievance adjusted, without intervention of an employee organization, provided the adjustment shall not be inconsistent with the terms of a collective bargaining agreement then in effect. The employee organization certified or recognized as the exclusive representative shall be given prompt notice of the adjustment.*

The important point to remember is that in both the public and private sectors, either by legislation or executive order, *the right to grieve is clearly enunciated and protected.*

THE BASIS AND NATURE OF GRIEVANCES

The situations out of which grievances arise and the nature of the grievances themselves are of such a great variety and involve such a multiplicity of considerations that they defy tabulation. They are limited only by the variety of circumstances that might arise in the employment relationship and by the real or imagined grievances arising therefrom. In order at least to give the reader some flavor for the sources and the nature of grievances, a number of broadly illustrative grievance situations are presented. Again, these examples are not exhaustive of all grievances.[3]

ABSENTEEISM

- An employer fired an employee for excessive absences. The employee filed a grievance stating that there had been no previous warnings or discipline related to excessive absences.
- An employer fired an employee for excessive absences. The employee disputed the discharge and brought evidence that absences were related to a shop injury suffered earlier and that his personal physician had notified the employer that the date of return to work was unascertainable.
- As a result of failure to report to work following a holiday, coupled with a poor work attendance record, the employer discharged an employee. The employee contested the discharge on a just-cause basis.

---

[3]From my own arbitration experience over almost three decades, and *Labor Arbitration Reports*, BNA, variously. For more illustrations of past grievances, see Prentice-Hall's *Industrial Relations Guide.*

APPEARANCE

- A truck driver was discharged for wearing a beard. He filed a grievance charging discrimination and lack of just cause.
- An employee was disciplined for wearing a wig in a meat-packing plant in disregard of a plant rule banning wigs for sanitary and safety reasons. The employee grieved the disciplinary action as unreasonable and in conflict with the Department of Agriculture minimal rules.
- A bus ticket agent was discharged for refusing to trim his hair. The employer based the discharge on a plant rule that required male employees to trim hair covering the ears and extending below the collar line. The employee grieved contending lack of just cause.

ASSIGNMENT

- The employer assigned the fabrication and installation of a support structure for a whirlpool bath to millwrights in his employ. As a result, employees who were pipe fitters filed a grievance claiming that they should have been assigned the work.
- A laborer partway into his shift was assigned some work of a higher-paying classification. When he received his weekly paycheck, he noticed that he had been paid at the laborer rate for the hours worked in the higher classification. He filed a grievance when the employer refused to adjust his pay.
- The employer assigned the dismantling, repair, and assembling of valves to instrument mechanics in his employ. Machinists in his employ filed a grievance claiming that the work should have been theirs, based on custom and practice.
- It had been the practice to assign work of vacationing helpers to other helpers. The employer assigned a journeyman machinist to fill the position of a machinist helper while the latter was on vacation. A grievance was filed on behalf of the helpers affected, protesting the action of the employer.
- A detective sergeant was temporarily assigned to the job of assistant detective chief. His next paycheck revealed no change in pay to that of the higher-paying position. He filed a grievance when informed by his employer that he would not receive the higher pay.

BARGAINING UNIT

- An employee voted in an NLRB-conducted election in which the union was certified as the bargaining representative. Later, this same employee was promoted to "acting reservations manager." Soon after, the company fired him. He filed a grievance claiming the protection afforded bargaining-unit employees under the labor agreement and protesting his discharge.

BEHAVIOR

- A male employee used foul language to a female employee and was discharged. The employee filed a grievance claiming that discharge was not based on just cause, since foremen set the tone for employees by using similar language in the presence of female employees.

- An employee in a plant where horseplay was widespread squirted a fellow employee with a fire extinguisher. The employer fired him for violation of a plant rule. The employee filed a complaint.

- A twenty-year employee who had not been previously warned was fired for drinking beer on the job. The employee filed a grievance claiming lack of just cause.

- An employee who had an altercation with another employee was discharged, while the other employee was not disciplined. The employer based his action on the discharged employee's being the aggressor in the altercation. The employee filed the grievance charging unequal treatment.

- An employee posted unauthorized inflammatory notices pertaining to the employer on the union bulletin board in violation of company orders. After repeated warnings from the employer concerning other notices posted by the grievant, he was discharged. The employee disputed discharge.

- An employee of long-time service in the company went into what was described as a screaming temper tantrum upon being denied two weeks' leave after returning from his annual vacation. He was terminated as a voluntary quit. He then filed a grievance stating the action of company was precipitous and premature.

- The company had a plant rule requiring inspection of female employee's large purses. An employee of long seniority refused to allow this inspection of her purse. As a result, she was discharged. She filed a grievance stating that the discharge was unwarranted and unreasonable.

- An employee was apprehended stealing company property and was discharged forthwith. The employee filed a grievance claiming too-severe discipline and lack of progressive discipline before discharge.

CALL-OUT AND CALL-IN

- The contract called for a four-hour guarantee at an overtime rate for call-outs. An employee was called to work at 6:00 A.M. He worked to 8:00 A.M. and then continued through the regular 8:00 A.M. to 4:30 P.M. work shift. The employer paid the employee two hours at the overtime rate for call-out plus his regular eight-hour pay. The employee filed a grievance for the four-hour guarantee for call-out plus his regular-shift pay.

- An employee was called from his home, after finishing his regular shift, to load a trailer. He completed the loading work in 38 minutes and then submitted a claim for the call-in guarantee of four hours' pay at the overtime rate. This was disallowed by the employer and a grievance ensued.

- Three employees were required to make emergency repairs during their lunch break. They submitted a claim for call-in pay. The employer denied the request. A grievance was filed.

- As a result of a computer breakdown, employees came to pick up paychecks on a holiday rather than at the scheduled payday. The employees filed for extra pay under a call-in clause requiring call-in pay for employees reporting to "work" and finding none. The employer refused. A grievance resulted.

CLASSIFICATION

- An employer required a cleaning-room foreman to perform minor clerical duties incidental to his other duties. The foreman filed a grievance claiming that this required that he be placed in the clerk classification for the clerical duties.
- Employees in a job that underwent a new job description, resulting in a change of job classification with a pay rate of 10 cents an hour below their current rate, filed a grievance when the employer refused to redcircle their current pay rate.
- The employer established the wage for a new job of operating an EDM machine, which produces dies for die makers, at a lower rate than the wage for skilled die makers. Employees hired into the new job filed a grievance claiming a skilled die maker's pay rate.
- Employees classified as "production layout artists" claimed they had the ability to do work of the higher classification of "creative artists." As a result, they asked to be reclassified at the higher classification. This was refused by the employer. The employees filed a grievance.

CONTRACT

- Under the contract, unless sixty-day notice is given prior to the termination date of the contract, the contract is automatically renewed. In this particular instance, the union failed to give the sixty-day notice prior to the reopener date. The employer then assumed that the contract was automatically renewed and refused to negotiate changes with the union. The union went out on strike. The employer, on the assumption that the no-strike clause of the contract had been automatically renewed, filed a grievance against the union claiming violation of the contract.

DAMAGES

- A union steward called an unauthorized strike at a construction site. The company presented the union with a statement of damages caused by the strike, claiming that the union was responsible for the act of its agent, the union steward. The union disclaimed responsibility and took the matter to the grievance procedure.

DAYS OF WORK

- The employer was required to place an employee in the job to which he is entitled within a maximum of ten days. Interpreting this as ten working days, the employer, on the tenth working day but the twelfth calendar day, placed an employee in the required job. The employee grieved stating it should have been within ten calendar days and requesting compensation for the two days' delay.

DISCRIMINATION

- An employer refused to withdraw written reprimands from an employee's file. The reprimands were imposed for failure of the employee to improve on his attendance record as required by the probationary agreement. The employee filed a grievance charging racial discrimination.
- A black employee was given a forty-five-day disciplinary layoff for violation of plant rules. The employee filed a grievance charging discrimination, since white employees guilty of the same rules violations were never given more than two weeks' layoff.
- An employer had separate lines of male and female progression. As a result, a job was awarded to a male applicant who had the qualifications instead of to a senior female applicant who had potential ability to perform the work. The female applicant filed a grievance charging sex discrimination in promotions.

FALSIFYING

- An employee who was almost blind in one eye had not stated the fact on his application. Subsequently, after employing the man, the employer found out about the blindness. The man was discharged for failure to disclose the condition on his employment application and as a hazard to other employees. The employee filed a grievance claiming that he could perform his work adequately.

GRATUITIES

- In the past, the employer had provided on his own an annual gratuity to his employees in the form of a family picnic outing. For economic reasons, he unilaterally discontinued the annual outing. His employees brought a grievance protesting this unilateral action.
- For a number of years, the employer allowed hunting privileges to employees on company-owned surplus lands. The employer then unilaterally discontinued the hunting privileges, and the employees affected filed an grievance protesting the action.
- For twenty years, employees had been bringing radios on the job. The contract contained the cluase, "past practice shall not be binding on either party." The employer unilaterally banned use of radios on the job. Employees grieved, stating that the employer could not unilaterally take such action.

HABITS

- It was found by the employer that an employee involved in the use of machinery smoked marijuana. The employer fired the employee on the assumption that he constituted a danger to the safety of other employees who were working on the same machinery. A grievance was filed maintaining just cause had not been shown.

HEALTH AND WELFARE

- The contract specifically stated that employees would pay a specified amount as their contribution toward dependent coverage. The premium was increased on dependent coverage. The employer increased the deduction from employees for dependent coverage by a pro rata amount of the overall increase in the premium. The employees grieved stating that the employer should pay the entire increase in the premium rate for dependents.

- The teachers and the board of education had a contract provision that required the district to provide the teachers full family health-care insurance, with the options as they become available. A pharmaceutical rider became available, but the board failed to add this to the insurance package. The teacher organization filed a grievance.

- The company had had a pension plan under which a number of employees had already retired. At the most recent negotiations, an agreement was reached on an increase in the pension benefits. The employer interpreted this as applying only to subsequent retirements. Retirees filed a grievance arguing that the increase was for all, past and present.

- An employer had a management right under the labor agreement to determine types and classes of insurance policies to be sold. He used this right to unilaterally eliminate several insurance policies. The Insurance Workers' Union filed a grievance claiming this was an abuse of management rights.

- Through an error, the clause on hospitalization insurance benefits was omitted from the labor agreement. An employee filed for the benefits and was denied by the employer on the basis that the contract contained no provision for them. The employee filed a grievance.

HOLIDAYS

- Christmas and New Year's are official holidays. In this incident, both holidays fell on Saturdays, a regular day off for shop employees. The employer refused to pay the holiday pay for the two holidays, since they fell on nonworking days. The shop employees, through their union, grieved the employer's decision.

- The employer's plant was partially burned down a week before the Thanksgiving holiday. The employer received permission from the insurance company to use some of the employees to do special clean-up work extending through the last scheduled workday before and after the holiday. When these employees filed for holiday pay for Thanksgiving, the employer refused to pay on the basis that the employees had not worked on a regular scheduled workday before and after the holiday. The employees filed a grievance claiming the holiday pay.

- Three employees worked on Washington's Birthday. The employer paid them regular overtime instead of premium holiday pay. They filed a grievance for the extra pay.

- The company refused to pay an employee holiday pay for July 4, which fell within his vacation period. The employee grieved, claiming holiday pay.
- The contract called for payment of holidays worked at time and a half plus holiday pay. An employee worked a shift from 12:01 A.M. to 8:00 A.M. on the holiday and claimed holiday pay plus time and a half for the hours worked. The employer denied the claim, arguing that the workday was 7:00 A.M. to 7:00 A.M., and therefore, for pay purposes the holiday began at 7:00 A.M. and not at 12:01 A.M. A grievance was filed.
- The employer is required to pay holiday pay to all "regular full-time employees and part-time employees." A probationary employee who was denied holiday pay filed a grievance.
- A wildcat strike took place on the last scheduled shift prior to a Memorial Day holiday. As a result, employees were not able to work the shift. The employer therefore did not pay them holiday pay, because they had failed to work the day prior to the holiday. The employees filed a grievance.
- The employer scheduled observance of a Memorial Day holiday falling on Saturday on the following Monday. The contract called for double time for working on holidays. Two employees worked on the Saturday. The employer paid them regular overtime rather than double time. The employees, claiming they should have received double time for working on the official holiday and not the employer-designated holiday, filed a grievance.

HOURS OF WORK

- In the past, employees had frequently left work before the end of a shift without permission. Under a lax supervision, this had never been questioned. The employer then instituted a strict policy requiring the service manager's permission to leave prior to the end of a shift. Several months after this change of policy, three employees left without permission and were given a one-day suspension. These employees grieved the suspension on the basis of long-established past practice.
- The labor agreement established a 7½-hour workday. It had been the practice to allow workers to quit a half-hour early. The employer issued an order requiring employees, effective the date of the order, to begin working a full 7½-hour day. The employees grieved this unilateral action.
- Machinists worked the Sunday midnight shift but, because of a time change, actually worked only seven hours. They claimed a full eight hours' pay, claiming that by the clock, there was eight hours' difference between the times of reporting and finishing the shift. The employer refused the eight hours' request. A grievance was filed.
- The employees on the first shift, upon reporting to work, found the plant door locked. They returned home and the next day applied for reporting pay. This was refused by the employer on the basis that the supervisor

had overslept but was there to open the plant within half an hour of starting time. A grievance ensued.

INCENTIVE

- A new incentive standard was unilaterally established by the employer. The union grieved the unilateral action.

INEFFICIENCY

- A head mixer in a bakery was discharged for omitting essential ingredients in a batch of cookie dough. He filed a grievance claiming that, in terms of his past record, the disciplinary action was too severe.
- An employee was discharged because of poor work, which was linked also to a negative attitude toward work, customer complaints about inadequate performance, and several prior warnings by the employer. The employee filed a grievance claiming the evidence was not sufficient to warrant discharge.

INSUBORDINATION

- A leadman refused to heed the supervisor's order to drill holes for fixtures in a "picture boat," and allegedly told the supervisor thereafter that he had changed his mind about going home so that he could whip the supervisor that afternoon. He was discharged. The leadman filed a grievance asserting lack of just cause.
- An employee refused to follow a work order that departed from specifications and was discharged. The employee filed a grievance claiming there was not just cause for disciplinary action, since he was following reasonably good judgment.
- An employee was given a legitimate order to mount a decal publicizing the union-employer status on a company car. The employee failed to comply with the order and was given a ten-day suspension. The employee filed a grievance stating that he felt the suspension was an excessive penalty.
- In order to perform repair work to a tachometer generator located in a box atop a hot strip mill, it was necessary for the employer to require that a motor inspector stand on an extension ladder. Because of the height, the motor inspector refused and was disciplined. He filed a grievance claiming that the employer had not shown just cause.
- An employee on two occasions refused to obey a supervisor's order to meet with him, unless a union representative was present at the meeting. As a result, the employee was discharged and subsequently filed a grievance protesting discharge.
- An employee of thirty-one years' seniority was suspended for his adamant refusal to obey an order of his foreman to return to work. At the time of the incident, the employer refused to let the employee have the assistance of his chief steward. The employee filed a grievance claiming improper suspension.

- A driver refused to allow a dispatcher to drive his truck, although ordered to do so by his superior. There was no question of health, safety, or legality involved. The driver was suspended. He filed a grievance protesting the employer's action.
- The employer scheduled overtime work for several of the employees, including the union steward. The union steward refused to work the overtime, used abusive language toward his supervisor, and instructed other employees not to work overtime. The supervisor directed the union steward to leave the company premises when he refused to work overtime. The union steward refused. The employer then discharged the union steward for insubordination. The union steward filed a grievance claiming he was fired because of his union activity.

JOB PARTICIPATION

- An employer posted a job opening, listing the job involved but not including the classification, wage rate, and shift assignment involved. A request was made that these items be included. The employer refused, claiming no need. The union filed a grievance stating that posted jobs must include characteristics of the position so that the potential bidder would be informed of the exact position he proposed to accept.

LAYOFF

- A firm became a subsidiary of another company but retained its corporate identity, and the contract it had been operating under with the union remained unchanged. It had been the practice in the past for the employer to continue production during inventory. After becoming a subsidiary, the employer abandoned the practice and put employees not involved in the inventory on temporary layoff. The union, on behalf of the affected employees, filed a grievance stating that the employer did not have the right to unilaterally take such action on the basis of past practice.

LEAVE

- An employee attended the funeral of his stepfather-in-law on personal leave. He then submitted a claim for funeral-leave pay for attending the funeral of a member of his "immediate family." The pay was refused by the employer. The employee grieved.
- During the time a city firefighter was on sick leave, he participated briefly in picketing by off-duty firefighters to protest layoffs of firefighting personnel. When he applied for sick-leave pay, the pay was denied by the employer. The employee grieved the employer's action.
- An employee was sentenced to serve a prison term for commission of a felony. He was subsequently discharged. Claiming that his leave-of-absence rights had been violated by the company, an authorized member of the union filed a grievance in his behalf. This was denied by the company, based on their claim that only the employee himself could file a grievance. The grievance then became a matter of whether another

authorized union member could file a grievance on behalf of a member incarcerated in prison.

- A traffic officer took paid sick-leave time to work for another employer. For this he was discharged. He grieved, claiming lack of just cause.
- An employee called in sick but was later seen by a member of management at a baseball game. The employee was fired for abusing sick leave. The employee then filed a grievance noting that she left the ballgame before it was over because she was sick and that the discipline was excessive.
- An employer failed to pay sick benefits during a strike. The employee affected filed a grievance claim for the sick benefits.
- A teacher was refused paid sick leave by her employer when she was rehospitalized for postdelivery complications arising from a pregnancy. She grieved.
- A female teacher who took leave to have a baby wanted the leave applied against her accumulated sick leave. The district denied this claim and applied the leave to maternity leave. The teacher filed a grievance.

Loss

- The tools of an employee, owned by him, were stolen from the company premises. The employee requested replacement by the employer, since the theft had happened on company premises. The employer refused. A grievance was then filed.
- During a strike, several employees lost articles from their lockers through theft. They applied for reimbursement for the lost articles. The employer refused payment, stating that it was not his responsibility. The employees filed a grievance requesting that the employer take the responsibility for what employees considered to be the employer's lack of security precautions.

Lunch Break

- Workers in the plant traveled from work stations to the main plant to eat their lunches. The lunch break had been set at one-half hour. The employer noticed that there was considerable abuse of the half-hour unpaid lunch break and docked workers' time for lateness. A grievance was filed.

Meals

- Under their labor agreement, employees working overtime were given free meals or extra pay. The employer initiated a program in which those working overtime no longer received payments but were provided a free meal cooked in a microwave oven. The employees grieved the employer's unilateral discontinuance of the payment in lieu of a meal.

NOTIFICATION

- Notification of discharge of an employee was made by the personnel manager, who gave the union president and chief steward a copy of the discharge letter. A grievance was filed protesting the discharge on the grounds that proper notification of the decision to discharge had not been given.
- The contract required a day's notice in lieu of pay in cases of reduction of working force or hours. Without giving proper notice, the company shut down the plant for the Martin Luther King funeral to avoid racial disturbance. The employees claimed pay for the day and grieved when it was not received.
- The contract called for two days' notice of any general layoff. The employer neglected to give the required notice. As a result, the employees affected filed a claim for the two days' pay. The employer denied the claim and a grievance was then filed.

OVERTIME

- A practice unprotested by the union was to include no more than a maximum of thirty minutes' travel time to a job site for the purpose of computing overtime pay. The actual time involved in traveling to the particular job site was forty-five minutes. But based on the unprotested past practice of the union, the employer counted a maximum of only thirty minutes. The employees filed a grievance, claiming the full forty-five minutes' travel time.
- An employee felt that another had been improperly given overtime that belonged to him. As a result, the aggrieved employee refused a scheduled overtime assignment. The employer fired the employee under a contract that prohibited strikes, slowdowns, or other interruption of work. The aggrieved employee filed a grievance protesting the discharge.
- Sunday overtime work was discontinued after a department was split. Employees affected filed a grievance protesting loss of the overtime work.
- An employer inadvertently violated the overtime-pay requirements. When it was discovered, he immediately changed the practice to comply. Employees who had not received the proper overtime filed a claim retroactive to the date the mistake was made. The employer refused the claims and paid back to the date the mistake was discovered. The employees filed a grievance.
- A rotation system of assigning overtime was used by the company. An employee failed twice to report for overtime. The employer thereupon refused him overtime the next time his name appeared. The employee grieved.
- City policemen reported for roll call at the beginning of a shift. The union filed a claim for overtime pay for the time involved in the roll call. The city denied the claim. A grievance was filed.
- An employer gave preference to an employee with 889 hours overtime

over an employee with 835 hours in a scheduled overtime. The second employee filed a grievance, claiming that the contract required that "low-houred" employees must be given first opportunity.

- An employee repeatedly refused to give a reasonable explanation for refusing to work Sunday overtime. As a result he was given a three-day disciplinary layoff. A grievance was filed protesting mandatory overtime for nonworking days.

PAY

- The union contract calls for compensation of employees while "engaged in meetings with company officials." After an arbitration hearing in which several employees were required as witnesses, the employees requested compensation for lost worktime. The company denied this request, stating that an arbitration is not a "meeting." The employees grieved the situation.
- Union committeemen were paid by the company for time lost from work. When a committeeman filed for pay for committeeman work performed when work was not scheduled, the employer refused to pay. A grievance was filed.
- Several employees at an army installation were engaged in work of a hazardous nature. They were denied hazard pay by their employer. They filed a grievance.
- Employees had to wait for their paychecks several minutes past quitting time. The practice had always been to pay during working hours. The employees filed for extra pay for the time they had to wait. This was denied by the employer, and a grievance was then filed by the employees.
- A teachers' strike was in progress. As a result of weather conditions, the school was closed for two days, during which the teachers continued to strike. At the conclusion of the strike, the teachers requested back pay for the two days the school was closed. The school refused. A grievance was filed.

PLANT RULES

- The plant had a posted rule barring employees from eating or drinking during unscheduled breaks. The employees filed a grievance, claiming the rule was arbitrary.
- Company rules relating to safety and conduct had been posted and operative for several years. The company was sold to another interest. Upon assuming control, the new management unilaterally changed the posted rules on safety and conduct. The result was that an employee was suspended for violation of the changed safety rules. The employee filed a grievance stating that the employer did not have the right to unilaterally change the rules and impose disciplinary action without discussion and notice of change to the union.
- An employer made a sudden change in several plant rules relating to disciplinary action. As an immediate result, there was an uneven application of the plant rules. During the process of change, three em-

ployees were discharged under the new rules. They filed a grievance stating the discharge was unreasonable and not based on just cause.

PROBATION

- In computing the probationary period of an employee, the employer excluded Saturday and Sunday work because he claimed this was not part of the basic workweek. The employee filed a grievance claiming the employer should have counted all workdays.
- A probationary employee was fired prior to completion of the probationary period. He filed a grievance disputing the discharge.

PROMOTION

- A senior employee was disqualified for promotion because of the results of an aptitude test. Since past use of tests had not resulted in junior employees being promoted over senior employees, he filed a grievance protesting the disqualification.

RATING

- An administrative assistant in the political-science department of a university obtained exceptional ratings in two evaluations. Following the last exceptional evaluation, the assistant was appointed union steward. On the next evaluation, the university employer rated him as average or below average on all value factors of the performance evaluation. The employee charged discrimination.

REDUCTION OF FORCE

- Contending that it would increase efficiency, an employer gave notice that the company would dissolve two departments and re-form them into a single new department with a reduced number of employees. The union, on behalf of the employees affected, filed a grievance stating that, even though the contract did not specifically prohibit the employer from taking such action, doing so required negotiation with the union on behalf of its members.
- The company found itself with a temporary material shortage and therefore found it necessary to temporarily lay off five employees. The five employees filed a grievance stating that the company could have anticipated delays in delivery of goods and thus prevented the need for the temporary layoff. The five employees asked for pay and allowances to compensate for management's error in not anticipating the shortage.

REPORTS

- The employer issued an order requiring production workers in the plant to fill out a daily production report. Four employees filed a grievance stating that they were not responsible for such reports under the labor agreement and their job descriptions.

REPRESENTATION

- An employee was summoned to an office meeting with his foreman. It was alleged that during the course of the meeting, the employee threatened the foreman. As a result, the employee was discharged. The employee then filed a grievance claiming that his grievance representative was not present during the meeting.

RIGHTS

- A teachers' union filed a grievance on its own behalf. The board of education refused to acknowledge the grievance, stating that only grievances on behalf of individual employees could be entertained. The union filed another grievance claiming that the employer had violated the right of the union to grieve over contract violations.

SAFETY

- Employees at the plant were required to change their footgear to steel-toed safety shoes. These were considerably more expensive, but the employer refused to compensate employees for the extra expense. A grievance protesting the extra cost was filed.
- An employee refused to wear protective equipment in a manner that the company felt proper. He was discharged. He filed a grievance claiming that the company had not shown just cause.
- An employee repeatedly refused to wear a hard hat in the safety-hat area after his supervisor asked, "Where is your hat?" and after he had been given a warning slip. The employer discharged the employee. The employee filed a grievance claiming lack of just cause.

SCHEDULING

- The employer unilaterally changed the starting time of an engraver etcher from 6 P.M. to 7 P.M. The employee filed a grievance claiming that the employer had failed to comply with notice requirements and priority requirements of the contract.

SENIORITY

- In taking over a plant, the successor employer reduced the force and, in so doing, laid employees off without regard to seniority. The union, which had the contract with the previous employer, filed a grievance claiming that the new employer was bound by the contract.
- An employee was hired during a strike. He was not able to report to work until the end of the strike and then was not assigned to a specific job

until some time later. The employer dated his seniority as of the date of assignment to the specific job. The employee filed a grievance claiming that his seniority in the specific job should have been from the date of hire during the strike.

- A junior employee was hired to fill the position of a laid-off senior employee. The senior employee filed a grievance protesting the action.
- An employee in a bargaining unit was promoted to foreman. At the time, he had accumulated ten years' seniority. Three years after his taking over the foreman's job, there was a reduction of force and he was returned to his old job. The employer dated the employee's seniority at the time of transfer back to the job as if he were a new hire with no accumulation of previous seniority. The employee filed a grievance.
- A strike occurred. After it ended, the employer began to rehire employees without regard to seniority. There was no clause in the contract requiring that seniority be used, but history and conduct supported this. The union filed a grievance.
- A senior employee was on vacation when a new job, that of set-up man, was posted. A junior employee successfully applied for the position. On his return, the senior employee filed a grievance asking that he be given the position on the basis of seniority.
- An employer laid off two mailing employees while retaining employees with less seniority. The laid-off employees filed a grievance claiming they had been improperly laid off.
- An employer awarded a job to a junior employee with technical college training instead of a senior employee with less education. The senior employee filed a grievance protesting the action.
- In a reduction in force, the employer allowed a supervisor to return to the bargaining-unit position he had held previously by bumping a less-senior unit employee. The employee bumped filed a grievance claiming improper use of seniority.

SHIFT

- The company had been operating on a sixteen-hour schedule with a 7:00 A.M. to 3:00 P.M. day shift and a 3:00 P.M. to 11:00 P.M. evening shift. The company unilaterally changed the schedule to twelve hours, and the shifts to 7:00 A.M. to 3:00 P.M. and 11:00 A.M. to 7:00 P.M. On behalf of the employees in the bargaining unit, the union grieved, stating that the employer did not have the right to change the shift without the approval of the union. The union asked that the schedule and shifts be returned to the earlier arrangement pending negotiations between the union and the company.
- An employer used outside help to perform unit work in the plant. The resulting effect on one employee was to bring about a change in his shift assignment. The employee filed a grievance claiming his shift should not have been changed.
- The employer unilaterally changed a fixed shift based on seniority to a rotation shift for employees. A grievance was filed protesting the elimination of seniority.

STRIKE

- Employees protesting incentive standards met with their foreman to discuss their grievance. Instead of returning to work after the meeting with the foreman, the employees insisted, over the foreman's direct order to the contrary, upon meeting with the grievance-committee chairman. This was during working hours. The contract had a no-strike clause. The employer discharged the workers for violating the contract. The employees grieved, claiming they had not gone on strike.
- The contract has a no-strike clause. Employees of the company went on strike anyway. Complying with the contract, the union disavowed the strike. The employer suspended the participants of the strike. A grievance was filed stating that the disavowal by the union of the strike was a bar to the employer's suspending employees on strike.
- State law prohibits public employees from striking. A local board of education decided to hold back a projected radio installation in district buses. Subsequently, mass illness was reported by employees. The district took action by disciplining employees for striking within the meaning of the state law. The employees filed a grievance arguing they had not struck in violation of the state law.

SUBCONTRACT

- The employer assigned work in the plant that he considered outside the bargaining unit to nonunit employees. The union immediately filed a grievance claiming that the work properly fell within their jurisdiction and therefore should have been performed by the unit employees.

SUCCESSOR FIRM

- The radio and equipment of a taxicab corporation was purchased, but the new owner did not assume the labor contract of the corporation. A dispute occurred involving the old contract, and the new owner refused to recognize the dispute because he felt he was not bound by the old contract. The union filed a grievance claiming that the contract went with the sale of the corporation.
- A business was sold. Under the previous owner, employees had the option of working on holidays at triple time. Under the new employer, employees claimed, they should not be deprived of income previously enjoyed. The new employer refused to be bound by practices of the earlier employer. Affected employees filed a joint grievance.

SURVEILLANCE

- The company had installed an incentive system. In order to evaluate the system, the company installed closed-circuit television to study the performance of incentive workers. There was no clause in the contract specifically forbidding such action. The workers being monitored filed a grievance stating that this was not a unilateral right of management under its management-rights clause.

TECHNICAL CHANGE

- The employer installed a motorized crane block to technologically improve operation. He also reduced the number of hookers on the operation from two to one. The hooker laid off filed a grievance requesting reinstatement on the grounds that (1) the crane block did not significantly reduce hooker duties, and (2) the increased workload for the remaining hooker required outside assistance.

TIME STUDY

- An employer unilaterally changed the time-study method, resulting in a possible change in earnings. The employees affected filed a grievance protesting the change.

TRANSFER

- A teacher was removed from a varisty basketball coaching position. The principal stated that this was his prerogative, since the position was outside the labor agreement. The teacher contested this interpretation and filed a grievance.
- The state health department ordered a safety shutdown that resulted in a temporary layoff. The employees laid off were transferred to lower-paying jobs temporarily. They claimed the rate of their regular jobs, which were at a higher rate. The employer denied the claims. A grievance was filed.

UNION

- During working hours, an employee asked the union president, who was a fellow employee, for a check-off card. The employer discharged the union president for improper organizational activities during working hours.

UNION SECURITY

- The labor agreement included a union-shop clause. Four members of the union employed in the bargaining unit refused to pay their dues. The union requested that the employer discharge these workers for failure to pay dues. The employer refused. The union brought a charge asking that the company pay the initiation fees and dues of the employees in arrears.
- In a non-right-to-work state, an employer failed to require new employees to join the union within thirty-one days, although there was a union-shop clause in the labor agreement. The union filed a grievance for compensation for loss of initiation fees and dues resulting from this action.

VACATION

- The contract provides for pro rata vacation benefits during plant shut-downs. Under the past agreements, the former union representative failed to require enforcement of this provision. In the most recent plant shutdown, the plant followed the past practice of ignoring the pro rata vacation-benefit provision. The new union leadership filed a grievance asking that the agreement be upheld under the clear language of the contract.

- An employee voluntarily resigned from his employment. At the time of his resignation, he was assured by a supervisor that he was entitled to pay for unused vacation time even though the contract contained no such guarantee. The employer refused payment of the vacation time. The employee then filed a grievance based on the supervisor's statement.

- The contract required paid vacations. An employee was on his two-week paid vacation when a wage increase took effect. The employer, however, computed the vacation-pay rate at the rate in force at the beginning of his vacation. The employee claimed that the rate increase should have been applied and filed a grievance.

- The contract called for a three-week vacation for ten-year employees. One employee worked nine months of a twelve-month fiscal year for twenty-seven years and then worked twelve months each year for four years. The employee was paid for a full twelve months for each of the thirty-one years. The employee requested the accrued vacation time for the last four years. His employer denied the request. A grievance was filed.

VENDING MACHINES

- As a result of malfunction of vending machines on the employer's premises, several employees lost money to the machines. The employer refused to refund money to employees who claimed they had lost money in the machines. The employees filed a grievance to regain their money.

WAGES

- The school board negotiated with the teachers' union a contract that provided for a wage reopener only. At the time the contract was reopened for wages only, the school board contended this meant only annual salaries. The teachers' union contended that "wages-only" reopener meant all economic matters—all compensation received by teachers, direct or indirect. A grievance was filed by the union.

- A districtwide labor agreement called for wage rates by established geographic areas. A contractor made an error in his bidding on a job and based it on a wage rate lower than that required for his area. When notified of this by the local business agent, he decided to use workers from his home base. The business agent, in order to maintain the employment for local people, agreed to allow the lower wage rate to be paid for that job. Several months later, the district council of the union, through a complaint by a competitor of the contractor, found out about the wage rate being paid and filed a grievance with the contractors' association requesting that the proper wage be paid retroactively.

Whole, Make Whole

- An employee was improperly terminated. As a consequence of an arbitration decision, he was later reinstated. In making the employee whole for the period of the termination, the employer refused to pay the employee for holiday pay for contract holidays that fell within the termination period. The employee filed a grievance stating that he was not made whole for all back pay and benefits.

Workmen's Compensation

- In computing workmen's compensation payments to eligible employees, the employer changed the basis of computation from the past policy of using gross earnings to a net-earnings method. This resulted in a reduction of the amount of payments. The employees filed a grievance asking that the former policy be reinstated and retroactive to the time of change of policy.

Workweek

- The boiler workers in the plant were on a rotation shift basis running over a five-day work schedule. The employer, while maintaining the rotation shift basis, placed the work of a seven-day work schedule. Employees filed a grievance claiming that this was not a reasonable exercise of the employer's rights under the management-rights clause of the labor agreement.
- The employer unilaterally changed the pay week, from Friday through Thursday with one-day-delayed payday, to Monday through Sunday with payday on the following Tuesday. The union claimed this was a negotiable item and filed a grievance.
- The employer unilaterally changed the workweek from Monday through Friday to Tuesday through Saturday. The employees filed a grievance stating that the employer had violated the contract, which required a Monday-through-Friday workweek "wherever possible."

SUMMARY

It can readily be seen that grievances arise from a vast number of circumstances and situations and take on a great variety of forms. Basically, grievances arise because:

1. A particular employee or group of employees has a complaint concerning a problem affecting him or them personally with respect to wages, hours, or other conditions of employment.

2. A union has a complaint that concerns:
   a. All bargaining-unit employees directly and their rights under the labor agreements
   b. The union's and its representatives' status
   c. General matters of contract observance and operation with only an indirect impact on the bargaining-unit employees
   d. Matters of principle vital to the labor-management relationship
3. An employer or association of employers attempts to both protect and enforce its rights under the labor agreement.

SELECTED REFERENCES

BNA Editorial Staff, *Grievance Guide.* Washington, D.C.: Bureau of National Affairs, Inc., 1972. An excellent source of materials on the problems of employers, unions, and workers in the day-to-day business of living under the union contract.

Crane, Bertram R., and Robert M. Hoffman, *Successful Handling of Labor Grievances.* New York: Central Book Company, 1965. Complete coverage of the various schools of thought as to what constitutes a grievance, methods of classifying and selecting grievance definitions, and what is not a grievance.

Industrial Relations Guide. Englewood Cliffs, N.J.: Prentice-Hall, Inc. Biweekly reports in this continuing series explain the impact of new developments and new trends in collective bargaining and arbitration. The basic text of the loose-leaf volume, updated periodically, includes a complete explanation of the nature of labor arbitration, plus descriptions of past awards and thousands of sample contract clauses. "New Ideas" articles are written by outside experts in the field on subjects of interest to management and labor alike.

Labor Relations Guide. Englewood Cliffs, N.J.: Prentice-Hall, Inc. This service, updated weekly, is particularly useful for business executives, lawyers, personnel managers, and consultants who want information that quickly and easily answers day-to-day labor-relations questions. Important decisions of the National Labor Relations Board, the Equal Employment Opportunity Commission, the Occupational Safety and Health Administration, and the courts are reported promptly in easy-to-understand language. The service includes an explanation of labor laws—Wage-Hour, the NLRA, the Civil Rights Act, Age Discrimination, Vietnam Era Veterans Reemployment Act, OSHA, garnishment, state labor laws, and others—and provides the full texts of federal laws and executive orders.

Peach, David A., and E. Robert Livernash, *Grievance Initiation and Resolution—A Study in Basic Steel.* Boston: Graduate School of Business Administration, Harvard University, 1974. An excellent analytical study of the grievance, ranging from environmental influences on problems and their resolution, to union influences on the challenge rate and the resolution process, and management influences on the grievance rate and resolution process. The authors conclude with a discussion of interrelationships and their implications for management.

Public Personnel Administration: Labor-Management Relations. Englewood Cliffs, N.J.: Prentice-Hall, Inc. Focusing on public-sector collective bargaining, this service explains laws, methods, rulings, clauses, and established precedents (including summaries of arbitration awards). Biweekly reports provide news of developments in this complex area. Sections of the basic text include "New Ideas," "Collective Bargaining Problems and Answers," "Annotated Public Employment Relations Laws and Regulations," "Union Contract Clauses," and Arbitration Awards Analyzed."

Wage-Hour Guide. Englewood Cliffs, N.J.: Prentice-Hall, Inc. This volume includes the texts of both the Equal Pay Law and the Wage-Hour Law. Information is provided on who is covered, who is exempt, wages and overtime, child labor restrictions, records-investigations, enforcement methods, government contracts, and related topics. A regular report explains current developments. A "Current Matter" section contains administrative opinions and digests of court decisions.

CHAPTER 17

GRIEVANCE PROCEDURE

The preceding chapter dealt with the sources and nature of the grievance. This chapter will treat the machinery established to process and resolve grievances, including all the steps short of grievance arbitration. Since grievance arbitration, the last step of the formal grievance procedure, involves a third party and is a judicial rather than a legislative step, it is given separate treatment in Chapter 18.

The main product of collective bargaining as envisioned by the Webbs was the establishment of industrial democracy in the workplace. Labor-management relations would have fallen short of this objective had collective bargaining been confined to the negotiation stage alone; negotiating the terms of the collective bargaining agreement establishes a constitution to guide the parties in their joint relations in the workplace but, as the Webbs recognized, is not enough to fully establish industrial democracy. To be really meaningful, the terms needed to be supplemented with a mechanism, whereby questions or problems arising in the day-to-day application of the labor agreement could be jointly and peacefully resolved.

In their classic work, *Industrial Democracy*, the Webbs, with their usual foresight, stated:

> *We must here plunge into a maze of complicated technical*
> *detail relating to these industries, each of which has developed*

> *its machinery for Collective Bargaining in its own way, and we despair of making the reader understand either our exposition or our criticism unless he will keep constantly in mind one fundamental distinction, which is all important.* This vital distinction is between the making of a new bargain, and the interpreting of the terms of an existing one. *Where the machinery for Collective Bargaining has broken down, we usually discover that this distinction has not been made; and it is only where this fundamental distinction has been clearly maintained that the machinery works without friction or ill-feeling.* . . . *This, it will be seen, is exclusively an issue of fact, in which both the desires and the tactical strength of the parties directly concerned must be entirely eliminated. For conciliation, compromise, and balancing of expediences, there is absolutely no room. On the other hand, it is indispensable that the ascertainment of facts should attain an almost scientific precision. Moreover, the settlement should be automatic, rapid, and inexpensive. The ideal machinery for this class of cases would, in fact, be a peripatetic calculating-machine endowed with a high degree of technical knowledge, which could accurately register all the factors concerned, and unerringly grind out the arithmetical result.*[1]

What the Webbs were talking about has since come to be known as *contract administration*. The vehicle for contract administration is the jointly negotiated grievance procedure.

After a labor agreement has been negotiated and the parties have signified their commitment to its provisions for a specified contract period of one, two, three, or more years, the process of giving meaning to the agreement begins. Management and the bargaining-unit representative *continue, in effect, to bargain collectively on a day-by-day basis* for the length of the contract period. Such bargaining does not involve negotiation of new terms or a new labor agreement. nor is it directed—although by agreement of the parties it can be—at altering the terms already negotiated in the contract. The administration of the agreement on a day-to-day basis is an interpretive process whereby the labor contract is applied, given meaning, and in effect transformed into a "living organism." The grievance procedure is the formal mechanism through which this transition is effected.

Not every day-to-day problem or question that might arise between employees and/or the union and the employer can be anticipated during the period when the terms of the agreement are being negotiated. The complexities of labor-management relations preclude the drawing up of such an all-inclusive, anticipatory labor agreement. Although both parties have sought to anticipate a problem through the negotiation of a particular

---

[1]Sidney and Beatrice Webb, *Industrial Democracy* (London: Longmans, Green and Co., 1902), pp. 182–84. (Emphasis added.)

clause or section of the agreement, they may discover that looking at the same clause or section later, under the pressure of an actual grievance, often results in a shift in their thinking. When negotiating, the parties are motivated by a desire to find an area of compromise in the language of the agreement. As a result, their view of the meaning of a particular clause or phrase or term may not anticipate all the varied applications to which it might be subject once it is applied. Also, as has been pointed out, the ambiguities in a contract may be deliberate: "The language is purposely indefinite because it is all the negotiators can agree to. Making a section of the agreement ambiguous may represent a decision by the negotiators to 'pass the buck' to those charged with administering the agreement."[2] It is thus that a union representative, responding to a complaint of one of his members, first looks at the particular clause in the agreement in terms of the way or ways it can be used to support the point of view of his aggrieved member. Management will also be looking at the clause in terms of how it may be used to protect its own interests. As a result, what seemed to be a consensus at the time of the joint negotiation may turn into a conflicting interpretation under the pressure of the separate interests and needs of the parties.

The grievance procedure provides management and the union with an institutional mechanism by which to dispose of complaints and charges of contract violation in an orderly and equitable manner. It provides a peaceful means of resolving misunderstandings, permits enforcement of the contract, and minimizes the use of strikes and lockouts. Indeed, industry would be chaotic if the strike or the lockout were the only means available to effect compliance with the contract. As William Whyte succinctly puts it, "If the grievance procedure works, the contract will work. If the grievance procedure does not work, then, of course, the contract does not work, and what you have is really jungle warfare."[3]

Not only is the grievance procedure crucial in vitalizing the agreement through the daily process of contract administration; it also performs an animating role in ensuring industrial democracy in the workplace by means of an open forum through which complaints and grievances may be peacefully resolved. Moreover, as Whyte notes, the grievance procedure

> ... is a social invention of great importance for our democratic society. . . . Nothing quite like this exists in most countries of the world. On the continent of Europe, for example,

---

[2]Sumner H. Slichter, James S. Healy, and E. Robert Livernash, *The Impact of Collective Bargaining on Management* (Washington, D.C.: The Brookings Institution, 1960), p. 695.

[3]William F. Whyte, "The Grievance Procedure and Plant Society," in *The Grievance Process*, Proceedings of a Conference (March 23–24, 1956), Labor and Industrial Relations Center, Kellogg Center, Michigan State University, p. 20. (Comment by Ken Bannon.)

> unions are organized on a much different basis. They are politi-
> cally oriented, and the tie of the worker to the local organiza-
> tion, such as it is, is very tenuous indeed. The things we call
> grievances, if handled at all, are generally handled in other
> channels. They get out of the plant and into the government
> sphere. On the other hand, what we have built up here is an
> essential part of democratic society. It is a means whereby the
> lone individual and the work group can take up their problems,
> have some means of redress, and furthermore, argue their prob-
> lems with people who are pretty close to those problems in the
> plant itself.[4]

Three major areas relative to the grievance procedure are the focus of
the remainder of this chapter: (1) the legal framework within which the
grievance procedure operates; (2) the substantive features of the grievance
procedure—initiator, scope, time limits, steps, costs, and variations; and
(3) some helpful hints for successful handling of grievances.

THE GRIEVANCE PROCEDURE AND THE LAW

PRIVATE SECTOR

Although the right to grieve is clearly enunciated in the Taft-Hartly Act,
there is no companion provision requiring that the right to grieve be
implemented by a formal grievance procedure. Section 201(c) alludes to
such a process but places main emphasis upon a terminal procedure for
final adjustment of grievances and/or questions regarding the application
or interpretation of agreements. Despite this omission, almost all private-
sector labor agreements include formal grievance machinery, owing to the
realization by both labor and management that unless they jointly establish a means of internally enforcing the contract terms and an orderly and
peaceful means of solving complaints of violations of the agreement, *only
chaos and resort to jungle tactics will ensue.* Instead of an instrument of
peace, the collective bargaining agreement *deteriorates into an instrument of open war.*

However, while Taft-Hartley does not require the parties to include a
negotiated grievance procedure in the labor agreement, it does address
itself in other ways to the grievance procedure once such a procedure is
included in the agreement. Under the terms of Section 9(a), grievance-

---

[4]*Ibid.*, p. 11. A. W. J. Thomson also notes that the grievance procedure may perform
important secondary functions as a diagnostic device, a medium of communication and
consultation, and a means of improving the quality of decision making. A. W. J. Thomson,
The Grievance Procedure in the Private Sector (New York: New York State School of Industrial and Labor Relations, Cornell University, 1974), p. 2.

procedure structures *must be broad enough* to meet two standards: First, the individual worker must be permitted to present grievances to his employer on an individual basis: "any individual employee or a group of employees shall have the right at any time to present grievances to their employer." Second, any employee has the right

> . . . to have such grievances adjusted, without the intervention of the bargaining representative, as long as the adjustment is not inconsistent with the terms of a collective-bargaining contract or agreement then in effect: Provided further, That the bargaining representative has been given opportunity to be present at such adjustment.

It is sometimes argued that this construction of the law as it relates to the grievance process encourages individual bargaining, provides a vehicle for weakening the practice of collective bargaining, and diminishes the ability of the bargaining agent to act for the entire unit of employees.[5] Offsetting this tendency are several practical considerations that tend to tie the bargaining-unit employee closely to the formal grievance procedure of the agreement and to his union representatives in handling his grievance. First, the majority of employees do not possess the expertise, nor do most employees want to take the time to develop the expertise, to process their own grievances under the terms or language of the contract. Second, there is the peer pressure that belonging to the union brings on bargaining-unit members to show their loyalty by utilizing their own organization to process the grievance. Third, the normal reluctance of the average employee to take on his superiors directly over a violation of the contract is somewhat overcome when he has the union acting as a buffer and an advocate in his behalf. Fourth, if the grievance must be appealed to higher levels of management, with the consequent need for more expert and knowledgeable handling, the union provides greater capability and resources to effectively represent the grievant than the individual employee has using his own resources only. It is for these reasons that, notwithstanding the language of Section 9(a), most employees with a grievance or complaint will opt to use their collective bargaining representative. Therefore, since the union is a formal party to the negotiated grievance structure of the labor agreement, it follows that most grievances will be processed via the formal grievance procedure of the contract.

Enforcement for most complaints of violations of the agreement proceeds from (1) a settlement of the grievance by the parties at one of the preliminary steps of the grievance procedure, or (2) a settlement through the final step of grievance arbitration. Even though the grievance pro-

---

[5]Benjamin J. Taylor and Fred Witney, *Labor Relations Law*, 4th ed. (Englewood Cliffs, N.J.: Prentice-Hall, 1983), p. 434.

cedure is in most instances the means used to enforce the terms of the contract, it should be made clear that *the employee is not without alternate means, if needed, to enforce his rights* under the contract. Two other avenues of enforcement are available if the labor agreement has been violated: (1) through the National Labor Relations Board, and (2) through the courts. Where there is no arbitration step in the grievance procedure, when an employer tries to force a solution in violation of the contract, or when a union representative refuses to properly represent the employee, *enforcement is possible either through the NLRB by claiming an unfair labor practice, or through the courts by charging a violation of a contractual right.* If a union that holds the position of exclusive bargaining representative of employees declines to process the grievance of a member of the bargaining unit, this is *tantamount to refusing representation,* which constitutes a violation of Section 8(b)(1)(A) of Taft-Hartley National Labor Relations Act.[6] Furthermore, Section 301 of the Taft-Hartley Act allows access to both state and federal courts for suits arising from violations of collective bargaining contracts. This means that "in the absence of an arbitration clause a court can be asked to decide whether to resort to arbitration or to the Courts."[7]

PUBLIC SECTOR: FEDERAL

Whereas LMRA 1947 includes no direct injunction requiring a formal grievance procedure to be included in collective bargaining contracts, there is no such ambivalence under the provisions of CSRA 1978, Title VII, governing collective bargaining for federal employees. Not only is there a statutory mandate that federal-employee contracts include a grievance procedure, but such a procedure shall be the exclusive vehicle, subject to certain conditions involving the nature of government operations, for handling violations of the collective bargaining agreement and for properly applying the laws, rules, or regulations affecting conditions of employment. In capsule form, the CSRA has the following to say about federal requirements for the grievance procedure:

Topic	**CSRA**
Grievance procedure mandated	Section 7121(a)(1) provides: ". . . **Any collective bargaining agreement shall provide procedures for the settlement of grievances.** . . ."

[6]Taylor and Witney, *Labor Relations Law*, pp. 434–35.

[7]R. W. Fleming, "Some Observations on Contract Grievances before Courts and Arbitrators," *Stanford Law Review*, 15, no. 4 (July 1963), 612.

Arbitration mandated

Exclusive grievance procedure

"Grievance" defined

Grievants

Section 7121(a)(1): grievances which "fall within its coverage"

Section 7121(a)(1) continues: "including questions of arbitrability."

This same section continues: "the procedures shall be the exclusive procedures for resolving grievances which fall within its coverage."

Section 7103(a)(2) says: "grievance" means any complaint—

(A) by any employee concerning any matter relating to the employment of the employee;

(B) by any labor organization concerning any matter relating to the employment of any employee; or

(C) by any employee, labor organization, or agency concerning—

(i) the effect or interpretation, or a claim of breach, of a collective bargaining agreement; or

(ii) any claimed violation, misinterpretation, or misapplication of any law, rule, or regulation affecting conditions of employment.

Section 7121(b) also provides that the negotiated grievance procedure shall "be fair and simple" and "provide for expeditious processing."

Section 7103(a)(9) says a grievance constitutes a complaint "by an employee," or "by any labor organization" concerning a matter of employment of the employee and "any employee, labor organization or agency," concerning application of the agreement, law, rule or regulation affecting conditions of employment. Section 7121(b)(3)(A) and (B) also assures the labor organization (the exclusive representative) the right to present grievances on behalf of any employee in the bargaining unit or on its own behalf and assures the employee the right to present a grievance on his own behalf as long as the exclusive representative is assured the right to be present during the proceedings.

Section 7102(a)(9) assigns to this phrase a broad meaning that includes "breach of the collective bargaining agreement" or of any "law, rule, or regulation affecting conditions of employment." However, the expression "fall within its coverage" is also conditioned by exclusions and exceptions relating to the special characteristics of the public sector explicitly identified in this statute. Section 7121(a)(1) says: "Except as provided in paragraph 2 of this subsection, any collective bargaining agreement shall provide procedures for the settlement of grievances." Paragraph 2, referred to above, says: "Any collective bargaining agreement may exclude any matters from the application of the grievance procedure which are provided for in the agreement." The parties, therefore, through negotiation, may choose to limit the scope of the grievance procedure by excluding certain matters from its coverage. Section 7121(c) directly excludes certain matters from access to the grievance procedure. These are claimed violations of Subchapter III of Chapter 73 (relating to prohibited political activities), retirement, life insurance, health insurance, a suspension or re-

Alternatives to grievance procedures

moval under Section 7532 (in the interests of national security), examination, certification, appointment, or the classification of any position which does not result in the reduction in grade or pay of an employee.

Section 7121(a)(1) provides the grievant a choice of an alternative channel of appeal to the grievance procedure. By so doing, the exclusivity of the grievance procedure for resolving grievances that fall within its purview is modified. Section 7121(a)(1) identifies two areas where aggrieved employees may utilize the negotiated grievance procedure, or if they choose, a statutory procedure. This section states: "Except as provided in subsections (d) and (e) of this section, the procedure shall be the exclusive procedures for resolving grievances which fall within its coverage." Section 7721(d) identifies one alternate: "An aggrieved employee affected by a prohibited personnel practice under section 2302 (b)(1) of this title which also falls under the coverage of the negotiated grievance procedure may raise the matter under a statutory procedure, but not both." Prohibited practices referred to above include discrimination against an employee or applicant for employment on the basis of race, color, religion, sex, national origin, age, handicapping conditions, marital status, or political affiliation; soliciting or considering information without the knowledge of an individual who is under or requests consideration for any personnel action; granting preference not authorized by law, rule, or regulation to an employee or applicant; granting preference to a relative; taking or failing to take a personnel action as a reprisal. Section 7121(e) provides that "Matters covered under sections 4303 and 7512 of this title which also fall within the coverage of the negotiated grievance procedure may, in the discretion of the aggrieved employee, be raised either under the appellate procedures of section 7701 of this title or under the negotiated grievance procedure, but not both." Section 4304 refers to actions to reduce in grade or to remove an employee for unacceptable performance. Section 7512 applies to actions involving a removal, a suspension for more than fourteen days, a reduction in grade, a reduction in pay, and a furlough of thirty days or less. Both Section 2302 and Section 4303 matters are appealable to review by the Merit Systems Protection Board.

Grievability and arbitrability questions

The question of the grievability or arbitrability of the subject matter of grievance complaints is also not ignored by CSRA. Section 7121 mandates that the agreement *shall* provide procedures for the settlement of questions of arbitrability. These questions are to be determined by the arbitrator.

PUBLIC SECTOR: STATE AND MUNICIPAL

The majority of the states and municipalities, through statutes or orders, have followed the lead of CSRA 1978, Title VII, or simply CSRA, in explicitly authorizing or requiring negotiated grievance procedures. This is in contrast to the NLRA, which is silent on the subject, although by intent it encourages the establishment of grievance procedures. Section 1173–8.0(f) of New York City's Collective Bargaining Law incorporates the grievance procedure in its statement of policy: "It is hereby declared to be the policy of the City that written collective bargaining agreements with certified or designated employee organizations should contain provisions for grievance procedures." Under the Minnesota state law,

Section 179.65(4), public employees are given the right through their bargaining representative to "meet and negotiate in good faith with their employer regarding grievance procedures and the terms and conditions of employment." Hawaii's Public Employment Relations Act, Section 89–10(a), states that the negotiated labor agreement "may contain a grievance procedure and an impasse procedure culminating in final and binding arbitration, and shall be valid and enforceable when entered into in accordance with provisions." Finally, it should be noted that many of the state statutes and orders under pressure to find alternatives to strike action have incorporated nontraditional techniques into the grievance procedure. These are treated more fully in Chapter 19.

THE GRIEVANCE PROCEDURE

In 1979, formal grievance procedures were included in more than 95 percent of private-sector labor agreements, around 90 percent of the labor agreements covering state and municipal workers, and in excess of 82 percent of the labor agreements covering federal employees. It is fairly safe to assume that as of the present day, close to 100 percent of labor agreements—private, municipal and state, and federal (required by law since 1978)—include formal grievance procedures. Studies show that for the most part, the mechanical aspects of public grievance procedures are found to be similar to those of private procedures. Some areas in which differences have been noted are these: (1) Private- and federal-employee labor agreements have been more specific and more comprehensive than state and municipal agreements; and (2) the scope of the grievance procedure is more limited in the federal, state, and local sectors than in the private sector. Finally, the trend over time has been for grievance procedures, as incorporated into contract language, to become more detailed and formal, not only in the newer agreements of the public sector, "but also in the older established procedures of the private sector."[8] In what follows, the reader is introduced to some of the more common features of grievance procedures by the use of examples from a broad sampling of labor agreements. Where there is a marked difference between public and private grievance procedures, this will be brought out specifically in the illustrations. Otherwise, the examples used are indicative of the common features of grievance procedures, although in detail there are variations, whether in the public or private sector.[9] The illustrations are organized

---

[8]Thomson, *The Grievance Procedure in the Private Sector*, p. 13.

[9]No attempt is made to identify the clauses used as examples of particular contracts. The purpose of the illustrations is to show types of language and procedures, not to personalize the sources. The examples were drawn from a broad cross section of industries plus agreements in the public sector.

under the following headings: scope, grieving party, steps, time limitations, expedited procedure and recompense for time involved.

Scope Provisions establishing the scope or coverage of the grievance procedure fall into two general classifications, limited and unlimited.

Most of the grievance procedures are limited in scope. Usually these confine the grievance that might be appealed to specific matters of the labor contract, its interpretation, conflicts between clauses, and the application of the specific terms of the agreement to specific cases.[10] Examples of such a restricted scope follow.

- A grievance is a difference of opinion with respect to the meaning and application of the terms of this agreement and/or the respective supplementary agreements.
- The term *grievance* as used herein shall mean disputes arising over the interpretation or application of any of the provisions of this collective agreement, including disputes arising over the termination of the employment of an agent.
- In the event that any difference arises between the company and the union, or any employee, concerning the interpretation, application or compliance with the provisions of this agreement, such differences shall be deemed to be a grievance and shall be settled only in accordance with the grievance procedure set forth herein.
- Grievances, within the meaning of the grievance procedure, shall consist only of disputes about wages, hours of work, and working conditions, as provided in this agreement; about the meaning and application of this agreement; and about alleged violations of this agreement.

Procedures that are less limited in scope allow other types of employee complaints to be processed, such as those conflicts that arise because the contract is silent, or because the issue is too unusual to be covered by the contract, or for any number of other reasons. Illustrations of some of these matters are:

- Grievances pertaining to rates of pay, hours of work, or conditions of employment.
- Any questions or problems which might arise concerning working conditions.
- Should any difference of opinion, controversy, or dispute arise between the parties hereto, such differences of opinion, controversy, or dispute shall constitute a grievance.
- A grievance is a matter of personal concern or dissatisfaction to an employee arising from the terms or conditions of employment, the consideration of which is not covered by other systems for agency review and the resolution of which has not been made at the normal superviso-

[10]The Bureau of National Affairs. *Collective Bargaining Negotiations and Contracts.* Washington, D.C.: Section 51:1, 1983.

ry level. Before a matter of personal concern or dissatisfaction (i.e., a complaint) becomes a grievance within the meaning of this section, the parties hereto encourage attempts at informal resolution as set forth in Section 9 of this article. Employee grievances include, but are not limited to, such matters as:

a. Working conditions and environment.

b. Relationships with supervisors and other employees and officials.

c. Implementation of personnel policies, practices and provisions of this agreement.

- Employee grievances do not include *questions of policy* in the areas itemized above. They may, however, include questions of the application of such policy to an individual employee or to a group of employees.

Who May File a Grievance   It goes without saying that all contracts provide for the initiation of grievances by individual employees or groups of employees. The same privilege is not accorded universally to the management or the union. Less than half of the contracts allowed either Management or the Union to initiate grievances.[11] Some illustrative clauses are:

- The union and/or any employee or group of employees shall have the right to present a grievance to the company.
- Grievances may be originated by a complaint of an employee or the union.
- Grievances must be initiated by employees (either singly or jointly); *they may not be initiated by the union.* The union may, however, present a grievance on behalf of an employee or employees who request the union to act for them if they are identified by name.
- Grievances may be presented by the company to the local lodge.

Steps in the Grievance Procedure   Grievance procedures are structured and tailor-made so as to provide a fair hearing for an employee at progressively higher levels of management. Although all procedures are generally similar in this respect, it is obvious that because some firms or agencies are larger, with a more complex management structure, progressive appeal to higher levels of management will involve more steps than the procedures of small and less-complex firms or agencies. Collective bargaining agreements, *while containing many general features in common from one bargaining group to another, must also be tailored in their specific details, primarily work rules, to fit the needs of the specific parties involved.* The same reasoning applies to the specifics of grievance-procedure structure. The number of steps required to achieve the objectives of grievance processing will depend upon such factors as the nature of the bargaining units, past experience in negotiation between the par-

[11]*Ibid.,* Section 51:2.

ties, the policies of management and the union, the size of the company and the union, patterns established in similar situations in the industry, the happenstance of personalities and their backgrounds, and any number of other factors that influence the results of a particular contract negotiation. Thus, a perusal of grievance provisions in a wide variety of labor agreements shows anywhere from *two-step procedures to as many as six- or seven-step procedures, if the arbitration step is included. The most common number of steps found in grievance structures is three, and the next most common is four.*

The following illustrations of grievance procedures reflect the general features of the step-by-step approach to the resolution of grievance complaints but, of course, do not and are not intended to reflect the specific tailoring of the steps to the needs of each situation. Time requirements at each step are omitted in order to highlight the step sequence to higher levels of appeal.

Two-Step Procedures

If at any time a difference arises between the union and the company regarding the true intent and meaning of a provision of this contract, or a question as to the performance of any obligation hereunder, a conference shall be held between a representative of the union and the company in an attempt to settle said differences. If, after such conferences, the matter is not settled, either party may institute arbitration proceedings.

Three-Step Procedures

Step 1	After the complainant or the union has had an opportunity to become aware of the event complained of, he or the union shall discuss it in person with the appropriate foreman; a member of the workmen's committee may accompany the complainant if he so desires.
Step 2	Present the grievances in writing to the company.
Step 3	Demand arbitration of the grievance if it is arbitrable.

Four-Step Procedures

Step 1	Discussion between the shop steward accompanied by the aggrieved employee, at the employee's discretion, and the overseer of the department.
Step 2	If the grievance is not adjusted after its presentation to the overseer, it shall be reduced to writing, dated, and signed by the employee involved and the shop steward. The grievance shall then be discussed between the shop committee for the mill in which the dispute arose and the union business agent on the one side and the representative of the plant (and such assistants as he may desire) on the other side.

Step 3   If the grievance shall not have been adjusted [under Step 2] it shall be taken up between a representative of the union on the one side and representatives of the company on the other side.

Step 4   Any grievance not adjusted may be submitted by either party to arbitration.

Five-Step Procedures

Step 1   The grievance shall be taken up between the employee and his immediate supervisor in an effort to settle the matter. The employee may request his shop committeeman to be present at this time if he so desires.

Step 2   If not adjusted under Step 1, the grievance shall be submitted to the shop steward or to a shop committeeman who shall discuss the matter with the employee's immediate supervisor if either believes the grievance has any merit.

Step 3   If the matter is not thus settled, the grievance shall be reduced to writing and submitted to the plant superintendent, after which it shall be discussed at a meeting of the company and the shop committee where a satisfactory settlement shall be sought.

Step 4   If not adjusted under Step 3, the grievance shall be submitted to higher officials of the company and the union and they shall try to work out a mutually satisfactory settlement.

Step 5   If the grievance is not settled, it shall be submitted to an Arbitration Board.

Six-Step Procedures

Step 1   Discussion between the aggrieved employee and his immediate supervisor, with or without the employee's steward, as the employee elects.

Step 2   Discussion between the aggrieved employee, his steward, and the location manager. Upon request of the steward, the Step 2 hearing shall include the representative of the local lodge.

Step 3   Discussion between representatives designated by the local lodge and representatives designated by the district manager. If the company's answer does not resolve the grievance, it shall be reduced to writing by the local lodge.

Step 4   Discussion between representatives designated by the local lodge and representatives designated by the labor relations department of the company.

Step 5   Step 5 may be invoked only at the option of the local lodge which appealed the grievance. Discussion between representatives designated by the grand lodge and representatives designated by the labor relations department of the company.

Step 6   An arbitrable grievance which has not been settled under the above-described procedure may be appealed to arbitration by the grand lodge automotive coordinator or the company.

Time Limitations on Appeal Steps There is considerable variation among grievance procedures as to the time limitations in appealing and receiving answers at each step in the grievance procedure. These range all the way from grievance procedures that incorporate no time limitations or merely state that the grievance should be handled expeditiously at each step, to grievance procedures that are very detailed in stating time limitations at each phase. Then, too, there is considerable variation, even among those agreements with time limitations, as to the length of time established, some extending over a considerable time period and some confining the time sequence to short periods. Four cases are used merely to illustrate the variation one might find among different contracts in the time span from the beginning of the grievance procedure to the final step, if used.

One way of determining time and step sequences in any particular contract situation is to consider two requirements: (1) To gain commitment to final decisions of the parties at lower levels, *the procedures should not be so short as to bypass or ignore important contributors.* (2) *On the other hand, the procedures should not be so long as to make the grievance process unnecessarily cumbersome and time consuming.* Moreover, while the absence of time limits may have some merit in terms of flexibility and simplicity of the grievance procedure, these are more than offset by the advantages provided by the more timely, systematic, and just treatment of grievances that such time limits help to provide. For illustrative purposes only, several procedures of different lengths are described:

Example 1

Step 1	No time limit.
Step 2	No time limit.
Step 3	If matter not settled within five (5) days, appeal may then be made to Step 4.
Step 4	Arbitration.

Example 2

Step 1	Each party recognizes the value of processing grievances promptly.
Step 2	If not settled at Step 1, reduce to writing within twenty-four (24) hours.
Step 3	Appeal to Step 3 may be made if settlement at Step 2 not reached within forty-eight (48) hours. Step 3 grievance meeting to be held within seventy-two (72) hours.

Step 4   If unsettled at Step 3 meeting, then Step 4 meeting to be held within ten (10) days.

Step 5   If unsettled at Step 4, appeal to arbitration must be made within ten (10) days.

Example 3

Informal   Discuss with foreman within five (5) days of occurrence or knowledge of occurrence.

Step 1   If no satisfactory settlement at informal step within two (2) days, then appealed to Step 1, but no later than three (3) days. Written grievance presented and must be answered within two (2) workdays. If unsettled, may be appealed to Step 2 within two (2) days.

Step 2   Must be reviewed by management within four (4) workdays with the union. Company must answer within four (4) workdays of this meeting. If answer unsatisfactory, appeal to Step 3 must be made within four (4) workdays.

Step 3   Parties must meet within ten (10) workdays of appeal. Company must answer within five (5) workdays of meeting. If answer is unsatisfactory, appeal to arbitration must be made within fifteen (15) days.

Step 4   Arbitration.

Example 4

Step 1   Grievance must be filed within sixty (60) days after it arises. Grievance to be reviewed within fourteen (14) days of submission. Management decision to be made within seven (7) business days of review.

Step 2   If decision unsatisfactory at Step 1, appeal to Step 2 may be made within twenty (20) business days of written notice of management decision at Step 1.

Expedited Procedure   In approximately two-thirds of agreements, there are included special procedures for expediting the handling of the grievance.[12] *Expediting is usually in the form of special time limits, or of starting at a later step in the procedure rather than going through the preliminary steps.* Subjects for which agreements most commonly provide an expedited procedure are *discharges, suspensions, general policy or group grievances, grievances filed by the company, safety or health matters, time study and incentive rates, plantwide or areawide grievances, hiring, issues requiring technical assistance, and benefit plans.* Some illustrations of these special procedures are as follows:

- **If the dispute involves a matter of general application, the initial step shall be Step 3. The initial step shall also be Step 3 in any case where**

[12]*Ibid.*, Section 51:3.

the grievance has arisen from the action of an official other than the immediate superior.

- Discharges or disciplinary actions are to be taken to the manufacturing manager. Appeals from his decision are to go directly to Step 3 of the grievance procedure.
- Discharge and discipline matters not settled directly by the manager-industrial relations and the union are to go directly to Step 4.

Costs of Grievance Processing   About half of agreements allow pay for representatives who present, investigate, or handle grievances.[13] Illustrative of such provisions are the following:

- Where Steps 1 and 2 of the grievance procedure take place during working hours, the company will pay on a straight-line basis for time actually lost by the shop steward, the union committeemen and the employee involved. The company shall not be bound to pay for the time lost in attending Steps 3 and 4 of the grievance procedure.
- Total union group at any [grievance] meeting shall not exceed eight persons. Committee members shall be paid for actual working time while attending such meetings. Time spent in meetings outside working hours shall not be considered as time worked.
- Grievances shall be handled during working hours without loss of pay to the grievance committee, union stewards, or employees involved.

EFFECTIVE GRIEVANCE HANDLING

As with negotiations, the variety of situations that arises in the handling of grievances precludes a formal approach. Each grievance, while similar in some aspects to other grievances, also has its own peculiar characteristics, either as to the details of the problem giving rise to it or as to the personalities involved in it. As a substitute for formulas for effective grievance handling, the reader is given a list of what might be called "grievance-procedure homilies." This list is a composite of the sound kinds of admonition and advice that experience in the field has found essential to successful grievance handling:

HOMILIES FOR MANAGEMENT

- Establish clear-cut policies, understood by all supervisors and employees.
- Authority to handle grievances should be given to the supervisor, and the limits of such authority made clear.

[13]*Ibid.*, Section 51:4.

- A responsible management representative should provide time for the grievant to tell his/her full story in private and without interruption. Give him/her your full attention. End on a friendly note.
- Show your concern for the grievant's problem by following through promptly on any action required by a settlement.
- No grievance should be considered too trivial for your attention.

Homilies for the Union

- Exercise a firm but fair hand in screening grievances for appeal. A poor grievance results in a lost grievance, a dissatisfied union member, a loss of valuable time, and a waste of union money.
- Take care to distinguish between gripes and grievances.
- Don't let grievances become political issues or let union politics influence your work.
- Level with the grievant on his/her case, and be sure the grievant levels with you. This may save later embarrassment and loss of face.

Homilies for Both Parties

- Be sure information on the grievance is complete and accurate.
- Know your labor agreement; check it often. Remember that it may take on a different meaning when applied to different grievance situations.
- Prepare each grievance as if it were to be appealed and presented before an arbitrator.
- Observe carefully all procedural steps required by the grievance procedure. Remember, failure to do so may result in having the case thrown out by an arbitrator without ever hearing the substance.
- Present your full position at the inception of the grievance procedure. Anything added to your position later may be considered new evidence and not admissable.
- As soon as a procedural error or a question of arbitrability arises, enter an objection.
- Settlement at the lowest step in the grievance procedure pays off in time, expense, and emotions.
- Keep the grievant fully informed of the course of a grievance.
- Control your emotions. It is not who is right, but what is right. Tantrums, vindictiveness, personal dislikes, provoking the other party, petty jealousies, and high-pressure tactics weaken your case.
- Delay can be costly as well as disruptive. Process grievances with promptness and dispatch.
- Facts! Facts! Facts! Do not base your case on hearsay. Do not allow verbal statements and hearsay testimony to substitute for written proof and firsthand testimony.
- Never horsetrade one grievance for another. Grievance settlements establish precedence. Settlement on grounds other than merit may return to haunt you.

- Accept settlement graciously. Tomorrow you must go back to living with each other.
- Keep adequate written records to ensure consistency and effectiveness.
- Saving face is important to the grievant, the employer, and the union. It can mean the difference between an amicable and a hostile settlement.
- Always use recognized channels. The agreement is your creation. Maintain the integrity of the agreement by religiously following its procedures.
- Remember, the grievance procedure is intended to resolve, not create, conflict.

Remember that these are only checkpoints for grievance handling, generally drawn from the experience of those on the front line; they in no way cover all possible types of problems arising in human relationships. They are indicative of both the nature of the human problems that arise and what seems to work in handling such problems, but it must be remembered that each situation is a combination of different personalities and problems, and no two are exactly alike. The successful handler of grievances must at one and the same time understand contract law and be an expert in human behavior.[14] Too often, those who are in closest contact with the grievance at its origin and have the best chance to solve it at an early stage have neither characteristic, but are in that spot because of technical competence relative to the product or service of the particular business. In these days of comprehensive labor agreements and laws bearing on human rights and dignity, it no longer behooves management to hire supervision for technical competence only. Today's supervisor, besides being technically competent, *must be at least aware of behavioral psychology,* if not a student in the field.

THE CBO SYSTEM: PREPARING FOR FUTURE NEGOTIATIONS

With the signing of the new contract, the period of testing this contract through its daily application commences. The grievance procedure is the instrument for processing questions concerning the meaning and application of the new agreement. But the grievance process serves another purpose. It is the source of bargaining information relative to how well the contract is performing during its application and if changes in the con-

---

[14]See Thomson, *The Grievance Procedure in the Private Sector,* pp. 14–19, for a discussion of "What Constitutes a 'Good' Grievance Procedure?" For sample private-sector clauses, complete with the names and locations of the companies and unions that negotiated them, see Prentice-Hall's *Industrial Relations Guide.*

tract dictated by that application will be required at the next round of negotiations. The bargaining information that the grievance procedure provides comes from two sources. The first source includes the many incidents where the problems of applying the contract are solved before becoming formal grievances. The second source comes from the formal grievance settlements. It is vital to have a feedback system to assure proper flow of vital bargaining data preparatory to the next negotiation. Chapter 7, "Gathering and Assembling Bargaining Information," addresses the means used to gather and record this flow of data resulting from the application of the agreement. Gathering such information is a continuous process from contract to contract. Upon the consummation of one contract, the gathering of bargaining data from the grievance procedure begins for the next contract negotiations.

SELECTED REFERENCES

Begin, James P., and Joseph C. Ullman, *Negotiated Grievance Procedures in the Public Sector,* Reprint no. 24. New Brunswick, N.J.: Institute of Management and Labor Relations, Rutgers University, 1971. Three articles, two by the authors jointly, including "The Structure and Scope of Appeals Procedures for Public Employees," "The Private Grievance Model in the Public Sector," and "Negotiated Grievance Procedures in Public Employment."

Brandt, Floyd S., and Carroll R. Daugherty, *Conflict and Cooperation.* Homewood, Ill.: Richard D. Irwin, 1967. A excellent casebook with major emphasis on grievance administration. The authors lean heavily on the many cases in which Professor Daugherty was involved. Provides an excellent format for establishing a learning-experience approach to grievance administration.

Crane, Bertram R., and Roger M. Hoffman, *Successful Handling of Grievances.* New York: Central Book Company, 1965. A detailed and thorough coverage of every aspect of grievance handling, from the nature of the grievance to the grievance machinery and labor agreements, and finally ending with the achievement of grievance control and proper grievance handling.

Davey, Harold W., Mario F. Bognanno, and David L. Estenson, *Contemporary Collective Bargaining,* 4th ed. Englewood Cliffs, N.J.: Prentice-Hall, 1982. Chapter 7 is highly recommended reading. The authors' experience in grievance administration is well put to use in this highly informative chapter on contract administration.

Fossum, John A., *Labor Relations—Development, Structure, Process.* Dallas, Tex.: Business Publications, Inc., 1982. Chapter 13, devoted to contract administration and Chapter 14, devoted to grievance arbitration are recommended reading.

Industrial Relations Guide. Englewood Cliffs, N.J.: Prentice-Hall, Inc. Biweekly reports in this continuing series explain the impact of new developments and new trends in collective bargaining and arbitration. The basic text of the looseleaf volume, updated periodically, includes a complete explanation of the nature of labor arbitration, plus descriptions of past awards and thousands of sample contract clauses. "New Ideas" articles are written by outside experts in the field on subjects of interest to management and labor alike.

Kochan, Thomas A., *Collective Bargaining and Industrial Relations—From Theory to Policy and Practice.* Homewood, Ill.: Richard D. Irwin, 1980. In Chapter 12, the author examines carefully the nature of grievance procedures and their relationship to the bargaining system, and advances criteria for the evaluation of grievance procedures.

Kuhn, James W., "The Grievance Process," in *Frontiers of Collective Bargaining,* eds. John T. Dunlop and Neil W. Chamberlain. New York: Harper & Row, 1967. A thorough discussion of the grievance process as a power base, and problems and opportunities in grievance handling.

Labor Relations Guide. Englewood Cliffs, N.J.: Prentice-Hall, Inc. This service, updated weekly, is particularly useful for business executives, lawyers, personnel managers, and consultants who want information that quickly and easily answers day-to-day labor-relations questions. Important decisions of the National Labor Relations Board, the Equal Employment Opportunity Commission, the Occupational Safety and Health Administration, and the courts are reported promptly in easy-to-understand language. The service includes an explanation of labor laws—Wage-Hour, the NLRA, the Civil Rights Act, Age Discrimination, Vietnam Era Veterans Readjustment Act, OSHA, garnishment, state labor laws, and others—and provides the full texts of federal laws and executive orders.

McPherson, Donald S., *Resolving Grievances—A Practical Approach.* Reston, Va.: Reston, 1983. An excellent study of the grievance process, including grievance arbitration, with case simulations.

Najita, Joyce M., *Guide to Statutory Provisions in Public Sector Collective Bargaining—Grievance Adjustment Procedures.* Industrial Relations Center, University of Hawaii, Honolulu, 1975. An excellent coverage of grievance-adjustment procedures under state statutes, ordinances, rules, and regulations.

Public Personnel Administration: Labor-Management Relations. Englewood Cliffs, N.J.: Prentice-Hall, Inc. Focusing on public-sector collective bargaining, this service explains laws, methods, rulings, clauses, and established precedents (including summaries of arbitration awards). Biweekly reports provide news of developments in this complex area. Sections of the basic text include "New Ideas," "Collective Bargaining Problems and Answers," "Annotated Public Employment Relations Laws and Regulations," "Union Contract Clauses," and "Arbitration Awards Analyzed."

Rehmus, Charles M., ed., *Developments in American and Foreign Arbitration.* Washington, D.C.: Bureau of National Affairs, Inc., 1968. Chapter 1 includes papers delivered at the 1968 meetings of the National Academy of Arbitrators concerning American grievance procedures compared to the British and Canadian.

————, "Positive Contract Administration," in *ASPA Handbook of Personnel and Industrial Relations,* eds. Dale Yoder and H. G. Heneman, Jr. Washington, D.C.: Bureau of National Affairs, Inc., 1979. The authors examine the role of the supervisor in contract administration, the grievance procedure as the essence of positive contract administration, and positive contract administration as an element in the prevention of grievances.

Taylor, Benjamin J., and Fred Witney, *Labor Relations Law,* 4th ed., chap. 15. Englewood Cliffs, N.J.: Prentice-Hall, 1983. A comprehensive statement of the legal nature of the grievance procedure as it has evolved through the Wagner and Taft-Hartley acts. (See Chapter 21 for the public sector.)

Thomson, A. W. J., *The Grievance Procedure in the Private Sector.* Ithaca, N.Y.: New York State School of Industrial and Labor Relations, Cornell University, 1974. In pamphlet form, this is a very basic and informative account of the function, development, structure, operation, and problems of the grievance procedure.

U.S. Department of Labor, *Grievance Procedures* (1964) and *Grievance and Arbitration Procedures in State and Local Agreements* (1975). (See annotated references, Chapter 7.)

Wage-Hour Guide. Englewood Cliffs, N.J.: Prentice-Hall, Inc. This volume includes the text of both the Equal Pay law and the Wage-Hour law. Information is provided on who is covered, who is exempt, wages and overtime, child labor restrictions, records-investigations, enforcement methods, government contracts, and related topics. A regular report explains current developments. A "Current Matter" section contains administrative opinions and digests of court decisions.

Werne, Benjamin, *Administration of the Labor Contract,* Chs. 1, 2, and 3. Mundelein, Ill.: Callaghan & Company, 1963. The author provides a most exhaustive and comprehensive study of arbitral interpretation and application of contract clauses. In his coverage of hundreds of arbitration decisions, the author finds one overriding factor standing out: the importance of precise, clear, and correct language.

Yoder, Dale, and Paul D. Staudohar, *Personnel Management and Industrial Relations,* 7th ed. Englewood Cliffs, N.J.: Prentice-Hall, 1982. Chapter 15 discusses the grievance procedure within the framework of the collective bargaining relationship of the parties.

CHAPTER 18

GRIEVANCE ARBITRATION

In Chapter 2, the point was made that in the last decade, the statement *collective bargaining is an institution in its own right* has taken on real and unmistakable meaning. It now seems appropriate, in view of the last few years' activity, to add that *grievance arbitration has also come of age.* A president of the prestigious National Academy of Arbitrators, Bert L. Luskin, succinctly stated his own point of view:

> *Arbitration has come of age and with it have come the carpers, snipers, and sensation seekers. With one notable exception, each and every attack on the process and those who administer it has come from persons and groups who have absolutely no knowledge of the process, its history, its purpose, and its aims.*
>
> *. . . I do not believe, however, that there has been a single proposal advanced that can serve as a worthy substitute for honest, effective administration of good grievance procedure or the arbitration process.*[1]

Although the coming of age of grievance arbitration received its stimulus under the War Labor Board policy of World War II,[2] requiring

---

[1]Bert L. Luskin, *Arbitration Comes of Age* (Amherst: Labor Relations and Research Center, University of Massachusetts, 1967), pp. 1, 8.

[2]For a full account, see Paul Prasow and Edward Peters, *Arbitration and Collective Bargaining*, 2nd ed. (New York: McGraw-Hill, 1983), chapter 1. U.S. Supreme Court deci-

the adoption of grievance-arbitration clauses in labor agreements, this distinctive use of arbitration in concept is not new. The Webbs, as already noted, recognized early the need for a judicial approach to problems of contract interpretation. In their monumental study, *Industrial Democracy*, they noted:

> . . . *This vital distinction is between the making of a new bargain and the interpreting of the terms of an existing one. Where the machinery for Collective Bargaining has broken down, we usually discover this distinction has not been made.* . . . This, it will be seen, is exclusively an issue of fact, in which both the desires and the tactical strength of the parties directly concerned must be eliminated. . . . *It is indispensable that the ascertainment of facts should attain an almost scientific precision. Moreover, the settlement should be automatic, rapid, and inexpensive.*[3]

And as related in Chapter 2, an agreement resulting from the settlement of the Cloakmakers' strike of 1910 established, among a number of other important provisions, a board of arbitration: one representative from each side and attorneys from the two groups. The board was charged with considering and settling all grievances, and its rulings were to be final and binding.

Recognition of the need for distinction between the handling of disputes over new contract terms and disputes arising from interpretation of the contract was also recognized early in the railroad industry. The Newlands Act of 1913 first made the distinction. The Transportation Act of 1920 continued the distinction by authorizing a system of regional boards of adjustment on each railroad, to which disputes involving contract interpretation could be referred if unsettled at the local level. Under the Railway Labor Act, as originally established, the twofold division—between disputes over changes in the contracts and disputes involving interpretation of the contract or arising from disciplinary action—was continued. The Railway Labor Act of 1926 included sections authorizing the establishment of boards of adjustment to deal with disputes involving interpretation of the contract. This was followed in 1934 by amendments to the act, which replaced the regional boards of adjustment with a permanent adjudicating agency, the National Railroad Adjustment Board.[4] It was from such a background that the War Labor Board activities of World

---

sions such as the Trilogy also added to the impetus given by the WLB activities. *Ibid.*, chap. 13.

[3]Sidney and Beatrice Webb, *Industrial Democracy* (London: Longmans, Green and Co., 1902), pp. 182–84. (Emphasis added.)

[4]Reed C. Richardson, *The Locomotive Engineer, 1863–1963* (Ann Arbor: Bureau of Industrial Relations, University of Michigan, 1963), pp. 410–12.

War II created the impetus for the broad usage of grievance arbitration today.

In this chapter, use of the term *arbitration* is confined to its use in conjunction with the grievance procedure. Thus, the term *grievance arbitration* is used to describe the special function of arbitration as a part of the contract-administration process. Moreover, grievance arbitration refers to voluntary rather than compulsory arbitration—that is, the use of arbitration as a final appeal step in the grievance procedure through the voluntary agreement of the parties. This voluntary agreement becomes a part of the language of the negotiated agreement and therefore a contractual obligation of the parties for the term of the agreement. This use is in contrast to *compulsory arbitration*, which is imposed upon the parties rather than resulting from their voluntary agreement. Distinctions will also be made among various constructs of voluntary arbitration, such as *single-arbitrator* arbitrations, *tripartite board* of arbitration, *ad hoc* arbitration, and *permanent* arbitration (single arbitrator or panel of arbitrators).

The use of a quasi-judicial process such as grievance arbitration indicates a recognition by the parties that more is to be gained by a judicial solution to problems of contract interpretation than by resorting to such overt actions as lockouts and strikes. In adopting grievance-arbitration clauses in their contracts, the parties are agreeing under contract that this process will be followed in lieu of the right to lock out or to strike. But it is even more than this. The acceptance of grievance arbitration is an act of support for the concept of self-government in the workplace and an act of faith in the free-enterprise concept, since the probable alternative to self-government is government intervention in the affairs of both parties.

A measure of the broad acceptance of grievance arbitration in matters of contract interpretation and administration may be seen in the usage statistics for both the public and private sectors of the economy. In the private sector, negotiated grievance procedures, including clauses providing for grievance arbitration, are almost universally prevalent. A study based on agreements between agencies and unions in the federal sector found, in the LAIRS (Labor Agreement Information Retrieval System) file, that as of May 1, 1975, 90 percent of the agreements, covering 93 percent of the federal employees, contained provisions for grievance arbitration.[5] In the state and local sectors, nine out of ten agreements between government organizations and unions contained provisions for grievance arbitration.[6] The trend in federal-, state-, and local-sector agreements toward

---

[5]*Negotiated Grievance Procedures and Arbitration in the Federal Government*, U.S. Civil Service Commission, November 1975, p. 1.

[6]*Grievance and Arbitration Procedures in State and Local Agreements*, U.S. Department of Labor, Bureau of Labor Statistics, Bulletin 1833, 1975, p. 1.

duplication of the prevalence of arbitration procedures in private-sector agreements is clear, and further emphasizes the coming of age of grievance arbitration in labor agreements.

It is the purpose of this chapter to complete the discussion that began in Chapter 16 with the *grievance* and continued in Chapter 17 with the *grievance procedure,* by considering the nature and mechanics of *grievance arbitration* as the terminal step in the grievance procedure. First to be considered is the legal environment within which grievance arbitration operates in both the private and public sectors. Next, a detailed examination is made of types of language in contracts directed to all aspects of grievance arbitration. The contract must also be considered as a factor in the overall legal environment of grievance arbitration. Finally, as in the chapters on negotiation and grievance procedure, some selected bits of advice in the form of arbitration homilies are noted as a way to be effective in presenting arbitration cases.

LEGAL ENVIRONMENT

The Courts

The legal environment of grievance arbitration is a matter of law resulting from court decisions, from statutes, from executive orders, and from the trade agreement. In the discussion in Chapter 4 of arbitrators as third parties to the collective bargaining process, the legal status of grievance-arbitration decisions was explained. The decision of the arbitrator is not only final and binding by contractual agreement but may be enforced through appeal to the courts. It may be overturned by the courts only if it involves a misuse of authority or procedural error by the arbitrator. The courts do not inquire into the reasoning of the arbitrator or the decision based upon the reasoning. Court inquiry is confined to whether or not the arbitrator has exceeded or abused his authority. Justice William O. Douglas, writing the majority opinion in the "Trilogy" decision of the Supreme Court, clearly stated the case for private arbitration in collective bargaining. The flavor would be lost by any attempt to paraphrase. On the matter of the equity of grievance claims, the Court stated:

> The question is not whether in the mind of a court there is equity in the claim. Arbitration is a stabilizing influence only as it serves as a vehicle for handling every and all disputes that arise under the agreement.
>
> . . . The function of the court is very limited when the parties have agreed to submit all questions of contract interpretation to the arbitrator. It is then confined to ascertaining whether the party seeking arbitration is making a claim which on its face is governed by the contract. Whether the moving party is right or

wrong is a question of contract interpretation for the arbitrator. In these circumstances the moving party should not be deprived of the arbitrator's judgment, when it was his judgment and all that it connotes that was bargained for.

The courts therefore have no business weighing the merits of the grievance, considering whether there is equity in a particular claim, or determining whether there is a particular language in the written instrument which will support the claim. The agreement is to submit all grievances to arbitration, not merely those the court will deem meritorious.[7]

The Court then made clear its refusal to review the merits or equity of an arbitration award:

The refusal of courts to review the merits of an arbitration award is the proper approach to arbitration under collective bargaining agreements. The federal policy of settling labor disputes by arbitration would be undermined if courts had the final say on the merits of awards.

. . . As we there [American Manufacturing Co. case] emphasized, the question of interpretation of the collective bargaining agreement is a question for the arbitrator. It is the arbitrator's construction which was bargained for; and so far as the arbitrator's decision concerns construction of the contract, the courts have no business overruling him because their interpretation of the contract is different from his.[8]

Finally, the Court outlined the situation under which it would review an arbitration case:

. . . Nevertheless, an arbitrator is confined to interpretation and application of the collective bargaining agreement; he does not sit to dispense his own brand of industrial justice. . . . When the arbitrator's words manifest an infidelity to this obligation, courts have no choice but to refuse enforcement of the award.[9]

STATUTE

It is not only the courts that have addressed themselves to the legal meaning, and perimeters of grievance arbitration. By statute, the use of griev-

---

[7]*Steelworkers v. American Manufacturing Co.*, 363 U.S. 564 (1960).

[8]*Steelworkers v. Enterprise Wheel and Car Corporation*, 363 U.S. 593 (1960). Similarly, the National Labor Relations Board, although not going quite so far, has adopted the policy of deferring to arbitration awards involving conduct allegedly consisting of both an unfair labor practice and a violation of contract, if certain specified conditions have been met. See Benjamin Aaron, *Contemporary Issues in the Grievance and Arbitration Process: A Current Evaluation*, reprinted from *Collective Bargaining Today* (Washington, D.C., Bureau of National Affairs, Inc., 1971), p. 163.

[9]*Ibid.*

ance arbitration has been not merely encouraged but made a part of public policy. This may be witnessed in the Railway Labor Act of 1926, in the provisions of the Labor Management Relations Act of 1947, in CSRA 1978, Title VII, and in state statutes.

As noted earlier, adjudication of appealed grievances is a process of long standing in the railway industry. The Railway Labor Act, in Section 3 of Title I, provides for the establishment of a "National Railway Adjustment Board." In Section 3, under Subsection (i), the nature of the work to be handled by the adjustment board is delineated:

> *(i) The disputes between an employee or group of employees and a carrier or carriers growing out of grievances or out of the interpretation or application of agreements concerning rates of pay, rules, or working conditions, including cases pending and unadjusted on the date of approval of this Act, shall be handled in the usual manner up to and including the chief operating officer of the carrier designated to handle such disputes; but, failing to reach an adjustment in this manner, the disputes may be referred by petition of the parties or by either party to the appropriate division of the Adjustment Board with a full statement of the facts and all supporting data bearing upon the disputes.*

If a deadlock occurs on the board with respect to the settlement of a case, the act provides further that the board shall select a neutral person "to be known as 'referee,' to sit with the division as a member thereof and make an award." The act further provides that the awards of the adjustment board "shall be final and binding upon both parties to the dispute, except insofar as they shall contain a money award" and may be enforced through the district court of the United States, where the findings of the board "shall be prima facie evidence of the facts therein stated. . . ."

In the private sector (excepting Railway Labor Act coverage), the Labor Management Relations Act of 1947 supports a terminal step for grievance appeals as a matter of public policy. As a part of the charge to the Federal Mediation and Conciliation Service, Section 203(d) states:

> *(d) Final adjustment by a method agreed upon by the parties is hereby declared to be the desirable method for settlement of grievance disputes arising over the application or interpretation of an existing collective-bargaining agreement. The [Mediation] Service is directed to make its conciliation and mediation services available in the settlement of such grievance disputes only as a last resort and in exceptional cases.*

The Taft-Hartley also makes clear that one of the obligations the government assumes in promoting industrial peace is to use its facilities to furnish assistance to employers and the representatives of the employees in "formulating for inclusion within" their agreements provision for "final adjustment of grievances or questions regarding the application or interpretation of such agreements. . . ."[10] Section 7121(b)(3)(C) of CSRA 1978, Title VII, mandates arbitration as a terminal step of the grievance procedure. It requires that any "grievance not satisfactorily settled shall be subject to binding arbitration which may be invoked by either the exclusive representative or the agency." It is important to note that the grievance procedure must include the arbitration step, the arbitration decision is binding, and arbitration may only be invoked by the exclusive employee representative or the agency. Section 7121(a)(1) also provides that the grievance procedure shall include procedures for determining questions of arbitrability. The arbitrator thus becomes the final determiner within the framework of the grievance procedure as to whether matters appealed to the grievance procedure are within the scope of the grievance procedure and thus arbitrable. His decision can be appealed to the Authority. Section 7122 provides that either party may file with the Federal Labor Relations Authority, an exception to an arbitration award only under these conditions:

(1) because it is contrary to any law, rule, or regulation; or

(2) on other grounds similar to those applied by Federal courts in private sector labor-management relations; the Authority may take such action and make such recommendations concerning the award as it considers necessary, consistent with applicable laws, rules, or regulations.

This is in contrast to private-sector appeals from arbitration awards when the courts will only proceed if the arbitrator has been guilty of procedural error or of exceeding his authority. The courts will not examine the substance of the decision—only questions related to procedural error and exceeding authority. The CSRA, on the other hand, allows the Authority to examine the substance of the award in relation to law, rule, and/or regulation.

State statutes vary with respect to mandating or not mandating terminal arbitration in the grievance procedures negotiated by state or local agencies with labor organizations. These statutes also vary as to whether they apply to all groups engaged in collective bargaining or to specific groups. A survey of state statutes that address the use of grievance procedure and grievance arbitration indicates that two states prohibit terminal grievance arbitration, seven states mandate a terminal grievance arbitration step, and twenty-two states include specific language in their statutes permitting the inclusion of terminal grievance arbitration in contracts covering state and/or municipal employees.[11]

[10]Taft-Hartley, Title II, Section 201 (c).

[11]The author's extrapolation from *Summary of State Laws*, Government Employee Relations Reporter. Washington, D.C., Sections 51:505 to 51:530, 1981.

LEGAL FRAMEWORK: THE LABOR AGREEMENT

The previous discussion, whether referring to congressional, court, or executive-branch action, has stressed one point: uniform support for a terminal step in the grievance procedure—arbitration—that permits the process to operate with minimal interference from the outside except for matters irrelevant to the contract or where authority under the contract has been abused or exceeded by the arbitrator.

Attention now turns to the collective bargaining agreement and grievance arbitration. The purpose of this section is to inform the reader about the manner and the language by which the agreement, a legal document, incorporates the terminal step of arbitration into the formal grievance procedure. Emphasis is not upon the union or industry where the particular clause originated, but upon the basic language and construction of grievance-arbitration clauses. The illustrations used are ordered somewhat chronologically to the grievance-arbitration procedure, so as to follow step by step through the entire process from the request for arbitration to the final decision of the arbitrator. This outline is not exhaustive of all variations in grievance-arbitration provisions but is indicative of the general language and structure of such provisions.

TIME LIMITS ON REQUEST FOR ARBITRATION

Following the practice of setting time limits in moving from one step of the grievance procedure to another, most agreements set a definite time limit within which the grieving party must request arbitration. As the following examples indicate, this time limit may vary considerably.

- If the grievance is not settled, either party may, within 15 days after the reply of the Director is due, by written notice to the other, request arbitration.
- If no satisfaction has been reached in the first two steps, then the grievance may be submitted to arbitration upon written notice within thirty days after delivery of the Company's Second Step answer.
- If such efforts fail to produce a mutually satisfactory understanding, the Council [labor organization] may, within six (6) months following the date of the occurrence or situation which is in dispute . . . be referred to arbitration.
- Any grievance which remains unsettled after having been fully processed . . . may be submitted to arbitration . . . provided such request is made within 60 days after the final decision of the Company has been given.
- Within and no later than one (1) year after the Union's notice of intent to arbitrate a grievance has been made . . . the Union may notify the American Arbitration Association to proceed with the selection of an

Arbitrator under its Voluntary Labor Arbitration rules; provided the Union shall not be deemed to have forfeited its grievance by reason of its failure to notify the Association.

WHAT MAY BE SUBMITTED TO ARBITRATION

In most instances, the issues referable to arbitration are identical to issues subject to the grievance procedure or are put in general terms as being matters covered by the contract. In some instances, however, the parties have specifically excluded certain issues from the arbitration procedure.

- The provisions of this Article [Arbitration] shall be applicable only to discipline or termination grievances and to grievances involving disputes concerning the application or interpretation of this contract or the application or the interpretation of the business practices, rules, regulations, now or hereafter in force in accordance with this contract.
- The Umpire shall have no power to . . . establish or change any wage; nor to rule on any dispute . . . regarding Production Standards. The Umpire shall have no power to rule on any issue or dispute arising under the Waiver Section or the Pension Plan, Insurance Program and Supplemental Unemployment Benefit Plan Section, except with respect only to the question of whether a discharged employee should receive a supplemental allowance.
- Grievances not concerning the application of the provisions of this Contract and grievances concerning general rates of pay shall not be arbitrable.
- Any dispute, difference, disagreement or controversy of any nature or character, whether or not a grievance between the Union and Company which has not been satisfactorily adjusted . . . shall be promptly referred to arbitration.
- In the event that parties shall be unable under the Grievance Procedure herein provided, to resolve any dispute growing out of the application or interpretation of any provisions of this Contract, such dispute shall be submitted to arbitration upon the sole issues of interpretation or application.
- [Public sector] It is agreed that arbitration of grievances only applies to the interpretation or application of this agreement. Arbitration does not extend to the interpretation or change of the agency or higher regulations or policy. Arbitration does not extend to grievances filed under agency procedures.

A good indication of the relative numbers of different types of issues appealed to arbitration may be gathered from the FMCS report on numbers of closed arbitration-award cases reported to the service for the fiscal year 1981. Total cases amounted to 8,101.[12]

[12]Federal Mediation and Conciliation Service, *34th Annual Report, Fiscal Year* 1981.

General Issues (Overtime other than pay, Seniority, Union officers, Strikes and lockout, Working conditions, Discrimination, Management rights, and work scheduling)	24%
Economic: Wage Rates and Pay Issues (Wages issues, Rate of pay, Severance pay, Reporting, Call-in and call back, Holidays, Vacations, Incentive, Overtime)	11%
Fringe Benefit Issues (Health and Welfare, Pensions, Other)	3%
Discharge and Disciplinary Issues	40%
Technical Issues (Job posting and bidding, Job evaluation)	5%
Scope of Agreement (Subcontracting, Jurisdictional disputes, Foreman, Supervision, Mergers, Consolidations, Other)	3%
Arbitrability of Grievances (Procedural, Substantive, Other)	10%
Not Elsewhere Classified	4%

WHO MAY REQUEST ARBITRATION

Although it may seem a simple matter, agreements do vary as to who—the union, the employer and/or the employee—may initiate arbitration. Employee initiation unilaterally is the exception rather than the rule, for a very simple reason: Arbitration is costly and time consuming. As a result, the union either retains to itself the right to request arbitration or requires that an employee initiating arbitration have its approval. In a few instances, employees may take the initiative alone.

- No individual employee himself may invoke Step 4 [arbitration].
- . . . such matters thus arising may be submitted to arbitration at the request of either the Agent or Union, or both.
- If the union or the Town is not satisfied with the decision of the Personnel Board, it may . . . submit grievance to arbitration.
- Any and all matters in dispute . . . which have not been adjusted pursuant to the procedure therein provided, shall be referred to arbitration.
- [Public sector] If the employee or union is dissatisifed with such decision, he or the union may request arbitration.

In the federal sector, CSRA, Section 7121(b)(3)(C) states that binding arbitration may be invoked by "either the exclusive representative or the agency."

SELECTING THE ARBITRATOR

Agreements vary in two general ways in selection of the arbitrator: (1) the method of selection, and (2) the type of arbitration—ad hoc single arbitrator, permanent arbitrator, tripartite arbitration board, or some other variation.

- The dispute shall then be submitted for final and binding determination to a single arbitrator, who shall be such person as may be mutually agreed upon.
- [Public sector] The question in dispute shall then be referred to an arbitrator selected by the parties from a panel or panels submitted by the American Arbitration Association, provided that the parties may mutually agree on a different method of selecting an arbitrator than that herein set forth.
- The arbitrator shall be agreed upon by the Local Management and the Regional Direction. If they cannot agree on an arbitrator . . . the moving party may request the Federal Mediation Service to name seven (7) arbitrators. The arbitrator shall be selected from such list in the following manner:

  (1) Within ten (10) calendar days from receipt of the list of arbitrators the Union or the Company . . . shall strike the names of three (3) on this list of seven (7) arbitrators;

  (2) The other party shall then strike three (3) names within the next ten (10) calendar days; the remaining name shall be the arbitrator.

- The parties shall jointly request the Director of the FMCS to submit a list of five (5) arbitrators. From this list the Grand Lodge Automotive Coordinator shall first strike three names. The Company shall then select the arbitrator from the remaining two names.
- . . . if the parties cannot agree upon any member of such list the Arbitrator shall be designated by the head of said Service [FMCS].
- In the event that the first two arbitrators are unable to agree on the appointment of the third arbitrator, then they will, together, ask the American Arbitration Association for a list of five persons, each fit to act as a neutral arbitrator. The names of these persons shall be arranged in alphabetical order upon two sheets of paper. The Company and the Union shall each take one sheet and cross out not more than two names. The first name not crossed out on both lists shall be the third arbitrator. . . .
- In the event that these two [employer-union-representative board] are unable to reach a decision within seven (7) days, then in that event a third person shall be chosen by the committee to act as an arbitrator and chairman of the committee. This committee shall act as a board of arbitration and the decision of such board shall be final and binding upon the parties to this agreement.
- The parties shall select a permanent arbitrator who shall serve subject to conditions mutually specified by the parties in agreement with the arbitrator.
- The impartial chairman shall have only the functions set forth herein and shall serve for one year from date of appointment provided he continues to be acceptable to both the Union and the Corporation.
- [Public sector] Such arbitration shall be conducted by an arbitrator designated from a standing panel of three (3) arbitrators maintained by the Office of Collective Bargaining in accordance with applicable law, rules, and regulations.

- The third arbitrator [neutral] shall be chosen from the seventeen-man permanent panel agreed to by the parties by alternately striking names until one remains and he shall be immediately notified.
- The question as to which party will strike first shall be determined by the toss of a coin.

In private-sector agreements, both the Federal Mediation and Conciliation Service and the American Arbitration Association are used widely as a source of names of arbitrators who, after being investigated and approved, have been placed on their arbitration panels. In the federal sector, the FMCS is used heavily as a source of arbitrator names; in the state and local sectors, almost 90 percent of the agreements call for use of either state or local labor agencies or the American Arbitration Association. Complete information on the AAA and FMCS may be obtained by writing to these organizations.

PREHEARING PRESENTATIONS

In most instances, the matter of submission of prehearing material or statements is left to the predilection of the parties or the desires of the arbitrator. In some cases, the parties choose to make these a formal contract commitment.

- The parties shall be mutual agreement select an arbitrator and shall execute a submission agreement. If the parties fail to agree on a joint submission each shall submit a separate submission and the arbitrator shall determine the issue or issues to be heard, provided that said issue is arbitrable in accordance with this Section.
- The charging and defending parties shall prepare brief written statements of the grievance which outlines the respective positions of the parties and shall deliver such statements to the Arbitrator and the other party at least seven (7) calendar days prior to the arbitration hearing.
- The Union and the Employer shall prepare a written submission agreement which shall be presented to the Board. The submission agreement shall specify the issue in dispute and the section or sections of the Agreement that are involved. In the event that the parties cannot agree on a joint submission agreement, then each party shall make its submission separately and supply the other party with a copy of such separate submission.
- [Public sector] Following selection of the arbitrator and his acceptance, the parties will prepare a joint letter submitting the matter in dispute. The joint letter of submission shall stipulate that the arbitrator, in arriving at his award, shall be limited to the interpretation or application of this agreement or agency policy and regulations; and shall not extend to changes, or proposed changes, in the Agreement, policies or regulations. The letter may contain mutually agreed-upon stipulations of fact and may be accompanied by documents the parties mutually agree

should be submitted to the arbitrator prior to the hearing. Either party may submit pre-hearing and/or post-hearing briefs, provided a copy of such briefs is furnished the other party.

ARBITRABILITY

A question that is important from time to time is whether the issue submitted is arbitrable within the agreement or the authority of the arbitrator. This may involve either procedural matters or substantive matters. Procedural matters are usually related to improper procedures through the preceding grievance steps or exceeding the time limits for appeals. Substantive matters usually refer to the type of issue being appealed to arbitration. In the private sector, the only appeal route over a disputed issue of arbitrability is to the courts. In the federal sector, a regular appeal process is established to the Federal Labor Relations Authority. Appeals to the courts in the private sector over an arbitrability issue have resulted more recently in the courts' deferring, at least in the first instance, to the arbitrator himself. The reasoning behind this is "that this issue is itself a dispute between the parties to be resolved through the procedure voluntarily established by them."[13]

- In the event that either party takes the position that a certain matter is not arbitrable, the question of arbitrability shall be submitted to arbitration together with the dispute on the merits of the matter before the arbitrator.
- The arbitrator shall have exclusive authority to determine whether he has jurisdiction over any matter submitted to him for arbitration. Any case appealed to the arbitrator on which he determines he has no power to rule shall be referred back to the parties without decision or recommendation.
- [Public sector] Questions that cannot be resolved by Union or Management as to whether or not a grievance is on a matter subject to arbitration under this Agreement may be referred to the Federal Labor Relations Authority decision.[14]
- Failure of the charging party to act within the applicable time limit specified for any step in the grievance procedure or the time limit herein above specified [arbitration] will constitute waiver of the charging party's right to further consideration of the case.
- In the absence of a written request for arbitration within 15 days after receipt by the union of the third step answer, the grievance shall be settled in accordance with the company's answer.

[13]Arnold Zack, *Understanding Grievance Arbitration in the Public, A Report to the Division of Public Employee Labor Relations,* United States Department of Labor, 1974, p. 9.

[14]Most of the reported cases have been submitted voluntarily to the arbitrator rather than to the Authority.

The Hearing

In most instances, the time, place, and conduct of the hearing are worked out by the parties and/or the arbitrator. Since the hearing is a quasi-judical process, less formal than a regular court session and not confined to the strict rules of procedure and evidence of the courts, the detailing of the hearing in the contract becomes rather difficult and, for good reason, is not often resorted to. One of the advantages of the arbitration process in lieu of court action is its viability and flexibility to respond to the human problems of the work relationship, as well as the contractual and legal problems. At the close of a hearing, the parties do not simply walk away from each other. The next day, they must continue to live with each other. The greater flexibility and procedural permissiveness of the arbitration process allow it to be tailored somewhat in each hearing to both the legal problem and the employer-employee problem, although consideration of the employer-employee problem must be within the allowable perimeters of the legal problem.

Each arbitrator has his or her own way of conducting a hearing, but the general procedures are similar. The arbitrator will usually open the hearing for settling of any preliminary issues that need to be attended to, such as agreement on the issue to be arbitrated, permission for publication of the decision, the format to be followed, whether witnesses are to be sworn, and any other procedural matters of importance to the arbitrator or the parties. Joint exhibits are often presented by the parties at this stage in the proceedings. This is followed by the parties' opening statements anent the issue and the case at arbitration. The opening statement usually consists of a review of the background of the case and what each party intends to prove. It is explanatory, rather than argumentative. Usually, the grieving party will be asked to go first. But if the case involved discharge or discipline, with the employer having the burden of proof to show "just cause," the arbitrator will usually have the employer start first.

Following the opening statements, the parties, in the same order, are permitted to proceed with their full arguments, including witnesses and exhibits to be presented in support of their positions. The choice of when to introduce exhibits is a matter of party preference. Some introduce them at the beginning and then refer to the exhibits as witnesses or arguments are presented in sequence of the development of the case. Objections, if any, to the admissibility of exhibits are entered as the exhibits are submitted. Each party has the opportunity of cross-examining witnesses and cross-examining again, if necessary. This proceeds in an orderly way, but often, depending on the case, in a rather informal give-and-take manner. The important requirement is that the arbitrator be given adequate information on which to base a well-thought-out and fair decision.

The hearing may last for just a few hours or it may run for several days, depending on the complexity of the issues and the presentations of the parties. At the conclusion of the presentation of their positions by the parties, there is usually a summing-up orally by each party of the main points on which its case rests; or, in some instances, if there is to be a written posthearing brief submitted by each party, both may forego a formal summation of their arguments. Before the hearing concludes, the arbitrator and the parties, if the contract does not already specify, come to agreement on submission of posthearing briefs. If they are to be submitted, a date for exchange of the briefs must be established. The easiest way I have found is for the parties to submit two copies of their briefs to the arbitrator, to be posted on a given date, and then for the arbitrator to send each party the other party's brief.

- Within 30 days after the filing of statements with the permanent arbitrator, the permanent arbitrator shall hold an oral hearing at which both parties shall have the privilege of being represented and to present oral, documentary, or physical evidence; to present testimony of witnesses and to examine the witnesses of the other party.

- At any time before the commencement of the arbitration hearing, either party may demand that the proceedings be recorded by a court reporter, in which case the arbitrator shall make arrangements to secure the attendance of a court reporter to record all the testimony and all the proceedings. The reporter shall transcribe the notes of the hearing within twenty (20) calendar days from the completion of the hearing and a copy of the transcript shall be furnished the arbitrator and the party requesting the court reporter. . . . The cost of the transcript for the arbitrator and for the party requesting it will be borne by the party requesting the transcript.

- Any hearing by an arbitrator shall start within three (3) scheduled working days after the arbitrator accepts the assignment and such hearing shall not exceed a period of three (3) calendar days.

- The arbitrator shall follow rules of procedure agreed to by the parties, but in the absence of the agreement thereon, the rule of the voluntary labor arbitration tribunal of the American Arbitration Association shall govern.

- Each party to a case submitted to arbitration will do everything in its power to permit early selection of and decision by the Arbitrator. The parties shall cooperate in arranging with the selected Arbitrator for the time and place that, subject to the Arbitrator's convenience, will best serve for the quickest and least costly disposition of the matter.

- The arbitrator shall hear and decide only one grievance in each case. He shall not be bound by formal rules of evidence. He shall be bound by and must comply with all of the terms of this Agreement. He shall have no power to delete or modify in any way any of the provisions of this Agreement. He shall have the power to make appropriate awards.

- [Public sector] The arbitration hearing shall be held between the hours of 0800–1600 hours, Monday through Friday, excluding holidays.

- [Public sector] Hearings are administrative proceedings and not court proceedings. An arbitrator will explain the procedures to be followed by

- [Public sector] Hearings are administrative proceedings and not court proceedings. An arbitrator will explain the procedures to be followed by both parties at the outset of the hearing.
- Rules of evidence are not applied stricly, but the arbitrator shall exclude irrelevant or unduly repetitious testimony.
- Decisions on admissibility of evidence or testimony will be made by the arbitrator.
- The arbitrator will give the parties opportunity to cross-examine witnesses who appear to testify.
- The arbitrator may exclude any person from the hearing for contumacious conduct or misbehavior that obstructs the hearing.
- There shall be no posthearing submissions to the Arbitrator by either of the parties.

TIME LIMITS ON ARBITRATOR'S DECISION

- The . . . arbitrator will issue the decision within ten (10) days following the date the oral hearing is scheduled.
- Any decision by the arbitrator shall be handed down within fifteen (15) days after the conclusion of the hearing. The parties may mutually agree to extend any or all of the foregoing time limitations.
- The arbitrator shall, within forty-eight (48) hours of the completion of such hearing, provide the parties with an oral record of his award, to be followed by a written statement of his recommendation as soon as time permits.
- The arbitrator shall render his decision in writing within thirty (30) days after the conclusion of the hearing.
- The arbitrator shall render in writing his or her decision within ninety (90) days after the record of the case is closed.

THE ARBITRATOR'S DECISION

The importance of the arbitration step in the grievance procedure is the finality and terminal nature of the award or decision. Although this is the implied objective in the parties' invoking arbitration rather than resorting to a strike, lockout, or other overt action or litigation, almost all agreements in the private sector drive the point home by way of specific language. The same pattern is evident in federal agreements wherein binding arbitration is mandated by CSRA 1978 and among state and municipal-sector agreements wherein over 80 percent with arbitration clauses opted for binding arbitration as the terminal step of the grievance procedure.[15]

- **The arbitrator's decision shall be final and binding on the Company, the Union, and the employee or employees involved.**

[15]The author's extrapolation from a *summary of BNA's, State Labor Laws, Government Employee Relations Reporter*, Sections 51:505–51:530, 1981.

- The arbitrator shall have the authority to interpret and apply the provisions of this Agreement, but shall not have the authority to amend or modify this Agreement or to establish new terms and conditions of this Agreement. There shall be no stoppage of work on account of any controversy which may be made the subject of arbitration and the decision of the arbitrator shall be final and binding on the Company, the Union, and the employee.
- An arbitration award shall be final and binding as to all issues involved in the grievance.
- [Public sector] The decision or award of the arbitrator shall be final and binding to the extent permitted by and in accordance with applicable law and this agreement. The arbitrator shall confine himself to the precise issue submitted for arbitration and shall have no authority to determine any other issues not so submitted to him.
- [Public sector] The party requesting arbitration will determine whether the arbitrator's award will be advisory or binding.
- [Public sector] . . . When an issue has been subjected to binding arbitration, either party may file exceptions to any award with the Federal Labor Relations Authority, under regulation prescribed by the Authority.
- [Public sector] In the event an arbitrator's award is appealed by the Union or management to the Federal Labor Relations Authority, then the award shall be stayed pending the Authority's final determination.
- Either party to an arbitration, upon receiving a final award by a panel arbitrator, may petition the Arbitration Review Board to appeal the decision of the panel arbitrator.

In a few agreements, provision is made not for review of an arbitrator's decision, but for a request for clarification:

- If clarification of the arbitrator's decision is deemed necessary, either party may request clarification from the arbitrator and a copy of the request shall be given to the other party.
- Any dispute between the parties as to the interpretation or construction to be placed upon the award made . . . shall be submitted to the impartial arbitrator who made the award, who may thereupon construe or interpret the award so far as necessary to clarify the same, but without changing the substance thereof, and such interpretation or construction shall be binding upon all parties.

ARBITRATOR AND ARBITRATION COSTS

Two types of costs are usually involved in arbitration hearings: (1) the fee and expenses of the impartial arbitrator; and (2) the costs other than for the arbitrator, such as legal counsel, time off from work for witnesses and officials presenting the two sides of the case, and transcripts, to name a few. Although contracts are usually explicit about the method of bearing the cost of the arbitrator, they are not always explicit about how the other costs will be handled, leaving this matter to direct arrangement between the parties or to established practice. Predominantly, the parties split the cost of the aribtrator equally. Payment of lost time for employees whose presence is necessary at the hearing varies. Legal costs and transcription costs are usually the responsibility of the party receiving the service. Some variations of these more common procedures are included below:

- The arbitrator's fee shall be divided equally between the Company and the Union.
- In the event of arbitration each party shall pay the fee of its arbitrator [a tripartite board] and all costs of preparing and presenting its case. The cost of the third arbitrator and all other reasonable costs of the arbitration proceeding shall be shared equally by the parties.
- All expenses and fees incurred by the impartial arbitrator . . . shall be divided equally and paid in equal portions by the Union involved, the contractor or contractors involved, and/or the individual Employer.
- The expenses and fees of the arbitrator shall be paid by the party requesting arbitration if the specific award sought is not granted by the arbitrator; if the specific award sought is granted, such fees and expenses shall be paid by the other party.
- . . . the fees and expenses of said arbitration shall be paid by the party against whom the decision is rendered.
- The costs of arbitration will be borne by the party who requests arbitration.
- [Public sector] The costs of the arbitrators shall be borne equally by the parties up to $1,000 per grievance. Additional costs above $1,000 shall be paid by the city.
- [Municipal level] The costs of arbitration shall be borne as follows: one-third by the employee organization and two-thirds by the County.
- [Public sector] The fees and expenses of the arbitrator shall be borne equally by the Fire Department and employee concerned; provided, if the union is a party to the dispute, such fees and expenses shall be borne equally by the Fire Department and the union.
- [Public sector] One-half of such compensation [arbitrator] shall be paid by the Authority. The other one-half shall be paid by the union, less the sum of $10 for each grievance appeal to the impartial arbitrator by an individual employee, which sum shall be paid by the individual employee.
- Each party shall bear the expenses in respect to its own witnesses. Each party shall pay one-half of the aggrieved employee's time lost from work for appearance at the arbitration proceedings.
- [Public sector] The employee's representative, appellants, and witnesses shall be on a pay status without charge to annual leave while participating in the arbitration proceedings if they are government employees and the hearings are conducted during the regularly scheduled tour of duty.
- Each party shall be responsible for costs of presenting its own case to arbitration.
- If an employee or other witness is called by the company, the company will reimburse him for time lost. If an employee or other witness is called by the union, the union will reimburse him for time lost.
- [Public sector] The employee serving as the Union representative, the

aggrieved employee and the employee witnesses who have direct knowledge of the circumstances and factors bearing on the case shall be excused from duty to participate in the arbitration proceedings without loss of pay or charge to annual leave.

GRIEVANCE-ARBITRATION HOMILIES

In keeping with the pattern established in the chapters on negotiation and grievance procedure, the reader is presented with advice drawn from experience in the field on how to be effective in the handling of arbitration cases. Although not exhaustive, the homilies listed here emphasize some of the more important requirements in the proper presentation and processing of arbitration cases.

- Don't take cases without merit to arbitration.
- Organize well. Prepare well. Facts are what count.
- The person to convince with the merits of your case is the arbitrator, not the other party.
- Be sure that the submission statement or statement of the issue says what you want it to say. The way the issue is worded dictates the kind of consideration the arbitrator must give to the case. An improperly worded issue can result in a decision contrary to what you seek and may be contrary to the weight of evidence or the obvious merits of the case.[16]
- Know your labor agreement and any laws, regulations, or orders that may be pertinent. Be sure you have firmly in mind their relationship to each other.
- Assemble factual support for your case in the form of documents, records, and witnesses for the purpose of hard proof. Don't attempt to "snow" the other party or the arbitrator by the volume of your exhibits and testimony.
- Do not try to influence the arbitrator on any grounds other than the merits of the case.
- Do not overemphasize, exaggerate, make wild claims, engage in personalities, bicker with the other party, withhold facts, distort, belabor points, fail to show respect for the position of the arbitrator, take your case lightly, badger witnesses, or attempt to belittle the other party.
- Be sure you make clear to the arbitrator all the surrounding circumstances pertinent to the case. Remember, until the hearing, the arbitrator must be assumed to be a stranger to the case. He can make a decision based upon only the information the parties provide him. He does not second-guess.
- Even if the arbitrator does not request such information, be sure that he has relevant material in advance, such as a copy of the contract, a statement of the issue, or any other information that is not argumentative but is relevant to an understanding of the case.

---

[16]For an excellent discussion of the significance of the submission agreement to the outcome of a case, see Prasow and Peters, *Arbitration and Collective Bargaining*, chap. 2.

- Do not approach the arbitrator with the merits of your case or in any way compromise his position as a neutral prior to the hearing.
- Be sure you have clearly in mind what you have to prove. Next, find facts or reasoning necessary to prove your point. Then organize your arguments and documentations in an orderly way. When you present your case, move smoothly from point to point. This will create a good impression.
- Anticipate the other party's arguments and prepare to counter them.
- Be sure you know what you will ask your witnesses and what their answers will be.
- Do careful research on past practice. It may make the difference between proving and not proving your case. Remember, past practice that is applied equitably and not in violation of the clear language of the contract may be used to give the contract meaning. But when it is a matter of past practice versus the clear meaning of the contract, go with the latter in preparing your case.
- Be sure, in preparing your case from the contract language, that you carefully review the entire contract for relevant material. The arbitrator will undoubtedly go through such a process.
- When arbitrators are treating such terms as "just cause" or "reasonableness," the most common tests they apply are whether the accused party has been arbitrary (not governed by principle), capricious (using unpredictable conduct), and/or discriminatory (not treating all equally).
- Eyewitness and written records are much more substantial forms of proof than hearsay or verbal statements.
- Select your arbitrator carefully. Impartiality, integrity, and experience are the most important points to check. Never let an adverse decision from any particular arbitrator blind you to his competence and impartiality as an arbitrator. Go with impartiality and competence every time. It will pay dividends where you have a substantial case.
- Try to find out in advance how the particular arbitrator conducts the hearing. This will give you a key to the way you should prepare for the hearing.
- Don't go into a hearing with a chip on your shoulder or in fear of the arbitrator.
- Remember that an experienced arbitrator is not impressed with histrionics. He wants the facts, not the embellishments.

CONCLUSION

Voluntary grievance arbitration, by the widespread nature of its use, shows a general acceptance and preference over such alternatives as the strike, lockout, or compulsory settlement. This widespread acceptance and use does not mean that the process of grievance arbitration is without its problems. With the added pressure of increasing numbers of employers and employee groups in the public sector that are turning to grievance arbitration, several aspects of the process have come under close scrutiny and criticism. More and more effort and experimentation have been given to reducing costs, to reducing the time involved in grievance arbitration, and to increasing the number of qualified arbitrators. The efforts being made along these lines will be a part of the discussion of resolution of conflict in Part IV.

SELECTED REFERENCES

Baer, Walter E., *Labor Arbitration Guide.* Homewood, Ill.: Dow Jones-Irwin, 1974. An excellent guide by an authority on labor contracts, written in everyday language, concerning arbitration principles and procedures, with the main focus on grievance arbitration. Any individual involved or intended to be involved in arbitration matters would benefit by this study.

BNA Editorial Staff, *Grievance Guide.* Washington, D.C.: Bureau of National Affairs, Inc., 1982. Informative and useful, illustrating general principles of grievance resolution based on a series of examples from arbitration awards. From these examples the reader should secure a good picture of the kinds of points arbitrators consider in handling grievance appeals. Moreover, as the BNA staff emphasizes, care should be taken in attempting to apply the rulings to one situation. No two contracts are exactly alike; therefore, one should carefully check contract language before concluding that any particular ruling would apply.

Carlson, Robert, *Labor Arbitration—What You Need to Know.* New York: American Arbitration Association, 1973. Short but helpful; includes three chapters: (1) "So You Have a Labor Grievance," (2) "How to Select a Labor Arbitrator," and (3) "Preparing for the Arbitration Hearing." A useful appendix includes "The Jargon of Labor Arbitration," "Court and NLRB Decisions," a bibliography of useful readings, the AAA voluntary labor arbitration rules, AAA's expedited arbitration rules, and the U.S. Arbitration Act.

Davey, Harold W., Mario F. Bognanno, and David L. Estenson, *Contemporary Collective Bargaining,* 4th ed. Englewood Cliffs, N.J.: Prentice-Hall, 1982. Few books can boast of this calibre of authorship in the arbitration field. Davey's experience goes back to the War Labor Board days and spans the development of arbitration to the present. Chapter 8, a combined effort of Davey, Bognanno, and Estenson, should be required reading for anyone interested in the process of grievance arbitration.

Dennis, Barbara D., and Gerald G. Somers, eds., *Labor Arbitration at the Quarter-Century Mark.* Washington, D.C.: Bureau of National Affairs, Inc., 1973. For any party interested in a look backward and a look forward at the arbitration process, this volume of the *Proceedings of the National Academy of Arbitrators for 1972* is required reading. Bringing together some of the most experienced arbitrators in the country, the editors have given the reader the benefit of their views of arbitration as they have evolved and what these portend. In addition, some topics of current concern are the use and abuse of arbitral power, judicial review from the viewpoints of the arbitrator and the parties, changing life styles and problems of authority in the plant, and advancing the acceptability of arbitrators.

Elkouri, Frank, and Edna Asper Elkouri, *How Arbitration Works,* 3rd ed. Washington, D.C.: Bureau of National Affairs, Inc., 1978. This is the most frequently cited and certainly considered by most arbitrators as the most comprehensive source on grievance arbitration decisions and precedent. A must for the library of any aspiring arbitrator or student of the grievance-arbitration process. process.

Industrial Relations Guide. Englewood Cliffs, N.J.: Prentice-Hall, Inc. By providing numerous examples of grievances that reached arbitration, the "Arbitration Awards Analyzed" section of this volume offers a useful reference for anyone who wants to see how arbitrators have handled particular types of grievances in the past. This section can help guide the grievance-handler in the early steps of the grievance procedure or in preparing the case for arbitration. References are footnoted.

Labor Arbitration Awards. New York: Commerce Clearing House, Inc. A continuing service containing the full texts of current arbitration awards, published weekly.

Labor Arbitration Reports. Washington, D.C.: Bureau of National Affairs, Inc. Included in the *Labor Arbitration Reports* are awards of arbitrators, reports of fact-finding boards, and court decisions on labor arbitration. This is a continuing service, covering a period from 1946 to the present. Arbitrators are also listed, with biographical sketches.

Landis, Brook I., *Value Judgements in Arbitration—A Case Study of Saul Wallen.* Ithaca, N.Y.: New York State School of Industrial and Labor Relations, 1977. In the Forward, Robert Coulson, President of AAA, describes Saul Wallen as "an outstanding technician and a luminous human being," whose decisions "will serve as target flares for future generations of arbitrators and advocates."

Prasow, Paul, *The Arbitrator's Role,* Reprint no. 240. Institute of Industrial Relations, University of California, Los Angeles, 1974. Professor Prasow discusses the role of the arbitrator in grievance-arbitration matters.

Prasow, Paul, and Edward Peters, *Arbitration and Collective Bargaining. Conflict Resolution in Labor Relations,* 2nd ed. New York: McGraw-Hill, 1983. This book represents the effort of the academician-arbitrator and the professional mediator to provide a theoretical basis for understanding the arbitration process. It is based on empirical analysis of the arbitration process, but not to examine the arbitration awards as such. Rather, the analysis is of the reasoning behind the awards, in order to identify criteria that might be translated into a body of common law governing judicial interpretation and enforcement of collective agreements. Prasow and Peters have made a major contribution by cutting through the verbiage of arbitration decisions to extract the common elements that constitute the formative basis of common-law development. Furthermore, the sections dealing with the grievance-arbitration process on such matters as the submission agreement, the semantics of contract language, the role of past practice, and evidence and proof should be required reading for every aspiring participant in arbitration procedures.

Rehmus, Charles M., ed., *Developments in American and Foreign Arbitration.* Washington, D.C.: Bureau of National Affairs, Inc., 1968. The 1968 annual meeting of the National Academy of Arbitrators delves into such questions as the role of law in decisions based on the language of the negotiated contract, grievance-arbitration matters that are also subject to the remedial processes of the NLRB, the influence, if any, of the arbitrator's need for joint acceptability of his professional services and the arbitration process, and the use and misuse of tripartite boards in grievance arbitration. B. J. Luskin and David Cole, respectively, address themselves to the increasing acceptability of arbitration and the changing attitudes and increased maturity of labor and management representatives.

Taylor, Benjamin J., and Fred Witney, *Labor Relations Law,* 4th ed., chaps. 15, 21. Englewood Cliffs, N.J.: Prentice-Hall, 1983. An excellent examination of the legal status of grievance arbitration and the role it plays in collective bargaining in both private and public sectors.

U.S. Department of Labor publications. See those annotated in Chapter 7 as *Arbitration Procedures,* 1966; *Grievance and Arbitration Procedures in State and Local Agreements,* 1975; *Understanding Grievance Arbitration in the Public Sector,* 1974; *Negotiation, Impasse, Grievance and Arbitration in Federal Agreements,* 1970.

Updegraff, Clarence M., *Arbitration and Labor Relations,* 3rd ed. Washington, D.C.: Bureau of National Affairs, Inc., 1970. Chapters III through VIII are especially useful in providing an account of the steps of the arbitration process, from selection of arbitrator to submission of agreement, to legal rules of evidence, to the hearing, and finally to the arbitrator's award. Excellent reference source.

Yaffe, Byron, ed., *The Saul Wallen Papers: A Neutral's Contribution to Industrial Peace.* Ithaca, N.Y.: New York State School of Industrial and Labor Relations, 1974. This book is not only to honor a man of great compassion and effectiveness as a neutral in labor-management disputes, but to bring some insight into the views of Mr. Wallen to those who are interested in the process of conflict resolution. Two areas of major emphasis are arbitration and mediation.

OTHER REFERENCES

The reader is also referred to the publications and proceedings of the National Academy of Arbitrators, the American Arbitration Association, the Federal Mediation and Conciliation Service, and the Society of Professionals in Dispute Resolution. These publications reflect the experience of the active arbitrators. Their addresses are:

National Academy of Arbitrators
Office of the Secretary
Graduate School of Business Administration
The University of Michigan
Ann Arbor, Michigan 48109

American Arbitration Association
140 West 51st St.
New York, N.Y. 10020

The Federal Mediation and Conciliation Service
United States Government
Washington, D.C. 20427

SPIDR
C/o American Arbitration Association
1730 Rhode Island Avenue, N.w.
Washington, D.C. 20018

PART IV

COLLECTIVE BARGAINING PROCESS: Resolution of Conflict

So long as the parties to a bargain are free to agree or not to agree, it is inevitable that, human nature being as it is, there should now and again come a deadlock, leading to that trial of strength and endurance which lies behind all bargaining. We know of no device for avoiding this trial of strength except a deliberate decision of the community expressed in legislative enactment.

Sidney and Beatrice Webb, *Industrial Democracy* 1902

CHAPTER 19

RESOLUTION
OF CONFLICT

Collective bargaining, as covered in Parts I, II, and III, is viewed as a joint process by which labor and management in a free society resolve their differences with a minimum of conflict. Two aspects of collective bargaining have been considered: first, the negotiation of contract terms that will cover the relationships of labor and management for a specified period of time; second, the means used to administer the agreement on a day-by-day basis.

Approximately 25 million workers and their employers operate under the constitution of the workplace known as the collective bargaining agreement. The process works, and works well. This is attested to by the lack of viable alternatives to collective bargaining to develop in a free society and by the large portion of the total agreements that are renegotiated regularly without strife.

Jack Conway notes:

> At this moment, collective bargaining has larger claim to vitality and utility than ever before in the history of the American society. Neither side of the American bargaining table is haunted by an uneasiness over what has been called the end of ideology or the exhaustion of the uses of collective bargaining.[1]

---

[1]Jack Conway, *Ideological Obsolescence in Collective Bargaining* (Berkeley: Institute of Industrial Relations, University of California, 1963), p. 3. Printed for private circulation.

NEED FOR IMPROVEMENT

Nevertheless, there has been ever-present on the labor-management scene a desire on the part of the advocates of free collective bargaining to discover techniques and methods collective bargaining can adopt to resolve conflict more effectively. Some of the more important reasons for the search for improvement of the collective bargaining process are these:

1. Collective bargaining in the traditional sense—negotiation, grievance procedure, and grievance arbitration—works well but not perfectly. Impasses occur. Crisis bargaining continues in some negotiations. Personal animosities develop. And the strained relations accompanying such situations could result in work stoppages and other interferences with the flow of production and services. The Bureau of Labor Statitstics notes, in addition, that "while legal bans and public opinion may deter strikes, shorten them, make them suicidal ventures for any sponsoring organization, and possibly result in the discharge of all strikers, they cannot entirely prevent strikes in a free society."[2]

2. As long as there is unresolved labor-management conflict, there will be economic pressure to find improved collective bargaining techniques and methods for its resolution. The company loses production and income. The employee loses employment and wages. Government agencies are under public pressure when they fail to provide tax-financed services. Federal and state governments lose tax revenue. The government employee, denied the right to strike, seeks an equitable alternative to this denied right. This mix of motives to resolve labor-management conflict in both private and public sectors, while not enough to override the need to strike in every case, remains a powerful force to encourage the development of constructive methods and techniques to bolster the effectiveness of traditional collective bargaining.

3. Off scene, there is always the spectre that if there should be a major breakdown in the ability of traditional free collective bargaining to resolve conflict, or if collective bargaining should not prove viable in its ability to adjust to changing times and institutions, the public or the government will be forced to move in the direction of compulsion. Every step in the direction of compulsion is a step toward the demise of free collective bargaining.

4. The special challenge is to find ways and means to prevent or resolve conflict in specific problem areas of work without weakening the basic fabric of free collective bargaining. Such problem areas are those with a critical impact on the health, welfare, or safety of the public and those, such as the federal, state, and local public sectors, where most

[2]*Work Stoppages—Government Employees, 1942–1961*, U.S. Bureau of Labor Statistics, Department of Labor, Report no. 247, 1963, p. 1.

employees have no statutory right to strike. In these areas, denial of the right to strike has not eliminated strikes. Moreover, without the right to strike or a suitable alternative, negotiation often becomes an exercise in frustration. Wingsinger of the Machinists notes the frustration of representatives of federal government workers: "Since Federal workers cannot strike, the representatives cannot exert the kind of leverage that makes collective bargaining work in private industry. They come to the bargaining table as supplicants, not as equals."[3] The special challenge then becomes one of finding alternatives to the strike (as distinguished from the right to strike) while at the same time preserving the incentives in traditional collective bargaining to resolve conflict.

TYPES OF CONFLICT

It should also be noted that "conflict" in labor-management relations is a multifaceted concept. It is not easily classified. It can be overt or covert. The latter type, because it is less easily identified, may be more damaging. Moreover, the conflict may arise at the organizing stage, during the negotiating stage, or during the period when the contract is in the process of being administered. Conflict in labor-management relations may also vary according to its source: It may be motivated by economic or financial considerations (wages, overtime, vacations, holidays, pensions, insurance); by matters of principle (management rights, union and employee rights); by personal reasons (discharge, discipline, promotion, rapport between supervisors and employees); by institutional problems (survival needs of the union and the company or agency as institutions); by political desires (internal company or union politics or federal, state, or local politics related to conflict situations); or by legal requirements (establishing precedent, determining the meaning of a contract).

Looked at in another way, the conflict may vary as to participants: an individual employee and one or more members of management, an individual or group of employees and the employer, the bargaining representative (union or association) and the employer, or any number of combinations of these individuals and groups. Finally, if overtly expressed, the conflict may be evinced by anger, animosity, coolness, or physical violence. Overtly expressed conflict may also assume the form of picketing, boycotting, taking excessive but legal sick leave, enforcing rules and regulations to the letter (ticketing by police, prescribing all possible tests in a hospital, establishing strict safety rules), or performing duties perfunctorily (bus drivers driving but collecting no fares). Other more covert

[3]William W. Wingsinger, "There Is No Alternative to the Right to Strike," *Monthly Labor Review*, September 1973, p. 58.

ways conflict may be demonstrated are by committing sabotage (causing a breakdown in machinery or defective products), effecting slowdowns, being deliberately inefficient, sowing seeds of dissension, or denigrating a product or firm.

THE STATUTES AND RESOLVING CONFLICT

Statutory attention to resolving conflict between labor and management is of much longer standing than the right of workers to organize and engage in collective bargaining activities. As early as 1888, legislation providing for voluntary arbitration and investigation was enacted to assist in the adjustment of disputes in the railroad industry. This was followed by the Erdman Act in 1898, inaugurating the policy of government mediation and conciliation of railway labor disputes. This legislation was replaced by the Newlands Act in 1913. Arbitration was retained, and a full-time Board of Mediation and Conciliation was established. But equally significant, or perhaps more significant, a distinction evolved between resolving negotiation disputes and resolving disagreements over the interpretation of contract language.

From these early statutes and the experience gained in their application, much of the contemporary legislation aimed at resolution of conflict was derived and expanded: the Railway Labor Act, Wagner Act, Taft-Hartley Act, Civil Service Reform Act, and the various statutes enacted by forty states.

Part IV should, therefore, be viewed as an extension of preceding discussions that have been concerned with traditional collective bargaining as viewed through the processes of contract negotiations, grievance handling, and grievance arbitration. The common themes of all the techniques of conflict resolution to be covered in this chapter are (1) a basic commitment to the efficacy and desirability of free collective bargaining, and (2) a dedication by the believers in free collective bargaining to develop ways and means of increasing the effectiveness of collective bargaining without destroying the basic instrument. This writer hastens to disclaim the presumption that any single technique or combination of techniques among those to be discussed constitutes a cure-all for labor-management conflict. Each method has its merits in a given situation and at a given period of time. Choice of any of the techniques or any combination of techniques must be carefully weighed against the particular circumstances involved in the conflict situation.

It should be emphasized that the procedure used in the techniques is also only a means to an end. The solution of conflict vitally depends upon the disposition of the parties toward peaceful labor-management relations.

RESOLUTION OF CONFLICT: NEGOTIATIONS

Attention is first directed to wide-ranging techniques and methods broached but never tried, those used and later abandoned, and those now operative. Introduced over several decades but at an accelerated rate during the last two and a half, their purpose has been to improve the effectiveness of traditional collective bargaining in the resolution of contract negotiation disputes. Simkin notes that "only a cynic could deny the fact of substantial progress in collective bargaining techniques over the past 30 years."[4] This trend has continued to the present.

The format followed emphasizes the nature of the tool or technique rather than the particular area of its use. Because of the wide variation in techniques, finding a simple means of classification and a systematic method of presentation is extremely difficult. Some techniques are formal; some are informal. In some instances, the particular technique allows flexibility of action; in others, it is quite inflexible. Some techniques are part of a structured process; others are unstructured. Some of the techniques are the result of actions of the parties themselves; some are the results of legislation or administrative orders; others are the work of a government agency, such as the Federal Mediation and Conciliation Service. Some are traditional techniques, such as arbitration, mediation, and fact finding. Others reflect the increasing flexibility being introduced in attempts to develop more viable ways of resolving labor-management disputes and to depart from the previous sacrosanct separation among the traditional techniques. Neutrals are used in some cases as resource and technical experts; in other situations, neutrals are used to resolve conflict through a binding decision. In some instances, the technique involves only the parties themselves; in others, a neutral or neutrals from the private sector are involved; in still others, the intervention of a government body occurs. Finally, the technique may be aimed at preventing conflict, or it may be aimed at resolving conflict evinced by an impasse or overt action such as a strike.

Mediation   The mediator has no authority to dictate a solution. The mediator acts as a catalyst to resolve a dispute by peaceful means through the use of his or her office, providing a positive environment for impasse resolution. Through knowledge of the issues and settlement patterns, the mediator is often able to break a deadlock by introducing innovative solutions.

Preventive Mediation   The mediator is involved well in advance of negotiations. Techniques include—the parties individually or jointly—

---

[4]William E. Simkin, "Positive Approaches to Labor Peace," *Industrial and Labor Relations Review*, Cornell University, October 1964, p. 37.

encouraging and establishing labor-management meetings and committees, sustaining liason before and after the contract is signed to smooth out unsolved problems, and conducting training seminars. The objective is to turn an ineffective relationship into a problem-solving relationship.

Relations by Objectives   RBO is a process of (1) identification of problems, (2) establishment of target goals or objectives necessary to correct the problems, (3) joint discussions on implementation, and (4) consensus on an action program. The key to the success of RBO is establishing a systematic framework for solving problems through interaction.

Early-Bird Negotiations   Establishing negotiations far enough ahead of the contract deadline so as to be able to discuss items in a calmer, more deliberate environment instead of the last-minute crisis bargaining ending so often in impasse is, of course, beneficial to both parties. An example is the negotiations between the New York hotel industry and the Steelworkers' Union in 1974. One variation is to allow the new contract to take effect at the date of ratification.

Postnegotiation Technique   The parties agree to postpone issues that might result in impasse to the time of the calmer and more deliberate atmosphere of special postnegotiations.

Continuing Joint Labor-Management Study Committees[5]   The parties establish these committees outside the limited time of the negotiation period. The objective is to create a better overall climate for negotiations by functioning informally, by keeping no records, by keeping the proceedings confidential, by having the discussions free and open and without commitment, and by not seeking conclusive consensus. Objectives are: easing of communication problems, creating a forum for innovation and creativity, encouraging frankness and realism, generating mutual trust and confidence, anticipating any crisis problems, making time available to determine facts, personalizing relations between management and union representatives, and encouraging more mature bargaining at the table.

[5]James J. Healy, ed., *Creative Collective Bargaining* (Englewood Cliffs, N.J.: Prentice-Hall, 1965); Simkin, "Positive Approaches to Labor Peace"; R. W. Fleming, "New Challenges for Collective Bargaining," *Wisconsin Law Review*, May 1964; Richard P. McLaughlin, "Collective Bargaining—The New Trend," *Labor Law Journal*, August 1964; Frederick R. Livingston, "Avoidance and Settlement of Disputes," BNA, No. 572 (1967) Di-D7; FMCS *Annual Report* for Fiscal Year 1965; "The Kaiser-Steelworkers Agreement," *Monthly Labor Review*, December 1959 (also February 1961); Kelly, "Techniques for Minimizing Crisis"; Executive Order 10946, Title 3, "Establishing a Program for Resolving Labor Disputes at Missile and Space Sites"; Clark Kerr and George Halverson, *Causes of Industrial Peace under Collective Bargaining: A Study of Lockheed Aircraft Corporation and the International Association of Machinsts*, Reprint No. 17, University of California, Berkeley, 1950. Kerr notes, "One technique for expeditious settlement has been on-the-spot investigation of grievances by the union's business representative and a representative of the company's Industrial Relations Office . . . only the essential issues are left for higher levels," p. 17.

Mediation-Arbitration   "Med-arb," has been used successfully by Sam Kagle, and by state governments, such as Wisconsin, by combining both mediation and arbitration functions in one individual. This technique is a procedural blending of mediation first, with arbitration authority granted, in reserve, to the neutral in order to proceed to binding arbitration if mediation is not successful. Parties pledge not to strike or lock out. It utilizes the best of both mediation and arbitration procedures and, most importantly, it "gives the med-arbiter muscle."

Mediation–Fact finding   Proscription of the right to strike by a number of states and the federal government has impelled the use of mediation–fact finding. Mediation–fact finding is to be distinguished from the traditional process of mediation followed by fact-finding. The former is a continuous process, carried out by one mediator or mediation board, in contrast to the two separate steps of the latter. The emergency provisions of the Taft-Hartley Act 1947 would be an example of the latter: a process of two separate steps, handled by the mediation services in the first step and the emergency board in the second step. In the mediation–fact-finding technique, the neutral acts as a catalyst in the mediation step, followed by fact finding with recommendations in the fact-finding step. The Washington, South Dakota, and Georgia statutes provide examples of this technique.

Partisan Mediation   This technique is characterized by the strong role essayed by a partisan group. An example is the strong role of the central labor councils in the San Francisco–Oakland Bay Area. No AFL-CIO union goes on strike without the approval of the central labor council. Before approval is forthcoming, a waiting period is triggered during which other unions that might be affected are contacted. The council uses its services to attempt to bring about agreement through mediation.

Mediation to Finality   This technique is mentioned here only to clear up any confusion concerning real meaning. In the 1967 railroad dispute, the final action taken by Congress was the establishment of a board to decide the issues. Donald Cullen notes, "Although the administration delicately termed this last step 'mediation to finality,' few observers could discern how it differed from compulsory arbitration."[6]

Fact finding   Fact finding in the traditional sense has also been used much more frequently by the proscription on the right to strike in the public sector. Nothing has hastened such usage more than the realization, especially of state governments, that, despite the proscription, public employees do strike. Fact finding may be in two forms: with recommendations and without recommendations. Moreover, fact finding with recom-

[6]Donald E. Cullen, *National Emergency Strikes*, ILR Paperback No. 7, October 1968, p. 75.

mendations may also be subdivided into binding recommendations and advisory recommendations. The Taft-Hartley Act, Section 206, provides for a board of inquiry in national emergency disputes "to inquire into the issues involved in the dispute and to make a written report to him [the President]." LMRA Section 213(a)—Conciliation of Labor Disputes in the Health Care Industry—provides for the appointment of a board of inquiry to investigate a dispute and render a written report of "the findings of fact together with the Board's recommendations for settling the dispute." Section 7119(c)(5)(A) of the CSRA 1978, Title VII also provides for the Federal Service Impasses Panel to use whatever methods and procedures are necessary to resolve an impasse, "including factfinding and recommendations." The majority of fact-finding recommendations are advisory only, and may or may not be made public.

Fact finding with Authority to the Governor to Render Recommendations Final and Binding   Nevada law provides that, where fact finding is instituted, if parties do not agree to final and binding recommendations, the governor, upon request of either party, may order that the "findings and recommendations on all or any specified issues of a factfinder in a particular dispute will be final and binding."

Fact Finding with Mediation   Connecticut law provides for fact finding with nonbinding recommendations but authorizes the fact-finder to mediate if desired. Oregon law allows the fact-finding committee to attempt mediation at any time prior to the submission of its findings and recommendations.

Fact finding–Public Referendum   The fact-finder's recommendations are tied to public referendum by allowing either party to place the recommendations on the next special ballot or regular election, the results to be retroactive.[7]

Arbitration   This refers to the use of voluntary arbitration as a terminal procedure in contract negotiation (interest) disputes. Although, until the last decade or two, government representatives and others have steered clear of terminal arbitration procedures, this use of arbitration is not without historical precedent. The reader is referred to the Amalgamated Street Railway Union and to the following industries: anthracite coal mining, hosiery, men's clothing, newspaper, book and job printing, electrical, and hotel, to cite a few. David Cole also recalls that in the first twelve years following World War II, he was involved at least fifty times in arbitration of interest disputes. More recent increase in the use of arbitration to resolve interest disputes has received impetus not only from more flexible attitudes toward varied techniques of using arbitration, but

---

[7]Sam Zagoria, "Referendum Use in Labor Impasses Proposed," *LMRS Newsletter,* September 1973, pp. 2–4.

also from the increasing preference of labor leaders since the 1960s for using alternatives to the strike. A reminder: Arbitration, as used in this section, refers to interest arbitration and is to be distinguished from grievance arbitration, discussed later in this chapter. A significant step was taken by the steel industry in the use of interest arbitration in 1973. The parties, through what is known as the Experimental Negotiation Agreement, agreed to submit all issues remaining unresolved to final and binding arbitration no later than April 20, 1974. Some contract items such as local working conditions, union membership, check-off, cost-of-living adjustments, no-strike, no-lockout, and management rights were excluded as issues for arbitration. The 1974 accord has been renewed at each contract negotiation period since that time. There have been no strikes. This shift in attitude toward interest-dispute arbitration is significant. Increasingly, practitioners are becoming convinced that arbitration in the areas of contract negotiation must become more viable and flexible if it is to meet the needs of the negotiating parties. This line of thinking views arbitration of interest disputes as a process in which adjustment, accommodation, and acceptability will be more common goals, rather than a win-lose type of adjudication. In skilled hands, it will also be considered as a "continuation rather than a replacement for the negotiation process."[8] More latitude is being allowed during the arbitration procedure for simultaneous or alternative use of other techniques. This is illustrated by several variations of arbitration use that follow immediately.

Public Members of an Arbitration Board Use Industry and Union Members as a Sounding Board   The public members of the tripartite arbitration board use the industry and union board members as a sounding board "against which the public members could rattle ideas, concepts, and specifics" in arriving at a decision acceptable to the parties.[9]

Arbitration Prehearing Negotiation   This technique allows the parties to an arbitration to sit down with alternate members of a bipartite arbitration panel, using the leanings of the neutral member to initiate further negotiations.

Arbitration cum Mediation   This technique permits the arbitration board, at its option, to resort to mediation any time during the arbitration process.

Arbitration cum Negotiation   The arbitrator or the arbitration board using this technique if not successful in settling a dispute would be given authority to remand some issues back to further negotiation by the parties.

[8]Charles M. Rehmus, "Binding Arbitration in the Public Sector," *Monthly Labor Review*, April 1975, p. 54.

[9]William E. Simkin, "Limitation of Arm's-Length or Adversary Arbitration," *Monthly Labor Review*, September 1973, p. 56.

Final-Offer Arbitration   Receiving most of the attention during the
last decade in the literature on the subject is a process termed variously
final-offer, last-offer, final-position, either-or, one-or-the-other, and *force-
choice arbitration* of interest disputes. This process has elicited much
interest among those seeking alternatives to the strike in the public-employee areas, but has also been recommended by its advocates for wider
use. The essence of final-offer arbitration is simply that in making a decision on a contract negotiation dispute, the arbitrator or board must select
one or the other of the final offers of the two parties. There are variations,
but the most common approach is for each party to offer a final package of
the unresolved issues at the point of invoking arbitration. The arbitrator
must then choose one of the two packages. The arbitrator has no flexibility
to vary the items within the packages or to modify the terms in a way he or
she might consider more fair and reasonable. Other variations of final-
offer arbitration provide for two final positions from each party, or allow
the arbitrator some flexibility in the decision other than just choosing one
of the last-offer positions. The Indiana, Michigan, Ohio, and Oregon statutes provide examples of the use of this technique.

Critical Nature of Service: Terminal Arbitration   In determining
the impasse procedures to be activated, Alaska includes a rather novel
approach to regular terminal arbitration. Public employees are classified
into three groups, according to the service they perform, under Section
23.40.200 of their Arbitration Act:

(1)   Those services which may not be given up for even the shortest
period of time;
(2)   Those services which may be interrupted for a limited period but not
for an indefinite period of time; and
(3)   Those services in which work stoppages may be sustained for extended periods without serious effect on the public.

In definition of these areas, the first group includes police, firemen, and
employees of jails, prisons, other correctional institutions, and hospitals;
the second group includes public-utility, snow-removal, sanitation, and
educational-institution employees; and the third group includes all other
employees. The Alaskan act provides that the first group may not strike
and that binding arbitration is the terminal procedure. The second group,
after mediation and a majority vote to strike, may strike on a limited basis,
but if the strike endangers the health, safety, or welfare of the public, the
matter may end in binding arbitration the same as with group 1. Group 3
employees may engage in a strike upon a majority vote of the employees
in the collective bargaining unit. The interesting aspect of the Alaskan act,
and perhaps a forerunner of things to come, is that a serious attempt has
been made to differentiate on a public-impact basis between the situations

when the right to strike should be allowed and when it should be prohibited. The act separates employees functionally in terms of the critical or noncritical nature of the service they perform. For too long we have retained the artificial distinction of critical versus noncritical on the basis of public- versus private-sector employees. These artificial distinctions should give way, and are slowly doing so, to more meaningful criteria in which critical and noncritical are based upon the actual service or productive effort and its impact on public safety, health, or welfare, regardless of the location of the work, whether in the public or the private sector.

Bag of Tools Although still not as formalized as other impasse procedures, this approach—also variously known as the *choice-of-procedures, mutual-anxiety, arsenal-of-weapons, multiple-tool,* and *uncertainty approach*—has received revived interest more recently. This interest has resulted in legislation such as that of Massachusetts, in congressional hearings on emergency disputes in transportation, and in increasing emphasis in professional writings. Most of the interest to date in the use of a multiple-tool approach has related either to impasses of major public concern or to emergency strike legislation. However, it is also receiving more attention as a possible impasse procedure in public-sector disputes.

The logic behind the bag-of-tools of multiple-tool approach is that, if no uncertainty is raised in the minds of the parties as to the procedures they might be faced with in case of impasse, then they avoid responsible bargaining in good faith and move perfunctorily through the legislated emergency-procedure steps to what they anticipate will be a favorable government handout. If uncertainty *is* introduced as to what procedures the government might eventually take, ranging from compulsion to a continuation of a work stoppage, then there might be an incentive for the parties to use the regular bargaining process rather than risk a negative result because of the impasse procedure selected. The way the multiple-tool approach would operate would be for the government to establish an impartial, independent, widely representative, and knowledgeable board with authority to utilize any one of a number of tools in attempting to resolve the impasse. The tools suggested range from those of a more compulsory nature to those with little or no compulsion. The following list, while not exhaustive, is representative of the types of choice:

1. A system of graduated penalties
2. Extending the no-strike period through use of an injunction
3. Further mediation
4. Advisory arbitration
5. Compulsory arbitration—all issues

6. Compulsory arbitration—issues at impasse only
7. Fact finding with recommendations—nonbinding
8. Fact finding with recommendations—binding
9. Final-offer arbitration
10. Partial strike or lockout
11. Nonstoppage procedure
12. Seizure
13. Unlimited strike allowed
14. Limited strike allowed

It is interesting to note that both the Taft-Hartley emergency procedures and the CSRA, Title VII, impasse procedures are flexible enough to provide for the bag-of-tools approach. Section 210 of Taft-Hartley provides for a final step that the president of the U.S. must take if the emergency dispute is not settled at the termination of the 80-day injunction. It reads: ". . . the President shall submit to the Congress a full and comprehensive report of the proceedings, including the findings of the board of inquiry . . . , together with such recommendations as he may see fit to make for consideration and appropriate action." Appropriate action in the hands of Congress certainly allows for the multiple-tool approach, among others, should Congress adopt the concept. The Railway Labor Act does not include such a provision, although it has been the practice of the president when he has exhausted all the procedures to place the dispute in the lap of Congress if it remains unsettled. Under the CSRA the resolution of impasse is of such major concern that, rather than its just providing for emergency procedures, a special panel, the Federal Service Impasses Panel, was established with direct responsibility for handling disputes not resolved by the normal procedures of CSRA. Section 7119 of CSRA provides for mediation and, with the approval of the panel, for binding arbitration of negotiation impasses. Beyond this, the panel is authorized to:

> recommend to the parties procedures for the resolution of the impasse; assist the parties in resolving the impasse through *whatever methods and procedures,* including factfinding and recommendations, *it may consider appropriate to accomplish the purpose of this section.* [Emphasis added.]

Admittedly, the Impasses Panel has not administered its functions through a bag-of-tools plus uncertainty approach. The reason for coverage here is that the framework effects such an approach should the Impasses Panel choose to go in that direction. Functionally, the activities and approach of the panel fit more closely to the next technique to be discussed—the *superneutral* or what might be called the *variable-technique* approach.[10]

Variable-Technique Approach   The reason for separating this from the bag-of-tools approach is that the bag-of-tools technique emphasizes the uncertainty created by the authority's selecting at some point one of a number of tools or techniques available to it that the parties, until that point, would have had no way of predicting. Hence the possibility that, as a result of the uncertainty, they might deem it more advisable to negotiate to a settlement. In contrast, under the variable approach, a neutral or an impasse board has a number of techniques at its option and uses them in any way it deems most productive at any particular stage of the negotiations. This means that it may use mediation, move to fact finding with recommendations, remand the matter to negotiations based on the recommendations, move back to the mediation, proceed to some form of arbitration with flexibility for the parties to continue negotiations, or turn to mediation while the arbitration is in process. The point is that it is an ad hoc procedure in which success depends upon the willingness of the parties to use various techniques and upon the ability of the neutral to handle with expertise and a good sense of timing and judgment the movement from one technique of impasse resolution to another.

Support for such a process, whether it is called the variable-technique, the arsenal-of-weapons approach, the superneutral, or the pragmatic and flexibile administration approach, should be forthcoming in the now-emerging climate of approval of more flexible approaches to conflict resolution. It is in a sense the breaking of the old conventional lines of demarcation that imposed a strict separation between the traditional impasse techniques of negotiation, mediation, fact finding, and arbitration, in order to permit the viability and flexibility in techniques of impasse settlement necessary to handle effectively today's types of impasse problems. It should also be emphasized that responsibility for much of the shift and change in attitudes that effect a more flexible approach to impasse resolution results from the new challenges of public-sector unionism and collective bargaining. David Cole points out that the variable-technique procedure has been used, and he vigorously supports a voluntary version of it:

> My strong preference is for an indefinite combination of all these procedures, together with any others the parties may devise that they believe may be helpful. I would favor a course in which they move by agreement step by step from one procedure to another until their differences are ended. I would exclude

---

[10]See Don H. Wollett, "Mutual Anxiety: A California Proposal," *Monthly Labor Review*, September 1973, pp. 50–51, for another approach wherein uncertainty is also the main focus.

> *nothing nor would I compel them to go forward if either chooses
> not to do so. This is because of the very nature of agreement
> making. . . . My suggestion is a combination of all the possible
> procedures to be used step by step, with emphasis on the con-
> stant mutual desire of the parties to move ahead.*[11]

Nonstoppage Strike Another technique has been around a long time but has not found much usage. Chamberlain notes that he arrived at the nonstoppage-strike proposal independently, but subsequently found three other, prior instances in which a similar proposal had been made: Marceau and Musgrave, in "Strikes in Essential Industries: A Way Out," *Harvard Business Review,* May 1949; Goble, in "The Non-Stoppage Strike," *Labor Law Journal,* February 1951; and Bakke, in a radio address over station WTIC, Hartford, June 15, 1952.[12] From time to time the nonstoppage strike, sometimes called the *statutory strike, semistrike,* or *income-work time gradual pressure strike,* has received renewed attention. The first known application of the technique was in 1964 as a result of an agreement between the Dunbar Furniture Company and the Upholsters International Union, AFL-CIO.

In contrast to a regular stoppage strike, the nonstoppage strike requires the parties to continue production while being subject to financial forfeits for the time the dispute remains unresolved. Several different proposals have been made for invoking the nonstoppage-strike process: by statute through the use of an injunction procedure, by voluntary agreement of the parties, or by voluntary agreement of the parties and congressional approval. The goals various writers identify are to ensure continued production; to attempt to promote collective bargaining by the disputants; to establish a way for the parties to fight it out without negative impact on customers, the community, or the public generally; a way of taking the public out of the middle; and a method by which there can be an accurate countdown of losses to the parties as a result of the continuation of the dispute.

The assumptions on which the nonstoppage approach is based are that an incentive to settle differences will be provided by requiring the parties to forfeit income to a lesser degree than in a full strike but nevertheless enough to be significant, and that, even though each party will receive some advantages by continuation of production and employment, both will also incur some losses.[13]

---

[11]David Cole, "The Evolving Techniques," *AFL–CIO Federationist,* May 1974 (a reprint).

[12]Neil W. Chamberlain, assisted by Jane M. Schilling. *Social Responsibility and Strikes* (New York: Harper & Row, 1953), p. 279.

[13]Cyrus F. Smythe, "Public Policy and Emergency Disputes," *Labor Law Journal* (Chicago: Commerce Clearing House, 1963), p. 830; Kenneth G. Slocum, "Working Strikers," *Wall Street Journal,* May 20, 1964, pp. 1, 15; Damon W. Harrison, Jr., "The Strike and Its

Labor-Management Cooperation   Another tool, certainly not new but receiving increasing attention as the union movement has matured and the economy has experienced "unrelenting economic stress,"[14] has been experimentation with various forms of union- or labor-management cooperation. As Yoder and Staudohar note, "Several programs have been in operation almost half a century, on several railroads, in clothing, electrical manufacturing, ladies' garments, carpet weaving, glass, street railways, and the cloth hat and cap industry."[15] Cooperative efforts between labor and management assume many forms and address many different problems of mutual interest. They are implemented, in some instances, through informal discussion committees and, in other instances, through formal committees. They are composed variously of representatives of labor, unions, management, the public, and government bodies. They are established through contractual negotiations in some instances. In other instances, they are formed outside the contractual arrangement by the parties or by public or governmental groups. They may be joint consultation committees within plants; local, interfirm committees; industry committees. They may also be regional or national area committees, labor-management committees, or community committees, depending upon the nature of the problem they are established to address. And without attempting to list all of the purposes for such committees, cooperative committees are formed to address mutual problems of skill upgrading, employment, quality of work life, flexible work schedules, productivity, training, legislation, labor-management conflict, community renewal, community environmental difficulties, worker satisfaction, communication, public relations, security, labor-management sharing arrangements, health and safety, security and retirement, to name a few.[16]

Alternatives: The Public Employment Experience," *Kentucky Law Journal*, Vol. 63 (1975), 464–65; David B. McCalmont, "The Semi-Strike," *Industrial and Labor Relations Review* (New York: New York School of Industrial and Labor Relations, 1962), January, pp. 191–211; George W. Goble, "The Non-Stoppage Strike," *Current Economic Comment* (Urbana: University of Illinois, Bureau of Economic and Business Research, August 1950), pp. 3–11; LeRoy Marceau and Richard A. Musgrave, "Strikes in Essential Industries: A Way Out," *Harvard Business Review*, Vol. 27, May 1940, 27; Chamberlain, *Social Responsibility and Strikes*, pp. 279–86; Stephen H. Sosnick, "Non-Stoppage Strikes: A New Approach," *Industrial and Labor Relations Review* (New York: New York School of Industrial and Labor Relations, Cornell University, 1964), pp. 73–78; "The Right to Strike and the General Welfare," Committee on the Church and Economic Life, National Council of Churches of Christ in the U.S.A. (New York: Council Press, 1967), pp. 4–39.

[14]Irving H. Siegel and Edgar Weinberg, *Labor-Management Cooperation, The American Experience* (Kalamazoo, Mich.: W. E. Upjohn Institute for Employment Research, 1982), p. 1.

[15]Dale Yoder and Paul D. Staudohar, *Personnel Management and Industrial Relations*, 7th ed. (Englewood Cliffs, N.J.: Prentice-Hall, 1982), p. 281.

[16]One of the most comprehensive studies of cooperation is Siegel and Weinberg, *Labor-Management Cooperation*, noted earlier.

Whether the technique is identified as joint labor-management committees, continuous bargaining, early-bird bargaining, preventive mediation, or cooperation, the key to the arrangement is that it provides a promising mutual benefit through a program of solving problems jointly. Experience has demonstrated that cooperation cannot be imposed from the outside. It is achieved through a joint decision that working together to achieve certain common goals, whether the goal is labor-management peace or improved efficiency of operation, is preferable to the alternate choices facing labor and management.

RESOLUTION OF CONFLICT: CONTRACT ADMINISTRATION

The principal concern of this section of Chapter 19 is not with conflict that results in strikes or work stoppages. When a contract includes grievance procedures with arbitration as the terminal step, as most of them do, the parties have already agreed that the terminal step of arbitration is to be a substitute for, not an alternative to, the right to strike or lock out. As a substitute for the strike, the grievance procedure *is*, by its very nature, one of the techniques developed by the parties for resolving conflict anent the meaning and application of the contract. The better the grievance procedure serves this purpose, the better collective bargaining functions. Therefore, just as there is continuing attention paid to tools and techniques to resolve negotiation impasses, so there is continuing attention paid to reducing conflict in collective bargaining by discovering ways to improve the functioning of the grievance or contract administration system. This has led to experimenting with some of the techniques used in the resolution of conflict in negotiations and with other measures aimed at rendering the grievance system more efficient in matters of timeliness, cost, and quality.

Grievance Handling

Lowest-Level Approach   The lowest-level approach is not a formal technique but rather a combination of actions taken to maximize settlement of grievances orally at the shop level. The program requires the following:

1. Top leadership of both the union and management must agree that the best settlement is a settlement at the shop level, and preferably before the grievance is reduced to writing.
2. Those normally involved at higher levels of the grievance procedure must actively support the lowest-level settlement policy through their willingness to move down to the problem in order to assist in

the shop-level settlement, instead of allowing the problem to move up to them.

3. All involved must commit themselves to a program of immediate response, frank discussion, factual but equitable judgment, and expedited settlement.

4. An active training program must be established to provide information continuously to lower supervisors and union stewards as to contract content and meaning.

The whole idea of the lowest-level approach is that of a "grass-roots" resolution process in contrast to an "institutional" resolution process. The UAW-International/Harvester experience has been that it can work and that it can also improve relations between the parties at the same time.

Grievance Mediation   Use of mediation at some point in the grievance procedure, prior to grievance arbitration, has in some instances been a successful technique and has been incorporated into a few labor agreements. Its use has appeared in several forms. In cases where a backlog of unsettled grievances has occurred, a form known as "intensive mediation" has been successful. An oft-repeated example is the time David Cole, with the assurance of full authority, plunged into an International Harvester-UAW backlog of thousands of grievances pending arbitration and dramatically reduced it through the technique of intensive mediation. In the Coos Bay region of Oregon, a federal mediator was called in to help reduce a backlog of some 150 grievances through intensive mediation. Avoiding a decision-making role, the mediator, through intensive mediation over a period of two weeks, "got the parties back on the track" and at the same time resolved more than 120 of the grievances.

Mediation is also used in a more conventional sense when it is formally recognized in the agreement as a step in the grievance procedure prior to arbitration. It is a distinct step in the sense that the mediator does not also act as arbitrator, as in med-arb; his job is to facilitate the settlement of the grievance by making suggestions or by advising the parties. He does not make a decision as the arbitrator does. His is the usual function of a mediator—to persuade, to facilitate, to act as a catalyst, not to force.

The coal industry has served as another experimental source in the use of grievance mediation. In November 1980, Stephen B. Goldberg and Jeanne M. Brett, jointly funded by the Department of Labor and the J. L. Kellogg Research Professorship, began an experiment in grievance mediation in the coal industry to determine whether "mediation could resolve a substantial proportion of grievances more promptly, less expensively, and more satisfactorily than arbitration."[17] The mediation step was inserted

---

[17]Stephen B. Goldberg and Jeanne M. Brett, "An Experiment in the Mediation of Grievances," *Monthly Labor Review*, March 1982, pp. 23–30. See also, for an example of

after the final internal step of the grievance procedure. At this point, the parties would have the option of going to mediation rather than arbitration. Mediation was to be conducted in an informal atmosphere, facts would be elicited without the usual rules of procedure or evidence applying, no record would be kept, and the grievant would participate fully. If settlement were not possible, the mediator would render an advisory opinion as to how the grievance might fare at the arbitration level. The mediator could not serve as an arbitrator, nor could any of the contents of the mediation sessions be used at the arbitration session.

A somewhat similar approach observed by the author, absent mediation, is to invite a neutral in at the final step of the grievance procedure prior to arbitration to render an advisory arbitration opinion as to the merits of the grievance. The advisory opinion cannot be used or cited if the grievance is pursued to arbitration.

Grievance Handling *cum* Fact-Finding   Sam Kagel underscores an inherent weakness all too evident in grievance handling, which frequently leads to appeal to arbitration when such a step is not really necessary. This is the failure, in preparing for an arbitration hearing, to obtain the facts necessary to settle the grievance until forced to. Kagel supports a fact-finding step that is triggered at the point where the grievance is reduced to writing. The advantage of such an interim step in the grievance procedure is that it disciplines the parties to obtain their facts earlier in the procedure and thus may obviate the continuing to arbitration of many unnecessary grievances. Such a step is already evident in some agreements in public- and private-sector contracts. The following are illustrative.[18]

- (a)   One factfinder shall be designated by the employer and one factfinder shall be designated by the union.
- (b)   The object of the factfinders is to thoroughly investigate the grievance so that their report could be the basic source of stipulated facts concerning the grievance.
- (c)   The factfinders shall put into writing all the facts upon which they agree and these will be considered stipulations.
- Upon request of the grievant and the union, the unresolved grievance will be referred to advisory fact-finding. A single fact-finder will be used. If the Board and union are unable to agree upon a fact-finder within 7 days, a panel of 5 or 7 names will be obtained from the American

grievance mediation, *Grievance and Arbitration Procedures in State and Local Agreements*, U.S. Department of Labor, Bulletin 1833-1975; and *Collective Bargaining Negotiations and Contracts*, BNA No. 626, (Washington, D.C.: Bureau of National Affairs, Inc.), no. 626, 1968, 1969.

[18]See *Grievance and Arbitration Procedure*, U.S. Department of Labor, Bulletin 1833; and Sam Kagel and John Kagel, "Using Two New Arbitration Techniques," *Monthly Labor Review*, November 1972.

Arbitration Association, and starting with the grievant the parties shall alternatively strike names until a single name is left.

- The committee, after deliberate and thorough review of all available testimony and information, shall make its findings and recommendations to the parties in writing.
- The findings and recommendations of the advisory committee may be made public by either party. The findings and recommendations of the advisory committee are not binding upon either party but shall serve as a basis for further good faith efforts on the part of both parties to negotiate and settle any remaining issue.
- The advisory panel shall review the grievance and within 20 days from date of appointment of third member, recommend a solution to the Mayor and City Council. The Mayor and City Council shall render the final decision.

Grievance Handling and Joint Study Committees   As a final note under grievance handling, it should be indicated that the joint labor-management committees discussed in this chapter also serve an important function in developing an atmosphere for both negotiations and grievance handling in which facts and objectivity become highlighted and problems are anticipated. The emphasis is not on a litigious stance by the parties, but upon personal relations, understanding, and a commitment to peace. The FMCS annual reports emphasize the continuing value of joint study committees as a tool in preventing collective bargaining conflicts of all types.

GRIEVANCE ARBITRATION

Criticisms raised with respect to grievance arbitration are not usually directed at the basic value of the technique. Indeed, grievance arbitration, noted in Chapter 18, is almost universally included as the terminal point in the grievance procedure and is the basic reason for there being few work stoppages over issues submitted to the grievance procedure. Peter Seitz notes that "Grievance Arbitration (despite the banshee-like howlings of a few dyspeptics . . .) is a marvelously acceptable and generally satisfactory institution."[19]

Most of the criticisms have been directed at the mechanics of grievance arbitration. As with other legal processes, there are many contrasting opinions as to what grievance arbitration does not do and what it ought to do. Some people feel that the process is too expensive; others point out

---

[19]Peter Seitz, "How to Succeed in Killing Arbitration without Really Trying," *Seminar on Collective Bargaining, 1967—Emerging Characteristics* (Jamestown, N.Y.: Jamestown Community College Press, 1968), p. 95.

that it is much less expensive than following the alternate route, that of resorting to the courts. Some accuse arbitrators of unnecessary delay; others pin the delay mainly on the parties themselves. Some think that delay can be reduced by drastically reducing or eliminating opinions; others argue that it is the obligation of the arbitrator to articulate his logic and reasoning to effect an acceptable award and to clarify contract intent for similar instances that might arise. Some persons think that the transcript of proceedings and the posthearing brief should be eliminated; others respond that in some complicated cases, the transcript is a positive need, and that the transcript is a device to keep witnesses honest and the arbitrator's award relevant to the issue presented. Criticism is also raised that there are too few arbitrators; a response is that there are not too few arbitrators but too few *qualified* and *experienced* arbitrators *acceptable* to the parties. Then there are those who criticize arbitrators for not being legalistic enough—for introducing problem solving to arbitration; others respond that the arbitration process is a problem-solving and a legalistic process, and that with good judgment, both can be used without weakening the process.

While not an exhaustive list, these attitudes indicate something of the give-and-take of published and verbal comments on grievance arbitration. The substance of the complaints, proposals, and discussions concerning grievance arbitration generally centers upon two major needs: (1) to increase the number of qualified, experienced, and acceptable arbitrators; and (2) to reduce the time and cost of arbitration. It is to meet these two general needs that most of the innovative activity of the Federal Mediation and Conciliation Service, the National Academy of Arbitrators, the American Arbitration Association, the Society of Professionals in Dispute Resolution, and the parties themselves is directed.

More Qualified, Experienced, and Acceptable Arbitrators To place the matter in proper perspective, it should be pointed out that there is some controversy over whether there is a shortage of arbitrators, even of qualified arbitrators. This question arises because of the reluctance of the parties to use younger, newer, or less experienced arbitrators even when they are qualified—indeed, many of these arbitrators have been accepted for the panels of the AAA and FMCS. Since final selection of the arbitrator who will hear the case is still a matter of mutual agreement between the parties, inclusion on a list submitted to them by the services (FMCS and AAA) does not mean selection by the parties. Because of questions such as this, the efforts to increase the number of arbitrators acceptable to the parties involve both an encouragement to the parties to use less experienced but qualified arbitrators already in the field, and also an attempt to increase the numbers of trained and qualified arbitrators in the field as a whole. It is a program, then, of increasing acceptability, increasing quality, and increasing numbers.

Two projects illustrate the attempts of various interested groups to increase the number of trained arbitrators. In a project funded by the Labor-Management Services Commission, the Department of Labor initiated training programs at UCLA and Berkeley to increase the numbers of experienced third-party neutrals. Each program, consisting of fifteen candidates, was a combination of classroom training and on-the-job or counterpart training. Experienced arbitrators directed the programs, and more were recruited to assist in the apprenticeship aspects of the program. Cooperation of referral agencies in fact finding and arbitration was obtained in order to ensure immediate exposure and experience for the candidates upon graduation.[20]

Another program, one of several sponsored by the NAA, AAA, and FMCS, was established in cooperation with Cornell University. Under this program, nine daylong sessions, one a month, were scheduled. Twenty practitioners from labor and management and seven attorneys were selected, based on criteria that included preferences (although not exclusively) for younger persons, five years' experience with labor or management or both in labor relations work, location in western New York, and no discrimination as to race, creed, color, or national origin. Exceptions could be made for highly qualified persons. In addition to the nine academic sessions, each trainee was assigned to accompany an experienced arbitrator to hearings (with approval of the parties) and to prepare an award for the evaluation of the experienced arbitrator after a formal award had been made in the case.[21]

Another approach to increasing the use of less-experienced but qualified arbitrators has been promulgated by the FMCS under its ARBIT system (Arbitration Information Tracking System). Although ARBIT was designed primarily to provide a more immediate response to those using the FMCS arbitration services, it also includes features that it is hoped will stimulate the use of newer arbitrators. ARBIT contains complete biographical information on each arbitrator, which is automatically updated with each case the arbitrator decides. Further, as requests are made to FMCS for arbitration panels from which the parties may choose the arbitrator they will use, an "active memory" in the ARBIT system ensures that there will be an equitable distribution in referrals among all names on FMCS lists. This means that newer arbitrators will have as much opportunity as older ones to have their names submitted by the FMCS to the parties on the panel referrals. (Usually, seven names are submitted.) Including the name of a newer arbitrator on these panels does not guarantee

---

[20]W. J. Usery, Jr., "Some Attempts to Reduce Arbitration Costs and Delays," *Monthly Labor Review*, November 1972, p. 5.

[21]James F. Power, "Improving Arbitration: Roles of Parties and Agencies," *Monthly Labor Review*, November 1972, pp. 19–20.

that he will be selected, of course, but it does increase the odds in his favor by presenting his name more frequently to the parties. Each time a newer arbitrator is selected and decides a case, his biographical data reflect this new information, thus increasing even more his opportunity to be again selected.

The mediators in the field, because of their constant contact with the parties, may also be a positive force in encouraging the use of newer arbitrators, by suggesting names when it is appropriate. Experienced arbitrators, too, have a responsibility. The NAA, AAA, and FMCS consider the responsibility of regular arbitrators to train newer ones important enough to include it as an obligation in their new *Code of Professional Responsibility for Arbitrators*, Section 1(C)(1) of which states, "An experienced arbitrator should cooperate in the training of new arbitrators." Through their *Code*, the three groups also seek to ensure high-quality performance among arbitrators by establishing standards that spell out not only ethical principles but what is considered good practice in the arbitration profession. The FMCS, while encouraging the use of newer arbitrators, has also instituted a quality-control program through the use of stricter criteria for new arbitrators seeking to be added to the FMCS roster. This means that while encouraging the use of newer arbitrators by listing them on its roster, the FMCS is also attempting to ensure that they will be qualified. The final check upon quality performance by arbitrators is through the parties themselves. This is simply a matter of exercising their right of choice to exclude arbitrators who, in the opinion of the parties, do not do a good job in terms of quality and/or the time consumed to render decisions.

Reducing Time and Cost of Grievance Arbitration   A number of programs have been instituted to reduce the time and cost involved in grievance arbitration. Through ARBIT, the FMCS has been able to provide panel names to the parties much faster. The AAA has also established an expedited procedure for the arbitration process itself. And the parties have begun to incorporate expedited arbitration procedures in their agreements.

The FMCS ARBIT system has already had phenomenal success in reducing the time it takes to respond to a party requesting an arbitration panel. For years, the average interval between a request and the forwarding of a panel of arbitrators was twenty days. In the first two years of ARBIT, the time was reduced to fifteen days, and by the end of fiscal year 1984, it was 6.4 days. The new standard of expediting panel names to parties is one working day.

Along with this, the FMCS through ARBIT is pledged to:

Establish better controls of arbitration activities

Create a capability of maintaining the new response-time standards even
with increased work load

Respond more precisely to requests

Ascertain national arbitration requirements

Determine substantive trends

These standards are all conducive to a speedier and better referral service
by FMCS and, through this, a reduction in both time and cost involved in
grievance arbitration.

The American Arbitration Association has also been significantly
involved in establishing expedited arbitration procedures. In response to
concern over rising costs and excessive delays, a subcommittee of the
AAA in 1971 recommended the establishment of an expedited grievance-
arbitration procedure "under which cases could be scheduled promptly
and awards rendered no later than five days after the hearings.[22] In return
for eliminating certain features traditionally associated with grievance
arbitration, the parties were assured that they could obtain quicker decisions at some cost savings. The Expedited Labor Arbitration Rules of the
AAA include appointment of the arbitrator by the AAA rather than selection by the parties; selection of the place and time of hearing by the AAA;
oral notice of a hearing not less than twenty-four hours in advance; elimination of transcripts or briefs; expeditions handling of hearings in whatever manner will permit full presentation by the parties; and no filing of
documents after the hearing. The award, in writing, is to be made promptly—unless agreed upon otherwise by the parties, within five business
days after the closing of the hearing. If the arbitrator determines that an
opinion should accompany the award, it should be in summary form.
Other features added by the AAA in New York are that Fridays are set
aside on a regular basis for hearings, and that the parties must be available
when called.

The concept of expedited grievance arbitration received a major
boost by the steel-industry settlement in August 1971. For the first time, a
two-year experimental expedited arbitration procedure (renewed each
contract since 1974) was founded, to be implemented on a regional intercompany basis. The procedure provides two routes for appeal of grievances to arbitration. All grievances may be appealed either to expedited
arbitration or to regular arbitration. Regular arbitration would proceed in
the traditional way under the agreement. To handle expedited cases, an
arbitration panel was established in each of twelve major steel areas.
Arbitrators selected for these panels were drawn from relatively young
lawyers in practice or on university staffs. An administrative officer was

---

[22]Expedited Labor Arbitration Rules of the American Arbitration Association.

established for each locality to receive referrals to arbitration from the parties and to assign a member of the panel on an alphabetical rotation basis.

The coal industry uses an expedited procedure called, in their agreement, "Immediate Arbitration." Under this procedure, the first three steps of the grievance procedure may be bypassed, an arbitration hearing held within five days, and a bench decision rendered on the spot, to be followed by a written decision within ten days.

Another technique labor-management groups use more frequently is to establish panels of rotating permanent arbitrators for regular cases. Although the specifics vary, the basic idea is for the parties, with the aid of such organizations as the FMCS and the AAA, to select a group of arbitrators who then, for the length of the agreement, on a rotational or random selection basis, handle all grievance arbitration. The use of a permanent arbitrator is not new. What seems to be new about the process described here is that the parties are attempting to secure the best of a combination of a permanent arbitrator and an ad hoc arbitrator system. Advantages anticipated from the permanent-arbitrators panel system are (1) experienced, well-qualified arbitrators on tap at all times, (2) a reduction of both time and costs by establishing a quick selection process and by using arbitrators who have a familiarity with the particular industry and contract, and (3) maintaining of some flexibility and fresh faces by rotating the cases among several arbitrators.

Finally, it should be noted that cost cutting and time saving in grievance arbitration may be assisted and encouraged by the AAA and FMCS, but their impact is limited. Control of costs and time is most effective when instituted by the parties themselves. Suffice it to say that costly and time-consuming procedures do not have to be endured by the parties. The parties *do* choose the arbitrators; they *do* spell out the grievance procedures in their agreements; and they may further control cost and time by joint agreement as to guidelines for hearings, transcription, documentation, and period of time for the decision.

The AAA has introduced some sound advice in its *9 Ways to Cut Arbitration Costs*:

1. *Arbitration should be prompt.* An important "hidden" cost in labor arbitration is the time lost to executives, union representatives, and workers. The cost of legal fees can also be significant. All of these items can be reduced by expediting the procedure. Furthermore, the "back pay meter" may be ticking while you are waiting for an eventual decision. Even where financial risk is not involved, a quick decision is usually better because keeping a grievant on the hook is bad for employee relations.

2. *Don't order a transcript unless you really need it.* Court reporting is expensive. Transcripts delay the award. The arbitrator can't start writing his opinion until he gets the record. Furthermore, arbitrators

feel obliged to read every word. That means study time at the per-diem rate. In some cases, transcripts are worth what they cost. But most of the time they serve only to double the total expenses of arbitration.

3. *Question the arbitrator's fee if you think it is too high.* The arbitrator is serving the parties. He should be paid a fair fee. Under AAA pro-cedures, you are told his per diem rate in advance of his appoint-ment. By reducing travel time, the number of hearings and study time, you have some control over the amount of arbitrator's fee. When necessary, ask the AAA to speak up about an unreasonably high fee.

4. *Clarify the issues before the first hearing.* Why spend hours of hear-ing-room time establishing facts that aren't really in dispute? When parties come in prepared with the names and seniority dates of griev-ants, amounts of money involved and other details of record, it not only cuts hearing-room time but shortens the arbitrator's study time as well. In labor arbitration, the matter has already gone through the grievance procedure. A badly organized presentation serves no good purpose.

5. *Sometimes, parties don't really need long opinions.* Parties can ask the AAA to request the arbitrator to simplify or eliminate his opinion. In a few cases, it may be appropriate for the arbitrator to handwrite his award and a brief opinion at the close of the hearing, delivering it to the parties at once. If you don't need an opinion as a guideline for the future, consider the possibility of eliminating it. The arbitrator's bill will be substantially smaller. The dispute may be resolved sooner.

6. *Avoid unnecessary citations.* When parties indulge in needless cita-tions they only compel the arbitrator to "go to the books" himself. That takes study time. Citation of awards by other arbitrators may be necessary in some situations. But be accurate. Don't rely on digests or headnotes alone. Above all, be selective.

7. *The labor arbitrator is an experienced professional.* Exercise restraint in submitting arguments about procedural matters. Generally, a sim-ple but accurate presentation of your facts and arguments will put the sophisticated arbitrator in a position to make a decision.

8. *Don't break your date with the arbitrator.* When a hearing date is set, keep it. Don't ask for postponements unless absolutely necessary. The arbitrator is a professional man whose time means money. He may be turning down another case on the day when your hearing is scheduled. Some arbitrators make a charge for postponements on short notice. This custom will grow unless parties exercise restraint.

9. *Find out about an arbitrator before you select him.* A man who never arbitrated a job evaluation dispute, for instance, may have to be edu-cated at your expense. Look up the arbitrator in the Summary of Labor Arbitration Awards and other reporting services. This will give you a better idea of his qualifications. If it's an AAA case and you need more information, don't hesitate to ask.[23]

---

[23]Reproduced by permission of the American Arbitration Association.

CONCLUSION

Much of the attention in the 1980s has been directed to the possible impact upon collective bargaining of bankruptcy procedures used primarily in the industries that have been deregulated, and of the appearance of concessionary bargaining in both the deregulated industries and other industries hit hard by the recession. What permanent effect such developments will have on collective bargaining is difficult to predict. If the past is indicative of what the future may hold for collective bargaining, the prediction must be that collective bargaining as a product of a free society will prove adaptable to whatever changes are necessitated as long as this free society continues. Moreover, these immediate developments in collective bargaining should not be allowed to impede the remarkable progress in turning collective bargaining around from a process that, in the 1950s, was said by some to be doomed to failure, to a viable and positive process marked by innovative and tradition-breaking ways to insure that collective bargaining does work, a positive approach to collective bargaining.

SELECTED REFERENCES

Aaron, Benjamin, and K. W. Wedderburn, eds., *Industrial Conflict—A Comparative Legal Survey.* New York: Crane, Russak & Co., 1972. A comparative legal survey of industrial conflict in the United States, Great Britain, Sweden, West Germany, France, and Italy.

Blackman, John L., *Presidential Seizure in Labor Disputes.* Cambridge, Mass.: Harvard University Press, 1967. In the foreword, John T. Dunlop notes that relatively little is known about seizure as one of the arsenal of tools in resolving conflict that vitally affects the public interest, and yet there have been seventy-one instances of its use. Professor Blackman provides a definitive account of the experience in these seventy-one seizure situations.

Chamberlain, Neil W. assisted by Jane M. Schilling, *Social Responsibility and Strikes.* New York: Harper & Row, 1953. For the reader who is interested in the social implications of the strike, this is a classic in the field. From the initial point of defining social responsibility, the author moves to a thoughtful consideration of public opinion and strikes, social control of strikes, and social and legal sanctions.

Davey, Harold W., Mario F. Bognanno, and David L. Estenson, *Contermporary Collective Bargaining,* 4th ed. Englewood Cliffs, N.J.: Prentice-Hall, 1982. Professor Davey and his colleagues offer the reader what is probably the best all-around analysis and review of collective bargaining in the contemporary period and the challenges that face collective bargaining in the future. Detailed, thoughtful, and combining the practical experience of the trio of authors, *Contemporary Collective Bargaining* is a must on the reading list of anyone aspiring to understand this institution in its contenporary and future setting.

Dunlop, John T., "The Function of the Strike," in *Frontiers of Collective Bargaining*, eds. John T. Dunlop and Neil W. Chamberlain. New York: Harper & Row, 1967. Professor Dunlop explains the functional classification of strikes and the decline of the strike. More important, he anticipates the developments that are now taking place: "The parties to collective bargaining may be reasonably expected to experiment more and to devote their attention to the design and perfection of procedures and machinery to resolve disputes."

"Exploring Alternatives to the Strike," *Monthly Labor Review*, 96, no. 9 (September 1973), 35–66. Included in this section are a series of articles based on papers presented at the fifth annual Collective Bargaining Forum of the Institute of Collective Bargaining and Group Relations. An excellent and informative series by some of the field's most astute professionals in both the academic and practicing areas. Addressed in the papers are such topics as the role of the strike, alternatives in the public sector, alternatives in the private sector, and alternative techniques. The articles range through all the traditional forms of alternatives such as mediation, fact finding, and arbitration, but even more important, they delve into new uses and combinations such as med-arb, binding arbitration in interest disputes, partisan mediation, mutual anxiety, and binding fact finding.

Fleming, R. W., "New Challenges for Collective Bargaining," *Wisconsin Law Review*, May 1964. Concise discussion of new techniques being used to resolve problems of technological change and to render resolution of conflict a more rational, continuing process.

Flynn, Ralph J., *Public Work, Public Workers*. Washington, D.C.: The New Republic Book Co., 1975. Through interviews and case histories, Flynn probes the feelings of government workers that are moving them to a new militancy, especially at the state and local levels. The author states that the first step toward a solution to the disorder of strikes is a new national law for public workers, on the order of the Wagner Act.

Gomberg, William, "Special Study Committees," in *Frontiers of Collective Bargaining*, eds. John T. Dunlop and Neil W. Chamberlain. New York: Harper & Row, 1967. Interesting and informative discussion of special study committees (joint study committees) with emphasis on the historical perspective. The author refers to such committee efforts as the National Civic Federation, the Protocol of Peace, the Cleveland Ladies' Garment Industrial Experiment, the Chicago Amalgamated Experiment, and the Pequot Mills Experiment.

Healy, James J., ed., *Creative Collective Bargaining*. Englewood Cliffs, N.J.: Prentice-Hall, 1965. The most definitive work to date on innovative and creative approaches to the improvement of the collective bargaining process. Included are discussions of such plans as the American Motors Progress-Sharing Plan, General Motors, United Air Lines, New York Hotel Industry, Electrical Contracting Industry, Hart Schaffner & Marx, International Harvester, Swift and Company, Allegheny Ludlum, Armour Automation Committee, West Coast Longshore, Basic Steel Human Relations Committee, and the Glass-Container Industry.

Hutt, W. H., *The Strike-Threat System—The Economic Consequences of Collective Bargaining*. New Rochell, N.Y.: Arlington House, 1973. A penetrating and provocative analysis of the strike, in which Professor Hutt concludes that fear of strikes inflicts far greater damage on the economic system than actual strikes do. The author reiterates an earlier view that the "mere right to disrupt the continuity of the productive process is having deplorable effects, regarding both the size of real income and equity in the distribution of income."

Indik, Bernard P., and Georgina M. Smith, *Resolution of Social Conflict through Collective Bargaining: An Alternative to Violence?* Reprint no. 22. Institute of Management and Labor Relations, New Brunswick, N.J.: Rutgers University, 1960. The authors examine the similarities and differences between the labor movement and the racial movement and the possibility of transferring the working elements of collective bargaining to the racial scene as a possible way of reducing conflict. They conclude "it does seem reasonable to expect that some modified bargaining scheme, adapted to the civil rights revolution, can provide a device, or an armament of devices superior to calling national guardsmen or police riot-control groups."

Knowles, K. G. J. C., *Strikes—A Study in Industrial Conflict.* Oxford: Basil Blackwell, 1952. This book stands as a classic on the strike and covers the British experience from 1911 to 1947.

Lester, Richard A., "An Alternative Strike Procedure," in Neil W. Chamberlain, ed., *Sourcebook on Labor,* p. 756. New York: McGraw-Hill, 1958. A sort of presidential bag-of-tools approach to emergency strikes with ad hoc hearings, voluntary arbitration, fact finding, injunction, and seizure with financial penalities as options.

Maggiolo, Walter A., *Techniques of Mediation in Labor Disputes.* Dobbs Ferry, N.Y.: Oceana Publications, 1971. Complete description of the philosophy of mediation, the mediator, the mediation function, and when to use the mediator.

McPherson, William H., "Grievance Mediation Under Collective Bargaining," *Industrial and Labor Relations Review,* 9, no. 2 (January 1956). Professor McPherson, on the basis of successful use of mediation prior to the grievance-arbitration step, advocates that more employers and unions should experiment with the technique.

Northrup, Herbert R., *Compulsory Arbitration and Government Intervention in Labor Disputes—An Analysis of Experience.* Washington, D.C.: Labor Policy Association, Inc., 1966. Professor Northrup provides an informed basis by which those interested in compulsory arbitration may measure its usefulness.

Seaton, Douglas P., *Arbitration of Public Employee Collective Bargaining Agreements: Different Methods, The Recent Experience of Other States, Implementation Issues.* St. Paul: State of Minnesota, 1981. One of the more thorough treatments of interest arbitration in public-sector negotiations.

Siegel, Irving H., and Edgar Weinberg, *Labor-Management Cooperation, The American Experience.* Kalamazoo, Mich.: W. E. Upjohn Institute For Employment Research, 1982. The authors, noting that the adversarial relationship of labor and management has not precluded efforts at cooperation, predict that industrial relations in America will become increasingly hospitable to cooperation. This is a most thorough study of American cooperation between labor and management by two very able researchers. It is highly recommended reading.

Simkin, William E., *Mediation and the Dynamics of Collective Bargaining.* Washington, D.C.: Bureau of National Affairs, Inc., 1971. The former director of the FMCS brings to the reader his unusual perception of the mediation process and its function in crisis bargaining, emergency disputes, preventive mediation, fact finding and mediation, and the use of mediation in public-employee disputes.

Stephens, Elvis C., "Resolution of Impasses in Public Employee Bargaining," *Monthly Labor Review,* 99, no. 1 (January 1976), 57–58. Professor Stephens reports on the developments in impasse resolution and the types of issues in dispute.

Stern, James L. et al., *Final-Offer Arbitration.* Lexington, Mass.: D. C. Heath, 1975. The authors describe and analyze what has happened in Pennsylvania, Michigan, and Wisconsin in dispute-resolution procedures for public safety employees. Called upon for information are the labor and management negotiators and neutrals involved in dispute resolutions in these states. From this study the authors project future trends and speculate about possible consequences of transferring various procedural arrangements to other bargaining situations. The study provides an excellent view of the final-offer arbitration technique.

Stern, James L., and Barbara D. Dennis, eds., Industrial Relations Research Association Series, *Proceedings of the Twenty-Seventh Annual Winter Meeting,* December 28–29, 1974, pp. 307–8. Papers delivered by Charles M. Rehmus and R. Theodore Clark, Jr., concerning legislated interest arbitration in the public sector.

Stevens, Carl M., "Mediation and the Role of the Neutral," in *Frontiers of Collective Bargaining,* eds. John T. Dunlop and Neil W. Chamberlain. New York: Harper & Row, 1967. Professor Stevens spells out the functions and tactics of mediation.

Tanimoto, Helene S., *Guide to Statutory Provsions in Public Sector Collective Bargaining—Impasse Resolution Procedures,* Occasional Publication No. 95, Industrial Relations Center, Honolulu: University of Hawaii, 1973. Excellent coverage of the statutes, ordinances, and personnel rules and regulations covering all the states and the District of Columbia as they apply to impasse procedures. Three major techniques are considered: mediation, fact finding, and arbitration. Included in the appendices is a chart of employees covered under state statutes and orders.

––––––, **and Joyce M. Najita,** *Guide to Statutory Provisions in Public Sector Collective Bargaining—Strike Rights and Prohibitions,* Industrial Relations Center, Honolulu: University of Hawaii, 1974. A state-by-state examination of the right to strike under state statutes.

Vaughn, M. David, Chariman, *Collective Bargaining in a Changing Environment,* (A Course Handbook). New York: Practicing Law Institute, 1982. Although designed as a course handbook for a program sponsored by the Practicing Law Institute, October to December 1982, this booklet contains a wealth of material on subject relating to collective bargaining and to managing conflict. Topics include concession bargaining, deregulation, new tools for bargaining, new technology, and emerging issues.

Wisconsin Center for Political Policy, *The Effect of Senate Bill 15 Amendments to the Municipal Employee Relations Act.* Madison: Center for Political Policy, December 1980. A comprehensive analysis of the impasse-resolution procedures included in the Wisconsin Public Employees Collective Bargaining statute. These procedures include mediation, fact finding, interest arbitration, med-arb, and combinations thereof.

Yaffe, Byron, and Howard Goldblatt, *Factfinding in Public Employment in New York—More Promise Than Illusion,* ILR Paperback No. 10, New York State School of Industrial and Labor Relations, Ithaca, N.Y.: June 1971. Yaffe and Goldblatt are part of a five-state study to evaluate the usefulness of fact finding as a strike deterrent in public employment. In concluding their study, the authors note that William E. Simkin's comments about successful fact finding are borne out by their survey: "Where fact-finding has been successful, I would suggest—but cannot prove—that the factfinder has mediated deliberately, instructively or surreptitiously." Their conclusion is that the New York situation affirms that where fact finding is so viewed, it is a relatively successful mechanism in resolving bargaining impasses.

Yoder, Dale, and Herbert Heneman, Jr., eds., "Employee and Labor Relations," *ASPA Handbook of Personnel and Industrial Relations.* Washington, D.C.: Bureau of National Affairs, Inc., 1976. This section of the PAIR handbook includes an article by Harold Davey on "Third-Party Mediation, Arbitration." Based on the author's more than thirty years' experience in the field and extensive research, the article is well worth the reader's attention.

Note: Again the reader is referred to the wealth of current material to be found in the publications and Proceedings of groups and institutions, such as: AAA's *Quarterly Arbitration Journal;* the Services published by Prentice-Hall, the Bureau of National Affairs, and Commerce Clearing House; Proceedings published by the National Academy of Arbitrators, the Industrial Relations Research Association, and the Society of Professionals in Dispute Resolution; public-sector journals published by such groups as the Public Service Research Foundation and by Baywood Publishing Co., Inc.; governmental publications such as the *Monthly Labor Review;* and publications of various academic institutions, such as Cornell's *Industrial and Labor Relations Review* and Berkeley's *Industrial Relations.*

CONCLUSION

The following observations represent the author's view as to the underlying themes of this book:

First, collective bargaining in all its aspects—negotiation, contract administration, and special strengthening techniques—has achieved a degree of acceptance and widespread respectability unmatched at any other time in its evolution.

Second, collective bargaining is both a product and a function of a free society. The rejection of alternate or substitute ways, based on compulsion, of resolving labor-management problems is a refreshing expression of faith in the free-society approach to the resolution of such problems.

Third, the negativism of the late 1950s and early 1960s toward collective bargaining, when even its continuation was questioned, has been replaced by a positiveness that finds expression in directing resources and efforts toward its improvement rather than in destroying the institution of collective bargaining.

Fourth, the most effective approach to training people for involvement in the various activities concerned with collective bargaining is through the learning experience. The various processes involved in collective bargaining—negotiation, grievance, grievance arbitration—are so inextricably woven into human relationships that one must experience the process in order to gain expertise.

Fifth, effectiveness in collective bargaining activities results from more-than-adequate preparation and experience. But preparation and experience alone are not sufficient. It is the function of the collective-bargaining-by-objectives methodology to add a third ingredient—a systematic and orderly approach to negotiations. Because it is a methodology, it is equally effective in any negotiation situation, not just that of collective bargaining. Not only does CBO introduce system into collective bargaining negotiations, but by the discipline it introduces, the level of preparation it requires, and the tangible goals that it produces, CBO provides a positive approach to collective bargaining negotiations.

COLLECTIVE BARGAINING BY OBJECTIVES:
Simulation Exercises and Negotiation Games

INTRODUCTION

Development of expertise in collective bargaining negotiation is more than a process of reading about and listening to others tell about the practice of negotiation. These are important tools in learning and developing expertise but leave some important gaps in the learning process. Collective bargaining is, as much as anything else, a process that requires a sense of feel for what is going on. The sense of feel is acquired through involvement in the process of collective bargaining, not in just reading about it. The closest substitute for actual experience in negotiating labor agreements is the use of simulation, a method of learning the writer has used effectively for a number of years. Tying simulation bargaining to the methodology of collective bargaining by objectives has greatly improved and enhanced the learning-experience results. The participants soon find that, by this approach, learning does not have to be painful; it may even be fun, and it can be highly motivational if placed in the proper framework. Participants quickly learn that negotiation requires the application of a number of interdisciplinary skills: accounting, economics, statistics, verbal and written communication, human behavior, labor law, labor relations, politics, and administration, to name a few. The author claims no monopoly on the best ways to use simulation in training potential negotiators, but offers this particular approach as one that obtains beneficial results. Nine steps carry participants as realistically as possible through all the stages of bargaining, from preparing for negotiations to the negotiations themselves, and then on to the testing of the negotiated agreement through its administration period.

THE GAMES

Two types of games are included, to be used according to the needs of those who participate in the simulation. These were selected to illustrate two basically different bargaining situations. The games use (1) a private-industry manufacturing firm and (2) a quasi-public transit system.

Information included in each game is sufficient for the purpose of placing participants in a simulation situation where the objective is to renegotiate an agreement between the employer and the union. Included is general information about the industry, information about the union and the employer, information about the labor relations between the parties during the time the labor contract has been in effect, and financial information. A copy of the contract that is to be renegotiated is also included. The participants should be held to the information provided in the game and not be permitted to manufacture additional information unless it logically derives from the game information or from researched and documented sources.

INSTRUCTIONS FOR USE OF THE SIMULATION EXERCISE

Step 1   Background

Participants should become aquainted as quickly as possible with the nature of the collective bargaining negotiation process and the tools needed for engaging in negotiations. At a minimum, the following should be covered, through reading and discussion, before embarking on the simulation exercise:

1. The evolution of collective bargaining (Chapters 1 and 2)
2. A description of the collective bargaining process (negotiation, contract administration, and techniques for resolving conflict)
3. The parties directly and indirectly involved in negotiations (Chapter 4)
4. The legal framework governing collective bargaining (Chapter 3)
5. The collective bargaining contract (Chapter 5)

To clarify and delineate the reading and discussions of the first four items, 1 through 4, above, the writer has found it useful for the participants to take a competency quiz. Participants are required to score above 90 percent, or the quiz is returned for more work. The purpose of the quiz is to help all participants reach the same level of knowledge concerning the negotiation process, the terms used, and the legal framework within which negotiations must function.

To aid the participants in acquiring a quick knowledge of what a collective bargaining contract contains, teams are organized, with three or four to a team and each team being provided with a private-sector contract and a public-sector contract. A list of topics usually found in negotiated contracts is given to each team. Each team is asked to determine what the particular contracts contain anent each topic—seniority, management rights, sick leave, vacation, promotion, premium pay, to name a few. After completing their assignments, the teams are convened to discuss their findings.

At this point, participants should also clearly understand the entire course that the simulation exercise will follow, from preliminaries to final agreement.

STEP 2   ORGANIZING BARGAINING TEAMS

This step may actually take place sometime during the initial orientation process of Step 1. Regardless of the size of the total group, the bargaining teams, for maximum participation and results, should be kept to about four participants each. After teams are organized, an even number of union teams and management teams should be designated and pairings made. From this point on, participants should identify only with the team they have been assigned to, and teams should relate only to the opposite teams with which they have been paired for the negotiations—that is, first management team to first union team, and so on. For maximum benefit, locations that are entirely separate from each other should be found for the various bargaining groups. The bargaining groups should be cautioned that each member must refrain from discussing with other groups what his group is doing until the whole exercise is completed.

STEP 3   MATERIALS FOR GAME
AND INTRODUCTION TO A SYSTEMATIC WAY
OF APPROACHING AND CARRYING ON
NEGOTIATIONS

Participants should be given the game being used for the simulation and referred to all other materials that will be available or sources to which they may turn in the process of the negotiations.

At this point, the participants should be asked to read Chapters 7 to 15 on the methodology of collective bargaining by objectives. The instructor should take time to be sure that they clearly understand the objectives procedure. The systematic way that this procedure leads them into the negotiations and supports them during the negotiations minimizes the mistakes they might make and will effect a much more positive approach.

STEP 4   PREPARATION FOR PRESENTATION
OF POSITIONS

Using the objectives approach, the bargaining teams should quickly develop their material—items, priorities, and objectives—from which can be derived the initial position that will be presentd to the other side.[1] This requires two steps in the process of establishing a complete list of items to be negotiated and the objectives for those items: (1) the initial position taken by the initiator party—usually, but not required to be, the union; and (2) the response of the other party. At this point it is well for the instructor to meet separately with the union teams as a group and the management teams as a group to explain different formats that may be used in presenting a position to the other party. Here, and at all points where convenient, the instructor emphasizes that the degree of benefit derived from the exercise is directly tied to the way in which the individual involves himself or herself in the role he or she has been assigned or has assumed.

The teams then establish a timetable for the presentation of positions and the beginning of actual negotiations. The importance of adequate preparation is emphasized at this point, since it is not customary for the parties to admit new items to the bargaining table once the negotiations actually begin.

STEP 5   NEGOTIATIONS

Bargaining groups should be completely separated from each other if maximum results are to be obtained. To put them into various corners of a large room only inhibits the learning experience.

Although the simulation process may be condensed and framed for short exposure situations of only one or two sessions, this may prevent maximum benefit in getting participants to feel the many aspects of negotiation. All too often, the simulation becomes a once-over lightly job when only one or two sessions are devoted to a simulation exercise. A much more productive approach is to allow as many as ten to twelve two-hour

---

[1]The instructor should check each CBO sheet before any exchange of positions to be sure it is completely filled out.

sessions, with all the outside sessions the groups find necessary. This involves enough depth of involvement so that participants not only see, but develop a sense of feel for, what the negotiation process really is: the frustrations of personality problems; the difficulties in verbally communicating with the other party; the slow, tedious, and time-consuming process of language construction; the emotionalism; and the strategies and techniques of negotiation, for example. For the full appreciation of these factors, a depth of exposure is required that brief simulation fails to achieve.

Once the negotiations begin, the most productive results can be obtained if the instructor at this point sheds his or her role and instead assumes any real role that the participants may require during the course of the negotiations: company official, union official, the NLRB, or the appropriate board, mediator, arbitrator, or legal counsel for either side.

During the negotiations, each participant should be asked to keep an individual log of the experience that not only relates what has happened but, more important, reveals an understanding of the forces in the negotiation process—personalities, economics, politics—that influence final results.

Participants should also be informed of the exact date when the contract will terminate, for two reasons: (1) This sets the time frame for the negotiations, and (2) it parallels the real situation by providing the participants with a date at which the 60-day period also terminates and at which time they may exercise all options allowed by the law, such as striking or extending negotiations if the contract has not been completed. The writer has also found that, in order to prevent artificiality from entering the negotiations in the latter part of the time period, it is best to inform the participants that, while a negotiated agreement should be their prime objective, the instructor will also accept a real impasse that meets with his or her approval.

Step 6 . Mediation Service

A highlight of the writer's own use of simulation has been to take the bargaining groups to the offices of the Federal Mediation Service for a simulation session in mediation. If one of the groups is at impasse—and quite often this is the case—this group becomes a live party to the mediation process, with the mediator functioning as he would with a real union-management situation. Other participants become observers. If a mediator is not available, the instructor should take the group through a mediation session. Participants should be asked to read Chapter 19.

Step 7   Testing the Agreement

At the conclusion of the negotiations, the bargaining groups should be asked to turn in a copy of the agreement (or a portion, if they were at impasse) and to read Chapters 16 to 18 of the text. The instructor should then carefully examine the agreements for problem areas in construction or omission, and formulate grievances to bring out these problems. Other grievances should also be formulated that show the workings of the agreement during the contract period. Through discussion relative to these grievance situations, the participants are easily brought to a realization of the importance of the construction and language of the agreement.

Step 8   Grievance Arbitration

An extension of Step 7's application of the contract is to involve the participants in an arbitration exercise in which they may play the roles of the parties and also that of the arbitrator. If time does not allow a full simulation of the arbitration process, the instructor should be careful to explain the process to the group.

Step 9   Windup

A general discussion of the negotiation session, observations as to what most influenced results, the use of experience gained in the use of various strategies and technniques as a base for the next negotiations, and an evaluation of the total learning experience gained through the simulation exercise should be the order of the day.

A MANUFACTURING GAME: PECK'S BREWERY

The Brewing Industry

Today, the brewing process is automated and standard throughout the world. Cereal, malt, barley, hops, and water are mixed and filtered into wort. The wort is boiled to liquefy the sugars into easily fermentable forms, then yeast is added to start the fermentation. Once fermentation is well on its way, the yeast is removed and the wort is transferred to an aging tank, where it lagers for several weeks. The brew is again filtered and packaged. Bottled and canned beer goes through a pasteurization process before being sent to market.

Breweries have for many years been a major source of tax revenue. Through the United States Brewers' Association, breweries have cooperated in policing themselves and accepting social responsibility through their antilitter and recycling programs.

The market is dominated by five national and several seminational breweries, with minor local competition from regional and local breweries. Breweries are closely regulated by federal and state agencies; so there is little difference in quality or price and only slight differences in product. The advantages of bulk purchasing and extensive distribution continue to give the larger breweries a pricing advantage, which has caused many of the regional breweries to go out of business. Competition among breweries is primarily based on the image their particular beer or company portrays. The image of a beer and its company is portrayed primarily through packaging, advertising, and slogans. Also, breweries have their own distinct labels to differentiate their product from that of their competitors. There is also continuous experimentation with ingredient blending, packaging, advertising, and marketing strategies by breweries.

Brewing companies advertise their product heavily through the mass media, especially television. Slogans play a major role in consumer recognition of brand names.

Quality is also a competitive factor. Some breweries emphasize the alcoholic strength of their beers; others their lightness. Quality is also determined by the brewing process. Although quality seems to be emphasized less than image, frequently quality and image are inseparable. For example, a brewery that stresses the use of natural spring water in its brewing process wants its beer to carry the image of quality.

Pricing is a major factor in brewery competition. Competition has intensified between regional and national breweries, and antitrust charges have been brought by regional breweries against alleged unfair pricing practices. The price squeeze on popular-priced brands of regional breweries has reduced their competitive advantage over national breweries because of rising costs and consumer price constraints. National brewers of premium beer, with greater operating and purchasing efficiencies, can brew and market more cheaply than regional brewers.

Brewery workers are semiskilled workers, with work ranging from general labor to cleanup to lead workers who determine minor variations and readiness of beer for bottling.

Unions are strong in the brewing industry, and pay rates on the average are higher than for food workers or all nondurable manufacturing workers. *The Brewers Almanac* and the Department of Labor publication, *Employment and Earnings,* may be reviewed for comparative wage rates.

The Milwaukee area has a total work force of approximately one million. The majority of the work force is classified as semiskilled, skilled, and professional workers. Milwaukee's unemployment rate generally approximates the national unemployment average.

Peck's Brewery

Peck's Brewing Company is a medium-sized brewery in the Midwest. The product is sold by lots to regional distributors, who sell to grocery stores, liquor stores. restaurants, and sports arenas.

Peck's beer is sold primarily in the Midwest states of Wisconsin, Michigan, Illinois, Ohio, and Indiana. Its primary target is Wisconsin, since it prides itself as a "home-grown" brew.

Peck's has its home office in Milwaukee, Wisconsin, and all Peck's beer is produced in the Milwaukee plant. The state of Wisconsin charges a tax of $2.50 a barrel (31 gallons) on all beer produced.

The company was founded in 1950 by Michael Robertson. Robertson's success emerged from two factors: (1) aggressive advertising, and (2) the image of a medium-sized company brewing exclusively for the Midwest. It was a family-owned concern until going public in 1965.

Peck's advertises in regional magazines and newspapers, on radio and on television. Recently, Peck's implemented spot television ads and advertising at the Milwaukee Brewers' baseball games. Since the slogan of Peck's beer is "back to nature," the TV ads are photographed in the wheat fields of Minnesota, the Iowa corn belt, or the pinewoods and lake regions of Wisconsin, thus stressing its Midwest origin. The ads and commercials are interspersed with bits of information on Peck's brewing procedure, emphasizing the quality Peck's brings to its customers.

EMPLOYEE RELATIONS

Employee relations at Peck's was fairly good for the first twenty-five years. However, in the midseventies friction developed between employees and management over wages, fringe benefits, and job security. The friction was intensified by the impersonal relationship that developed between management and the employees over the years, as Peck's grew from a 100-employee local brewery to the present 600-employee regional brewer. Peck's was able to restrict wages and fringe benefits because of the personal relationship between owner Michael Robertson and each of the employees, who knew him as "Mike." The employees enjoyed security in knowing Mike personally and feeling like part of the family. They also enjoyed company outings, bowling in the company league, and being able to go to Mike, knowing he would understand their problems.

By the midseventies, Robertson had become increasingly distant. The personal identification of the employees with the firm and its owner had diminished. The expanding social gap between management and employees caused employee pride in the company to lessen until almost everyone viewed his or her work as "just another job." There followed a steady increase in the number of complaints about the lower-than-average wage and fringe-benefit package and the lack of job security.

Peck's seemed ideal for union organization by the International Union of United Brewery, Flour, Cereal, Soft Drink and Distillery Workers of America (AFL-CIO). The International had long regarded Peck's as the

lone holdout in the Milwaukee area. Working slowly with Peck's production workers, the International Union, through Local No. 3, reached a
point in 1977 when it deemed it could successfully achieve bargaining
status. Consequently, an NLRB-sponsored election was requested upon a
30 percent showing of interested employees.

The union had underestimated the employees' loyalty to Peck's and
lost the election by a narrow margin, getting only 44 percent of the votes.
However, the union was not to be denied. Using some of the older, more
disgruntled employees as internal organizers, the union began a quiet
campaign. A second election was called eighteen months later. This time
the union won by a large majority. Local No. 3 was designated as the
bargaining representative for Peck's production employees. The membership of the union increased from 32 percent to 64 percent of the 500
production employees. Contract negotiations produced a contract.

EXEPRIENCE UNDER THE FIRST AGREEMENT

The contract was less than satisfactory to both parties. Management and
the union agreed that the grievance procedure was cumbersome and
needed modification. Both also agreed on the need for an effective pension plan.

Rank-and-file members of the union still complained about their
wages; although greatly improved, they were still below the brewery average. They also complained that the entire fringe-benefit package was not
competitive with industry norms, especially the insurance and holiday
provisions. The union asked for and received an additional holiday.
Union members also requested an increase in life insurance and a dental
plan. Both demands were rejected.

Grumbling was heard about the distribution of overtime, slack-time
leave, and the lack of a wage-maintenance program. Most of this com-
plaining could be traced to the slack production months of January and
February, when thirty employees were laid off for three days a week for
six successive weeks. The employees felt that a shorter workweek for
everyone would be preferable to this situation. Overtime distribution
could also be improved by allowing some choice in the working of overtime hours.

The layoffs in January and February also pointed out that the term
job security was interpreted differently by each side. The company defined the term as "importance to the company of the job performed by an
individual," whereas the union said it meant "seniority in the department." The term was arbitrated, and the company definition prevailed.

The company also had complaints about the contract. Because the
cost of arbitration was not specified, the company paid all costs for the
first three arbitration cases. The union assumed that Peck's would con-

tinue to pay all arbitration costs. Management accused the union of abusing this omission in the contract by taking frivolous cases to arbitration.

Management was also dissatisfied with the amount of work time that union stewards were using to conduct their business. The stewards presumed they could conduct most of their business on company time. Supervisors permitted this practice to continue, but requested that limits be established in the amount of company time stewards could use to conduct their business.

Management insisted that a "management rights" clause was necessary, as well as a revision of the "transfer and promotion" article. Some personnel changes management intended to implement were delayed several weeks while the union tried to challenge them through the grievance procedure.

The transfer and promotion clause prevented the company from hiring some well-qualified personnel from another brewery that was going out of business because some of Peck's employees were also "well qualified" and had to be given preference.

EXPERIENCE UNDER THE SECOND AGREEMENT

Approximately two years ago, the union and Peck's management reached agreement on a second contract. Several problems have developed since then. The negotiators will undoubtedly want to discuss these problems as well as matters which were not resolved during the preceding contract negotiations at the upcoming negotiations.

Due to increasing consumer demands for Peck's beer and in an attempt to reduce overtime costs, management informed the union that it is considering adoption of an expanded work schedule. This, according to management, will result in the implementation of shifts and/or an extended workweek of six or seven days. An extended workweek would establish Saturday and Sunday as regular workdays for some employees. The existing agreement does not provide for this type of scheduling, but management claims that the management rights clause permits the company to adjust the work schedule as necessary to manage operations. The union insists that, regardless of the management rights clause, implementation of such a work schedule would be a violation of Article 9—Hours of Work.

Peck's has purchased new high-technology equipment in order to automate the power plant. This equipment is scheduled to be operational July 1 of next year. The present power plant employees will be displaced by the new automated equipment. The new equipment will require only four highly technical employees to monitor the computerized system twenty-four hours a day, seven days; and four semitechnical troubleshooter employees. The power plant currently employs eighty-six semiskilled and unskilled employees. These employees and the union want to retain the remaining power plant jobs. They also want retraining, bumping rights, supplemental unemployment benefits, extended layoff rights, and severance pay for the power plant employees being displaced.

The Safety Committee was organized during the first contract on a tenuous foundation. Under the first contract, only one line was directed to the formation of the committee. Without a predetermined function or defined structure, the Safety Committee was forced to spend the contract period attempting to define its objectives and functions. Shifting from watchdog, then advisory, and finally to grievance functions, the committee awaited the conclusion of the second negotiations for its role to be defined. However, those negotiations failed to provide this definition. Increasing numbers of OSHA violations led the union to pursue the watchdog role to ensure proper record keeping and safety compliance. Management contends that these activities should remain under its unilateral control. Management advocates that the Safety Committee return to the advisory and grievance functions. As contract negotiations approach, union and management representatives again hope that the negotiations will clarify the role of the Safety Committee.

The union membership is very disgruntled over the outcome of an arbitration concerning payment for time worked on recognized holidays. Several employees worked on the Fourth of July holiday. They were paid eight hours for the time worked, plus four hours' overtime. The employees who worked grieved, requesting eight hours' holiday pay. The case went to arbitration, and the arbitrator ruled the company had properly paid the employees under the terms of the contract.

Employees have charged Peck's with employment discrimination through grievances and appeals to federal and state antidiscrimination agencies during the last three years. A black malting-department worker filed a grievance when rejected for a lead position. The grievance was dropped when the employee was awarded another lead position. Three discrimination cases are currently pending against Peck's. One is by a long-term female employee in the bottling department who filed a sexual harassment charge against her supervisor for making improper sexual advances. Peck's has also been named in the suit because it does not have an established policy pertaining to sexual harassment. Another suit involves a handicapped individual (fully qualified as a brewer at another brewery) who is unable to work at Peck's because of Peck's unwillingness to modify the building to allow the wheelchair applicant access to the facility. A Chicana (female) malting department employee has filed a discrimination suit based on Peck's former policy of not hiring Chicanos. Because of the former policy, Chicanos do not have sufficient seniority to compete successfully for higher-paying jobs. Chicanos also have a substantially higher layoff rate than other employees because of the former policy.

The criteria for promotions—merit and seniority—have resulted in employee mistrust of the selection process. The union claims that management has developed arbitrary, nonjob-related criteria disguised as merit factors. As a result, several grievances have been filed concerning management's selections for promotions.

Peck's financial condition has been cyclical during the last decade. The problems in the national economy have taken their toll. The union has been fairly understanding of the tight economic conditions during the first two negotiations. However, Peck's employees, like workers throughout the nation, are feeling the pinch of inflation and becoming more aggressive and militant in their demands for improvements in wages and fringe benefits.

Among the many issues left unresolved from the last negotiation was the development of layoff procedures that contain strong employee protections. The matter of work sharing was referred for additional study, but there is no evidence, in the opinion of the union, that these studies have been undertaken.

The issue of departmental versus plantwide seniority is evident from several grievances. Overtime, vacations, employee welfare benefits, and layoff procedures are subject to lengthy service criteria. Management wants to tighten these length-of-service requirements and establish rigid definitions for them. Union leaders and members claim these requirements are too extensive and not consistent with those of the industry or local firms.

Finally, both union and management believe a separate leave-of-absence article should be added to the contract. Jury duty, union business, extended illness or injury, and other conditions of this type are now handled case by case. Lengths of leaves, seniority accumulations, and job and wage guarantees are currently left to management's discretion. Union members want their negotiators to effect a system which assures uniform, equitable, and consistent application of leave-of-absence provisions. Union membership is now 77 percent of the bargaining unit; union representatives think it should be 100 percent.

Management insists that wage or fringe benefit increases negotiated this year must be offset by worker productivity increases. Union leaders are not opposed to improving productivity, but they do not want the bargaining-unit members to be exploited in the name of productivity improvements.

The economic cycles of the seventies and eighties and concurrent inflation have inflicted financial pressures on the company and its employees. Peck's has managed to stay afloat and has expanded sales through a more-effective advertising program and a policy of holding prices to a minimum in order to remain competitive within the brewing industry.

Peck's television ads proved to be far more productive in stimulating sales than anticipated. Whether this market will continue to grow and whether retail prices can remain competitive are crucial questions for Peck's. Peck's aggressive management must accept the challenge constructively. The union must consider Peck's viability in the marketplace while representing the rank-and-file members.

Contract

This CONTRACT made this FIRST day of May 1983 between the undersigned firm, Peck's Brewery, of Milwaukee, Wisconsin (hereinafter referred to as the EMPLOYER), party of the first part, and the Brewery Workers' Local Union No. 3, Milwaukee, Wisconsin, and the International Union of United Brewery, Flour, Cereal, Soft Drink and Distillery Workers of America (hereinafter referred to as the UNION), parties of the second part, as representative of the employees covered by this Agreement.

THEREFORE, in consideration of the mutual covenants hereinafter set out, the parties hereto covenant and agree as follows:

Article 1
Union Recognition

(a)   The EMPLOYER recognizes the UNION as the sole collective bargaining agent for its employees in the Brewery Department, Bottling Department, Malting Department and Power Plant, as hereinafter more specifically stated.

(b)   The EMPLOYER shall not interfere with the right of employees to become members of the UNION. The UNION shall not interfere or discriminate against employees who choose not to join the UNION.

(c)   The term "EMPLOYEE" or "EMPLOYEES," as used in this agreement, shall be construed to include only the classifications of employees specifically listed in this agreement and employed in the Employer's plant.

(d)   Upon written authorization of an employee(s), the EMPLOYER shall deduct monthly Union dues and initiation fees from employee earnings. The deducted monies shall be remitted to a designated Union official regularly.

(e)   The maintenance of membership Union Security system shall have an open period which begins ninety (90) days prior to the contract expiration and closes on the contract expiration date.

Article 2
Hiring New Employees and Seniority

(a)   Preference in hiring of new employees shall be given in accordance with the following, provided the applicant(s) are well qualified and physically able to perform the work:
(1)   Employees requesting transfer from one department to another.
(2)   Employees who were employed by the Employer during the preceding year.
(3)   Others experienced in the brewing industry.
(4)   Other applicants.

(b)   If an opening occurs in any department, the vacancy shall be posted for four (4) days.

(c)   Any employee who leaves one department to work in another department shall lose all seniority in the former department after thirty (30) days.

(d)   Temporary summer help may be used without meeting the requirements of paragraph (a) above, provided there are no employees laid-off who are willing and able to work and the duration of summer employment does not exceed fifty (50) consecutive work days. All temporary help shall be paid probationary wages. Employees converting from temporary summer help to full-time employment shall be considered as category (3) or (4) of paragraph (a) above and shall not be hired before applicants in categories (1) or (2) of paragraph (a).

(e)   When temporary employees are required in a department, laid-off employees from other departments shall be given first consideration for temporary employment. Acceptance or refusal of temporary work in another department shall not affect the job security of said employee in their own department. Temporary employment of laid-off employees shall be at the rate prevailing in the assigned department.

(f)   Promotions within departments shall be awarded according to the employees' merit and seniority in that department.

(g)   New hires shall complete a ninety (90) day probationary period. The grievance procedure is not available to probationary employees.

Article 3
Layoff and Recall

Employees shall be laid-off impartially according to length of service with the company. The last employee laid-off shall be the first recalled, and the first laid-off shall be the last recalled.

Article 4
Discharge

Employees may not be discharged, except for good cause, in the discretion of the Employer. The Union shall have the right to investigate. Causes for discharge shall include, but not be limited to, the following: dishonesty, misuse of brewing monies, willful destruction of brewery property, and inadequate moral conduct. No wages for time not worked shall be paid to discharged employees if the Union does not make its investigation within three (3) days. If no investigation is made, the discharge shall be final.

Article 5
Discrimination and Union Activity

The parties hereto agree not to use any subterfuge, coercion or intimidation, directly or indirectly, to evade or frustrate compliance with the spirit and terms of this agreement, nor cause the discharge or suspension of any Union member(s) because of Union activities.

Any employee on leave of absence for Union activities or as a full-time Union officer shall retain their seniority and shall on return to work be given their former position, if capable.

Article 6
Injuries and Illness

(a)   An employee who, through sickness or accident, cannot perform their work must report to the Employer and the Union, and shall after recovery be re-employed in their former position, provided such sickness or accident has not incapacitated the employee.
(b)   Regular employees shall accrue four (4) hours of sick leave per calendar month of service.

Article 7
Reporting Accidents and Injuries

All employees must in case of accident or injury report same to the Employee Relations Office and first-aid person; and procure names and addresses of all witnesses to the accident.

No employee shall refuse to go for medical treatment when directed by Management or first-aid person. An injured employee(s) shall be removed from the job until injuries are determined and first aid or doctor's care is supplied. Any mechanical defects shall be reported immediately.

Article 8
Safety

(a)   A joint Union-Management Safety Committee shall be established.
(b)   The Employer reserves the right to make such rules and regulations as may be necessary to secure safety and maintain proper order. Recommendations from the Safety Committee shall be considered promptly.
(c)   Safety appliances for any work of a hazardous or injurious nature as deemed necessary shall be furnished by the employer. Employee(s) shall use such isssued equipment.
(d)   Gas masks shall be furnished to employees working in tanks or vats. As a safety measure, an employee shall be stationed outside tanks or vats while an employee(s) is varnishing, kotizing or mamutizing inside the tank or out.

Article 9
Hours of Labor

(a)   Eight (8) hours shall consist of a day's work. The work week shall consist of five (5) days starting on Monday which shall be consecutive except where interrupted by a holiday. Work shall not begin before 7:30 A.M. nor later than 9:00 A.M. The starting time shall be prescribed by the Employer and the hours worked shall be consecutive, except for one-half (½) hour break for lunch which shall be between 12:00 noon and 1:00 P.M. as assigned by the Employer.

(b) All work performed at the request of the Employer in excess of eight (8) hours in any day shall be paid at the rate of time-and-one-half (1½).

Article 10
Holidays and Leave

(a) The following nine (9) holidays shall be recognized under this agreement:
   (1) New Year's Day
   (2) Good Friday
   (3) Memorial Day
   (4) Fourth of July
   (5) Labor Day
   (6) Thanksgiving Day
   (7) Christmas Eve
   (8) Christmas Day
   (9) Employee's Birthday

Any employee must have worked ninety (90) days for the Employer prior to a holiday to be eligible for holiday pay. Any qualified experienced employee working one (1) day in the week in which a holiday falls shall receive holiday pay.

These holidays shall not be considered part of the regular work week if no work is done.

If work is performed on any of these holidays, it shall be paid at the rate of time-and-one-half (1½), and these days shall then be considered part of the regular work week.

Employees shall perform holiday work in seniority rotation.

When an employee is called for jury duty, the Employer shall pay the employee an amount equal to the regular jury duty pay paid by the jurisdiction for a period of fifteen (15) days.

Article 11
Vacation

Vacations shall be given to all employees in the continuous service of the Employer, as follows:

1 year = 1 week
5 years = 2 weeks
15 years = 3 weeks
20 years = 4 weeks

Vacation pay shall be the average weekly wage for a period of twelve (12) months in the calendar year immediately preceding the effective date of this contract, but shall, in no case, be less than the employees' base pay for a 40-hour week.

Employees shall receive a maximum of three (3) days pay in the event of the death of the following: Natural Mother or Father, Spouse, Child, Mother-in-Law, or Father-in-Law.

Article 12
Insurance and Pension

(a) Medical insurance shall be provided for the payment of thirty (30) days hospitalization per year in a semi-private room, scheduled payment of benefits for various services and outpatient emergency room service for all employees, premiums paid by the employer. Employees may purchase coverage for their spouse and dependent children (to age 19) at the employer group rate.

(b) Major medical coverage—$1,000 deductible per person, per year, may be purchased at group rates by the employees for themselves, their spouse and dependent children (to age 19).

(c) Non-contributory pension plan—Employer shall contribute five percent of the employee's annual earnings to the pension fund. Employees shall be eligible to participate after three (3) years employment and shall be fully vested after fifteen (15) years of employment.

(d) The Employer shall provide each employee with $2,000.00 of term life insurance at the Employer's expense. Employees may purchase additional life insurance in increments of $1,000.00 to a maximum of double their annual wages. This additional insurance shall be paid for by the employee at the Employer's group rate.

Article 13
Union-Made Malt and Other Materials

Union-made malt and all other union-made materials shall be given preference—price, quality and availability being equal and contract commitments permitting.

Article 14
Hauling Materials

It shall be the duty of the employees covered by this agreement to haul all bulk material required in the brewery, including hops, grains, etc., also all packages and containers such as kegs, cases, bottles, cans, etc.; said materials to be hauled from railroad cars, freight stations, boat terminals, warehouses, etc., and delivered to platform as directed.

Article 15
Wages

(a) Payment of wages due employees shall be made by the Employer every other Thursday for work performed during the previous two (2) calendar weeks, except when regular pay day falls on a day not worked, pay checks shall be distributed on the previous day.

(b)   The wage schedules which follow shall become effective May 1, 1983 and May 1, 1984 respectively.

	WAGE RATES	
EMPLOYEES	5-1-83 Hourly	5-1-84 Hourly
BREWING DEPARTMENT		
Lead Worker	10.11	10.32
Assistant Lead Worker	8.65	8.83
Regular Worker	7.23	7.37
First Year Worker	6.03	6.16
Extra Help	5.29	5.40
MALTING DEPARTMENT		
Lead Worker	9.72	10.09
Assistant Lead Worker	7.89	8.21
Regular Worker	7.02	7.30
First Year Worker	6.01	6.25
Extra Help	5.00	5.20
BOTTLING DEPARTMENT		
Lead Worker	9.68	10.07
Assistant Lead Worker	7.85	8.16
Regular Worker	6.93	7.21
First Year Worker	5.78	6.01
Extra Help	4.81	5.00
POWER PLANT DEPARTMENT		
Senior First Worker	10.29	10.70
First Worker	9.14	9.50
Operators	7.31	7.61
Maintenance	7.31	7.61
Helpers	5.78	6.01

(c)   Probationary wages shall be eighty-five percent (85%) of the hourly rate for the classification(s) specified in b. above.

Article 16
Military Service

Should any employee covered by this agreement be called to active military service in the armed forces of the United States, such employee shall be considered on leave of absence and shall be entitled to all rights of re-employment as provided by federal law.

Article 17
Limitation of Union Responsibility for Unauthorized Strike

Except as otherwise provided in this agreement, during the term of this agreement, the Union guarantees the Employer that there will be no authorized strike, work stoppage, or other concerted interference with normal operations by its employees. The Employer guarantees that it shall not lock out its employees. For the purpose of this Section an authorized strike, stoppage, or other concerted interference with normal operations is one that has been specifically authorized or ratified by the General Executive Board of the International Union.

Should an unauthorized strike, stoppage, or other concerted interference with normal operations take place, the International Union shall in no event be liable, financially or otherwise, provided that the International Union within twenty-four (24) hours after actual receipt of notice in writing or by telegram from the Employer that a strike or work stoppage has commenced shall notify the Employer in writing or by telegram that such strike, work stoppage or other concerted interference with normal operations is unauthorized and that a copy of such notice has been sent to the Local officers with instructions to bring it to the attention of the employees involved. The Local Union whose members are involved in such unauthorized action shall not be held to its legal liability therefore, if any, provided it meets the following conditions. But in any event the Local Union agrees to:

(a) Promptly post notices in conspicuous places at the affected plant and at the Local Union office stating that such action is unauthorized.

(b) Promptly order its members to resume normal operations. The employees who instigate or participate in unauthorized strikes or stoppages in violation of this agreement shall be subject to discharge or discipline, in which event their recourse to the grievance and arbitration procedures shall be limited to the question of whether they did instigate or participate in such strike or concerted activity.

Article 18
Separability

Should any part hereof or any provision herein contained be rendered or declared illegal, invalid, or an unfair labor practice by reason of any existing or subsequently enacted legislation or by any decree of a court of competent jurisdiction or by the decision of any authorized Government Agency, including the National Labor Relations Board, the remaining portions hereof shall not be affected thereby; provided, however, in such contingency the parties shall meet and negotiate with respect to substitute provisions for those parts or provisions rendered or declared illegal, invalid, or an unfair labor practice.

Article 19
Arbitration of Grievances

(a) Grievances by individual employees relating to the interpretation or application of this contract shall be first taken up by the employee affected and their immediate supervisor or by the shop steward and immediate supervisor. If they fail to arrive at a mutually satisfactory adjustment within five (5) days, unless extended by mutual agreement, the matter shall be referred to the Secretary of the Local Union, who shall attempt to adjust it by negotiations with the Employer's representatives. If a mutually satisfactory adjustment is not arrived at by them within an additional five (5) days, unless extended by mutual agreement, the matter shall be submitted to a Board of Arbitration upon written request of either party.

(b) The Board of Arbitration herein referred to shall be chosen and shall operate as follows: Two (2) arbitrators shall be appointed by the Union and two (2) by the Employer within five (5) days, unless extended by mutual agreement, after the receipt of the request for arbitration. In the event that a majority is unable to agree upon the disposition of the case, a fifth neutral arbitrator who shall be Chairperson of the Board shall be designated by the aforesaid four (4) arbitrators.

Should the four (4) arbitrators be unable to agree upon the neutral arbitrator within five (5) days, unless extended by mutual consent, the neutral arbitrator shall be designated, upon written request of either party, by the American Arbitration Association. The Board of Arbitration as so constituted shall determine the matter at issue by decision in writing signed by at least three (3) of its members. The decision shall be final and binding upon the parties.

(c) There shall be no strike or lockout while arbitration is pending; provided, however, that in the event one party should fail or refuse to appoint arbitrators or should take any action to prevent arbitration or should fail or refuse to comply with a decision of the Board of Arbitration within three (3) days after its receipt, the party in default shall automatically lose its case and in addition to whatever other remedies may be available to the party not in default, the first clause of this paragraph shall not be binding upon such party.

(d) Discharges may be made the subject of grievances and arbitration.

(e) The Chairperson of the Board of Arbitration shall be reimbursed for time and expenses by the party losing the decision.

Article 20
Management Rights

The Employer retains any right(s) not modified, curtailed, or restricted by this agreement. These shall include, but not be limited to:

(a) The right to direct and control the work force.

(b) The right to direct or expand production and install/implement technological change.

(c) The right to construct new facilities, relocate existing facilities, or close present facilities.

Article 21
Termination

This contract shall become effective May 1, 1983 and shall continue in effect through April 30, 1985 and renew itself automatically thereafter for periods of one (1) year unless either party serves written notice upon the other not less than sixty (60) days before the end of the initial period or any subsequent period of its desire to terminate or modify this contract.

TABLE A-1
Income Statement, 10-Year Trend (Expressed in thousands)

	1984	1983	1982	1981	1980	1979	1978	1977	1976	1975
Sales	99,901	89,197	81,088	74,393	70,182	68,138	64,893	61,803	60,003	56,607
Cost of Good Sold	84,500	74,300	67,009	61,150	59,100	56,210	52,600	50,001	48,600	45,325
Labor*	14,201	11,350	10,999	10,276	10,000	9,900	9,860	9,750	8,748	7,847
Raw Materials and Overhead	70,299	62,950	56,010	50,874	49,100	46,310	42,740	40,251	39,852	37,478
Gross Profits	15,401	14,897	14,079	13,243	11,082	11,928	12,293	11,802	11,403	11,282
Selling and Administration Expense	6,622	6,406	6,140	5,959	5,098	5,010	4,969	4,957	4,789	4,822
Depreciation Expense	2,695	2,607	2,464	2,384	1,939	2,088	2,151	2,065	2,031	1,998
Other Operating Expense†	4,004	3,873	3,800	3,443	2,881	3,101	3,381	3,187	3,065	2,960
Income Before Taxes	2,080	2,011	1,675	1,457	1,164	1,729	1,792	1,593	1,518	1,542
Income Taxes	832	804	670	583	466	692	717	637	607	617
Net Income	1,248	1,207	1,005	874	698	1,037	1,075	956	911	925

*"Labor" includes payroll for both regular time and overtime, and fringe benefits.
†"Other operating expense" includes interest expense.

TABLE A–2
Peck's Balance Sheet, 10-Year Trend (Expressed in thousands)

	1984	1983	1982	1981	1980	1979	1978	1977	1976	1975
Cash & Marketable Securities	8,320	7,900	7,363	6,920	6,150	5,879	5,190	4,640	3,280	3,010
Accounts Receivable	9,896	9,790	9,433	9,098	8,200	7,125	6,420	5,660	4,100	2,945
Inventory	9,949	9,030	8,990	8,700	7,693	7,533	7,350	7,000	6,951	6,732
Other Capital Assets	4,244	3,791	3,722	3,610	3,255	2,829	2,740	1,670	1,600	1,513
Total Capital Assets	32,409	30,511	29,508	28,328	25,298	22,366	21,700	18,970	15,931	14,677
Plant & Equipment	60,011	58,301	56,721	52,644	49,089	44,711	40,250	38,739	35,900	35,627
Accumulated Depreciation	33,318	30,623	28,016	25,552	23,168	21,229	19,141	16,990	14,925	13,371
Net Plant & Equipment	26,693	27,678	28,705	27,092	25,913	23,482	21,109	21,749	20,975	22,733
Other Assets	3,140	2,972	2,800	2,620	2,368	2,001	1,902	1,839	1,580	1,271
TOTAL ASSETS	62,242	61,161	60,807	58,040	53,579	47,849	44,711	42,558	38,486	38,681
Current Liability	17,570	17,572	18,423	17,798	15,893	12,658	11,170	10,124	7,220	8,193
Long-term Debt	10,720	10,702	10,505	9,409	7,562	5,599	4,810	4,728	4,520	4,513
Other Liability	313	300	291	280	269	250	276	272	251	234
Total Liability	28,603	28,574	29,219	27,487	23,724	18,507	16,251	15,124	11,991	12,940
Common Stock & Additional Paid-in-Capital	10,961	10,917	10,900	10,860	10,836	10,830	10,821	10,700	10,554	10,554
Retained Earnings	22,678	21,670	20,688	19,693	19,019	18,512	17,639	16,734	15,941	15,187
Total Liability & Stockholders' Equity & Retained Earnings	62,242	61,161	60,807	58,040	53,579	47,849	44,711	42,558	38,486	38,681
Average Shares Outstanding	45,000	45,000	42,000	40,000	38,200	36,800	34,000	32,600	31,400	30,000

Note: The appropriate accounting methods which minimize taxes were used in all cases (i.e., depreciation methods, inventory valuation methods, etc.).

TABLE A–3
Statement of Retained Earnings, 10-Year Trend (Expressed in thousands)

	1984	1983	1982	1981	1980	1979	1978	1977	1976	1975
Beginning Retained Earnings	21,670	20,668	19,693	19,019	18,512	17,639	16,734	15,941	15,187	14,362
+ Net Income	1,248	1,207	1,005	874	698	1,057	1,075	956	911	925
− Dividends	240	225	210	200	191	184	170	163	157	150
Ending Retained Earnings	22,678	21,670	20,688	19,693	19,019	18,512	17,639	16,734	15,941	15,187

TABLE A–4
Average Hourly Earnings By Classification

	AVERAGE HOURLY RATE	NUMBER OF EMPLOYEES IN CLASSIFICATION
Leadman	$10.16	26
Assistant Leadman	8.40	30
Regular	7.29	288
First-Year Worker	6.14	40
Extra Help	5.20	30
Senior First Man	10.70	15
First Man	9.50	15
Operators	7.61	21
Maintenance Men	7.61	20
Helpers	6.01	15
	$7.86	500

TABLE A–5
Employees by Years of Service and Average Age

YEARS OF SENIORITY*	NUMBER OF WORKERS†	AVERAGE AGE
20 or more	26	51 years
15–19	130	38
10–14	160	33
5– 9	40	27
4	30	25
3	20	22
2	20	22
1	28	21
11– 1	46	20
	500	

*In calculating years of service, employees with fractional years of service are placed in next lower category (i.e., employees with 14 years 11 months of service are in 10–14 year interval.
†Eighteen percent (18%) of all production employees are women.

TABLE A–6
Peck's Brewery Accessions and Turnover

	Total Accessions	SEPARATIONS		Total
		Voluntary	Involuntary	
1984	46	9	20	29
1983	40	16	16	32
1982	36	10	20	30

A MASS TRANSIT GAME: MADISON MASS TRANSIT AUTHORITY

THE MASS TRANSIT INDUSTRY

The United States mass transit industry has grown tremendously during the last decade. The growth can be attributed to the increased population, the flight from urban cities to suburbia, and increased federal funding.

Congress recognized its importance in 1964 when it began appropriating funds to be awarded to local mass transit authorities through the grant application process. Capital expansion and operating assistance grants were given to mass transit properties on an 80/20 ratio (federal funding contributed 80 percent and the local transit property contributed 20 percent). The Urban Mass Public Transit Administration (UMPTA) distributes the funds to the local transit properties based on their grant applications.

Larger transit properties with professional staffs and greater local funding bases receive the majority of the grants. However, all mass transit properties may submit grant proposals for review. Because of federal funding, the transit industry is closely regulated by federal and state regulations.

The transit industry is composed of three types of properties, as follows:

> **Class 1**   serves an area with a population greater than 1,000,000
>
> **Class 2**   serves an area with a population greater than 500,000 through 1,000,000
>
> **Class 3**   serves an area with a population not less than 50,000 through 500,000.

Mass transit throughout the United States has made tremendous technological progress since its inception as the horse-drawn trolley. Several types of equipment operate today. For example, San Francisco operates antique cable cars, electric cars, standard diesel-powered buses, and the completely computerized, highly reliable Bay Area Rapid Transit System (BART).

Improved technology has caused labor-management disputes over job security because fewer employees are required to operate the equipment. The majority of the employees in transit were semiskilled; but the introduction of computerized systems in several cities displaced the semiskilled employees with higher-skilled technicians and transit professionals. Labor has been forced to make concessions because of technological improvements in transit systems. Many of these disputes have

been argued in various federal courts under Section 13(c) of the Urban Mass Transit Act (1964)—49 U.S.C. 1909(c). Section 13(c), which pertains to labor-management relations in mass transit, is particularly important in high population areas where mass transit is a vital element of the transportation network.

Transit industry unions have traditionally been powerful. Pay scales of Class 1 systems are competitive and frequently among the highest in the local labor market. Class 2 property wages are competitive, but somewhat lower than Class 1 wages. Unions exist in the majority of transit properties throughout the United States.

MADISON MASS TRANSIT AUTHORITY

Madison Mass Transit Authority (MMTA) is a Class 2 property in the northeastern United States. Madison has never been without a transit system. Its history can be traced back to the horse-drawn trolley.

Although MMTA existed for decades, it never flourished. MMTA has had several owners. It was privately owned by the Walters family from its inception until the late 1960s when it was purchased by the City of Madison. MMTA struggled under city management for approximately six years until MMTA became a dependent of the state government. A nine-member board of directors (citizens of the four-county service area) and a general manager (selected by the board) have the authority to manage MMTA today.

The reorganization of MMTA brought increased UMPTA funding for operating and capital expenses. Although federal funding was available earlier, Madison could not compete for grants because the city did not have matching funds. In 1973 the state legislature enacted a mass-transit tax bill designed to assist MMTA to expand its service. The transit tax, in the form of ½ percent sales tax, was collected in the four-county MMTA service area. Although the tax bill was passed in 1973, the tax revenues did not reach MMTA until 1975 when $1.2 million was added to MMTA's accounts. Upon receipt of these tax revenues, MMTA began an expansion program. New diesel-powered buses were ordered to replace the dilapidated buses. The board of directors approved a plan to purchase property for a new facility, which included maintenance shops, operations buildings, and administration offices. The existing facilities were in such ill repair that state and federal Occupational Safety and Health (OSHA) officials had issued several citations for OSHA violations. The maintenance department received the majority of citations.

MMTA receives its funding from the following sources: 25 percent from fare-box collections, 30 percent from the state transit sales tax, and 45 percent from federal grants. Two conditions have direct impact on the percentage distribution: (1) the board of directors can increase fares; this

may be negative or positive depending on the economy; and (2) federal funds may be increased or decreased as the political climate changes in Washington.

EMPLOYER-EMPLOYEE RELATIONS

MMTA employer-employee relations have been good. During the early days, when the system was owned by the Robert A. Walters family, it always produced a profit. The fundamental reason for its success was the Walters' genuine concern for their employees, which assured a competitive wage and fringe benefit package for them. Employees were proud of their transportation system and encouraged ridership. The system added new buses as necessary, and the maintenance facilities were always clean, freshly painted, and had the best equipment available. The relationship discouraged union organization among the employees. After the Walters family sold its interest in the company, ridership declined and the system deteriorated.

The system was near bankruptcy when it was purchased by the city. The transit employees became city employees, inheriting the wages and benefits of city employees.

A wage-and-benefit study was conducted by an independent consultant. The results of the study produced the conclusion that the transit employees were overpaid in comparison with other city employees performing similar duties and responsibilities. The City Council immediately froze the transit employees' wages. The wage freeze continued after the reorganization of MMTA as a four-county service system because Madison city employee wage-and-benefit plans were adopted by the MMTA board of directors. The transit employees were angry. The Amalgamated Transportation Workers Union (ATWU) immediately began an organizing campaign. Local 128 of ATWU won the representation election with 83 percent of the vote. Contract negotiations began which produced the attached contract.

Although representatives of Local 128 and the board of directors negotiated intensely for a satisfactory contract, the contract has proved less than satisfactory for both parties. Management thinks that union officials have exploited the contract's union recognition article through their solicitation of grievances from the membership. Work assignments are a management right. However, the previously mentioned problem has created an environment which enables negotiation of work assignments through the grievance procedure. The union has grieved numerous unilateral work-rule additions and modifications which it believes unreasonable.

The wage freeze forced many employees to moonlight because the combination of inflation and frozen wages created personal financial

crises. Management disciplined several employees for moonlighting based on a broad interpretation of the contract relating to moonlighting.

Slowdowns, work-to-rule actions, and two wildcat strikes occurred. Management considers contract language pertaining to these behaviors as ineffective. Union members claim that the six-month probationary period is too long and denies employees negotiated benefits. The union charges management with arbitrarily terminating probationary employees.

The union claims that management has violated the seniority article because it has posted inaccurate seniority lists in an untimely manner. Individuals claim many seniority-list errors (dates and classifications) have been ignored by management. Several grievances have been filed by union members who have been disciplined for time violations. All of these grievances assert that the management interpretation of "reasonable time" is too broad. A discharge arbitration concerning this issue is pending. Management is concerned about the ambiguous contract language and time limits for filing grievances.

Employees are dissatisfied with sick pay and maximum sick leave accrual. Union members have challenged the requirement of working the day before and after a holiday to receive holiday pay. Management believes the requirement is necessary to control employee absenteeism and assure service to the public during holidays.

The union claims that vacation calculations are unfair. They assert that the percentage of allotted workdays that one must work before receiving vacation is excessive and inflicts hardship on the employees.

The percentage increases for new employees during the first twelve months of employment are viewed as noncompetitive in the local labor market. Bus operators claim five years is too long to wait for senior operator pay. They also say that senior operator pay should be a higher percentage of regular operator pay. Maintenance employees claim their wages are substantially lower than similar workers in other industries throughout the area. The resignations of several highly skilled maintenance workers in favor of other local employment at substantially higher wages during the last twelve months gives credence to this complaint.

Management recently learned from a reliable source that the maintenance workers and the rest of the bargaining unit have a serious dispute over the union's plan to request an across-the-board percentage increase for all employees in the forthcoming negotiations. The Teamsters may be successful in organizing a new maintenance-workers bargaining unit if Local 128 does not resolve the internal dispute.

Management believes they cannot continue to operate a transit system with a Cost of Living Adjustment (COLA) in the contract. Management expects the union to propose a reduction in the COLA computation formula which would increase COLA payments. Recent contract settlements between several Class 1 properties and their respective bargaining representatives include COLAs of this type. Therefore, this will be a high-priority bargaining item for both parties.

Although the majority of the work force is relatively young, employees have expressed concern about the present retirement plan. An age discrimination suit has been filed by an employee who was forced to retire at sixty-five. Several sex discrimination cases are currently pending arbitration, and the Equal Opportunity Commission is investigating a sexual harassment case.

Maintenance and clerical (stockroom, etc.) personnel receive coveralls and laundry service. In addition, they want a tool allowance. Bus operators want their uniform and cleaning allowance increased.

Management claims the run selection–run assignment article is too restrictive and not conducive to controlling operating costs. Bus operators claim that the assignment of routes and equipment is arbitrarily based on friendship rather than seniority.

MMTA wants to eliminate the extra board operators and hire part-time operators with restricted fringe benefits. Management believes part-time operators would reduce labor costs and enhance management's flexibility in assigning and scheduling work. Mass transit unions have traditionally opposed part-time operators. Therefore, the union can be expected to vigorously oppose this item.

Travel time is an issue because of the current contract language. Pay for total travel time is interpreted by management. The union disagrees with management's interpretation.

Regular bus operators want the twelve-hour spread reduced because they assert dispatchers arbitrarily assign extra work. The primary concern of operators is that overtime is not based on the overtime list, but on the dispatcher's subjective discretion.

The miss-out article is unacceptable to management because of the spiraling cost of replacement pay. Management terminated an operator for excessive miss-outs on the grounds that Article 25 (c)(2)(e) gives management that right. The union disagrees, claiming the miss-out article stipulates miss-out penalties and that, in this case, management is in violation of the contract. The union requested a discipline review hearing; the hearing officer upheld the termination. The union recently voted to take the case to arbitration.

ECONOMIC CONDITIONS

The financial condition of MMTA is uncertain because of increasing costs and taxpayer pressure to reduce taxes. MMTA received approximately $67 million in federal funds and approximately $30 million in local sales-tax revenues during the past decade. In spite of this, they are at an economic crossroad. MMTA has increased individual ride fares and special passes three times in the past four years. Financial forecasts indicate that current fares and passes are priced at a maximum return and additional increases would result in decreased fare-box revenues. Management claims that if the union demands a high-cost contract settlement this could result in an unreasonable fare increase which ultimately could reduce ridership and force layoffs of bargaining-unit employees.

Although sales tax collections increased moderately during the last three years, it is uncertain if the trend will continue because of the sluggishness of the economic recovery. Economic conditions and the Washington political climate, which is intermittently hot and cold to mass transit, create an uncertain future for federal funding. Management insists that wage-and-benefit increases must be offset by productivity increases if MMTA is going to continue operating.

Therefore, both labor and management must come to the bargaining table fully prepared to bargain from a factual, not emotional, perspective.

Contract

This contract is made this FIFTH day of JANUARY, 1983, between the undersigned agency, the Madison Mass Transit Authority (hereinafter referred to as the EMPLOYER), party of the first part, and Local No. 128 of the Amalgamated Transportation Workers of America (hereinafter referred to as the UNION), party of the second part, as representative of the employees specified within this Agreement.

Therefore, in consideration of the mutual covenants hereinafter defined, the parties hereto covenant and agree as follows:

Article 1
Union Recognition and Bargaining Unit

a.　The Employer recognizes the Union as the exclusive representative for the purpose of Collective Bargaining, with respect to wages, hours, and working conditions, for all bus operators, parts, maintenance, and clerical employees.

b.　The Union representative may receive and discuss employee complaints and grievances on the Employer's premises.

Article 2
Recognition of Management

a.　The Employer shall continue to exercise exclusively the right to establish policy; to manage its business; to determine the qualifications for and selection of managerial and supervisory personnel; to determine the number of employees that it will retain in its service at any given time; to make rules and regulations governing the operation of its business and the conduct of its employees; and to otherwise exercise full control except as expressly limited by the terms of this Agreement.

Article 3
Employee Cooperation and Non-Discrimination

a. Employees shall work for the best interests of the Employer. Employees shall operate vehicles and equipment carefully and with utmost regard for passengers' safety, to prevent equipment loss, and for the public interest. Employees shall maintain a neat and clean appearance and shall be courteous and respectful to the public. No employee shall accept employment with another employer during the term of their employment which in any way interferes in their employment with the Employer or is in competition with the Employer.

Article 4
Strikes and Lockouts

a. The Union shall take no action to interrupt the service of the Employer as long as the Employer complies with and fulfills all terms and conditions of this Agreement. The Employer shall not engage in any lockouts.

Article 5
Probationary Period

a. Employee shall be defined as: person employed by the Employer in a regular full-time job. Such employee shall serve a six (6) month probationary period at the time of hire. Upon satisfactory completion of probation, the employee shall receive all rights of full-time regular employees including the grievance procedure. Such employee shall be eligible for employee benefits the first of the month following thirty (30) days of full-time regular employee status.

b. During the probationary period the Employer is the sole judge of ability, competency, fitness and qualifications to perform work. This judgment shall not be subject to the grievance or arbitration procedure.

Article 6
Seniority

a. Employees shall have system-wide seniority in one of four departments: Operations, Parts, Maintenance, and Clerical. The seniority lists shall be posted on work area bulletin boards. Lists shall be updated as needed, and a copy shall be furnished to the Union upon request.

b. Seniority shall continue to accrue during layoff or approved leave of absence. Leave of absence time shall not be considered as time worked for any purpose except accumulation of seniority.

c. Continuity of service shall be broken and seniority shall terminate for the following reasons:

1. Voluntary resignation
2. Discharge
3. Failure to return to work within twenty (20) days of a layoff recall notice
4. Absence without leave for five (5) consecutive days
5. Layoff of ten (10) months.

Article 7
Layoffs

a. The Employer shall not layoff any employee(s) unless there is a reduction in service. Before any layoff, the Employer and the Union shall meet on the validity of the layoff.

1. A ten (10) day advance notice of layoff shall be given to each affected employee. Regular force reductions shall be in the reverse order of the department seniority list.
2. When regular force is increased, laid off employees in the classification being increased shall be recalled in the reverse order of layoff.

Article 8
Discipline

a. *Oral and Written Reprimands*   Oral and written reprimands shall be given to the employee by their immediate supervisor for infractions of Employer work rules.
b. *Suspension*   Explanations of an employee suspension(s) shall be given to the employee in writing. The Union shall be notified in writing of the suspension within a reasonable time after the action is taken.
c. *Discharge*   When the Employer discharges an employee(s), an explanation of the discharge shall be given to the employee(s) in writing. The Union shall be notified in writing of the discharge within a reasonable time after the discharge.

Article 9
Grievances

a. A grievance is defined as any controversy between the Employer, its employees or the Union over interpretation or application of this Agreement. Grievances must be filed in a timely manner.
b. Upon receipt of a grievance, the parties shall meet promptly and attempt to resolve the grievance.
c. At the conclusion of the grievance hearing, a written decision shall be rendered as soon as possible.

Article 10
Arbitrations

a. Only grievances alleging a violation of this Agreement or a claim of unjust termination may be processed to arbitration.

b. Every reasonable effort shall be made to avoid arbitration. If the grievance is not resolved, it shall be jointly submitted to a Board of Arbitration composed of three (3) persons, one (1) chosen by the Employer, one (1) chosen by the Union. The two (2) shall select a third neutral who shall act as Chairperson of the Board.

c. Each party shall bear the expense of its own arbitrator and shall jointly bear the expense of the Chairperson.

Article 11
Court and Jury Duty

a. Employee(s) called to court shall be paid their regular rate of pay.

b. Employee(s) shall be released from work for jury duty, but shall not suffer any reduction in pay. Payments received for jury duty, provided the employee makes a reasonable effort to report for whatever work the Employer can make available, shall be exchanged for the employee's regular full-time payroll check.

Article 12
Sick Leave and Bereavement Leave

a. Regular full-time employees who have completed at least six (6) months of service shall receive six (6) hours of sick leave credit for each full month of service to a maximum of twenty (20) days of sick leave.

b. An employee who is absent from work because of illness or injury shall be paid sick pay at the rate of six (6) hours pay per day, beginning with the first (1st) day of hospitalization or injury or on the second (2nd) day of absence for non-hospitalized illness or accident.

c. Proof that injury or illness necessitated absence may be required by the Employer.

d. Employees shall be allowed one (1) day bereavement leave for members of the immediate family. Employees may use accumulated sick leave at the rate of six (6) hours per each day for additional bereavement pay.

Article 13
Equal Employment Opportunity

The Employer and the Union agree that there shall be no discrimination of any classes protected by federal, state or local laws.

Article 14
Holidays

a. The following seven (7) Holidays will be observed:

New Years Day   **Thanksgiving Day**
Memorial Day   **Christmas Day**
Independence Day   **Employee's Birthday**
Labor Day

Employee(s) shall receive eight (8) hours pay at their straight-time rate for each holiday.

Article 15
Vacation

a. Employees shall receive vacation with pay as follows:

    After one (1) year of continuous service—one (1) week
    After three (3) years but less than seven (7) years of continuous service—two (2) weeks
    After seven (7) years but less than twelve (12) years of continuous service—three (3) weeks
    After twelve (12) years but less than twenty (20) years of continuous service—four (4) weeks

b. Service shall be calculated from the employee's anniversary date. During each anniversary year, an employee who works ninety-five (95) percent or more of schedule work days shall be entitled to a full vacation. Employees who work up to seventy-five (75) percent but not less than fifty (50) percent of scheduled workdays shall have vacation pro-rated according to the percentage of days worked. Those who work less than fifty (50) percent of scheduled workdays shall not receive vacation for the anniversary year.

c. Pay for each week of vacation due shall be computed on the basis of regular weekly hours which the employee would have worked during said vacation.

Article 16
Physical Exams

a. Employer shall allow employees pay for time not worked for Employer-requested physical examinations. Examination times shall be scheduled by the Employer.

b. Pre-employment physical examinations and physical reexaminations shall be performed by qualified professionals designated by the Employer.

Article 17
Insurance

a. The Employer shall require all employees covered by this Agreement, hired on or after January 1, 1983, to participate in the Group Life Insurance Program commencing with the first day of the calendar month following the end of their probationary period.

b. Except as provided in Section c of this Article, the Employer agrees to pay to the Health and Insurance Benefits Trust Fund the amount indicated below for each employee covered by this Agreement beginning with the first day of the calendar month following sixty (60) days of continuous employment. Present employees shall receive said benefit immediately or upon completion of the sixty (60) days of probationary service, whichever is applicable based on their status.

c. The monthly amount to be paid by the Employer shall be thirty-eight dollars ($38.00) for single coverage; seventy-two dollars ($72.00) for two persons; and one-hundred twenty dollars ($120.00) for family coverage.

Article 18
Wages

a. Starting rates for bus operators, maintenance, parts and clerical employees shall be less than the basic rate of pay for their first twelve (12) months of service in accordance with the following schedule:
    1. First three (3) months of service—85% of basic rate
    2. Second three (3) months of service—90% of basic rate
    3. Third three (3) months of service—93% of basic rate
    4. Fourth three (3) months of service—96% of basic rate
    5. Thereafter basic rates as shown in Section b.

b. Basic Wage Rates

Class of Service	Straight Time Wage Rate
Bus Operator	$8.45*/hour

*Effective April 1, 1984, Senior Operators shall be paid fifteen cents (15¢) per hour more than a regular operator. A Senior Operator is defined as a bus operator who has more than five (5) years of continuous service.

Maintenance	Straight Time Wage Rate
Journey Mechanic	$10.60/hour
Helper	8.50/hour
Laborer	7.74/hour
Steam Cleaner	8.25/hour
Service Employee	7.74/hour
Janitor	7.31/hour
Bus Cleaner	7.25/hour

Clerks	Straight Time Wage Rate
Parts	$7.86/hour
Courier	7.10/hour
Farebox Counter	7.48/hour

A cost of living adjustment (COLA) based upon the change in the Consumer Price Index (CPI) of the Bureau of Labor Statistics, all cities figure, shall be paid semi-annually beginning July 1, 1983. For every five-tenths (.5) of one percent change in the CPI in excess of seven percent (7%) one-half percent (½%) shall be added to the employees' wages.

Article 19
Pension

a. Employees who retire must meet the following criteria:
    1. Twenty (20) years of continuous service with the Employer;

2. The employee is working or on an authorized leave of absence at the time of retirement;
3. Employee is eligible to retire under Social Security rules.

Article 20
Leave of Absence

a. Leaves of Absence without pay may be granted to employees for a period not to exceed thirty (30) days in any year.
b. An employee elected or appointed to a full-time position in the local or International Union shall be given a leave of absence for the duration of the term of office. Said leave may be extended not to exceed thirty (30) days upon written request. Upon return from leave the employee shall be reinstated without loss of seniority, privileges, benefits, and at the current wage rate.
c. Upon request of the Union President, officials of the Union or members appointed to serve on a committee shall be granted time off from work without pay for Union business.

Article 21
Run Selection—Run Assignment

a. All regular schedules and runs subject to bidding shall be posted at least seven (7) days before going into effect, except in emergency cases, runs shall be temporarily assigned to bus operators until the seven (7) day posting is satisfied. A copy of runs shall be given to the Union seven (7) days before posting. There will be a general bidding date in regular runs at least four (4) times a year.
b. Seniority shall prevail in the assignment of runs on general bidding days.
c. Regular schedules for new runs that are not operated in connection with existing runs shall be posted at leave five (5) days before taking effect and shall be subject to bidding.
d. On all "change days" the Employer shall post a list with the type of bus normally assigned to the route. The Employer shall assign equipment on an impartial basis to bus operators. This shall not be construed to limit or restrict in any manner the right of the Employer to change equipment.

Article 22
Extra Motor Coach Operators

a. An employee(s) assigned as an extra board bus operator(s) shall be paid at the regular straight-time hourly rate from the reporting time until the operator is released or until the operator commences assignment. Extra board bus operators shall be guaranteed two (2) hours for reporting for a work assignment.
b. No report time shall be allowed to bus operators on show-up when relief is granted.
c. Extra board bus operator shall have one (1) day off each week.

d. Regular bus operators shall not be used for extra work when qualified extra board bus operators are available.

e. Work assignments shall be posted on a daily register showing the total work time for each assignment and the running total work time of each bus operator for the pay period.

Article 23
Time Allowances

a. Preparatory time—Bus operators shall be allowed ten (10) minutes preparatory time for each pullout from the garage.

b. If a bus operator's schedule requires reporting to the garage before or after they begin or end their driving assignment at some point other than the garage, the operator shall be paid for time spent traveling from the garage to the pullout assignment and for the total time spent in traveling to return from destination point to the garage.

Article 24
Overtime

a. Regular bus operators shall be paid one and one-half (1½) times their regular straight-time hourly rate for all work before or after their regular run provided they have worked all of their scheduled runs.

b. Regular bus operators who work on their regularly scheduled day(s) off and have worked the preceding five (5) days shall be paid at the rate of one and one-half (1½) times their regular straight-time hourly rate. Bus operators who have worked part of a shift and have been properly excused for the shift or who are off on official business for the Employer or the Union shall be considered to have worked their assigned work for that shift.

c. Regular bus operators who work in excess of a twelve (12) hour spread shall be paid at one and one-half (1½) times their regular straight-time hourly rate.

d. Regular bus operators who want extra work shall sign the overtime list. Extra work will be rotated among all regular bus operators who have signed the overtime list and are available for extra work.

Article 25
Miss-Outs

a. A miss-out is defined as:

1. Each failure of a bus operator to report for duty at the scheduled place and time according to the duty schedule; and

2. Each failure of a bus operator to report either personally or by telephone at the time designated by the dispatcher after missing-out.

b. Two (2) minute lee-way shall be allowed on morning report, only.

c. The penalty for miss-outs shall be as follows:

1. Regular Bus Operators—for each miss-out the operator shall lose their run and pay for the day of the miss-out.

2. Extra Board Operators—

a) First miss-out in a thirty (30) day period, the operator shall either be assigned to other work or be released after serving one (1) hour penalty time.

b) Second miss-out within a thirty (30) day period, the operator shall be subject to the penalties specified for the first miss-out and may, at the Employer's discretion, lose their next regular assignment.

c) Third Extra Board miss-out within a thirty (30) day period, the operator shall be subject to penalties specified for the first and second miss-outs, and to such further discipline as may be deemed appropriate.

d) An operator who does not report in person or by telephone within one (1) hour of any miss-out will be charged with an AWOL and subject to any of the above specified penalties.

e) If any operator misses their run or work assignment while enroute to work by bus being seven (7) or more minutes late on its scehdule, they shall be permitted to take bus on its return trip and shall be paid for the full time of the run or work assignment provided the operator immediately notifies the dispatcher of being late and also furnishes a detailed report of the incident and reason for delay.

f) This article shall not be construed to limit or restrict in any manner the right to terminate a bus operator for excessive miss-outs.

Article 26
Uniform and Tool Allowance

a. Upon completion of training, bus operators shall be issued three (3) shirts, two (2) pairs of trousers, and one (1) windbreaker. After the completion of the probationary period and upon request, a bus operator shall be issued a voucher for the remainder of the one-hundred thirty-five dollar ($135.00) annual uniform allowance less the cost of items previously issued. Thereafter the uniform allowance shall be one-hundred thirty-five ($135.00) per year. It shall be available on the anniversary date of the employee's qualification as a bus operator.

b. No operator shall be allowed to work unless reporting in uniform. The uniform shall be designated by the Employer.

c. Authorized maintenance and clerical employees shall be provided suitable coveralls with laundry paid by the Employer.

Article 27
Duration of the Agreement

This Agreement shall become effective January 5, 1983 and shall continue in effect until January 5, 1985 and thereafter shall renew itself automatically for a period of one (1) year each subsequent January 5 unless either party serves written notice on the other of their intention to reopen the Agreement for termination or modification no less than ninety (90) days prior to the expiration date of said Agreement.

TABLE B–1
**Employees Based on Seniority
and Average Age**

YEARS OF SENIORITY	NUMBER OF EMPLOYEES	AVERAGE AGE
Less than 1	36	22 years
1	44	22 years
2	45	23 years
3	50	25 years
4	65	30 years
5–9	197	34 years
10–14	51	39 years
15–19	63	43 years
20 or more	51	55 years

Notes:
1. Seventeen percent (17%) of maintenance and clerical employees are women.
2. Fifteen percent (15%) of bus operators are women.
3. Four hundred fifty-five (455) employees are bus operators and one hundred forty-seven (147) are maintenance, parts, and clerical employees.
4. Partial years of service were rounded off to the closest full year of service, i.e., 9 years and 10 months = 10–14 years; 9 years and 4 months = 5–9 years.

Definitions

1. *Extra Board*—maintained for the purpose of assigning work not being performed by a regular bus operator.
2. *Change or Bid Day*—days when bus operators are given an opportunity to change or select their work assignment by exercising their seniority.
3. *Report Time*—the time an operator is due to report for work.

TABLE B–2
MMTA Labor Turnover* and Accissions

YEAR	TOTAL TURNOVER	VOLUNTARY TURNOVER[†]	INVOLUNTARY TURNOVER[‡]	ACCISSIONS[§]
1984	243	157	86	201
1983	172	80	92	160
1982	150	79	71	138

**Labor Turnover—the gross movement of workers into and out of employment status within individual establishments.*

[†]*Voluntary Turnover—includes resignation, failure to respond to a recall notification, retirement, and other separation actuibs bit initiated by Management.*

[‡]*Involuntary Turnover—includes discharge, layoff, and other separation actions implemented by Management.*

[§]*Accissions—includes new hires, recalls from layoffs, rehires, and other actions which restore employment status to an individual.*

TABLE B–3
MMTA Balance Sheet
Assets
(Expressed in thousands)

	1975	1976	1977	1978	1979	1980	1981	1982	1983	1984
Current Assets:										
Cash	271	285	141	134	87	—	—	180	188	19
Short-Term Investments	238	250	422	627	1,529	4,756	635	607	930	180
Receivables:										
Sales Tax	*	*	*	1,195	2,805	809	3,846	6,418	6,723	7,094
Federal Operating Grants	219	230	2,716	1,145	4,176	3,004	5,457	4,303	3,974	4,149
Federal Capital Grants	158	166	505	13,175	3,201	2,523	20	1,811	355	40
Other	53	55	48	53	24	85	525	597	117	242
Total Receivables	938	987	3,831	16,329	11,823	11,178	9,849	13,128	11,171	11,525
Parts and Supplies at lower of average cost on market	64	68	87	134	211	339	872	1,371	1,335	1,365
Prepaid Expenses	22	23	20	62	53	59	152	135	144	85
Total Current Assets	1,024	1,079	3,940	16,525	12,087	11,576	11,508	15,421	13,767	13,175
Property, Plant and Equipment at Cost:										
Land and Land Improvements	105	111	130	165	198	265	2,802	3,916	4,656	4,430
Buildings	471	496	493	556	609	570	571	800	805	14,480
Motor Coaches	1,113	1,171	3,353	4,154	15,583	15,583	15,492	16,150	16,178	21,233
Other Property and Equipment	99	104	185	364	899	1,579	2,177	2,575	2,915	3,536
Construction	—	—	—	—	—	—	—	1,096	9,320	550
	1,787	1,881	4,161	5,239	17,288	17,996	21,043	24,537	33,874	44,230
Less Accumulated Depreciation	(372)	(391)	(473)	(861)	(1,890)	(3,489)	(5,056)	(6,771)	(8,610)	(10,510)
Net Property, Plant and Equipment	1,416	1,490	3,688	4,378	15,398	14,508	15,987	17,765	25,265	33,720
	2,441	2,569	7,628	20,903	27,485	26,083	27,495	33,186	39,032	46,895

*No sales tax.

321

TABLE B-4
MMTA Balance Sheet
Liabilities and Equity
(Expressed in thousands)

	1984	1983	1982	1981	1980	1979	1978	1977	1976	1975
Current Liabilities:										
Checks written in excess of cash in bank	136	769	228	1,000	—	—	—	—	—	—
Accounts Payable	744	1,151	1,718	1,055	550	2,618	65	18	16	15
Accrued Liabilities	1,283	1,018	980	1,847	690	450	215	244	146	139
Accrued Insurance Claims	164	190	249	110	—	—	—	—	—	—
Long term debt due within one year	26	45	43	153	—	—	—	—	—	—
Total Current Liabilities	2,353	3,172	3,209	4,164	1,240	3,068	280	262	162	154
Long Term Debt Due after one year	902	1,146	1,151	1,317	2,531	3,092	12,759	2,714	—	—
Equity:										
Contributed Capital:										
Federal Grants for Capital Expenditures	32,878	23,435	17,041	23,381	18,096	17,378	5,186	5,310	2,408	2,287
Less Accumulated Amortization	(8,073)	(6,600)	(5,336)	(8,380)	(3,489)	(1,890)	(861)	(731)	—	—
Net Contributed Capital	24,801	16,834	11,706	15,001	14,607	15,448	4,325	4,579	2,408	2,287
Retained Local Equity	18,840	17,880	17,120	10,068	7,705	5,837	3,538	73	—	—
Total Equity	43,640	34,714	28,826	25,069	22,312	21,325	7,863	4,652	2,408	2,287
	46,896	39,032	33,186	30,550	26,083	27,485	20,903	7,628	2,569	2,441

TABLE B–5
MMTA Statement of Revenues and Expenses
(Expressed in thousands)

	1984	1983	1982	1981	1980	1979	1978	1977	1976	1975
Operating Revenues:										
Passenger Fares	4,178	3,305	1,586	1,628	1,759	1,608	1,176	1,504	1,275	1,206
Special Service Fares	58	43	30	15	59	257	253	—	—	—
Advertising	86	77	90	85	63	65	36	—	—	—
Other Income	886	605	391	495	219	152	56	58	123	25
	5,151	4,030	2,097	2,223	2,099	2,081	1,520	1,562	1,398	1,231
Operating Expenses:										
Transportation	11,448	10,303	8,541	7,940	7,876	3,695	2,080	1,101	768	825
Maintenance	7,872	7,117	6,055	4,081	2,476	1,479	901	450	225	319
Planning	915	1,100	1,209	920	651	1,301	205	20	17	25
Administration	2,460	1,679	2,100	2,541	2,210	900	701	352	174	250
Depreciation	2,112	1,943	1,900	1,801	1,780	1,100	400	140	65	70
	24,846	22,142	19,806	17,283	14,993	8,475	4,287	2,064	1,249	1,489
Operating Loss:	(19,695)	(18,112)	(17,709)	(15,060)	(12,894)	(6,395)	(2,767)	(502)	150	(258)
Non Operating Revenues:										
Sales Tax	13,773	13,253	13,548	12,177	10,037	8,109	5,553	194	146	144
Federal Operating Assist. Grant	4,649	4,564	4,900	6,195	3,337	3,300	1,328	1,115	—	—
	18,422	17,817	18,448	18,372	13,374	11,409	6,881	1,309	146	144
	(1,273)	(295)	738	3,312	480	5,015	4,114	807	(4)	114

4. *Report*—the time bus operator is required to remain on duty until assigned to additional work or released. This is all paid work time.

5. *Preparatory Time*—time allowed for readying equipment for service prior to pulling out.

6. *Travel Time*—time spent in traveling from the garage to the assignment embarkation point and/or time spent in traveling to return from the assignment to the garage.

7. *Spread Time*—elasped time between the beginning and end of a split run.

8. *Pull-In Time*—time assigned for the movement of a vehicle from its last scheduled stop to the garage where operator picked up equipment.

9. *Pull-Out Time*—time assigned for the movement of a vehicle from the garage to its first scheduled passenger pick-up point.

10. *Split Run*—a run that is completed in intermittent periods and contains one unpaid period or release from duty.

11. *Straight Run*—a regular run that has continuous pay time from starting time until work is completed.

12. *Relief Point*—a designated point on the route where bus operators may be scheduled to begin or terminate the whole or some part of their run.

RECOMMENDED REFERENCES

American Public Transit Association, *Comparative Labor Practices.* Washington, D.C.: APTA, 1225 Connecticut Avenue NW, Suite 200.

———, *Labor Information Series.* Washington, D.C.: APTA.

———, *Management Seminar.* Harvard, Pennsylvania: John A. Dash and Associates.

Bureau of National Affairs, *BNA Policy and Practice.* Washington, D.C.: Bureau of National Affairs, Inc.

Schultz, Charles L., *The Public Use of Private Interest.* Washington, D.C.: The Brookings Institute.

Urban Mass Transportation Act (1964), Section 13(c); amended by Public Law 91–453, 91st Congress, October 15, 1970.

SUBJECT INDEX